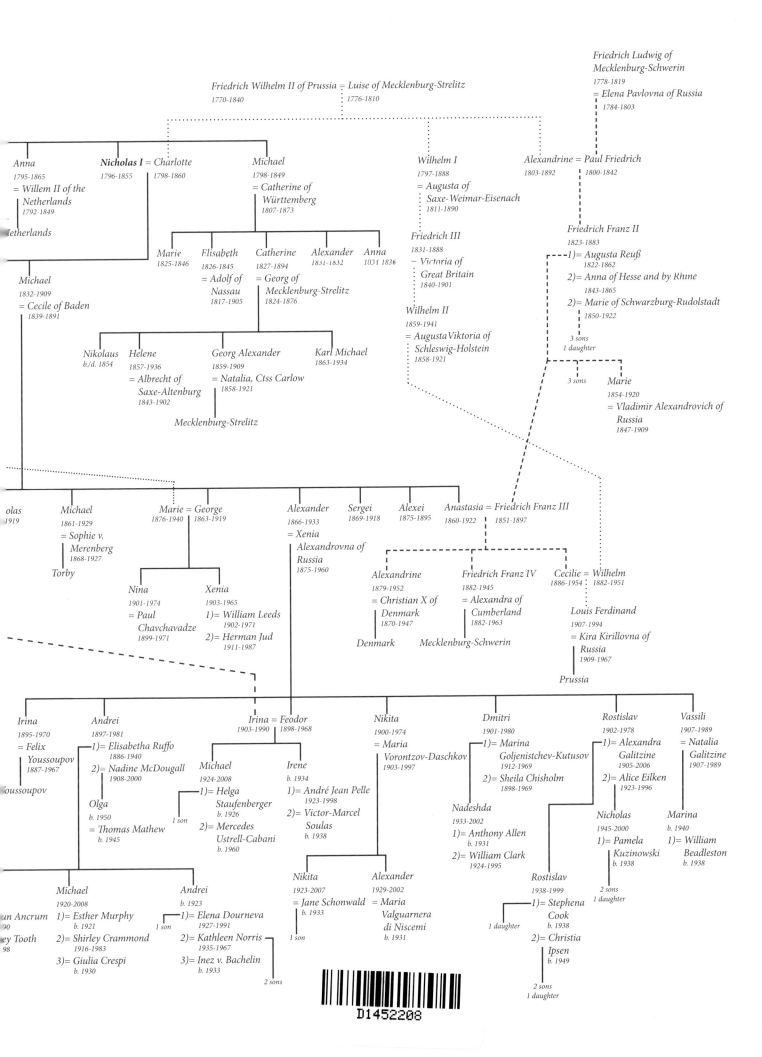

Friedrich Wilhelm II of Prussia = Luise of Mecklenburg-Strelitz
1770-1840 · 1776-1810

Friedrich Ludwig of
Mecklenburg-Schwerin
1778-1819
= Elena Pavlovna of Russia
1784-1803

Anna
1795-1865
= Willem II of the
Netherlands
1792-1849
Netherlands

Nicholas I = Charlotte
1796-1855 · 1798-1860

Michael
1798-1849
= Catherine of
Württemberg
1807-1873

Wilhelm I
1797-1888
= Augusta of
Saxe-Weimar-Eisenach
1811-1890

Alexandrine = Paul Friedrich
1803-1892 · 1800-1842

Michael
1832-1909
= Cecile of Baden
1839-1891

Marie
1825-1846

Elisabeth
1826-1845
= Adolf of
Nassau
1817-1905

Catherine
1827-1894
= Georg of
Mecklenburg-Strelitz
1824-1876

Alexander
1831-1832

Anna
1031 1836

Friedrich III
1831-1888
– Victoria of
Great Britain
1840-1901

Wilhelm II
1859-1941
= AugustaViktoria of
Schleswig-Holstein
1858-1921

Friedrich Franz II
1823-1883
1)= Augusta Reuß
1822-1862
2)= Anna of Hesse and by Rhine
1843-1865
2)= Marie of Schwarzburg-Rudolstadt
1850-1922
3 sons
1 daughter

3 sons

Marie
1854-1920
= Vladimir Alexandrovich of
Russia
1847-1909

Nikolaus
b./d. 1854

Helene
1857-1936
= Albrecht of
Saxe-Altenburg
1843-1902

Georg Alexander
1859-1909
= Natalia, Ctss Carlow
1858-1921

Karl Michael
1863-1934

Mecklenburg-Strelitz

olas
1919

Michael
1861-1929
= Sophie v.
Merenberg
1868-1927

Torby

Marie = George
1876-1940 · 1863-1919

Alexander
1866-1933
= Xenia
Alexandrovna of
Russia
1875-1960

Sergei
1869-1918

Alexei
1875-1895

Anastasia = Friedrich Franz III
1860-1922 · 1851-1897

Nina
1901-1974
= Paul
Chavchavadze
1899-1971

Xenia
1903-1965
1)= William Leeds
1902-1971
2)= Herman Jud
1911-1987

Alexandrine
1879-1952
= Christian X of
Denmark
1870-1947

Denmark

Friedrich Franz IV
1882-1945
= Alexandra of
Cumberland
1882-1963

Mecklenburg-Schwerin

Cecilie = Wilhelm
1886-1954 · 1882-1951

Louis Ferdinand
1907-1994
= Kira Kirillovna of
Russia
1909-1967

Prussia

Irina
1895-1970
= Felix
Youssoupov
1887-1967
Youssoupov

Andrei
1897-1981
1)= Elisabetha Ruffo
1886-1940
2)= Nadine McDougall
1908-2000

Olga
b. 1950
= Thomas Mathew
b. 1945

Irina = Feodor
1903-1990 · 1898-1968

Michael
1924-2008
1)= Helga
Staufenberger
b. 1926
2)= Mercedes
Ustrell-Cabani
b. 1960
1 son

Irene
b. 1934
1)= André Jean Pelle
1923-1998
2)= Victor-Marcel
Soulas
b. 1938

Nikita
1900-1974
= Maria
Vorontzov-Daschkov
1903-1997

Dmitri
1901-1980
1)= Marina
Goljenistchev-Kutusov
1912-1969
2)= Sheila Chisholm
1898-1969

Nadeshda
1933-2002
1)= Anthony Allen
b. 1931
2)= William Clark
1924-1995

Rostislav
1902-1978
1)= Alexandra
Galitzine
1905-2006
2)= Alice Eilken
1923-1996

Nicholas
1945-2000
1)= Pamela
Kuzinowski
b. 1938
2 sons
1 daughter

Vassili
1907-1989
= Natalia
Galitzine
1907-1989

Marina
b. 1940
1)= William
Beadleston
b. 1938

Michael
1920-2008
1)= Esther Murphy
b. 1921
2)= Shirley Crammond
1916-1983
3)= Giulia Crespi
b. 1930

un Ancrum
90
ey Tooth
98

Andrei
b. 1923
1)= Elena Dourneva
1927-1991
1 son
2)= Kathleen Norris
1935-1967
3)= Inez v. Bachelin
b. 1933
2 sons

Nikita
1923-2007
= Jane Schonwald
b. 1933
1 son

Alexander
1929-2002
= Maria
Valguarnera
di Niscemi
b. 1931

Rostislav
1938-1999
1)= Stephena
Cook
b. 1938
1 daughter
2)= Christia
Ipsen
b. 1949
2 sons
1 daughter

Romanovs Adrift

The Russian Imperial Family

in 1913-1919

By Greg King & Penny Wilson

Afterword by Katrina Warne

ISBN: 978-1-944207-10-6

EUROHISTORY.COM

Eurohistory & Kensington House Books
6300 Kensington Avenue
East Richmond Heights, CA 94805
USA
Email: books@eurohistory.com & eurohistory@comcast.net
Phone: 510.236.1730

Greg King & Penny Wilson
Romanovs Adrift: The Russian Imperial Family in 1914-1919
ISBN: 978-1-944207-10-6

Cover artwork by David W. Higdon & Henry Wong

In memory of Jon Phillips ...

Acknowledgements

Greg King would like to thank Janet Ashton, Paulette Blum, Professor Joseph Fuhrmann, Brien Horan, Roger King, Susan Meslans, and Debra Tate for their advice and support.

Penny Wilson would like to thank Matt Crouch, Simon Donoghue, Gino Gonzalez, Gio Gonzalez, Nicole Flaherty, Christopher Kinsman, Tricia and Jim Manara, Haley McIntyre, Edward and Mary O'Hanlon, Stephanie O'Hanlon, Jamie and Lindsey Phillips, Georgia Phillips, Charlotte Phillips, Jennifer Rider, Jisel Schell, Joshua Sweeten, Basil Trenham, Cassian Trenham, Tom Wilson, and Teddy Yelland.

We also thank Arturo Beéche, Galina Korneva, Coryne Hall, Marlene Eilers Koenig, Professor Ilana Miller, Katrina Warne, and Sue Woolmans for generously sharing information with us. David W. Higdon and Henry Wong are thanked by the authors for their design of the covers.

Author's Note

This book covers the lives of eighty members of the Romanov Dynasty between 1913-1919. The cast of characters is thus immense. For the ease of readers, we have divided these Romanovs into their eight respective branches. The Emperor headed the premier line, the Nikolaievich branch, which consisted of himself, his wife, and his children. There were six Grand Ducal branches (Alexandrovich, Vladimirovich, the Junior Alexandrovich Line, Nikolaievich, Konstantinovich, and Mikhailovich), three junior branches (Oldenburg, Leuchtenberg, and Mecklenburg), and the five Grand Duchesses who had entered into foreign marriages. To further help identify our subjects, we have freely used patronymics in an effort to avoid confusion between those with identical Christian names.

For most of the period covered in this book, Russia used the Julian calendar rather than the Gregorian Calendar in use in the West. This meant that dates in the Nineteenth Century were twelve days behind those in the West, and thirteen days behind those in the West during the Twentieth Century. Because the bulk of this book is set before 1918, we have given dates according to the Julian calendar; for those subjects living in the West, and for particularly important events, we have given dates according to both the Julian and the Gregorian Calendars.

Contents

Tsar Nicholas II on the shore of the Gulf of Finland.

Prologue

In 1913, the Romanov Dynasty celebrated the tercentenary of its rule in Russia. Three hundred years earlier, and following wars, palace coups, and a string of pretenders – a period known as "The Time of Troubles" – a body of elected nobles in Moscow voted to offer the vacant throne to Ivan the Terrible's great-nephew by marriage, young Michael Romanov. A delegation found him hiding at the Ipatiev Monastery in Kostroma; it took some convincing before the sixteen-year-old Michael accepted their offer, but he was duly crowned in Moscow, the first of the eighteen Romanovs who would rule Russia over the coming centuries.

On a cold February day in 1913, it was Michael's successor, Nicholas II, who held the throne. He had reigned since 1894, nineteen years marked by political turmoil, assassinations, military defeat, and revolution. In 1905, circumstances compelled the Emperor to grant his country an elected parliament, the Duma, thus ending autocratic rule. Reform gradually followed, sometimes with Imperial consent and often despite its opposition, and the immense Russian Empire began to emerge as a world power, with a growing economy and, for Nicholas, a welcome decrease in violent dissent. More than ever, he believed that *"the landowners, the nobility, and the army"* remained loyal; those opposed to the throne were *"Jews, students, landless peasants, and some workers."*[1]

Nicholas was not only Russia's Emperor: he was also head of the House of Romanov. In 1913 there were eighty members of the dynasty, divided between eight branches. The Emperor headed the premier line, the Nikolaievich branch, which consisted of himself, his wife, and his children. There were six Grand Ducal branches (Alexandrovich, Vladimirovich, the Junior Alexandrovich Line, Nikolaievich, Konstantinovich, and Mikhailovich), three junior branches (Oldenburg, Leuchtenberg, and Mecklenburg), and the five Grand Duchesses who had entered into foreign marriages. They were a curious mixture of *noblesse oblige* and privileged snobbery, often struggling – like the Empire itself – to come to grips with a Twentieth Century world. Previously, attitudes of public service, loyalty, and discretion had characterized this collection of Grand Dukes and Duchesses, but under Alexander II morals loosened and ideas of personal enrichment took hold. Alexander III further eroded their support by eschewing court ceremonies and depriving many of his relatives of important leadership roles, a pattern that ultimately came to full fruition under Nicholas II. Alexander III, one relative later commented bitterly, *"had broken up the family"* to the point where unity among the Romanovs was impossible.[2]

Without responsibilities, many Romanovs hurled themselves into pleasure: public scandals and marital indiscretions became common. Grand Duke Alexander Mikhailovich complained of the *"discontent and lack of discipline"* among his relatives, who often *"displayed a complete disrespect for the wishes of the Emperor and showed an extremely bad example to Russian society. If Nicky was not able to bring his own relations to their senses, he could hardly count on a greater success with his ministers, generals, and chamberlains. Obviously, we stood on the threshold of moral decadence."*[3] Most of the Grand Dukes, insisted Infanta Eulalia of Spain, *"neither understand the aspirations of the democracy nor sympathize with them, for, reflecting the glory of Autocracy, they are more firmly convinced than any other Royal Persons in Europe that a gulf divides them from the rest of mankind. And this conviction is so deep that they appear to believe that the most ordinary actions are ennobled by the mere fact that they are performed by persons in whose*

Grand Duchesses Maria, Tatiana, Anastasia and Olga Nikolaievna.

veins flows the Imperial blood."[4]

A twenty-one-gun salute fired from the Fortress of St. Peter and St. Paul awoke the Imperial capital of St. Petersburg on February 21, 1913. Later that morning the entire Imperial Family would travel by carriage from the immense Winter Palace to the Cathedral of Our Lady of Kazan for a *Te Deum* – it had been nearly a decade since they had last all appeared in public – and it would be a rare chance to see the Emperor's usually cloistered children. But the mood in the streets was scarcely festive: flags and bunting hung limply in the intermittent rain, and although thousands had turned out to watch the ceremonies, they were, complained a courtier, *"on the whole undemonstrative...a typical Petersburg crowd."*[5]

The procession began just before noon. Nicholas II rode in an open carriage, accompanied by his nine-year-old son and heir, Tsesarevich Alexei; behind them, in a second carriage, came Russia's enigmatic and aloof Empress Alexandra, riding with her mother-in-law Dowager Empress Maria Feodorovna. And, before the seemingly endless succession of Grand Dukes and Duchesses, Nicholas and Alexandra's four young daughters appeared. Grand Duchesses Olga, Tatiana, Marie, and Anastasia Nikolaievna, clad in white dresses and hats, were objects of admiration and of mystery, all but unknown to their father's subjects since their mother's increasing retreat from court and isolation in the Alexander Palace at Tsarskoye Selo.

An unwelcome incident at the cathedral earlier that morning overshadowed the magnificent *Te Deum*. As if flouting public opinion, Alexandra had sent her favorite, the already notorious Gregory Rasputin, an invitation to the ceremony. His appearance caused an uproar; when an angry official ejected the peasant,

the congregation as well as the crowd outside tittered with condemnatory looks and gossip. The ill-conceived invitation only served to reinforce widely held notions of the peasant's power over the Imperial couple.

The Imperial Family attending the Tercentenary celebrations at the Ipatiev Monastery in Kostroma.

Two days of receptions, dinners, and ceremonies followed the service, but to many onlookers mere curiosity had replaced loyalty. Sad whispers went through crowds at the sight of Tsesarevich Alexei being carried on the shoulders of a Cossack rather than walking; with Nicholas and Alexandra having made the decision to keep his hemophilia a secret, his frailty was ascribed to an accident the previous autumn. Society was disappointed that the Empress had not deigned to host a magnificent ball to mark the anniversary; when she left the Mariinsky Theatre during the first act of a gala performance of *A Life for the Tsar*, the auditorium rippled with resentment.

A grand tour of Russia followed, as the Imperial Family traveled down the Volga on a pilgrimage to the Ipatiev Monastery at Kostroma where Michael Romanov had learned of his election to the throne. At a few places the crowds seemed enthusiastic, but many noted that overwhelmingly they seemed uncomfortably sparse and silent. Prime Minister Vladimir Kokovtsov recorded nothing but *"shallow curiosity"* on the faces greeting the Emperor and his family.[6] But both Nicholas and Alexandra saw only what they wished to see: crowds of loyal peasants dedicated body and soul to the throne. *"Now you can see for yourself what cowards these state ministers are,"* Alexandra told one courtier. *"They are constantly frightening the Emperor with threats and forebodings of revolution, and here, you see it yourself, we only need show ourselves, and at once their hearts are ours."*[7]

Archduke Franz Ferdinand of Austria, Emperor Franz Josef's heir. Along with his wife Sophie, they were assassinated in Sarajevo on June 28, 1914. WWI began weeks later.

Nicholas II tried to use the ceremonies to win back popular support for the Dynasty, issuing idealized souvenir photographs and postcards of his family. He took this propaganda effort a step further, for the first time authorizing an adoring biography written by a trusted courtier; Nicholas read through the manuscript, personally approved every word, and excised sentences about the Duma that he believed challenged his conception of himself as all-knowing autocrat.[8] *The Reign of the Sovereign Emperor Nicholas Alexandrovich* offered a telling look at how the Emperor wanted to be viewed, and how he viewed himself. The Nicholas II appearing in the book was dedicated and selfless, a man possessed of superhuman insights and intellectual gifts who needed no politicians or state apparatus to guide him in his task of leading Russia to the glory he believed lay in store for them both.[9]

An assassin's bullets fired in Sarajevo in the summer of 1914 signaled the beginning of the end for the Romanovs. At first Nicholas, like many other heads of state, tended to ignore the storm clouds gathering over Europe. When officials warned that he must prepare for war, the Emperor insisted that they were *"exaggerating the gravity of the situation."* The Balkans had always been trouble, but no one was foolish enough to launch a war over them. Besides, Nicholas argued, Kaiser Wilhelm II *"had frequently assured him of his sincere desire to safeguard the peace of Europe and it had always been possible to come to an agreement with him, even in serious cases."*[10]

On July 15, Austria-Hungary declared war against Serbia and began bombarding Belgrade. Over the next few days Nicholas authorized partial mobilization of Russia's forces, canceled it, and reinstated it

Выходъ Его Императорскаго Величества Государя Императора на балконъ
Зимняго дворца къ народу послѣ молебствія 20-г Іюля 1914 г.

as his officials delivered dire warnings that the Empire would be humiliated if it failed to act in Serbia's defense. On the afternoon of July 17, Foreign Minister Sergei Sazonov arrived at Peterhof, explaining he'd just come from an urgent meeting with the Minister of the War and the Chief of the General Staff. All agreed that Nicholas

After the declaration of war, Nicholas II attended a Te Deum at the Winter Palace. He later came out on the balcony and addressed the gathered masses. He was greeted with loud cheers. It was the last time Russians would react to their Tsar in such a manner. Three years later they would violently sweep him off the throne.

could no longer delay an order for General Mobilization. Nicholas, Sazonov recalled, bowed his head in silence then, *"in a voice deep with feeling,"* said, *"This would mean sending hundreds of thousands of Russians to their deaths. How can one help hesitating to take such a step?"* Nicholas was pale; he said no more, as if stunned.[11]

A series of increasingly urgent telegrams between Tsar and Kaiser followed, with each desperately trying to save the peace without backing down and losing face. On the night of July 19, Nicholas left his family and retreated to his study in the Lower Palace at Peterhof. A little before eight Sazonov rang with an urgent message. The Tsar picked up the telephone and listened as his Foreign Minister announced that Germany had declared war on Russia earlier that evening. Stunned, Nicholas walked to the drawing room, where his family waited, and broke the news that war had finally come. Alexandra and her daughters burst into tears.

On July 20, Nicholas responded with his own declaration of war against Germany. Nicholas and Alexandra came to the Winter Palace for a *Te Deum*, during which the Emperor swore never to make peace as long as a single German soldier remained on Russian territory. The *"intensity was extreme,"* recalled Princess

A propaganda photo: Tsar Nicholas II dressed as a soldier ready for war.

Cantacuzene. When Nicholas and Alexandra arose from prayers in the immense Nicholas Hall, the crowd of 5,000 spontaneously broke into the national anthem. Nicholas *"was paler than usual, and seemed somewhat startled but not displeased,"* while Alexandra looked like *"a Madonna of Sorrows"* as they passed through the cheering room.[12]

Just after three o'clock in the afternoon, Nicholas appeared on the palace balcony, followed by the Empress. Tens of thousands had jammed Palace Square below: they greeted Nicholas with loud cheers, some falling to their knees. The Emperor tried to speak but the enthusiasm was wild. A voice below began singing the national anthem; in seconds thousands joined in, serenading the Imperial couple who bowed their heads in gratitude:

God Save the Tsar,
Mighty and Powerful,
Long May He Reign,
Reign for Our Glory,
O Orthodox Tsar!
God Save the Tsar!

Nicholas II had never before experienced such heartfelt and spontaneous loyalty from his subjects. After so many difficult years and trials, it must have seemed that his moment of triumph had finally came. In less than three years, these same cheering, nameless crowds would sweep the Emperor from his throne and bring an end to the proud Romanov Dynasty.

Chapter I

The Senior Nikolaievich Line: Nicholas & Alexandra

On a clear spring day in 1881, the twelve-year-old future Nicholas II stood in a study at St. Petersburg's Winter Palace, watching in silent horror as his grandfather Alexander II bled to death before his eyes. Despite years of reform – the Emancipation of the Serfs, judicial and military changes, and easing of press censorship – the Emperor faced a backlash, as liberals pushed for more concessions and would-be revolutionaries seemingly lurked behind every tree. They had pursued him for years. Even the Winter Palace wasn't safe: in 1880 Nihilists had managed to blow up a dining room, killing forty though Alexander II himself escaped injury.

The Emperor had spent the morning of Sunday, March 1, preparing an edict announcing the creation of an elected council drawn from local bodies known as zemstvos. Although Alexander II would retain autocratic power, he allowed that his people should have an advisory role in the country's affairs. In a happy mood, he attended a military review that afternoon, called on a relative for tea, and set off in his carriage for the Winter Palace. Armed with bombs, members of the radical Narodnaya Volya, The Party of the Peoples' Will, watched as the Emperor's equipage turned along the Catherine Canal. One bomb shattered the carriage but Alexander was unhurt; when he left the vehicle to ask about the wounded, another bomb exploded at his feet.

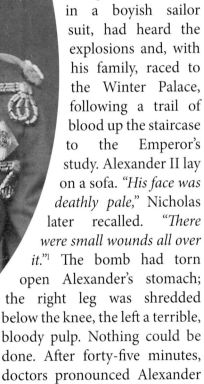

Tsar Alexander II.

Young Nicholas, clad in a boyish sailor suit, had heard the explosions and, with his family, raced to the Winter Palace, following a trail of blood up the staircase to the Emperor's study. Alexander II lay on a sofa. *"His face was deathly pale,"* Nicholas later recalled. *"There were small wounds all over it."*[1] The bomb had torn open Alexander's stomach; the right leg was shredded below the knee, the left a terrible, bloody pulp. Nothing could be done. After forty-five minutes, doctors pronounced Alexander II dead. His son and heir, now Alexander III, quickly left the grim chamber. For young Nicholas, the events of that Sunday were mute evidence that concessions brought chaos, and that if left unchecked liberalism was destined to destroy the Russian Throne.

1

Grand Duke Nicholas Alexandrovich and his mother, c. 1869.

Just over three decades later, Nicholas II greeted the new year of 1914. He had ruled since 1894, a small, mild-mannered, exceptionally polite yet inscrutable man who had taken his place as the eighteenth Romanov sovereign. Yet he compared poorly with his illustrious ancestors. Plagued by self-doubt, he stumbled through his reign, dogged by misfortune and damaged by self-inflicted wounds.

Nicholas was born in the Alexander Palace at Tsarskoye Selo on May 6, 1868, the first child of Tsesarevich Alexander Alexandrovich and his Danish-born wife Marie Feodorovna. The very day of his birth haunted the superstitious Nicholas throughout his life: in the Russian Orthodox Church, May 6 was the Feast Day of St. Job the Sufferer. The idea that, like Job, he was destined for tragedy became a self-fulfilling prophecy. *"I have a presentiment – more than a presentiment, a secret conviction, that I am destined for terrible trials,"* Nicholas once confessed. *"And I shall not receive my reward on this earth. How often have I applied to myself the words of Job: 'Hardly have I entertained a fear than it comes to pass, and all the evils I foresee descend upon my head.'"*[2]

Nicholas was the eldest of six children. A brother, Alexander, was born in 1869 but died the following year. Another brother, George, arrived in 1871, followed by sister Xenia in 1875, brother Michael in 1878, and sister Olga in 1882. Tsesarevich Alexander was an intimidating man and an intimidating father; gruff and powerful, he loathed any sign of weakness. He could be devoted and doting, romping with his children, taking them for long walks, and teaching them how to hunt for mushrooms in the forest, but he expected complete obedience. He saw young Nicholas's gentle character and diminutive figure as disappointments, even ridiculing his son, deriding him as unworthy of the Romanov name, and shouting, *"You are a little girlie!"* at him in front of playmates.[3] As a result, recalled Finance Minister Sergei Witte, Alexander's children were often uneasy and watchful in his presence.[4]

Marie Feodorovna, Nicholas's mother, offered refuge, but comfort came at a terrible price. Wanting an idealized family, she kept her children, especially her sons, emotionally dependent and immature. *"Never forget that everyone's eyes are turned on you,"* Marie Feodorovna warned her eldest son when he was nineteen, *"waiting to see what your first independent steps in life will be....Be polite and courteous so that you get along with your comrades without discrimination, though without too much familiarity or intimacy and never listen to flatterers."*[5] To this, Nicholas agreeably replied: *"I will always try to follow your advice, my dearest darling Mama. One has to be cautious with everyone at first."*[6]

From an early age, Nicholas struggled to reconcile these two conflicting parental influences, one harsh, the other indulgent. He learned to charm, to please, to conceal his true feelings, to treasure private family life and act obediently to avoid unpleasant scenes. Life was pleasant enough. Nicholas was brought up in the massive Anichkov Palace on St. Petersburg's Nevsky Prospekt, though following Romanov tradition he slept on a camp bed, took cold baths, and survived on questionable porridge and nursery puddings. Things darkened following his grandfather's assassination in 1881. Thinking St. Petersburg was unsafe and fearing revolutionary plots, the new Alexander III moved his family to the suburban palace of Gatchina, where at his insistence they crowded into a series of low-ceilinged rooms originally meant for the servants.

Nicholas Alexandrovich and his brother George Alexandrovich.

Alexander III inaugurated a reign so repressive that even newspapers were forbidden to print the word, *"Constitution."*[7] This repression was passed on to Nicholas. Contrary to popular opinion, he received an excellent education. He was intelligent and had a quick mind, yet Alexander III ordered that no instructor was allowed to question his son or even to grade his work.[8] Nicholas studied religion, Russian and world history, arithmetic, geography, Russian literature, science, grammar, and composition; learned English, German, and French; and heard lectures on economics, military tactics, political affairs, and international relations.[9] Konstantin Pobedonostsev, Ober-Procurator of the Holy Synod, cemented Nicholas's distaste for bureaucrats, the press, rebellious students, and self-interested politicians; only the *"absolute power of the sovereign,"* Pobedonostsev insisted, guaranteed Russia's future.[10]

In 1887 Nicholas entered the military, first serving in the elite Preobrazhensky Life Guards Regiment and rising to the rank of Colonel of the Horse Guards Artillery. He enjoyed the cautious camaraderie of life at the military camp of Krasnoye Selo, where he had a private villa: the regulated existence appealed to his sense of order, and he was happy to have all of his decisions made for him. In the fall of 1890, he embarked on a Far Eastern tour that ended prematurely after a thwarted assassination attempt in Japan.

Back in St. Petersburg, he took a mistress, ballerina Mathilde Kschessinska, and lived the frivolous, hedonistic life of a privileged prince.

Nicholas later complained that his father *"had never once mentioned the responsibilities that awaited him."*[11] And his sister Olga Alexandrovna insisted that the lack of preparation *"was my father's fault. He disliked the mere idea of state matters encroaching on our family life, but after all, Nicky was his heir."*[12]

Yet contrary to perception, Alexander III did try to introduce his son to his future duties. He named Nicholas chairman of the State Famine Relief Committee in 1891 after widespread crop failures, and in 1893 appointed his heir Chairman of the Trans-Siberian Railway Committee. He also asked Nicholas to attend sessions of the State Council and the State Finance Committee, and sit in on his weekly meetings with ministers. Nicholas, though, found most of the proceedings a bore, and his interest quickly waned: he once confessed that he couldn't understand how anyone could read state papers – *"I limit myself to one or two of the most interesting,"* he confided to his diary, *"and the rest go straight to the fireplace."*[13] As a result, Alexander III apparently gave up – at least for the time being. To Sergei Witte, the Emperor confided that his adult heir was *"nothing but a boy, whose judgments are utterly childish."*[14]

Father and son were utterly different in both appearance and character. The immense Alexander towered over his family and entertained relatives by tearing packs of playing cards in half; Nicholas, recalled his cousin the future Queen Marie of Romania, was *"small, almost frail looking. His eyes were kind, had a caressing expression, there was something gentle about him, and his voice was low pitched and soft."*[15] Charles Sydney Gibbes, who served as English tutor to Nicholas's children, noted his admirable qualities but lamented that he *"seemed incapable of inspiring fear. He knew very well how to guard his dignity and his emotions, and had no difficulties inviting sympathy and loyalty. But the kind, tender – one could say almost loving – expression in his eyes never intimidated."*[16]

From the left: George and Nicholas Alexandrovich, Xenia and Olga Alexandrovna, Marie Feodorovna, and Michael Alexandrovich.

Alexander III was a practical man, while his son was a romantic. The merits of Peter the Great revealed this difference. Alexander III once declared that he completely agreed with Peter's decision to have his only son and heir Alexei tortured and condemned to death for rumored treason. Nicholas, though, despised his renowned predecessor. *"He is the ancestor who appeals to me the least,"* he once said. *"He had too much admiration for European culture."*[17] Instead, Nicholas idolized Peter's father Tsar Alexei, and idealized the era he represented, a time of superstitious Orthodoxy and absolute power uncorrupted by liberal, western ideas.[18]

Intimidated by his father and coddled by his mother, Nicholas could never escape the fear that everyone doubted his abilities; in fact, this accounted for some of his otherwise inexplicable behavior in refusing to listen to the counsel of others, as if he felt the need to constantly prove the wisdom of his own judgment. Deeply religious, he was certain that all events, large or small, good or bad, were preordained; there was no point in fighting against Divine Fate. He sincerely believed that his own views were always correct and guided by God, recalled courtier Alexander Mossolov, and that *"he was in no way bound by his position"* to do *"anything that he did not want to do. In this his natural timidity played a part. He hated to have to investigate anything, to complain of anything, to stand up to anybody. Following out his fixed rule, he never worried and never grew heated, even in situations in which an outburst of temper would have been only too natural."*[19]

Tsesarevich Nicholas Alexandrovich, late 1880s.

Yet this apparent certainty hid persistent doubts. Nicholas knew that in many ways his judgment was lacking and *"he had no confidence in himself. He began to become aware of his lack of experience and education, and for that reason could not issue an order without immediately beginning to doubt its wisdom."*[20] The lack of self-confidence proved fatal. With his innate dislike of confrontations, he let others dictate to him. It was not that he always took their advice: rather, his passivity merely reinforced impressions that he lacked character.

Unfortunately for Nicholas, and for Russia, the one person who might have provided support instead became the most persistent of his critics. Nicholas first met Princess Alix of Hesse in 1884, when her sister Elisabeth married his uncle Sergei. *"Alix and I wrote our names on the back window of the little Italian house (we love each other),"* was Nicholas's diary entry recording their burgeoning feelings.[21] A childish romance on his part developed into something more mature five years later, when Alix spent six weeks in St. Petersburg. Escorting her to dinners, skating parties, and dances, Nicholas found himself ever more drawn to the shy, coldly beautiful golden-haired Alix. Others noticed his interest with apprehension, including Alexander and Marie Feodorovna, who found the Hessian princess stiff, overly serious, and obviously uneasy even at intimate family dinners.

As one of Queen Victoria's favorite granddaughters, Alix of Hesse seemed, at least on paper, eminently suitable as a future Russian Empress. Yet her character was quixotic. Born on June 6, 1872 to the future Grand Duke Ludwig IV and his British wife Princess Alice, Alix had grown up in the Hessian capital of Darmstadt. Mother and daughter shared more than a bloodline. Both were headstrong, prone to mysticism, inclined to depression, and beset with complaints of *"nervous exhaustion."* With the Victorian penchant for wanting to be useful and imbued with visions of social justice, Alice had swept into Darmstadt armed with *"improving"* ideas: charitable organizations, new schools, orphanages, and academies for training young women to enter the workplace. She meant well, though the good people of Darmstadt couldn't understand why their new Princess wanted to change them. Some of Alice's drive undoubtedly stemmed from unhappiness: she scarcely knew her husband when they married and soon found that they had nothing in common. She couldn't match his carefree sociability and didn't understand how he never read a book. Disillusion set in. Emotionally drift, Alice increasingly complained of fatigue, spending her days collapsed on a sofa. In her growing melancholy, Alice – like her daughter later – had her own "disreputable monk," in this case, a controversial theologian named David Strauss who openly questioned the basic tenets of Christianity.

Alice died of diphtheria in 1878. The effect of this loss on the six-year-old Alix has long been debated. Her youthful melancholy and constant mourning have figured prominently in attempts to unravel Alix's enigmatic character. It explains so much: her social unease, her seriousness, her exaggerated piety, and her own tendency to depression. It's a

Princess Alix of Hesse and by Rhine.

theory almost tailor-made for the future Empress of Russia, concise and comfortable. It's also questionable. The stark truth is that Alix had few memories of her mother; she was, after all, only six when Alice died. And with her prolonged lapses into emotional fatigue and retreat to comfortable isolation, Alice hadn't been a consistent presence in her daughter's life. The tears that followed her death weren't crippling: Alix still had her adoring father, her three sisters Victoria, Elisabeth, and Irene, her brother Ernst Ludwig to whom she was devoted, and her grandparents, including a very involved Queen Victoria.

But Alix developed into a preternaturally serious young woman. None of her siblings succumbed to the retreat that now characterized the young Hessian princess. Alix liked to be alone; she liked to brood; she liked to indulge her emotions. She was introspective to the point of alienation. She echoed the dangerous, indulgent melancholy of her mother and of her grandmother. *"You always play at being sorrowful,"* Alix's cousin Princess Marie Louise of Schleswig-Holstein once told her. *"One day the Almighty will send you some real crushing sorrows, and then what are you going to do?"*[22] Isolation suited Alix precisely because she was so uncomfortable around people; she even disliked extended family gatherings, fearing that everyone was secretly watching her, assessing her, and finding fault. Alix, said a cousin, *"seldom smiled,*

Princess Alix with her siblings Ernst Ludwig and Marie.

and when she did it was grudging, as though making a concession….No warmth emanated from her; in her presence enthusiasm wilted."[23]

Self-awareness was not generally one of Alix's strong suits, but even she recognized her own shortcomings. *"Of course I am gay sometimes,"* she told an acquaintance, *"and sometimes I can be pleasant, I suppose, but I am rather a contemplative, serious being, one who looks into the depths of all water, whether it be clear or dark."*[24] Growing up in Darmstadt, she had little social experience; she never learned the royal art of gracious small talk, of putting public obligation over personal comfort, and could not disguise her dislike of such duties. Unfamiliar faces sent her into a paralyzing panic complete with unbecoming blush. Confidences were rarely extended: Alix concealed her insecurities behind a veneer of smug superiority fed by an idiosyncratic education that left her convinced that she possessed a brilliant mind, even as she relied on emotion, not reason, when making decisions.

Perhaps such things were of little importance in a minor Hessian Princess, but they mattered immensely in a future Empress of Russia. Nicholas, though, saw none of it. *"My dream is to marry Alix H,"* he confided to his diary in 1892. *"I have loved her for three years already, and I constantly cherish the hope that, God willing, one day I will marry her."*[25] His parents resisted, as did Alix: in 1888 she'd been confirmed into the Lutheran Church, and the wife of the future Emperor of Russia had to be Orthodox. She took few things in life more seriously than God, even if hers was an oddly cold devotion, bereft of joy but viewed as a means to personal reflection and aiding others. No doubt aware of the influence they would wield over the country's future sovereigns, Alix's sister Elisabeth and her husband Grand Duke Sergei Alexandrovich did all in their power to promote the romance. Elisabeth had converted in 1891: rather strangely, she even assured her sister that no doctrinal issues separated the two

Princess Alix and Princess Marie of Hesse and by Rhine.

Princess Alice of Hesse and by Rhine with five of her children: Elisabeth, Irene, Ernst Ludwig, Alix (on her mother's lap), and Victoria.

faiths. When, in the autumn of 1893 Nicholas wavered, Sergei excoriated him for his lack of resolve, writing that Elisabeth *"was so disappointed and outraged by your letter that she asks me to tell you she considers this case decisively finished….If you have no strong character, no will or your feelings have changed, it's deplorable you haven't told me or my wife."*[26]

A chastened Nicholas tried again as letters flew back and forth between St. Petersburg and Darmstadt. Alix rejected the overtures: *"I have tried to look at it in every light possible,"* she wrote to Nicholas in November 1893, *"but I always return to one thing. I cannot do it against my conscience. You, dear Nicky, who also have such a strong belief will understand me that I think it is a sin to change my belief, and I should be miserable all the days of my life, knowing that I had done a wrongful thing."*[27] Nicholas replied with a passive-aggressive masterpiece: *"How am I to change my feelings after waiting and wishing for so long, even now after that sad letter you sent me?…Do not say 'no' directly, my dearest Alix, do not ruin my life already! Do you think there can exist any happiness in the whole world without you?"*[28]

Nicholas was equally adamant with his parents: if he couldn't marry Alix, he declared, he wouldn't marry at all. Faced with his intransigence, and falsely assured by Elisabeth that Alix would never change her religion, Alexander III and Marie Feodorovna finally agreed that Nicholas could make what they thought would be a futile proposal to the Hessian Princess when he attended the wedding of her brother Grand Duke Ernst Ludwig to their mutual cousin Princess Victoria Melita at Coburg in April 1894. Alix dreaded what was coming. *"I know,"* she wrote to Nicholas's sister Xenia Alexandrovna, *"Ella will begin again, but what is the good of it, and it is cruel always to say I am ruining his life."*[29]

Nicholas overcame the obstacles with the assistance of Alix's sister Elisabeth, the help of his aunt Grand Duchess Vladimir, and the prodding of Kaiser Wilhelm II. At first, Alix rejected Nicholas's proposal: her aunt Empress Friedrich confided that she swore *"to everyone that though she was very fond of him, she would never take him."*[30] But, as Nicholas admitted, the idea of sharing her house, and her beloved brother's affections, with the stubborn and brittle Victoria Melita weakened Alix's resolve and finally gave

A royal gathering in Coburg, Edinburgh Palais, 1894.

Front (and seated), from the left: Kaiser Wilhelm II, Queen Victoria, Princess Beatrice of Edinburgh, the Empress Friedrich, and Princess Feodora of Saxe-Meiningen. Second row, same order: Hereditary Prince Alfred of Saxe-Coburg and Gotha, Tsesarevich Nicholas Alexandrovich, Princess Alix of Hesse and by Rhine, Princess Victoria of Battenberg, Princess Irene of Prussia, Grand Duchess Marie Pavlovna Sr., and Grand Duchess Marie Alexandrovna (Duchess of Edinburgh and Saxe-Coburg and Gotha). Third row, same order: The Prince of Wales, Prince Henry and Princess Beatrice of Battenberg, Princess Louise of Saxe-Coburg and Gotha, Princess Alexandra of Edinburgh, Hereditary Princess Charlotte of Saxe-Meiningen, and the Duchess of Connaught. Fourth row, same order: Prince Louis of Battenberg, Grand Duke Paul Alexandrovich, Prince Philipp of Saxe-Coburg and Gotha, Count Mensdorff-Pouilly, Grand Duke Sergei Alexandrovich, Crown Princess Marie and Crown Prince Ferdinand of Romania, Grand Duchess Elisabeth Feodorovna, Grand Duke Vladimir Alexandrovich, and Duke Alfred of Saxe-Coburg and Gotha.

her a reason to accept his proposal. *"A wonderful, an unforgettable day in my life,"* Nicholas wrote in his diary. *"The day of my betrothal with my dear darling Alix....Oh God! A mountain has been lifted from my shoulders....I went about all day dazed. I could not believe that all this had happened to me."*[31]

Nicholas was happy, but others were less encouraged. The future Empress of Russia, commented her aunt Empress Friedrich, had *"a very haughty disposition, and would be much more inclined than supposed to take very seriously her position."* Alix, she said, *"is far too convinced of her own perfection, and she will never listen to other people's advice, besides which she has no tact."*[32] Count Osten-Sacken, formerly Russian envoy in Darmstadt, insisted, *"Princess Alix will be the misfortune and unhappiness of Russia!"*[33] And,

Tsar Alexander III in 1893, a year before his untimely death.

according to Sergei Witte, the former Master of the Darmstadt Court greeted word of the engagement with a succinct flourish: *"What a piece of good luck it is for Hesse that you are taking her away!"*[34]

That summer of 1894, Alexander III fell terminally ill with nephritis. Nicholas brought his fiancée to the Crimea, where his father lay dying, and Alix soon made her forceful personality felt. Incensed that doctors first made their reports to the Empress, Alix intruded into Nicholas's diary with objections and admonitions that he *"be firm"* and *"show your own mind and don't let others forget who you are."*[35]

Nicholas was far too polite to take Alix's advice that his mother be pushed aside, but the diary entry was indicative of things to come. Believing that her fiancé was too weak, she decided that her role was not merely to support him but also to warn him of perceived character deficiencies and prod him to become the man she wished him to be. The pattern established at Livadia that autumn of 1894, with Alix dictating to Nicholas, would continue unabated for the next twenty-three-years and proved fatal. Not even in his private life could he escape censure; two decades of such exhortations eroded what little confidence he possessed, until he finally believed his wife's incessant warnings that he was weak and lacked character.

When Alexander III died on October 20, Nicholas became Emperor. *"What am I going to do?"* he cried pathetically to his brother-in-law Grand Duke Alexander Mikhailovich.[36] The following day, Alix needlessly rushed her conversion to Orthodoxy, taking the name Alexandra Feodorovna. In his despair, Nicholas II made a grievous mistake, insisting that they marry as soon as possible. Had the new Alexandra Feodorovna lived in Russia as the year of mourning passed, she could have slowly come to know society and her husband's family, studied the language and her new religion, and learned about the pressures of life under such an intense microscope. Their sad

Laurits Tuxen's painting of the wedding of Nicholas II and Alexandra.

Surrounding the couple, from the left: King George I of the Hellenes, King Christian IX of Denmark, Dowager Empress Marie Feodorovna, the Princess of Wales, Queen Olga of Greece, Grand Duchess Marie Alexandrovna, the Duke of York, the Prince of Wales. Other royals in the background include: Grand Duchess Marie Pavlovna Sr. (partly obscured), Grand Duchess Elisabeth Feodorovna, Princess Irene of Prussia, Grand Duke Paul, Grand Duke Ernst Ludwig of Hesse and by Rhine, Grand Duke Sergei Alexandrovich, Grand Duke Michael Nikolaievich, Grand Duke Alexei Alexandrovich, Prince Heinrich of Prussia, Grand Duke Vladimir Alexandrovich, and Duke Alfred of Saxe-Coburg and Gotha.

wedding, an uncomfortable fusion of ceremonial vows wrapped in mourning, took place on November 14 in the Cathedral of St. Petersburg's Winter Palace. *"She comes to us behind a coffin,"* people whispered of their new Empress, *"and will bring bad luck."*[37] The morbid parallels between mother and daughter were eerie. Princess Alice had wed Alix's father in a gloomy ceremony just six months after the death of Prince Albert, as Queen Victoria wept copiously. Now, tears also spilled from Nicholas II's widowed mother as she watched her son wed a woman she struggled to welcome into her distraught family.

Nicholas settled into his new roles as Emperor and husband, but soon found himself beset with unexpected domestic difficulties. He spent the first months of his married life living under his mother's roof at Anichkov Palace, ensconced with Alexandra in the same rooms he had used as a child, until apartments could be renovated for the couple in the Winter Palace and in the Alexander Palace at Tsarskoye Selo south of the capital. A kind of strained détente, polite on the surface yet simmering with hidden animosities, characterized relations between the now Dowager Empress and her new daughter-in-law, as both women – proud, arrogant, stubborn, and emotionally dependent – fought for Nicholas's time and attention. There were uncomfortable scenes and petty squabbles over precedence and imperial jewels that magnified into near hostility. Tension between the two women were so bad that, in spring of 1895, when Nicholas asked his wife to join him in presenting his mother with a Faberge egg for Easter, Alexandra flatly refused.[38]

Alexandra's behavior caused Nicholas difficulties. She rejected friendly advice offered by the Dowager

Alix and her father Grand Duke Ludwig IV.

Empress and by Grand Duchess Vladimir, creating a growing schism with the Imperial Family. She showed little tolerance for the Romanovs and their admittedly indulgent manner of life, and slowly turned her husband against his family, insisting that his relatives be judged according to her own moral standards, even as she failed to fulfill her own duties as Empress. Much later, tutor Charles Sydney Gibbes blamed her difficulties on Alexandra's *"lack of theatrical sense. The theatrical instinct is so deeply ingrained the Russian nature that one often feels that they act their lives rather than live them. This was completely foreign to the Empress."*[39] It is little wonder that the acerbic Grand Duke Nicholas Mikhailovich – no admirer – once referred to Alexandra as *"the woman who wanted to set Christ straight."*[40]

The strength of royalty lies in its ability to charm and engender affection: Alexandra failed at both. Society found her cold, awkward, and obviously uncomfortable in her new role. Worse, she exacerbated the situation by openly complaining not only of the Romanovs but also of her new country and its aristocrats, condemning them as immoral, vacuous, and hedonistic. She tried to impose her own prim, bourgeois values on proud St. Petersburg, suggesting that ladies should focus less on dinners and balls and instead form sewing circles to knit charitable contributions. Her manner was unfortunate and unsubtle, driven by an insistence that she knew best: when society fought back, so did Alexandra, crossing names from imperial guest lists. If she meant to teach a lesson she failed: in the end, the Empress's petulant behavior alienated aristocrats, officials, and members of her husband's family – the very people whose support was so necessary for the throne's preservation.[41]

A fatal pattern was set in these first years of Nicholas II's rule, in which he increasingly retreated into seclusion at the expense of his ceremonial duties. How great a role Alexandra's growing discomfort with her role as Empress may have played in Nicholas's retreat has long been the subject of debate, but there is little doubt that he

Empress Marie Feodorovna and Tsesarevich Nicholas.

gradually faded from regular public view under her influence as she *"showed how much animosity she could entertain towards her uncles and aunts,"* especially when judging them according to her own standards of morality.[42] The Alexander Palace at Tsarskoye Selo became not only their shared domestic sanctuary but also an increasingly unreal microcosm of the world Nicholas found most assuring, a place of devoted courtiers and luxury almost studied in its deliberate manifestations of simplicity, as Alexandra sought to emphasize just how different she was to the flamboyant Romanovs. Here the couple raised their four daughters: Olga, born in 1895; Tatiana, born in 1897; Marie, born in 1899; and Anastasia, born in 1901.

Nicholas and Alexandra at Schloß Rosenau on their engagement.

In May of 1896 Nicholas II went to his coronation in Moscow. The most solemn religious rite of his entire reign, the ceremony reinforced Nicholas's conception of a divinely mandated autocracy and belief that he stood apart from other monarchs. Yet a few days after the ceremony, over 1,400 people were crushed to death awaiting an open-air feast on Khodynka Meadow. Nicholas's response to the tragedy hinted at what was to come. Although initially inclined to cancel the remaining celebrations, he bowed under threats by his four powerful uncles Vladimir, Alexei, Sergei, and Paul and agreed to continue as if nothing

had happened. Although Nicholas later announced that he would give the families of the deceased 1,000 rubles, he failed to honor his promise. The Khodynka disaster laid the groundwork for the troubled decades to come, in which loyalty and the myth of a benevolent tsar gradually eroded under the realities of Nicholas II's rule.

The response to Khodynka revealed the fatal flaw in Nicholas's character: he went through life attempting to placate and please, avoiding confrontations and uncomfortable situations. *"As a man,"* recalled one of his officials, *"he inspired, by a union of rare qualities of heart and charming traits of character, a sentiment of deep sympathy."* Everyone admitted his great charm, but Nicholas's tendency to vacillate often left his ministers frustrated. An official would leave a meeting pleased at his gracious reception only to learn that he had been fired by the time he returned home. Nicholas, said Alexander Izwolsky, had an *"instinctive fear"* of *"saying or doing anything disagreeable to a person in his presence. When he had decided to dismiss a Minister he lacked the moral courage to tell him so to his face, but, on the contrary, treated him with twice his usual courtesy and attention and then had recourse to a written communication."*[43]

From the day of his accession to the time he abdicated, Nicholas's routine rarely varied. He was a man of routines, someone who took personal comfort in a strictly ordered world. He usually rose before eight each morning and slipped from the bedroom he shared with Alexandra. Like his father, he adopted simple baggy breeches and a loose peasant blouse as his preferred clothing if he had no official events.[44] He read telegrams, scanned newspapers, and looked over the day's schedule; walked regularly at ten; then met with officials and ministers until luncheon. Another afternoon walk preceded additional meetings. At five he joined Alexandra for tea, then worked until dinner, finally retiring around midnight.[45] Nicholas was methodical in everything he did. The same sense of regulation and order that had surrounded Nicholas in childhood characterized his adult life. He alone possessed the keys to his private study, and only reluctantly handed them over when it was to be cleaned. Palace servants were forbidden to move a single object: from the books, souvenirs, maps, letters, and other trinkets scattered across his desk and the tables, Nicholas demanded that everything be exactly as he had left it, saying that he wanted to be able to enter the room even in the dead of night and know immediately where any object could be found. When he wrote a letter, Nicholas often labored over it for hours; each night, before going to bed, he habitually made entries in his diary. This obsession with order even dominated intimate family moments. Nicholas carefully watched as photographs were glued into albums: an extra drop of paste resulted in anxiety.[46]

Tsar Nicholas II reading at home in the Alexander Palace.

Order was one thing that eluded Nicholas II in his reign. When he first came to the throne, many took his youth and choice of bride as evidence that he meant to change the course of Russian policy by advancing liberal ideas. Such hopes vanished in January 1895, when the new Emperor received representatives of provincial *zemstvos* in the Winter Palace. The delegation from Tver had dared express a wish that Nicholas would listen to the voice of the people; Nicholas answered the perceived challenge to his autocratic powers by dismissing as *"senseless dreams"* any idea that the *"people"* should have any role in how Russia was governed.

Jealously rebuffing anything that smacked of sharing his power, Nicholas from the start regarded the official governing apparatus – the Imperial Senate, the State Council and its ministers, and even his own court – as barriers between him and his people. He trusted no one: he even refused to keep a private secretary, fearing any infringement on his prerogatives. He set ministers against each other, accepted and then just as quickly rejected advice, and was always watchful for criticism or threats to the autocracy.

For the most part Nicholas followed the path his father had laid out, though in 1899 he stunned the world by sponsoring the First International Hague Peace Conference. The idea of limiting armament and preventing military actions undoubtedly held a certain appeal for Nicholas, but considerations beyond mere benevolence had played an equally important role. The previous year Austria-Hungary had announced a major military increase and restructuring; perceiving this as a threat in the Balkans, Nicholas agreed that the best way to avoid a costly arms race was to promote disarmament. The results were negligible, though the conference did establish the International Court of Arbitration. Nicholas was even nominated for the first Nobel Peace Prize – an irony considering the chaos that soon enveloped his Empire.

I should not take this decision upon myself. So far my conscience has never deceived me. Therefore, in this case also, I intend to follow its dictates. I know you, too, believe that 'the Emperor's heart is in God's hand.' So be it. I bear a terrible responsibility before God for all authorities set up by me and at any time I am ready to answer for them to Him."[48]

Shortly after the turn of the century, driven by a reckless sense of mission, Nicholas tried to colonize Manchuria and Korea, a misadventure that brought 1904's Russo-Japanese War, the destruction of the Baltic Fleet, and the Empire's humiliating defeat a year later at the Battle of Tsushima. The war coincided with the spread of discontent across the country; continued unrest eventually forced Nicholas to toy with half-hearted concessions. In December 1904, he investigated the possibility of granting an elected assembly, or Duma, without any actual power. Then, on Sunday, January 9, 1905, Tsarist troops opened fire on hundreds of unarmed men, women, and children marching on the Winter Palace to appeal for better working conditions. Known as "Bloody Sunday," the day did incalculable damage to the Emperor's prestige, especially when he received a delegation of workers at Tsarskoye Selo a week after the tragedy and declared that he forgave *them* for the crime their brethren – *"a rebel mob"* – had committed against the throne in marching on the Winter Palace.[49] A few weeks later, Grand

Tsar Nicholas II and his cousin Prince Nicholas of Greece. Greek Nicky, as the prince was called by the family, visited Russia frequently, particularly after his marriage to Elena Vladimirovna.

The first decade of Nicholas's reign witnessed growing unrest. Along with strikes and protests calling for reform came political assassinations: Bobrikov, Governor-General of Finland in 1902; Sipyagin, Minister of the Interior, in 1902; and Phehve, Minister of the Interior, in 1904, were among the more prominent officials killed by revolutionaries. Nicholas stubbornly resisted calls for change, once angrily asking, *"What have I got to do with public opinion?"*[47] Amidst a wave of pogroms, he similarly rejected lessening Russia's notoriously anti-Semitic laws. *"An inner voice,"* he explained, *"more insistently repeats to me that*

Tsar Nicholas II during the earlier years of his reign.

Duke Sergei was blown to pieces by a terrorist bomb and full-scale revolution soon swept the country.

Attempting to appease hated public opinion while still preserving his powers, Nicholas revisited granting an elected representative body. The proposal lingered in limbo as the Empire continued to slide into chaos: the Black Sea Fleet mutinied, railways and factory workers went on strike, and demonstrators filled the streets, demanding change. At the end of August, Nicholas finally announced that he was granting a purely consultative Duma, without the right to initiate or even pass legislation. This did nothing to quell the unrest. By October 1905, Russia was paralyzed, with more than 2 million workers on strike; in a letter to his mother, Nicholas insisted that *"nine-tenths of the troublemakers are Jews,"* though he also included *"engineers, lawyers and such-like bad people"* in his litany of enemies.[50]

Sergei Witte, Chairman of the Council of Ministers, insisted that there were only two ways to avoid further chaos: Nicholas could declare a military dictatorship, or he could grant a real constitution and a parliament with legislative authority. This last idea was completely alien to the Emperor's way of thinking. *"I shall never, under any circumstances,"* he once said, *"agree to a representative form of government, because I consider it harmful to the people God has entrusted to my care."*[51]

Yet Nicholas, ever pliable to pressure, soon gave in. On October 17, 1905, he reluctantly signed a manifesto establishing the Duma and ending the autocracy. Prince Vladimir Orlov found the Emperor sitting at his desk in the growing twilight, tears streaming down his face. Thinking that he shouldn't intrude on such a personal moment, he began backing away when Nicholas stopped him. *"Don't leave me today!"* he sobbed. *"I am too miserable. I feel that in signing this act I have lost the crown. Now it is the end of everything!"*[52]

Nicholas hadn't yet lost his crown, but he had lost the autocracy. He knew it, though he was loath to admit the fact, and spent the next decade attempting to rewrite the past, clinging to a deluded insistence that the reforms had been freely granted and that his autocratic power was never lessened.[53] He emphasized his contempt by refusing to open the parliament at their new home in St. Petersburg's Tauride Palace but instead summoning the deputies to an elaborate court ceremony in the Throne Room of the Winter Palace, where they would be forcefully reminded of his authority. The first two Dumas were closed when they demanded new concessions; the election laws were illegally altered to ensure a more conservative Third Duma. Things seemed to be improving, yet a dire situation was unfolding in the Alexander Palace.

After four daughters, Nicholas and Alexandra were desperate for a son and heir, and they fell under the influence of questionable mystics and wandering holy men. An elderly, imbecilic woman, Matrëna the Barefooted, entertained the imperial couple with idiotic mumbles supposedly predicting a son. Next came Dimitri Kolbya, a crippled epileptic whose *"divine revelation"* consisted of shouts, groans, and unnerving high-pitched shrieks. When his prediction of a male heir failed to materialize, he, too, was sent packing.

But the most important of these mystics was "Monsieur Philippe," a disreputable former butcher and criminal from Lyon named Philippe Nazier-Vachot. In addition to supposedly possessing powers of invisibility, he also claimed that he could select the sex of an unborn child. Alexandra naïvely ate it up. In the summer of 1902, Philippe declared that the Empress was expecting a son. Everyone waited in anticipation; Alexandra even put on weight, although she

Empress Alexandra Feodorovna and Tsesarevich Alexei, c. 1905.

refused to let doctors examine her. After nine months and no child Alexandra suffered labor pains: a fertilized egg was discharged, allowing doctors to characterize the episode as a miscarriage. Not to be put off, Philippe advised the gullible Empress that she would conceive a son if only the Emperor ordered the canonization of Seraphim of Sarov, an ascetic Eighteenth Century hermit already rejected by the Orthodox Church for sainthood. Alexandra insisted: when a Bishop objected, he was stripped of his rank and exiled to Siberia. The head of the Orthodox Church protested, but Alexandra cut him off, declaring, *"Everything is within the Emperor's power, even the making of saints!"*[54] The Imperial couple eventually got their way by forcing a canonization that caused a scandal in the church.

Nazier-Vachot fell from favor, but by 1904, Alexandra was again pregnant. On July 30, 1904, she finally gave birth to a son, Tsesarevich Alexei. Discovery that he had inherited hemophilia left the parents distraught and seeking a miracle that could save their son, a quest that ended on November 1, 1905, when the imperial couple first met Siberian peasant Gregory Rasputin. Simple, unpretentious, and never able to rise above his peasant background, Rasputin bewitched and beguiled, mumbling half-learned Bible passages along with assurances that all of Russia loved the Tsar. A subservient Rasputin, grumbling before Nicholas and Alexandra and unaffectedly calling them "Papa" and "Mama," appealed to their vanity. Yet it was his presumed ability to alleviate Alexei's attacks of hemophilia that cemented his place at court. After several apparent "miracles," Alexandra was convinced that Rasputin's prayers kept her son alive.

Rasputin was nothing but a cynical charlatan who stumbled through his new life in St. Petersburg. He boasted about his friendship with the Imperial couple; bedded innumerable women; and drank to excess. No one knew that Alexei suffered from hemophilia; no one could understand why the Emperor and Empress tolerated this increasingly debauched peasant. The Empress rejected evidence of his misdeeds, unwilling to admit that her faith in the peasant had been misplaced. Belief in Rasputin as a man sent by God to save her son was, in fact, an unconscious emotional convenience meant to preserve Alexandra's fragile ego.

Nicholas liked Rasputin personally, but he never fell completely under his power. Unlike Alexandra, he was usually willing to admit that the peasant had a less savory side. Several times officials reported on this or that misdeed as the Emperor listened quietly, but inevitably he insisted that, *"Nobody has the right to interfere in my private business."* When Prince Vladimir Orlov objected, reminding the Emperor that his *"private life belongs to all of Russia,"* Nicholas shut down any further conversation, saying, *"If you love me, please don't speak to me about it ever again. It is too painful for me."*[55] To another official, he commented simply: *"I can do nothing about it."*[56] This impotence in the face of his strong-willed wife indicated that he couldn't or wouldn't stand up to Alexandra.

Nicholas was powerless because, after two decades of marriage, the more forceful Alexandra had reduced him to a shadowy figure repeatedly bowing to her will. The marriage was certainly passionate, but it also carried a dangerous element of unbalanced obsession. Extremely jealous of his

Tsar Nicholas II and his wife Alexandra Feodorovna.

official obligations, ties to the Romanov family, and even friendships, Alexandra isolated Nicholas until his circle of intimates was confined to a few courtiers and his wife's boudoir. Nicholas accepted it as idealized love precisely because it repeated the same smothering patterns that had characterized his relationship with his mother. He associated unconditional love with obedience, correction, and compliance. Over the years, Alexandra's constant warnings about his weakness eroded what little self-confidence Nicholas possessed. By the last weeks of his reign, after twenty-two-years of such hectoring, Nicholas had taken to repeatedly signing his letters to his wife, *"Your weak-willed hubby."* In attempting to reshape her husband according to her own desires, Alexandra made Nicholas entirely dependent on her and her opinions.

Alexandra wallowed in insecurities that took form in questionable claims of insomnia, heart palpitations and circulatory problems. Several times, Nicholas confessed to relatives that it took a toll, yet doctors who suggested psychological rather than organic causes were quickly replaced. In 1910, Alexandra spent some time in Germany, where she submitted to examination by several specialists. Kaiser Wilhelm II had Count Paul von Hintze, his military attaché in St. Petersburg, secretly collect the medical opinions. The physicians were unanimous that Alexandra had no organic problems; instead, she was suffering from *"a severe nervous disorder."* After noting complaints of *"weakness of the heart"* and *"general fatigue at the least bodily effort,"* the secret report concluded that Alexandra suffered from a *"pathological condition"* that the doctors vaguely deemed a *"hysterical illness."* Not that anyone had dared to suggest such a thing to her: *"Her Majesty took the greatest offense when advice or contrary medical opinions were offered to her."*[57]

There might have been a slightly hyperbolic touch to this report, but even Imperial physician Eugene Botkin admitted, *"I let my imagination run free in searching for different names for her condition."* Privately, he said that Alexandra was *"not entirely normal,"* and spoke of *"the pathological character"* of her complaints.[58] The medicines he prescribed – the barbiturate Veronal and Aconitum to relieve severe anxiety and Ignatia to control mood swings and emotional instability – testify to the psychological, not organic, nature of the Empress's problems.

Despite the turmoil in his private life, the Nicholas II of 1914 could face the future with some optimism. His Empire had successfully avoided becoming embroiled in the Balkan Wars of 1912-13 and the Russian economy was growing. Foreign investment was starting to transform industry; new labor laws went into force; and the government embarked on an ambitious project to ensure universal education by 1924. But then came the assassination of Archduke Franz Ferdinand and

Tsar Nicholas II and Kaiser Wilhelm II, with Grand Duke Alexei.

his wife at Sarajevo. Although extremely reluctant to go to war, Nicholas II faced a host of insistent ministers and military officials who argued that he must order mobilization against Austria-Hungary after Emperor Franz Josef rejected Serbia's half-hearted replies to his government's ultimatum. Nicholas initially agreed to mobilize his troops then tried to rescind the measure only to again change his mind a few hours later. On July 20, Germany declared war on Russia.

In a burst of patriotism, Nicholas II changed the name of the Imperial capital from the Germanic St. Petersburg to the Slavic Petrograd and watched as thousands of his soldiers marched off to war. An early Russian offensive in East Prussia quickly devolved into disastrous defeat, and it soon became apparent that the Tsarist Empire was hopelessly short of adequate troop transport, munitions, and even bullets for ordinary soldiers. Nicholas II began spending weeks at Stavka, the military headquarters established first at Baranovichi and then, with the Russian retreat, at Mogilev. *"It is difficult to believe that a great war is raging not far from this place,"* Nicholas wrote to Alexandra on September 22, 1914. *"Everything seems so peaceful and quiet."*[59] His presence was symbolic: at the beginning of the war Nicholas had named Grand Duke Nicholas Nikolaievich Jr. as Commander-in-Chief of the Russian Army. The Emperor, who had no practical experience with war or military planning, sat in on meetings, attended reviews,

Tsar Nicholas II at the front with Grand Duke Nicholas, in the car, towering over him.

and discussed options, but all decisions rested with the fiery Grand Duke.

Alexandra, too, joined the war effort, though she did so in her own peculiar way. Although presiding over relief organizations with an admirable sense of purpose, she seemed most interested in practical, not ceremonial, pursuits. She took Red Cross training along with her two oldest daughters, and worked in a hospital reserved for wounded officers at Tsarskoye Selo. It gave Alexandra purpose and served her psychological desire to feel needed but criticism followed. The public couldn't understand an Empress who bandaged shattered legs and sutured bloody wounds. People thought that she was debasing her position.

In early 1915, Russian soldiers steadily advanced against the Austrians in Galicia but the gains were temporary: an offensive launched by the Central Powers in May drove Tsarist soldiers back amid devastating casualties. By the beginning of the summer, nearly 1.4 million Russian soldiers had been killed or wounded, with nearly a million more taken prisoners-of-war. In August, Warsaw fell to the advancing Germans. Russia was in retreat, its army demoralized.

Alexandra used the crisis to campaign against Grand Duke Nicholas Nikolaievich. He had made no secret of his distaste for Rasputin, which earned the Empress's wrath. In letters to her husband, she insisted that the Grand Duke was always plotting, attempting to promote himself and diminish the Emperor – an unfounded charge she later repeated to her former sister-in-law Grand Duchess Victoria Feodorovna.[60] She urged her husband to remove the Grand Duke from power and assume Supreme Command himself – a move she had initially rejected in the worry that distance would lessen her influence over her husband.

In truth Nicholas II needed little persuasion. Despite his lack of tactical training, the Emperor believed that his place was with his army. During the Russo-Japanese War he had wanted to lead his men but let himself be dissuaded. Now, he hoped to atone for that mistake: however symbolic, his presence at the Front, he believed, would help lift morale. There were also practical considerations. Civilian and military authority was divided between the Emperor and the Grand Duke: by assuming Supreme Command, Nicholas II hoped to consolidate power and expedite decisions.

This was all well and good, but it ignored one problem: as an autocrat, Nicholas II's constant attention and action were crucial to the operation of his government. By removing himself from that role, he created a vacuum in leadership. When his ministers learned of the decision, ten of the thirteen officials signed a letter opposing Nicholas's proposal. If he insisted, they asked to be relieved of their posts. Nicholas saw in this not a warning sign but revolt, and angrily rejected their advice. They would resign only when he saw fit. *"In the moment of danger,"* Nicholas declared with finality, *"the duty of a sovereign is to be with his army and if need be, perish with it."*[61]

Gregory Rasputin.

Nicholas left for Stavka to assume Supreme Command carrying a triumphant letter from his wife, who assured him that Rasputin had blessed the decision. *"Our Friend's prayers arise night and day for you to Heaven,"* she wrote her husband, *"and God will hear them. It is the beginning of the glory of your reign. Our Friend said so and I absolutely believe it."*[62] In fact, it was the beginning of the end, but neither Nicholas nor Alexandra perceived the dangers that lay ahead.

While Nicholas's assumption of Supreme Command made a certain amount of bureaucratic sense, his impact at Stavka was negligible. He heard reports for an hour every morning, but most of his official duties consisted of assenting to his generals' advice. *"Strictly speaking,"* recalled Father George Shavelsky, *"that hour-long report session constituted all of the sovereign's work as supreme commander."*[63] Most of his time passed pleasantly: he lunched with officials and foreign representatives; took long walks or went driving in the afternoons; and occasionally received ministers visiting from Petrograd.

With Nicholas at headquarters, Alexandra now became the face of Imperial power. The Emperor made governmental decisions but those decisions were often influenced and coerced by his wife. In a letter to her husband, Alexandra assured Nicholas that she had *"trousers on, unseen,"* and was ready to lead the government in his absence.[64] Armed with undying earnestness and convinced of the superiority of her intellect, she plunged forward in an effort to be *"useful."* Alexandra's understanding of her adopted homeland was abysmal. *"Russia loves to feel the whip,"* she insisted to Nicholas, *"it's in their nature."*[65] In letters she urged Nicholas to crush all revolt, to become Peter the Great or Ivan the Terrible, to be more decided in his opinions. Yet she protested whenever Nicholas voiced an opinion different than her own. She didn't want him to be more autocratic; she wanted him to be more obedient to her will. Nicholas, she candidly said, *"is weak, but I am not."*[66]

A deadly self-delusion took hold. Alexandra scattered Rasputin's name throughout her letters, but she was the dominant partner in their relationship. The hysterical Empress in thrall to the Siberian peasant who dictated government appointments is a myth. Rasputin was crafty enough to sense what Alexandra wanted and simply parroted back her own views when quizzed on politicians and policies. She then used Rasputin's name to wrap her opinions in a mantle of divine sanction to her husband. It all meshed with emotional ideas that her marriage was some sort of religious mission, but it was an abusive mixture of faith and politics. The tragedy is that no one was strong enough to stop her.

Empress Alexandra Feodorovna.

Officials came, went, and were reshuffled for no apparent reason: in the eighteen months from September 1915 to the Revolution, Russia had four Prime Ministers, five Ministers of the Interior, four Ministers of Agriculture, three Ministers of War, three Foreign Ministers – on and on it went, a shocking and disreputable display that left the country paralyzed. Nicholas seemed unable to resist his wife's suggestions, which were often little short of demands, even when he knew her proposals would be catastrophic. Once, he even unbelievably confessed to adjutant Nicholas Sablin that he purposely made bad decisions precisely because they flew in the face of all advice that he had received. By doing so, Nicholas insisted, he would *"prove his own power."*[67]

Such was the case with Alexander Protopopov, who mumbled to himself, twitched, and shouted obscenities at the voices in his head: suffering from syphilis and slowly going insane, he had already been confined to asylums and suffered nervous breakdowns, but Alexandra wanted him made Minister of the Interior. When Nicholas resisted, she used Rasputin's name, suggesting that since the peasant liked him, Protopopov had all the necessary qualifications. The Emperor was uncertain. *"Our Friend's ideas about men are sometimes queer,"* he warned. *"All these changes exhaust the head. They happen much too often."*[68] Alexandra refused to back down and Nicholas gave in against his better judgment.

Protopopov was so incompetent that the Emperor wanted to remove him after only two months in office. *"It must be done,"* he warned his wife. *"Only please don't mix in our Friend! It is I who carry the responsibility and must choose accordingly."*[69] This wasn't what Alexandra wanted to hear.

Ignoring her husband's pleas, she immediately had Rasputin telegraph the Emperor warning of dire consequences if Protopopov fell from power. At the same time, she began her most insistent and shrill campaign: she wrote Nicholas two and sometimes three letters a day demanding that he keep Protopopov. Alexandra even traveled to headquarters to make her case in person. What happened next was probably the most serious argument of their married life: even the un-emotive Emperor admitted that their days together had been *"especially hard ones."*[70] Twenty years of Alexandra's constant recriminations and exhortations had left Nicholas perpetually apologetic; he seemed to actually fear opposing his wife. And so, to Russia's horror, the insane Protopopov remained in the second highest office in the land.

Tsar Nicholas II and Tsesarevich Alexei Nikolaievich.

Destructive decisions by Nicholas and Alexandra also undermined the authority of the Russian Orthodox Church. They allowed Rasputin to openly meddle in church affairs. His disreputable friends were promoted to positions of authority and his enemies exiled. The monk Varnava, who liked to be photographed in coffins and lived in scandal with a bevy of attractive young men, became a bishop over the church's objections. Another man, Bishop Alexei, had a mistress and engaged in blasphemous worship yet with Rasputin's backing he became the fourth most powerful official in the Orthodox Church. Two Rasputin protégés, Alexander Volzhin and

Nicholas Raev, were appointed in quick succession to serve as Ober-Procurator of the Holy Synod. Even worse scandal came when Alexandra urged her husband to name the notorious Bishop Pitirim as Metropolitan of Petrograd, the most powerful clerical position in the church. Not only was he Rasputin's ally but Pitirim was also an undisguised scoundrel: he ignored his monastic vows of poverty and chastity, blackmailed people, stole from the church treasury, and lived openly with his male lovers. Yet Alexandra deemed him clever and impelled Nicholas to promote him as Metropolitan. Soon the Alexander Nevsky Monastery echoed with gypsy choirs, wild orgies, and drunken midnight revels. When the Communist Revolution came, people so willingly turned against this bastion of traditional faith precisely because the Emperor, his wife, and Rasputin, had tragically erased the Church's remaining moral authority.

Nicholas II rarely discussed military affairs with his wife, though this did not stop Alexandra from volunteering her opinions and, inevitably, those of Rasputin. The Emperor begged his wife not to share military details with the peasant but she ignored her husband. *"He won't mention it to a soul,"* she insisted, *"but I had to ask His blessing."*[71] During the Brusilov Offensive in the spring and summer of 1916, Alexandra besieged her absent husband with Rasputin's advice. For Nicholas, it must have been frustrating to have his wife so pointedly reject his wishes; even worse, it must have been humiliating, as if an illiterate Siberian peasant somehow better understood the complexities of military strategy and munitions.

Russian losses in the Brusilov Offensive were appalling: some 1.4 million soldiers were killed, wounded, or taken prisoner but the action successfully crippled Austria, diverted German troops from the Western Front, and saved the French Army at Verdun. Then, just as Tsarist troops were advancing into enemy territory, Alexandra assailed her husband with demands that the campaign be halted. Letter after letter filled with demands followed, until Nicholas obeyed. Everyone suspected that Alexandra was behind the decision. Russia's German-born Empress, they whispered, must be secretly working with Rasputin to ensure a German victory – how else to explain such an inexplicable development?

Grand Duchess Marie Pavlovna Sr.

By the autumn of 1916, Russia was rapidly spiraling into chaos. Discontent in the army, the endless succession of ministerial appointments, moral disintegration among the Orthodox hierarchy, and the shadow of Rasputin all coalesced into a growing hatred against the Romanov Dynasty in general, and Nicholas – and especially Alexandra – in particular. Watching the latest newsreels in a cinema, one British visitor was shocked when the audience erupted in hisses when the Empress appeared on screen.[72]

Grand Duchess Marie Pavlovna was stunned when she heard *"people speaking of the Emperor and Empress with open animosity and contempt. The word 'revolution' was uttered more openly and more often; soon it could be heard everywhere. The war seemed to recede to the background. All attention was riveted on interior events. Rasputin, Rasputin, Rasputin – it was like a refrain: his mistakes, his shocking personal conduct, his mysterious power. This power was tremendous; it was like dusk, enveloping all our world, eclipsing the sun. How could so pitiful a wretch throw so vast a shadow? It was inexplicable, maddening, baffling, almost incredible."*[73] No rumor was too bizarre: obscene pamphlets and cartoons showed the Empress and Rasputin; people believed that he slept with Alexandra and her four young daughters. The Empress, it was said, believed herself to be a second Catherine the Great; she had reduced her husband to an impotent shell. Nicholas must divorce her and confine her to distant convent, voices warned, before she deposed him and took the throne for herself.

On the morning of December 17, 1916, the telephone beside Alexandra's chaise in the Mauve Boudoir jingled to life. The Empress was stunned: Rasputin was missing. *"Our Friend has disappeared!"* she wrote to her husband at headquarters.[74] In reply, Nicholas assured her that he was *"horrified and shaken,"* and made plans to return to Tsarskoye Selo.[75] But officials noted that his mood seemed lighter, as if a burden had been lifted from his shoulders.

It did not take the police long to learn what had happened. The previous evening, Rasputin had gone out with Prince Felix Yussoupov. The Prince denied all but soon the story unraveled in all of its grisly, theatrical detail: with the assistance of Grand Duke Dimitri Pavlovich, conservative politician Vladimir Purishkevich, an army doctor named Lazovert, and a young officer named Sukhotin, Yussoupov had arranged the peasant's murder in his palace. After having been poisoned, shot, and stabbed, Rasputin had been hurled into a frozen river, where he was located a few days later. Alexandra had Rasputin's body brought to Tsarskoye Selo for burial in a corner of the park on the morning of December 21. *"My family and I witnessed a sad scene,"* Nicholas wrote in his diary, *"the burial of the unforgettable Gregory, assassinated by monsters at the home of Yussoupov."*[76] That year, for the first time in memory, Nicholas and Alexandra sent no Christmas presents to the Grand Dukes and their families.[77]

Public opinion supported the murder, and

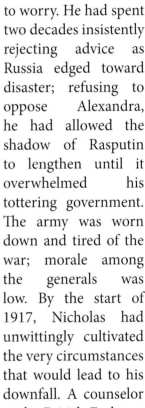

Grand Duke Dimitri with Tsar Nicholas II and Grand Duchess Tatiana Nikolaievna.

Nicholas was unable to punish either the popular Purishkevich or Lazovert and Sukhotin. Instead, he took half-measures against Grand Duke Dimitri Pavlovich and Felix Yussoupov. Dimitri was sent to his regiment in Persia, while Yussoupov was exiled to one of his family's estates in central Russia.

Nicholas had reason to worry. He had spent two decades insistently rejecting advice as Russia edged toward disaster; refusing to oppose Alexandra, he had allowed the shadow of Rasputin to lengthen until it overwhelmed his tottering government. The army was worn down and tired of the war; morale among the generals was low. By the start of 1917, Nicholas had unwittingly cultivated the very circumstances that would lead to his downfall. A counselor at the British Embassy reported back to London: *"I have never heard anyone say a good word about the Tsar or Empress, and their assassination is quite openly discussed. No one is shocked by it."*[78]

The constant fights, the perceived disloyalty of his relatives, Rasputin's murder, and the decades of admonitions from Alexandra – it had all left the Nicholas II of January 1917 close to a nervous breakdown, a situation exacerbated by the Imperial couple's drug use. Alexandra was addicted to barbiturates and varied prescriptions merely added to her lethargy and mental confusion. By now Nicholas and Alexandra were taking cocaine, hashish, and opium to relieve frequent headaches, toothaches, sleeplessness, and insomnia. This escalating spiral left the Imperial couple paranoid and unable to comprehend what was taking place outside the walls of their palace.

When Vladimir Kokovtsov, former chairman of the Council of Ministers, met Nicholas in early February, he was shocked at the Emperor's obvious decline. *"He had become almost unrecognizable,"* Kokovtsov remembered. *"His face had become very thin and hollowed and covered with small wrinkles. His eyes had become quite faded and wandered endlessly from object to object. The whites were of a decidedly yellow tinge, and the dark retinas had become colorless, gray and lifeless."*[79]

Chairman of the Council of Ministers Vladimir Kokovtsov.

grave, drawn features and furtive, distant gaze, the impenetrability of his thoughts and the thoroughly vague and enigmatical quality of his personality, confirm me in a notion which has been haunting me for months, the notion that Nicholas II feels himself overwhelmed and dominated by events, that he has lost all faith in his mission or his work, that he has so to speak abdicated inwardly and is now resigned to disaster and ready for the sacrificial altar."[81]

The last week of February 1917, rumors reached the government that Nicholas II would come to the Duma and make an important address. Hopes ran high that he might finally grant the country a responsible ministry. But then, on February 22 the Emperor abruptly changed his plans, announcing that he was leaving the capital for Stavka. The

Count Paul von Benckendorff, Grand Marshal of the Imperial Court, was so worried that one day he cornered Dr. Eugene Botkin. *"It can't continue this way much longer,"* Benckendorff said. *"His Majesty is a changed man. It is very wrong of him to attempt the impossible. He is no longer seriously interested in anything. Of late, he has become quite apathetic. He goes through his daily routine like an automaton, paying more attention to the hour set for his meals or his walks in the garden than to affairs of state. One can't rule an empire and command an army in the field in this manner."*[80] And French Ambassador Maurice Paleologue came away from a meeting at Tsarskoye Selo convinced of impending tragedy: *"The Emperor's words, his silences and reticence, his*

timing could not have been worse: workers at the Putilov Factory, Petrograd's largest steelworks, had just gone out on strike; within a day they would be joined by hundreds of thousands of hungry protesters and disillusioned students. When Nicholas finally returned to Tsarskoye Selo ten days later, it was a former monarch, a prisoner of the new Provisional Government, and the man who had unwittingly brought the proud 304-year-old Romanov Dynasty to its end

Chapter II

The Senior Nikolaievich Line: The Imperial Children

By 1914 Nicholas and Alexandra's children were fast growing up. Later, devoted courtiers wrote of *"their extreme simplicity, candor, freshness, and instinctive kindness."*[1] They were, declared the Empress's friend Lili Dehn, *"innocent children,"* with *"no idea of the ugly side of life."*[2] *"Unassuming and natural, without a trace of hauteur,"* wrote Anna Vyrubova.[3] And Baroness Sophie Buxhoeveden encapsulated such sentiments, insisting that the Imperial children *"were used to a quiet life,"* *"never quarreled,"* and never resented the isolation in which they were brought up.[4] Yet time has gradually revealed a more realistic version of their lives, illuminating individual desires, worries, and characters that combine to make Nicholas and Alexandra's children human beings instead of dutiful saints.

Grand Duchesses Tatiana, Maria and Olga.

They were all brought up simply, or as simply as a prince and princesses in a palace might be. Olga and Tatiana shared one bedroom, Marie and Anastasia a second; only Alexei had a private bedroom. Within the household, the two eldest girls were known as "the Big Pair," while Marie and Anastasia were "the Little Pair." They slept on the traditional folding army camp beds, made comfortable with quilted eiderdowns, took warm baths only at night, and helped maids clean their rooms. Hoping to avoid any precocious tendencies, Nicholas and Alexandra asked that courtiers address them not by titles but rather by their Christian names and patronymics; ever frugal, the Empress also insisted that they receive minimal allowances each month, from which they were expected to purchase personal items and gifts.

Olga, born on November 3, 1895, most closely resembled her father in character. As a baby, recalled Grand Duchess Marie Pavlovna, she was *"remarkably ugly, with a head too large for her small body."*[5] It was, along with a short nose that she joking called *"my humble stub,"* the one physical defect she could not overcome.[6] Olga had her father's chestnut hair and deep blue eyes set in a wide, typically Slavic face with a fair complexion; she went, as Lili Dehn noted, from being rather *"plain"* to a *"beautiful"* young woman by the time of the Tercentenary in 1913.[7] Graceful and energetic, she was a beautiful dancer, though she unfortunately had few opportunities to do so. She was also extremely conscious of her privileged position, and keenly felt the needs of those less fortunate than herself; when she later came into possession of a small part of her private fortune, she began regularly donating it to help others.[8]

Many concurred that Olga was the most thoughtful of the children. Her nanny Miss Eager later recalled how, on a trip to Germany, she had taken young Olga to a toy store, telling her to select an item for herself. Olga looked over the shelves and picked the smallest, cheapest toy she could find. Eager objected, explaining that the owner would undoubtedly be upset if she went away with such an insignificant item. *"But the beautiful toys belong to some other little girls, I am sure,"* Olga said. *"And think how sad they would be if they came home and found we had taken them while they were out."*[9]

Olga, remembered Gleb Botkin, son of Imperial physician Eugene Botkin, was *"by nature a thinker,"* with *"a sweetness about her which prevented her from affecting anybody in a depressing manner, even when she herself felt depressed."*[10] Olga liked to read, painted well, and was a gifted pianist, though her music teacher inevitably complained that she was lazy and practiced only when she wanted. She was also determined and had a tendency to stubbornness. With her straightforward character, she found it difficult to conceal her feelings and at times, everyone agreed, she spoke her mind too freely, and occasionally let loose with displays of irritated temper. Sometimes, recalled Buxhoeveden, she would *"turn suddenly cross when offended."*[11]

Tatiana, the second daughter, was born May 30, 1897. In character and appearance, she was most like her mother: tall, thin, elegant and extremely reserved. Pierre Gilliard called her *"less transparent, frank, and spontaneous"* than her siblings, as if Tatiana carefully guarded her actions.[12] She had dark auburn hair, fine features, a pale complexion, and wide-set, dark eyes that, Buxhoeveden insisted, *"gave her a poetic, far-away look."* Although quiet, Tatiana knew her own mind and could be stubborn, though she naturally concealed her feelings and tried desperately to please those around her. Her siblings called her *"the governess"* for her somewhat dominant manner. If a special was needed, all agreed that *"Tatiana must ask Papa to grant it."*[13]

Tatiana was the most social of the daughters and *"longed pathetically for friends."*[14] She was also the most popular of Nicholas and Alexandra's daughters, perhaps because she was the only one of the four sisters to take pains over her appearance: she loved clothing and *"liked admiration."* Many thought that her parents favored her over their other daughters, possibly because Tatiana was ever compliant and obedient.[15] When she was nineteen, Nicholas described his hope that she *"will remain as good, loving, and patient a girl as she is now, and be our consolation in old age."*[16]

Many noted Tatiana's obvious displays of overt piety, and both Gilliard and fellow tutor Charles Sidney Gibbes speculated that while she did not necessarily feel the same religious passion in her soul, she tried to do so to please her mother. Pleasing Alexandra, in fact, was what won her mother's favor, and Tatiana became the Empress's trusted confidant and selfless caregiver. She always abandoned her own interests to cater to Alexandra's whims, to sit with her, to read to her, *"to do anything that was wanted,"* Buxhoeveden recalled.[17] As Pierre Gilliard noted, Tatiana *"knew how to surround her with un-wearying attentions and never gave way to her own capricious impulses."*[18]

Marie, the third daughter, was born on June 14, 1899. Nicholas II was apparently so disappointed by

Standing, from the left: Grand Duchess Maria Nikolaievna, Princess nina Georgievna,, and Grand Duchesses Anastasia. On the floor are Grand Duchesses Olga and Tatiana Nikolaievna with Princess Nina Georgievna, and Princess Olga of Greece.

the arrival of yet another Grand Duchess that he had to take a solitary walk before he could face his wife.[19] Marie was widely acknowledged as the most beautiful of the four daughters. She had abundant, long brown hair tinged with blonde, a rosy complexion, and eyes so deeply blue that they were called *"Marie's saucers"* within the family. Of all the daughters, she was also the most even-tempered and jovial, simple in her tastes and always kind to those around her; her dream, she often said, was to marry and raise a large family.[20]

As a young girl, Marie was somewhat plump: her sisters, unfortunately, took advantage, calling her *"fat little bow-wow."*[21] Even Alexandra joined in undermining her daughter's self-confidence and *"often teased her"* about her weight.[22] Such ridicule played on Marie's gentle spirit, and she struggled with feelings that she was unwanted and unloved. When younger, Olga and Tatiana referred to Marie

as their *"step-sister,"* and this sense left the third daughter occasionally feeling alienated.[23]

Anastasia, the youngest of the four daughters, was born on June 5, 1901. *"I cannot help sharing your natural disappointment that a fourth daughter instead of a son has been born,"* King Edward VII wrote to Nicholas II.[24] She had fine auburn hair and vibrant blue eyes, but felt cursed by her lack of height. Everyone agreed that she was vivacious and intelligent, though also something of a terror. Perhaps she simply rebelled because, as the youngest girl, she was fighting for her own place within the family, but her outlandish pranks and wild behavior became legendary, especially among the hapless Romanov cousins she often tormented.

At a young age Anastasia would entertain old men with her witticisms; yet her humor, often pointed, *"found sensitive spots."*[25] There was something of

Tsesarevich Alexei Nikolaievich driving his miniature automobile.

a tomboy about her: she climbed trees, made faces, cheated at games, spat, scratched and kicked if she failed to get her way, and generally behaved abominably, yet she could also be extremely sensitive. *"Whenever I talked with her,"* recalled General Count Alexander von Grabbe, head of the Cossack *Konvoi* Regiment, *"I always came away impressed by the breadth of her interests. That her mind was keenly alive was immediately apparent."*[26]

None of the four daughters proved to be particularly brilliant when it came to their studies, though neither Nicholas nor Alexandra seemed to have taken much care when it came to selecting men of great accomplishment, skill, or intellect to teach their children. It was ironic, given Nicholas II's frequent complaints about how he felt betrayed by his own educational shortcomings. Children of previous Romanov sovereigns had been tutored by intellectual greats: renowned historians, artists, poets, lawyers, philosophers, and discoverers. Nicholas and Alexandra selected people like the unremarkable Swiss Pierre Gilliard, Yorkshire native Charles Sidney Gibbes, and ambitious palace official Vladimir Voyekov to teach their children. Perhaps this reflected the couple's lingering distrust of "intellectuals" in general; but as Pierre Gilliard noted, Alexandra – as her mother-in-law had done with Nicholas and his siblings – also distrusted anyone who might come between her and her children and influence them in any way.[27]

Olga was undoubtedly the most intellectual of the four sisters, with *"a remarkably quick brain,"* Gilliard said. *"She had good reasoning powers as well as initiative,"* and *"picked up everything extremely quickly."* Yet he was forced to note that Olga *"did not fulfill the hopes I had set upon her. Her fine intellect failed to find the elements necessary to its development. Instead of making progress, she began to go back."* He thought that Tatiana was *"not so gifted"* as Olga and less interested in intellectual pursuits, while Marie seemed to completely lack ambition. Anastasia had a fine brain but no taste for formal education.[28]

"Alexei was the center of this united family, the focus of all its hopes and affections," wrote Pierre Gilliard. *"His sisters worshiped him. He was the pride and joy of his parents."*[29] After four successive daughters, Nicholas was ecstatic over his son's birth on July 30, 1904. It was, Nicholas wrote in his diary, *"an unforgettable, great day for us, during which we were clearly visited by the grace of God. At a quarter-past one in the afternoon, Alix had a son, who in prayer we named Alexei. Everything happened at a remarkable pace….No words can*

adequately thank God for the consolation He has bestowed on us."[30]

Russia and its ruling family celebrated. *"I don't think that you have yet seen my dear little Tsesarevich,"* Nicholas said to Alexander Mossolov one day. *"Come along and I will show him to you."* They found the baby in the middle of his bath, *"lustily kicking out in the water."* Nicholas picked him up, cradling him in his hands and asking, *"Don't you think he's a beauty?"*[31] Six weeks later Alexei bled uncontrollably from his naval. After three days the bleeding stopped but over the following months, as Alexei began to crawl and tumble, his limbs were peppered with dark, ugly bruises. There was no longer any doubt: Alexei had inherited hemophilia.

From the left: Grand Duchess Maria Nikolaievna, Princess Victoria of Great Britain, Empress Alexandra Feodorovna, Tsesarevich Alexei, Grand Duchess Olga Nikolaievna, Grand Duchess Anastasia Nikolaieva, Grand Duchess Olga Alexandrovna, and Grand Duchess Tatiana Nikolaievna.

Nicholas seems never to have considered the possibility of a hemophiliac son. Alexandra, though, was well aware of her family's dangerous legacy. Queen Victoria had one hemophiliac son, Prince Leopold, Duke of Albany, who died from a hemorrhage after a minor fall on a staircase. The Queen had passed the mutated genes on to two of her daughters, Alexandra's mother Alice and the Queen's youngest child, Beatrice. Alexandra's brother Friedrich, called Frittie, had died at the age of three from the disease, while her sister Irene had two hemophiliac sons, Waldemar in 1889 and Heinrich, who died of the condition just weeks before Alexei's birth. Yet Alexandra had stubbornly dismissed the risks. A few weeks after her engagement, she told one of Queen Victoria's courtiers that she was ignoring *"all those horrid things which were said about cousins marrying,"* and the unpleasant implications of the *"disease which poor Frittie had."*[32]

Hemophilia brought with it uncertainty. Although an external cut could be bandaged, there were no treatments for internal hemorrhages; usually they stopped after a time of excruciating pain and pressure; when they did not, death could result. *"Your Majesty must realize,"* Professor Sergei Fedorov warned Nicholas, *"that the Tsesarevich will never be completely cured of his disease. The attacks of hemophilia will recur now and then. Strenuous measures of protection will have to be taken to guard the Heir against falls, cuts and scratches, because the slightest bleeding may prove fatal."*[33] The Imperial couple carefully kept their only son's disease a secret; not even the Emperor's sisters were told until several years after Alexei's birth. Nicholas accepted his son's condition passively, as indeed he did with all misfortunes: it was simply the inscrutable manifestation of God's will. Not so Alexandra. Knowing that she was responsible for passing on the condition to her son devastated Alexandra, and the guilt she felt eventually led to her belief in Rasputin.

With his fine features, auburn hair, and blue-gray eyes, Alexei closely resembled his mother.[34] Perpetually worried about accidents, Nicholas and Alexandra appointed two sailors from the Imperial Navy, Andrei Derevenko and Klementy Nagorny, to constantly watch over their son. Anna Vyrubova later recalled the invalid Alexei always asking Derevenko, *"Lift my arm...put up my leg...warm my hands."* Derevenko patiently and calmly did all he could to alleviate the boy's sufferings and keep him well, though Alexei naturally strained against his enforced safe mode of life. *"Can't I have a bicycle?"* he might beg, only to be told that he could not; ordinary climbs, games of tennis, and other physical activities brought their own worries. Sometimes, the denials were too much: *"Why can other boys have everything, and I nothing?"* Alexei might cry in despair.[35]

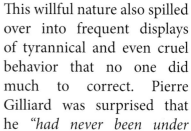

Tsar Nicholas II and Alexandra Feodorovna with their daughters Tatiana and Anastasia Nikolaievna visit Anna Vyroubova.

"He thoroughly enjoyed life — when it let him — and was a happy, romping boy," Gilliard recalled, adding that Alexei was charming, affectionate, and *"sensitive to suffering in others just because he had already suffered so much himself."*[36] Numerous people commented on this affinity for suffering and unusual thoughtfulness in the young boy,

and his illness undoubtedly deeply affected him. Tutor Charles Sydney Gibbes deemed him *"of a bright and amiable disposition,"* noting that his illness *"served but to heighten the sensitivities of his character and to deepen his sympathies."*[37] But illness also effected his education. *"His frequent illnesses made him rather backward at his lessons,"* Buxhoeveden recalled, *"but he was very clever, with a good memory, and when he was well he worked hard to make up for lost time."*[38] But while Gilliard agreed he had *"very quick wits and a keen and penetrating mind,"* Alexei was a difficult pupil, unaccustomed to the discipline of the classroom and at times hostile and even defiant with his tutors.[39] Gibbes later admitted that Alexei *"had no great love of books,"* but was instead *"by nature active rather than sedentary. Unfortunately his illness prevented his ordinary development."*[40]

This willful nature also spilled over into frequent displays of tyrannical and even cruel behavior that no one did much to correct. Pierre Gilliard was surprised that he *"had never been under any regular discipline."*[41] The young Tsesarevich was known to hit people in the nose; slap other children (including his sister Olga during a public appearance); order his cousins to jump into mud puddles; and call his father's officials names.[42] Once, the young boy entered his father's reception room and found a minister speaking to a colleague. *"When the Heir to the Throne crosses a room,"* Alexei loudly declared, *"Ministers ought to get up!"*

Nicholas II simply laughed it all off, saying, *"Later on, you will find it harder to deal with my son than with me."* [43] Even a commentator as sympathetic as tutor Charles Sydney Gibbes reluctantly admitted that *"his social environment prevented him from being as perfectly balanced as an ordinary child."*[44]

"Despite his good nature and compassion," said Anatole Mordvinov, one of Nicholas II's adjutants, Alexei *"promised to have a stubborn and independent character in the future. From his earliest days he did not like to obey, and would only do so, like his father, when he was himself convinced of it."*[45] And George Shavelsky, a priest attached to the Imperial suite, recalled that, *"incapacitated as he was, he was permitted and forgiven much that a healthy child would not have been….As a result he developed a mischievous streak, which often went beyond the bounds of what is acceptable."*[46]

Nor did Alexandra intervene. Although she tended to ignore her daughters, she doted on her son and could not bear to correct him. At a 1912 family dinner, Grand Duke Konstantin Konstantinovich was horrified when the eight-year-old Alexei refused to sit up properly, made fun of other guests, and licked his plate. Instead of her correcting this churlish behavior, Alexandra berated her daughter Olga for not better parenting her brother.[47] Other members of the Romanov Family were similarly disturbed by the Tsesarevich's actions, though no one dared say a word in protest.

Tsar Nicholas II and Tsesarevich Alexei.

Alexei thankfully began to grow out of this behavior, but the incidents only underlined a larger problem within the palace: for all of the legends of a devoted Imperial Family spending endless hours together in the Empress's boudoir over everlasting cozy teas, Nicholas and Alexandra were inconsistent parents.

Although all the children adored their father, Nicholas's burdens kept him *"from giving them as much time as he would have wished."* Gilliard had to admit that *"he did not see much of his children,"* and left responsibility for their care to Alexandra.[48] And Alexandra proved to be a most peculiar parent.

There is no doubt that Alexandra was a loving mother, but she was also an obsessive, selfish, and judgmental one who seemed most interested in isolating her children from perceived negative influences and the enemies her increasing paranoia led her to see lurking at every turn. She saw no reason why her daughters should not think and behave exactly as she herself had done at their ages: this largely meant suppressed gaiety, preternatural seriousness, and retreat from the world. Queen Marie of Romania saw that, when away from their mother, the four girls behaved quite naturally and were lively. When the Empress was present, though, *"they always seemed to be watching her every expression, so as to be sure to act according to her desires."*[49]

The pattern of obsessive love coupled with harsh judgments created emotional confusion, and – consciously or subconsciously – Alexandra sublimated the lives of her daughters to her own illnesses, using her health to demand subservient compliance. The four girls were expected to act as companions to their mother, to read to her, to do whatever she wished and to do it without a hint of protest. This wasn't so different from the way things operated in other royal households; it is of note only because it so contradicts the gauzy romantic legend surrounding the last of the Romanovs. It all took an emotional toll. *"I am always so awfully sorry when you are tired and you can't get up,"* Tatiana wrote to her mother in 1909.[50] In 1913, Olga complained in a letter to her grandmother, Dowager Empress Marie Feodorovna that her mother's heart, *"as usual isn't well. It's all so unpleasant."*[51]

Disappointment with their mother became an unspoken but shared connection between the Grand Duchesses. It is telling that, of the five children, all but Tatiana preferred the company of their father to that of their mother. Tatiana, Alexandra once wrote to Nicholas, was the only one of their daughters who understood her way of thinking.[52] As the eldest, Olga bore the brunt of her mother's criticism. *"You are growing very big,"* she warned her daughter in 1909, *"don't be so wild and kick about and show your legs, it is not pretty. I never did so when you age, or when I was smaller and younger even."*[53] In 1910, when Olga was fourteen and craving some measure of independence, she wanted her own room in the palace instead of sharing with her sister Tatiana; she also wanted to wear longer dresses. But she felt

Grand Duchesses Anastasia and Marie Nikolievna, Tsesarevich Alexei Nikolaievich, and Princess Elisabeth of Greece.

so constrained around her mother that she actually asked her ten-year-old sister Marie to write to the Empress suggesting these two "favors." Above all, Olga didn't want Alexandra to know that the ideas had come from her, and Marie was careful to suggest that her eldest sister was unaware of the proposals.[54]

As the most headstrong of the four daughters, Olga inevitably clashed with her mother, especially in her teenage years. Even when Olga was twenty, the Empress expected complete obedience and suppression of any independent thought. Olga, she complained to Nicholas in March 1916, *"is always most unamiable about every proposition."* When Alexandra insisted, her daughter sulked.[55]

"No young girls were ever asked to the Palace," Buxhoeveden recalled. *"The Empress thought that the four sisters should be able to entertain one another."*[56] *"Very few girls,"* Gilliard wrote, *"would have accommodated themselves so easily to a life such as theirs, a life deprived of outside amusements, and with no other source of distraction than those joys of family life."*[57] Heartwarming stories of how these privileged Grand Duchesses eagerly helped maids make their beds, shared jewelry with courtiers, and sat with soldiers of the guard asking after their families, reflect not merely their generous natures but also the desire to break free of the cloistered existence enforced by their mother. Attempting to later defend this isolation, Anna Vyrubova wrote that the Empress

"dreaded for her daughters the companionship of over-sophisticated young women of the aristocracy, whose minds, even in the schoolroom, were fed with the foolish and often vicious gossip of a decadent society. The Empress even discouraged association with cousins and near relatives, many of whom were unwholesomely precocious in their outlook on life."[58]

This unreasoned, wholesale exclusion of companions simply repeated Alexandra's own distrust and dislike of her husband's family and aristocracy. It also kept the Grand Duchesses immature. One courtier complained that the girls *"associated with no one and generally behaved like young savages,"* while another noted that they *"did not always behave in the way one might fairly have expected,"* and was surprised to hear the eldest daughters, even when young women, talking *"like girls of ten or twelve."*[59]

Grand Duchess Olga Nikolaievna.

Social life was confined to innocent flirtations with young officers from the Imperial yacht *Standart*, who often served as tennis partners, or the rare occasions when the Grand Duchesses were allowed to participate in some ceremony. All four of the daughters were appointed honorary colonel-in-chief of their own regiments of the Imperial guards, and happily attended parades and reviews, but only Olga enjoyed the benefit of appearing at a ball in her honor. For her sixteenth birthday in November 1911, Nicholas and Alexandra gave a dinner and ball at the new White Palace at Livadia for their eldest daughter.

Olga appeared for the first time in a long pink tulle gown, with her hair worn up as she happily moved among the guests on her father's arm.

One figure from outside palace circles did become a fixture in their lives: Rasputin. Unraveling precisely what the five children may have believed or thought about the Siberian peasant is nearly impossible; under their mother's tutelage they wrote him passionate, admiring letters, yet some evidence suggests that they were never as enthralled with *"Our Friend"* as Alexandra may have wished. It was inevitable that Rasputin's scandalous behavior would in time tarnish the Grand Duchess's admittedly blameless reputations, though aside from the more sensational claims the real trouble stemmed from their nurseries. Sophie Tiutcheva, their governess, repeatedly complained about the peasant and his visits to her young charges, to the point that a young Tatiana feared her mother would soon retaliate. *"I am so afraid,"* the twelve-year-old girl wrote, that the governess would say *"something bad"* about the peasant.[60]

Another incident came when nursemaid Maria Vishnyakova complained that Rasputin had tried to rape her in the spring of 1910. Alexandra dismissed her, but soon stories of Rasputin's malign influence and power over the Imperial Family spread. The actual facts behind the allegations were never entirely clear; most have accepted the word of Anna Vyrubova in the peasant's defense

35

– surely a shaky proposition given her own loyalty to Rasputin, desire to protect the Imperial Family, and penchant for both lying and distorting facts in her memoirs. The impact, though, weakened respect for the Throne.[61]

Repeated hemophiliac crises made Rasputin indispensable, at least to Alexandra. The worst came in 1912 when, while staying at the Polish hunting lodge of Spala, Alexei nearly died from an uncontrollable internal hemorrhage in his upper left thigh. Doctors confessed themselves powerless as the young boy screamed out, *"Mama, help me!"*[62] It is possible that doctors did secretly intervene: plans were discussed to slice open the swelling and relieve the pressure, but the risk was immense and no one would later admit to such an action.[63] The crisis might also have passed naturally, through spontaneous re-absorption: it had happened only two weeks earlier, with the initial swelling that led to the crisis at Spala.[64]

Yet for Alexandra, it was Rasputin who was to be thanked. To a hasty cable, he had replied, *"The Little One will not die. Do not allow the doctors to bother him too much."*[65] Within a day of its receipt, the Tsesarevich did indeed begin to recover. It was surely a coincidence, but the gullible Empress saw only a miracle.

Tsesarevich Alexei Nikolaievich on his pony.

By the winter social season of 1914 Olga was eighteen and Tatiana sixteen, ages that should have opened a new world of parties and balls to the sheltered young ladies. Olga enjoyed a brief appearance during the Tercentenary celebrations, and relatives in the Crimea offered small dances and dinners to entertain the girls, but the two eldest Grand Duchesses largely remained cloistered at Tsarskoye Selo. Their aunt Grand Duchess Olga Alexandrovna brought them to her St. Petersburg palace every week for small luncheons and informal dances, which helped relieve some of the isolation. *"I remember the girls enjoyed every minute of it,"* Olga later said.[66] Dowager Empress Marie Feodorovna also resented the way Alexandra kept her four daughters cloistered at Tsarskoye Selo. In January 1914, hoping to offer them a glimpse into the world, she gave an elaborate ball – her first in twenty years – for Olga and Tatiana Nikolaievna at the Anichkov Palace. Nicholas and Alexandra escorted their eldest daughters, though the Empress departed at midnight. Olga and Tatiana, though, refused to leave until half-past four in the morning, clearly relishing this rare opportunity to enjoy society beyond their mother's tightly-controlled universe.[67]

As they matured romantic rumors began to surround Olga and Tatiana. Olga had briefly

Empress Alexandra Feodorovna and her four daughters: Olga, Anastasia, Tatiana, and Maria.

Visiting with the Hessian cousins: Grand Duchesses Olga and Tatiana Nikolaievna, Tsesarevich Alexei Nikolaievich, and their cousins Hereditary Grand Duke Donatus and Prince Ludwig of Hesse and by Rhine.

fallen in love with an officer from the *Standart*, Paul Voronov, but there was no question of any serious romance. There were rumors that Olga might marry her father's cousin Grand Duke Dimitri Pavlovich, or Edward, the Prince of Wales (later Edward VIII and then Duke of Windsor); Prince Christopher of Greece was another possible suitor, while Prince Alexander of Serbia was said to be interested in Tatiana. By 1914, however, more serious marital plans were afoot.

In March, Crown Prince Ferdinand of Romania and his wife Marie (first cousin to both Nicholas and Alexandra) came to St. Petersburg with their son Prince Carol, second-in-line to the throne. They stayed at Tsarskoye Selo for several days, during which Olga was thrown together with Carol in the hope that romance would blossom. But, as Crown Princess Marie recalled, neither *"Carol nor Olga showed any sort of desire towards becoming more closely acquainted."* Marie had a private chat with the Empress, who *"talked very quietly, like a reasonable mother. We agreed with each other that neither of us could make any promises in the name of our children, that they must decide for themselves. The only thing we could do would be to create occasions when they could meet, which would certainly not be easy as our lives were lived so far apart."*[68]

The next "occasion" for an arranged meeting came in the summer of 1914, when the Russian Imperial Family paid a brief visit to their Romanian cousins at Constanza on the Black Sea. During the voyage aboard *Standart*, Olga pulled tutor Pierre Gilliard aside and pointedly quizzed him about the reason for the trip. When he tried to pretend that it was merely a diplomatic visit, she cut him off, saying she knew that it involved her potential marriage to Carol. *"Papa,"* she told Gilliard, *"has promised not to make me,*

Summer of 1914, Constanza, Romania. Standing, from the left: King Carol I of Romania, Grand Duchess Anastasia Nikolaievna, and Princess Marie, Prince Carol, Crown Prince Ferdinand, and Queen Elisabeth of Romania. Seated, same order: Grand Duchess Maria Nikolaievna, Empress Alexandra Feodorovna, Grand Duchess Tatiana Nikolaievna holding Princess Ileana of Romania, Crown Princess Marie of Romania, Tsar Nicholas II, Grand Duchess Olga Nikolaievna holding Prince Mircea of Romania. On the floor: Tsesarevich Alexei Nikolaievich and Prince Nicholas of Romania.

and I don't want to leave Russia. I should be a foreigner in my own country. I'm a Russian, and mean to remain a Russian." [69]

Nothing came of the idea, and a month after the Romanian visit World War I abruptly ended any such plans. If Alexandra had kept her daughters sheltered, she had at least also exposed them to the necessity of service. During stays in the Crimean, the Grand Duchesses had eagerly participated in an event known as the Day of White Flowers, during which they sold blossoms in aid of charities, and they had helped their mother sell small items – knitted blankets, embroidered handkerchiefs, watercolors – they had made at Alexandra's annual charity bazaar. The Empress had also taken regularly taken them to visits tubercular patients in the Crimea's many hospitals; when an official objected to the dangers of exposure, Alexandra declared, *"I don't think it will hurt the children, but I am sure it would hurt the sick if they thought that my daughters were afraid of infection."*[70]

These charitable attitudes took on a more serious form once the war began. Both Olga and Tatiana trained as Red Cross nurses and helped care for wounded officers in a private hospital established in the Catherine Palace at Tsarskoye Selo. They not only rolled bandages and read to the soldiers but also tended to their wounds and assisted in operations: they saw the devastation of war firsthand, and also experienced deaths when men died on the operating table.

The traumas deeply affected the two young ladies; Tatiana could more easily compartmentalize her life, once writing to her mother that she was *"sorry I'm not a man"* and thus able to take on a more active role.[71] But the suffering played havoc with Olga's nerves and led to a nervous breakdown. On one occasion Olga broke the glass in a lamppost; on another, she lashed out by destroying the fittings of a cloakroom in the hospital. By October 1915, losing weight and increasing pale, she was removed from active nursing and instead given a desk job in the hospital; depressed, she also began receiving regular injections of arsenic to combat what was described as anxiety – *"this is my treatment,"* Alexandra wrote to Nicholas, *"she must lie more, as goes about so pale and wearily."*[72]

Marie and Anastasia were too young to train as nurses, but they had their own hospital in the Feodorovsky Gorodok near the Alexander Palace at Tsarskoye Selo. Several times a week, they visited the wounded, questioned the men about their families, wrote letters for them, and joined in their games. As for Alexei, the Emperor decided that, despite his young age and delicate health, he should experience something of life at headquarters. Although Alexandra was reluctant, she realized that the Tsesarevich needed to gain something of the confidence his father lacked. At Mogilev, where Stavka had been established, he shared a room in the Governor-General's house with his father, took lessons, and met military representatives of Russia's allies. *"His presence,"* Nicholas assured Alexandra, *"brings light and life to us all....It is awfully cozy sleeping near each other. I pray with him every evening since the train, he says his prayers much too quickly and it is difficult to stop him."* At

Tsesarevich Alexei Nikolaievich.

luncheons, *"he sits on my left and behaves well, but is sometimes inclined to be rather gay and noisy."*[73]

There were reviews and occasional inspections of regiments, which the young boy thoroughly enjoyed. *"He sat with a serious face,"* Nicholas reported to Alexandra after a visit to Odessa, *"saluting all the time. Through the tumult of the crowd and the shouts of 'Hurrah!' I managed to hear women's voices calling out, 'The heir, the angel, the pretty boy!'"*[74] His father also took him to visit hospital wards full of the wounded. Alexei, recorded Gilliard, was deeply moved by the suffering he witnessed.[75] The experience of war did more to improve the boy's somewhat difficult character than any hours spent in the schoolroom.

Only in late 1916, after Rasputin's murder, did the specter of possible revolution seep into the lives of Nicholas and Alexandra's children. A courtier found the four Grand Duchesses sitting closely together on a sofa after hearing the news. *"They were cold and visibly terribly upset, but for the whole of that long evening the name of Rasputin was never uttered in front of me. They were in pain because the man was no longer among the living but also because they evidently sensed that with his murder something terrible and undeserved had started for their mother, their father and themselves and that it was moving relentlessly towards them."*[76]

Chapter III

The Alexandrovich Line: Dowager Empress Marie Feodorovna & Grand Duke Michael Alexandrovich

Dowager Empress Marie Feodorovna

By 1914, Nicholas II's mother Dowager Empress Marie Feodorovna was almost as much of a spectral phantom at court as was Empress Alexandra. Her withdrawal from Russian social life had been long and painful, but as the years passed she felt herself isolated from her son and his family and an alien in her own adopted country.

Born November 26 (New Style), 1847 as Marie Sophie Frederika Dagmar, she was one of the children of the future King Christian IX of Denmark and his wife Louise of Hesse-Kassel. Hers was a relatively impoverished childhood, at least by royal standards: though the family lived in the ostentatiously named Yellow Palace in Copenhagen, money was scarce, clothing was handed down, and education relegated to the cheapest tutors. Along with lack of money went a complete lack of etiquette: Christian's family lived comfortably and unostentatiously, with little interest in their titles or positions. Yet her father had been selected to one day sit upon

The Dowager Empress Marie Feodorovna with her son Tsar Nicholas II and his daughters: Olga, Tatiana, Maria, and Anastasia Nikolaievna.

the Danish throne, and equally glittering futures awaited four of the children: in 1863, daughter Alexandra wed Queen Victoria's eldest son the Prince of Wales, the future King Edward VII, and son Wilhelm was selected as the new King George I of the Hellenes. This same year, Christian succeeded to the Danish throne as well, which he occupied until 1906. As for young Dagmar, or "Minny" as she was called, she would one day sit upon the Russian throne as Empress.

In 1863, Prussia waged war with Denmark over the principalities of Schleswig-Holstein. Berlin's victory left the young Dagmar with an unreasoned hatred of all things German, despite the fact that both of her parents were of German ancestry. Never able to forgive this minor territorial loss, she spent the rest of her life waging a constant war against Prussia. *"I heard it at the dinner table twenty times every day!"* an exasperated Nicholas II once candidly confessed.[1]

Although life in the Yellow Palace had been happy, and protocol almost non-existent, the lack of money and the Schleswig-Holstein crisis left the young Dagmar ambitious. Petite, with dark hair and large, vibrant eyes, she was not as pretty as her sister Alexandra, but Dagmar soon faced the glamorous marital prospect of wedding Tsesarevich Nicholas Alexandrovich, eldest son of Emperor Alexander II of Russia. After some family machinations, she found herself betrothed to the delicately handsome young man known as "Nixa," but her happiness was not to last. Within a few months, the Tsesarevich fell ill and in April of 1865, he died of meningitis.

What happened next became a source of Romanov Family legend, as romantics asserted that the dying man had placed his fiancée's hand into that of his younger brother Alexander and asked him to look after her. Although the slightly awkward Alexander was less intelligent and less attractive than his late brother, Dagmar knew where her duty lay. For Alexander, the decision was more difficult, particularly as he was already in love with another lady at court. Yet in the end both followed the wishes of their parents. In June 1866, while on a visit to Copenhagen, Alexander proposed and Dagmar accepted.

Dagmar converted to Russian Orthodoxy and received the name Marie Feodorovna. On October 28, 1866, she wed Alexander in the Cathedral of the Winter Palace. King Christian IX and Queen Louise remained in Copenhagen, unable to afford the expenses demanded of the occasion, though they sent their son Frederik to see his sister wed. The usually terse Alexander confided details of the

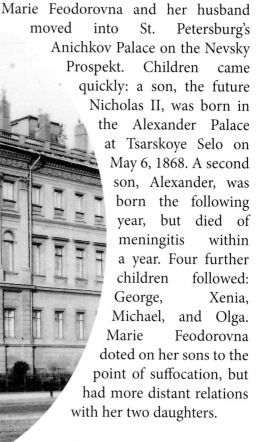

St Petersburg's Anichkov Palace.

wedding night to his diary: *"I took off my slippers and my silver embroidered robe and felt the body of my beloved next to mine....How I felt then, I do not wish to describe here. Afterwards we talked for a long time."*[2]

Marie Feodorovna and her husband moved into St. Petersburg's Anichkov Palace on the Nevsky Prospekt. Children came quickly: a son, the future Nicholas II, was born in the Alexander Palace at Tsarskoye Selo on May 6, 1868. A second son, Alexander, was born the following year, but died of meningitis within a year. Four further children followed: George, Xenia, Michael, and Olga. Marie Feodorovna doted on her sons to the point of suffocation, but had more distant relations with her two daughters.

On the afternoon of Sunday, March 1, 1881 Marie Feodorovna was preparing to go ice-skating when the sound of explosions rent the St. Petersburg sky. Everyone suspected the worst: that another attempt had been made on the life of Alexander II, and instinctively scattered Romanovs made a mad rush to the Winter Palace. The found a horrific scene in the Emperor's study: a Nihilist bomb had left Alexander II near death. In a letter to her mother Queen Louise, Marie Feodorovna wrote: *"Anyone who has not seen the appalling sight himself can never imagine anything like it! I can still see it before me, night and day! The condition was truly heart-rending! His face and head and upper body were untouched but his legs were completely crushed and torn up to the knees, so that at first I did not understand what I was actually looking at, a bleeding mass with half a boot on the right foot: all that was left of the left was the sole of his foot! Never in my life have I seen anything like it: no, it was horrible.*[3]

Alexander II died after forty-five agonizing minutes. Marie Feodorovna's husband became Alexander III and she, Empress. *"Our happiest and loveliest time is now past,"* the new Empress lamented. *"My peace and calm are gone; now I will only ever worry about Sasha [Alexander III]."*[4] Alexander III quickly turned his back on his father's liberal policies, which he believed had led to the tragedy. He also turned his back on St. Petersburg, moving his family to the immense suburban Gatchina Palace, which could more easily be guarded. Only during regular family holidays in Copenhagen could the Romanovs cast aside all etiquette and the nagging fear of assassination.

Tsar Alexander III and Empress Marie Feodorovna.

that accompanied her privileged position. *"Her whole personality was so attractive and sympathetic that she was loved by all who approached her,"* wrote the British Ambassador, *"and she had the great gift of putting everybody at their ease. Her sense of humor also did away with all constraint on the part of the guests, so that the conversation at these luncheons never flagged and was as a rule very amusing."*[5]

Marie Feodorovna, said her niece, was *"not very tall, but she held herself in such a way that she could have been taken for anything but an Empress."*[6] To atone for her small stature, she usually piled cushions on chairs, to make herself appear taller and more imposing. She spoke with an *"extremely musical"* voice that carried *"a curious, guttural timbre."*[7] Like her sister Alexandra, Marie Feodorovna determinedly ran after her faded youth but failed to catch it; she covered her face with creams and waxes and cloaked herself in scents so heavy that they continued to hang in rooms even after she had left.[8] She also smoked from morning to night, but wanted no one outside of her immediate family to know it; when a visitor was announced, she would simply curl her hand behind her, *"oblivious to the clouds of smoke arising like incense"* wafting around her head like a halo.[9]

Marie Feodorovna shared the Russian Throne with her husband for the thirteen years of Alexander III's reign. She made herself beloved, enjoying her role as Empress, wearing increasingly elaborate gowns from Worth in Paris, covering herself in ropes of diamonds and pearls, and presiding over what little of court life she could convince her reluctant husband to continue. With her love of pleasure, talent for conversation, and easy charm, Marie Feodorovna made the ideal Empress, a woman who recognized and even relished the responsibilities

At the beginning of 1894, Alexander III became ill. He lost weight, seemed lethargic, and suffered from a persistent cough. Doctors advised rest, and for a time it seemed as if he was recovering. But by early autumn, doctors diagnosed incurable

nephritis. On October 20, he died at the age of forty-nine while staying at Livadia. Marie Feodorovna was a widow at the age of forty-five. *"I am completely heartbroken,"* she confided to her diary.[10] The unwelcome changes came quickly: her eldest son took the throne as Nicholas II and, on November 14 – his mother's birthday – he wed his fiancée Alexandra, the former Princess Alix of Hesse and by Rhine, in a sad, somber ceremony at the Winter Palace.

"How hard for poor Aunt Minny to see another young Empress in her stead, with she still herself so much too young to be an Empress Dowager," German Empress Friedrich wrote presciently. *"It is a very difficult and painful position, at any rate for some years. However Nicky is such a good, dutiful and devoted son, he*

will make it easy for her, and she will not have to go through what I had to endure, and often still have. Alicky [Alexandra] is sure to be very good to her, even though she has grown up without a mother, and been a little spoilt, which has made her a little vain and conceited and affected at times, but she is very kindhearted, and when she becomes a little less indolent will, I am sure, do all she can to make matters easy for her mother-in-law."[11]

This optimism soon proved wrong. Relations between Marie Feodorovna and her new daughter-in-law remained cordial, yet resentments continually bubbled just beneath the surface. Marie Feodorovna, as her sister Alexandra, Princess of Wales confessed, had been *"very much annoyed"* when her son refused to abandon pursuit of the Hessian Princess.[12] Much is made of how uncomfortable Marie Feodorovna made Alexandra's life; in some respects, this was true. Marie Feodorovna was jealous of her hold over Nicholas, and resented having to cede her position and power as empress consort. Yet, the Dowager Empress was also a new widow, adjusting to a new life, with a son on the throne she instinctively knew lacked many of the qualities needed in a successful autocrat. Nicholas II thus spent the first year of his reign caught in this domestic drama, attempting to appease the two women he loved most and ease the tensions between them.

Above: Tsesarevich Nicholas Alexandrovich, Tsar Alexander III, Crown Prince Constantine of Greece, and Grand Duke George Alexandrovich.

At left: Alexander III and his family at Gatchina. Alexander III holding Olga Alexandrovna, with tsesarevich Nicholas Alexandrovich and Xenia Alexandrovna surrounding him. On the stairs: Marie Feodorovna, Michael Alexandrovich, and George Alexandrovich.

"I still believe that they tried to understand each other and failed," said Nicholas II's sister of her mother and her sister-in-law. *"They were utterly different in character, outlook, and habits."*[13] This much was true. Marie Feodorovna was pragmatic and practical; Alexandra was self-indulgent and prone to morose isolation. The contrast sharpens when examining how each woman dealt with the tragedies in their lives. Marie Feodorovna watched her father-in-law bleed to death before her eyes in 1881; lived through the fear of anarchist attacks; lost her beloved husband in 1894; had buried her second son, Alexander, within a year of his birth; and in 1899 watched as the remains of her son George were interred after he fell victim to tuberculosis. Yet unlike her daughter-in-law, she never isolated herself, never turned to mystics, never gave way to health complaints, and always did her public duties as Empress. That Alexandra could not make similar efforts left Marie Feodorovna puzzled and perturbed. *"She has splendid ideas,"* the Dowager Empress once said of her daughter-in-law. *"But she never tells me what she does or expects to do; when we two are together she always converses about everything but herself. I shall be very glad if she will only drop her reserve."*[14]

Tsar Alexander III, Empress Marie Feodorovna, and the Princess of Wales.

Above all, Marie Feodorovna knew what was expected of her role. If the job of Empress was to be a social butterfly, a leader of society, indulging in endless entertainments, she fulfilled those expectations admirably. Alexandra could not – or would not – do the same. Perhaps such functions were indeed frivolous, but at the Russian Court they mattered greatly. Marie Feodorovna understood the theatrical side of her role; Alexandra never did.

Alexandra would have been wise to befriend and respect Marie Feodorovna, not to compete with her or reject her well-meaning if meddlesome advice. Marie Feodorovna was already a respected figure at court; Alexandra was an unfamiliar face. By continually clashing with the Dowager Empress, Alexandra forced society and members of the Romanov Family to choose sides – and in this case, it was Marie Feodorovna who won the battle. *"Quite openly, my mother enjoyed being first lady in the Empire,"* recalled Marie Feodorovna's daughter Olga Alexandrovna.[15] According to the protocol of the Russian Court, a dowager empress took precedence over an empress consort. Marie Feodorovna served as patron of the country's charitable and educational institutions. Alexandra suggested that she would like this patronage given to her, but the Dowager Empress, insulted, refused. Marie Feodorovna tried to retaliate with her own act of petty vengeance. By tradition, the names of the reigning Emperor and Empress always came first in the Orthodox Church's prayers for the Imperial Family; the Dowager Empress insisted that, according to precedence, her name should come before that of her daughter-in-law. Nicholas, presumably beset by both mother and wife, declined to intervene in this struggle. Unwisely, Alexandra refused to let the situation go, taking the issue to the Holy Synod and asking for a ruling on whose name should come first. They sided with her, but the new Empress's humiliation of her mother-in-law only further alienated her from Marie Feodorovna and from the Imperial Court.

Nor was Marie Feodorovna above petty vengeance. It was customary for a dowager to turn over certain pieces of Imperial jewelry to a new empress, but Marie Feodorovna refused. Instead, she gave Alexandra a number of heavy, uncomfortable tiaras and necklaces from the reign of Catherine the Great. Nicholas once again found his time consumed with settling domestic squabbles between his mother and his wife. Alexandra demanded the jewels; when Nicholas asked his mother to hand them over, Marie Feodorovna again refused. Hearing this, Alexandra insisted that, even if she had the jewels, she would never wear them. Nicholas related this to his mother, who realized that the new Empress would have to don certain pieces on ceremonial occasions. To avoid a scandal, she hastily dispatched most of the jewels to her daughter-in-law, but the public soon learned of this unseemly battle.[16]

Krasnoe Selo, c. 1892.

Seated, from the left: Grand Duchess Xenia Alexandrovna, Grand Duchess Marie Pavlovna Sr., Grand Duchess Elena Vladimirovna, Grand Duchess Alexandra Josifovna, Empress Marie Feodorovna, Tsar Alexander III, Grand Duke Michael Nikolaievich, and Grand Duke Paul Alexandrovich. Next row, same order: Dukes Karl-Michael and George of Mecklenburg-Strelitz, Grand Duke Konstantin Konstantinovich (KR), Queen Olga of Greece, Grand Duke Sergei Mikhailovich, Tsesarevich Nicholas Alexandrovich, Grand Duke Vladimir Alexandrovich, Grand Duke Nicholas Nikolaievich Jr., Duke Alexander of Oldenburg, Grand Duke Dimitri Konstantinovich, Duke Peter of Oldenburg, and Duke George of Leuchtenberg. On the floor, same order: Grand Duke Alexei Mikhailovich, Grand Duke Michael Alexandrovich, Grand Duke Andrei Vladimirovich, and Grand Duke Boris Vladimirovich.

Yet, in the first decade of his reign, it was largely Marie Feodorovna, not Alexandra, who held more political influence over her son. When Nicholas came to the throne, everyone anticipated that it was his mother who would wield the greatest power. One author ranked her among the *"shrewdest political intriguers in Russia: she sees everything, knows everything, and is the one person to be reckoned with….Her son has always been like putty in her hands."*[17]

The Dowager Empress made a great show of reluctance whenever she intruded into her son's realm. *"I am sorry to have still to forward to you so many papers,"* she wrote apologetically.[18] And again: *"My heart bleeds to have to write you all these painful things, but if I don't tell you the truth, who will?"*[19] Unfortunately, recalled Foreign Minister Sergei Sazonov, Marie Feodorovna was *"too outspoken and impetuous. The moment she begins to lecture her son, her feelings run away with her, and she sometimes says the exact opposite of what she should; she annoys and humiliates him."*[20]

It became increasingly difficult for Nicholas to handle his mother's incessant requests without causing scandal. After so many years in power, she had surrounded herself with a group of wastrel friends and

The Dowager Empress on her yacht, the Polar Star.

untrustworthy officials who took advantage of imperial favor to rob the state.[21] When she begged Nicholas to loan one of her friends a million rubles to cover her debts, the Emperor was firm: *"I must tell you honestly that it is impossible,"* he wrote. *"I should like to see how she would have dared even to hint at such a thing to Papa, and I can certainly hear the answer he would have given her!"*[22] There were further scandals over missing funds from the Red Cross, hospitals, orphanages, and famine relief – all of which could be traced to the Dowager Empress's disreputable circle of friends.[23]

The Dowager Empress's last real forays into the political arena grew from the increasing chaos surrounding the rise of Rasputin, and the country's rapid spiral into disaster. In 1914, she complained to recently dismissed Prime Minister Vladimir Kokovtsov: *"My poor daughter-in-law does not perceive that she is ruining both the Dynasty and herself. She sincerely believes in the holiness of an adventurer, and we are powerless to ward off the misfortune which is sure to come."*[24]

By this time, Marie Feodorovna, having felt herself pushed aside by her son, no longer welcomed in his family, and no longer captivated by frivolous balls and extravagant dinners, began to spend longer periods of time abroad, visiting her sister in England as well as returning to her native Denmark. Together with Queen Alexandra, she bought a small, glistening white villa, Hvidøre, outside of Copenhagen, where they could retreat into a semblance of quiet life, although there was nothing quiet about her arrival. The Dowager Empress usually arrived with a *"retinue of 200 people. Servants, bodyguards, maids, and ladies-in-waiting all poured from the train as the fascinated crowd stood and stared....There were no tiresome problems about money."*[25] Days in Denmark, holidays abroad, and voyages on the Imperial yacht *Polar Star* now formed the Dowager Empress's isolated though idyllic world.

Marie Feodorovna was in London, visiting her sister Queen Alexandra, when World War I erupted. She quickly left to return to Russia, but found that German authorities insultingly blocked her train in Berlin. She was forced to turn back and travel via a different route through Denmark. She found her son's Empire swept

The Dowager Empress and her sister Queen Alexandra at Hvidøre, their Danish home.

up in war fever: in a misplaced burst of patriotism, Nicholas II changed the name of the capital from the Germanic St. Petersburg to the more Slavic Petrograd. *"As if we had not more important things to do than renaming our cities in such times!"* the Dowager Empress complained.[26]

The Anichkov Palace became the seat of the Dowager Empress's wartime activities (she left Gatchina and moved to Elagin Palace to be closer to the capital). As President of the Red Cross, she organized a bandage-rolling workshop at Anichkov and, recalled one participant, *"frequently dropped in to see how we were getting on, giving us always an encouraging compliment. Tea served daily at five ended our labor and we were sent home with a delightful feeling of being very useful and greatly appreciated. Sometimes she would put on one of our great white aprons and would sit for hours, working at the long tables, folding or packing."*[27] When visiting hospitals, recorded one witness, she went *"round the wards, laughing and joking, with an air of warm cordiality to the soldiers who were not in bed, speaking softly to those who were seriously wounded, once laying her hand with a gesture of infinite gentleness on the forehead of a boy who was obviously dying."*[28]

The Dowager Empress watched in impotence as her

The Dowager Empress and her granddaughter Grand Duchess Olga.

son stumbled from one disaster to another, naming and dismissing ministers, suffering military setbacks, and ignoring the looming scandal of Rasputin. In 1915, when the Emperor assumed Supreme Command of the Army, replacing the popular Grand Duke Nicholas Nikolaievich, the Dowager Empress was beside herself with outrage. *"What are we coming to?"* she asked. *"This is not at all like Nicky; he is lovable, he is honest, he is good – it is all* her *work....I can't understand anything any more. It is not my dear boy; he is too good to do such a thing....It is all* she; *she alone is responsible for all that is happening now. It is too awful."*[29]

Eventually, in May 1916, the Dowager Empress gave her son an ultimatum: *"Either me or Rasputin."*[30] Nicholas chose the peasant and his mother abandoned the capital entirely. She moved to Kiev, taking up residence in the Mariinsky Palace there, in a form of subtle protest against the Empress and her infamous "holy man." In the autumn of 1916, the Dowager Empress again tried to intercede with her son. She wrote to Nicholas, warning that Alexandra – under Rasputin's influence – was ruining the country. The Dowager Empress begged Nicholas to send Rasputin away, and to forbid Alexandra from *"interfering in affairs of state."*[31] Nicholas ignored the plea.

The Dowager Empress at Hvidøre, her Danish home.

The situation, already strained, deteriorated even further after Rasputin's assassination. Dowager Empress Marie Feodorovna was so distressed by Nicholas's response in exiling Grand Duke Dimitri Pavlovich that she wrote to her son, begging him to reconsider his actions. *"One should reach in oneself and forgive,"* she counseled. *"I am sure you are aware yourself how deeply you have offended all the family by your brusque reply, throwing at their heads a painful and entirely unjustified accusation. I hope also that you will alleviate the fate of Dimitri Pavlovich by not leaving him in Persia, where the climate is so dreadful. It is not like your kind heart to behave this way; it upsets me very much."*[32] But Nicholas was unmoved by his mother's letter.

Grand Duke Michael Alexandrovich

A scandalous liaison, illegal marriage, and vindictive punishments kept Grand Duke Michael Alexandrovich, Nicholas II's only surviving brother, from participating in the 1913 Tercentenary celebrations. Born November 22, 1878 at the Anichkov Palace, Michael had been spoiled and indulged by his parents, who clearly favored him over their other children. Sergei Witte remembered that Alexander III had made no secret of the fact that Michael, called "Misha" in the family, was his favorite son.[33] Closest to his sister Olga, who called him "Floppy" after his habit of flopping into chairs, Michael was genial and unpretentious.[34] After his father's death in 1894, Michael lived with his widowed mother at Anichkov Palace and at Gatchina before joining the Life Guards Horse Artillery Regiment. In 1899, on the death of his older brother George, Michael became heir presumptive and began to carry out public duties, attending the funeral of Queen Victoria in 1901. In 1902 he transferred to the Life Guards Cuirassier Regiment stationed at Gatchina.

Handsome and carefree, Michael was incredibly naïve. Alexander III once insisted that his youngest son *"believed without hesitancy anything and everything anyone told him."*[35] Another of his

Grand Duke George Alexandrovich.

Grand Duke Michael Alexandrovich.

friends recalled: *"I have never met another man so uncorrupted and noble in nature; it was enough to look into his clear blue eyes to be ashamed of any bad thought of insincere feeling. In many ways he was a grown up child who had been taught only what was good and moral. He did not want to admit that there was wickedness and falsehood in the world and trusted everybody."*[36] A British writer, who met him in 1914, described the Grand Duke as *"a truly masculine figure, a sportsman of the real English type,"* with *"a noble soul"* and *"most pronounced sincerity."*[37]

Michael detested the ceremony that accompanied his position: he liked to dance but drank only moderately, disliked rich food, and didn't smoke. Only three pursuits captured his interest. The first was his collection of fast motorcars. He kept two Packards at Gatchina, along with some smaller automobiles, but his favorite vehicle was a gray Opel open touring car. Michael liked to drive himself, racing at breakneck speeds along the roadways, but he had the unfortunate habit of nodding off when behind the wheel. Once he crashed his motorcar and it was only by a miracle that he escaped serious injury.

The Grand Duke's second interest was his estate, Brasovo, near Orel. *"He was never so happy as when at Brasovo,"* recalled his stepdaughter, *"and he would have enjoyed pottering around the land, taking a deep interest in the crops and livestock and the people dependent on the estate."* He took *"enormous pains over the peasants, especially any who were sick or in any sort of trouble,"* and seemed

Grand Duke Michael Alexandrovich and his sister Grand Duchess Xenia Alexandrovna.

genuinely dedicated to the welfare of those whom he regarded as in his care.[38]

Unfortunately, the Grand Duke's third and main interest seemed to be the pursuit of unsuitable romances. In 1902 he apparently fell in love with his first cousin Princess Beatrice of Saxe-Coburg and Gotha, and led her to believe that they might marry, despite the Orthodox Church's prohibition against a union between such close relatives. Never one to fight, Michael let the matter drop, deeply hurting Beatrice.[39] Soon, he was infatuated with Alexandra Kossikovskaya, Kamer Freilina to his sister Olga. Known as *"Drina,"* Kossikovskaya, said a contemporary, was *"not pretty, but clever and pleasant, and she gave him all her heart."*[40] Three years older than the Grand Duke, Drina was a commoner, daughter of a provincial attorney – and thus deemed unfit for a Romanov. *"Three days ago,"* Nicholas informed his mother in July 1906, *"Misha wrote asking my permission to marry. He said too that he cannot wait any longer than the middle of August. I will of course never give my consent to such a marriage."*[41] Marie Feodorovna was equally horrified, writing, *"We must do everything to save him from himself."*[42] She had Alexandra dismissed from service, and the Emperor made it clear that if Michael pursued her he would lose his place in the succession.[43]

Michael foolishly refused to abandon his beloved "Drina" and planned to secretly marry her. To prevent such a move, Nicholas II ordered Okhrana agents to follow the pair and prevent Kossikovskaya from leaving Russia.[44] Michael's interest soon waned: he now focused his attentions on Nathalia Wulfert, wife of one of his fellow officers.

Born Nathalia Sheremetievskaya in 1880 to a Moscow lawyer, "Natasha," as she was known, had an excellent private education. In 1902, she had married Sergei Mamontov, a musician who later worked for the Bolshoi Theatre Company. In 1903 she gave birth to a daughter, Nathalia, and for a time enjoyed her fashionable life in Moscow and her illustrious circle of friends, which included Sergei Rachmaninov and Feodor Chaliapin.[45] Soon, though, Nathalia grew bored of domestic life, and could be seen around Moscow in the company of men other than her husband. In 1905, a humiliated and compliant Mamontov granted her a divorce so that she could marry her then current lover, military officer Vladimir Wulfert.[46] In 1907, Wulfert was serving in the Life Guard Cuirassier Regiment at Gatchina under Michael Alexandrovich, and bewitching Natasha soon enough propelled herself into the Grand Duke's orbit. For a year, relations were apparently platonic, but by 1909 Michael and Nathalia had become lovers.

Opinions of Nathalia largely agreed: she was *"extraordinarily beautiful"* and *"exceedingly intelligent," "clever, pleasant, and very cultivated,"* while at the same time exceptionally *"ambitious"* and a woman who *"lived for flattery."*[47] Grand

Grand Duke Michael Alexandrovich and his sister Grand Duchess Olga Alexandrovna.

Duke Alexander Mikhailovich sounded the rare sour note, describing Nathalia as a *"supremely cold, dictatorial, majestic woman,"* with *"domineering brownish eyes"* that he compared to *"ice."*[48]

By late 1909, Nathalia had separated from Wulfert and was living in a Moscow apartment that her lover Michael had provided. Nicholas tried to thwart the romance, transferring his brother to a Hussar regiment at Orel, but Michael was unwilling to abandon Nathalia, who soon found herself pregnant with the Grand Duke's child. On July 24, 1910 she gave birth to a son, named George after Michael's late brother. As she was still married to Wulfert, Michael bribed officials to grant a retroactive divorce that allowed him to claim paternity and paid his lover's former husband a sum equivalent to some $2 million to renounce any claims over him.[49]

Nicholas II relented slightly, allowing Nathalia to live with Michael on his Orel estate and granting her son the surname "Brasov." Within a few months, the couple had moved back to Gatchina, where Michael had a large villa. On the Emperor's orders, agents of the secret police kept Nathalia under constant surveillance, which intensified whenever she went abroad.

In autumn 1912, Michael and Nathalia took their usual holiday in Europe, but unexpected news from Russia led them to a fateful decision when they learned that Tsesarevich Alexei was seriously ill at Spala in Poland. This gave Michael pause. If Alexei died, he would become his brother's heir presumptive again; in such a situation, it was unlikely that he would be allowed to continue his liaison with Nathalia. Having previously considered marrying his mistress and legitimizing their relationship and son, he now decided that he could not longer wait to act. In October the pair managed to evade Okhrana agents and slipped into Austria where, on the 16th, they were married in a Serbian Orthodox Church.[50]

Michael quickly admitted to the union, informing his brother that his action had been spurred by Tsesarevich Alexei's most recent illness and fears that he would be forcibly separated from Nathalia if he became heir. Nicholas II was furious when he received the telegram: *"He broke his word, his word of honor,"*

Grand Duke Michael Alexandrovich and his first cousin, and good friend, Princess Victoria of Wales.

he mumbled on reading the news.[51] The Dowager Empress was beside herself on learning of the marriage, writing to Nicholas: *"It is unbelievable – I can hardly understand what I am writing – it is so appalling in every way that it nearly kills me! I beg only this one thing of you: that it be kept absolutely secret to avoid another scandal! There have been secret marriages in the past which one pretended to know nothing about. I think this is the only way out – otherwise I won't be able to show my face anywhere for the shame and disgrace of it all!"*[52]

To this, Nicholas replied: *"May the Lord forgive him! Unfortunately, everything is over between him and me now, because he has broken his word. How many*

times did he tell me, without my asking, he himself gave his word that he would not marry her. And I believed him implicitly! What upsets me particularly is that he refers to Alexei's illness as having forced him to rush into this ill-considered step! He doesn't seem concerned with either your distress, or our distress, or the scandal this event will cause in Russia. And at such a time…just a few months before the Jubilee of the Romanov Dynasty!!! It's shameful and awful!"[53]

The Grand Duke's marriage was religiously valid, but illegal in Russia for the purposes of the succession. Nathalia was not only a commoner, something forbidden by the Fundamental Laws of the Russian Empire for valid dynastic unions, but she was also twice divorced, with two previous husbands still living. The marriage had also taken place without the Emperor's consent. Nicholas II responded by giving full vent to his wrath, as he explained to his brother-in-law Grand Duke Alexander Mikhailovich: *"If I fail to discipline my own brother,"* he asked, *"what right have I got to expect outsiders to obey me?"* Then, in rich words considering his own determined pursuit of the arguably unsuitable Alix of Hesse, he continued: *"We royalty must think of our task, not of our own personal desires and fancies. It is all very well to heap abuse on our system of marriages, but it is the only system that preserves our children from inheriting the traits of the commoner."*[54]

In December, Michael's financial assets were seized and placed under control of a specially appointed conservator; at the end of the month the Grand Duke was stripped of his right to serve as Regent for his nephew Alexei if the Tsesarevich prematurely came to the throne, and he was placed under "guardianship." On January 1, 1913, Nicholas stripped his brother of his military ranks and banished him from Russia.[55] Such a guardianship was ordinarily used only for people unable to care for themselves. As Michael complained to his brother, it *"has put me in the position of an imbecile or a madman and made my situation totally unbearable. As things are, even a short visit to Russia is impossible for me, for I shall be seen as a man who has been subjected to a humiliating punishment."*[56]

Instead, Michael remained in exile. Shortly before his marriage, he had transferred a considerable part of his fortune abroad, which allowed him to live in comfort. He and Nathalia moved to England, renting Knebworth House where they lived quietly with their son. For a time they enjoyed the whirl of social life in London, mixing with visiting Russian artists and aristocrats in an effort to maintain some ties to their native land. It seemed unlikely they would ever be allowed back into Russia. Nicholas II once described his sister-in-law as *"a cunning, wicked beast."*[57]

The war finally ended Michael and Nathalia's exile. Nicholas agreed to his brother's request that he be allowed to return to Russia – with his wife and son – and take up a position in the army. Promoted to the rank of Major-General, Michael was given command of the Caucasian Native Cavalry Division, a newly formed and unimportant regiment. Natasha and George lived in a villa at Gatchina; although Michael had a palace in the capital, Nathalia, as a morganatic spouse, was not allowed to live within its walls. Michael accepted this, but he did ask that Nicholas finally legitimize George. The Emperor agreed, creating the boy Count Brasov.

Neither Nicholas nor his wife would receive Nathalia. Writing of Michael, Alexandra confided to her husband, *"I am sure this war will make more of a man of him – could one but get her out of his reach! Her dictating influence is so bad."*[58] Michael got a firsthand taste of the fight when he commanded his troops during a harsh and difficult campaign in the Carpathian Mountains in January 1915. To Nathalia, he confided that he was *"ashamed to face the people, i.e., the soldiers and officers, particularly when visiting field hospitals, where so much suffering is to be seen."*[59] But Nicholas recognized his brother's heroic actions and awarded him the military's top honor, the Order of St. George. *"I am very glad for his sake,"* Nicholas wrote to Alexandra, *"as I think that this time he has really earned this military distinction, and it will show him that he is, after all, treated exactly as all the others, and that by doing his duty well he also gets a reward."*[60]

If Michael remained devoted to his wife, Nathalia proved somewhat more pliable. Her indiscreet relationship with Grand Duke Dimitri Pavlovich – which probably extended only to flirting –

Grand Duke Michael Alexandrovich and Nathalia Wulfert.

nonetheless wounded Michael's sense of honor, and undoubtedly exacerbated the ulcers from which he began to suffer. When she wrote to her husband how flattering she found the attention, Michael replied sadly: *"When I think about it my heart sinks and there's a nagging pain in my chest. It is a complicated feeling; there is frustration, jealousy, and deep sadness."*[61] And again, in July 1915, he warned Nathalia of *"the pain you have given me"* in writing of the relationship. *"I am now getting more and more convinced that I was right when I said your feelings toward me and your love have changed and that intense, undiluted feeling that used to be is no longer there and will never be again."*[62]

No break occurred: Nathalia assured her husband that the relationship was platonic, and that she allowed it because it fed her vanity. In truth there was little Michael could do: his military duties increased at the beginning of 1916, when he assumed command of the 2nd Cavalry Corps; a few months later, he led them in the Brusilov Offensive. General Alexei Brusilov found the Grand Duke *"an absolutely honorable and upright man, taking no sides and lending himself to no intrigues….He shunned every kind of gossip, whether connected with the services or with family matters. As a soldier, he was an excellent leader and an unassuming and conscientious worker."*[63]

Although Michael was heroic in battle, the Brusilov Offensive eventually proved to be a disaster. By

the time Nicholas II halted the action, his brother was all but debilitated with ulcers from constant worry over the situation, over Nathalia, and over the government's disintegration. In September 1915, he tried to warn Nicholas about Alexandra's *"dangerous influence"* over political affairs, but the Emperor dismissed such concerns.[64]

Michael tried again in the autumn of 1916, writing to his brother: *"I am deeply concerned and worried by what is happening around us. There has been a shocking alteration in the mood of the most loyal people…which fills me with a most serious apprehension not only for you and for the fate of our family, but even for the integrity of the state order. The public hatred for certain people who allegedly are close to you and who are forming part of the present government has, to my amazement, brought together the right, the left and the moderate; and this hatred, along with the demands for changes are already openly expressed."*[65]

Nicholas dismissed his brother's warning …

Grand Duke Michael with his wife and their son, Count George Brasov, named after his late uncle George Alexandrovich.

Chapter IV

The Vladimirovich Line

Marie Pavlovna, Grand Duchess Vladimir

With Empress Alexandra in self-imposed seclusion, and Dowager Empress Marie Feodorovna so often away from Russia, Marie Pavlovna, Grand Duchess Vladimir – armed with *"the graceful bearing of a great lady of the Renaissance"* – became the most powerful and influential lady in the Imperial Family.[1]

Born Princess Marie of Mecklenburg-Schwerin on April 22 (New Style), 1847, she was the daughter of Grand Duke Friedrich Franz II and his wife Princess Augusta of Reuss-Köstritz. In 1874, she married Grand Duke Vladimir Alexandrovich, third son of Emperor Alexander II after several years of determined negotiations. Having been raised a Lutheran, Marie refused to convert to Russian Orthodoxy. Eventually, Alexander II agreed that his son could marry the German Princess and, because Vladimir was at the time fourth in line to the throne, Marie was not required to change her religion.

The new Grand Duchess Marie Pavlovna, known as "Miechen" in the Imperial Family, initially had a difficult time adjusting to life in her new homeland. Vladimir was a difficult man and a difficult husband, headstrong and arrogant. *"What sort of husband shall I make?"* he had supposedly asked. *"I am drunk every night, and cure the headache of the next morning by getting drunk again!"*[2] Yet he and his wife shared much: both were dedicated to pleasure; loved art, food, wine, and entertaining; and were exceptionally proud. Although Marie Pavlovna lost her first son, Alexander, shortly before he reached the age of two, she gave birth to four surviving children: Kirill, in 1876; Boris, in 1877; Andrei, in 1879; and her only daughter, Elena, in 1882.

Grand Duke Vladimir Alexandrovich.

The Grand Ducal pair lived in splendor at the suburban palace of Ropsha (where Peter III had been assassinated) and at the Florentine-style Vladimir Palace overlooking the Neva in St. Petersburg, where Marie Pavlovna quickly cemented her reputation as a brilliant hostess. After the 1881 assassination of Alexander II and accession of Alexander III, her power increased. Fearful of Nihilists, the new Emperor retreated to the suburban palace at Gatchina and gradually reduced the number of Imperial entertainments. Marie Pavlovna stepped into this void, creating a second, rival Court that eagerly entertained St. Petersburg society. Her parties became legendary: leading artists, singers, dancers, and composers flocked to her palace, where French champagne flowed in streams and entertainments went on until dawn. One visitor recorded that the Grand Duchess received standing atop a thick white bearskin, *"her luxuriant, regal features clothed in the gorgeous blue robes of the native Russian costume, the gown and the head dress ablaze with jewels and the long velvet train carpeting the floor behind. She stood as the personification of Russian feminine beauty, enchanting in its touch of barbaric wildness and its tinge of Oriental voluptuousness."*[3]

Marie Pavlovna was, by all accounts, intelligent, charming, and clever as well as ambitious and spiteful. She was, wrote British Ambassador Sir George Buchanan, *"a grande dame in the best sense of that term, but without any pretensions as regards the strict observance of Court etiquette,"* a lady *"admirably fitted to play the part of hostess and to do the honors of the Court. With great conversational gifts, she was not only herself full of verve and entrain, but possessed the art of inspiring them in others."*[4] Another contemporary called her *"the only Grand Duchess of the old school left, and she certainly knows how to maintain, when*

Grand Duke Vladimir Alexandrovich and his bride Duchess Marie of Mecklenburg-Schwerin.

it is necessary, the dignity of her position....If she is not universally liked she is still considered, and her judgments taken into account."[5] *"There is a smartness about her that no one else can attain,"* Queen Marie of Romania insisted, while another niece declared that Marie Pavlovna *"had the greatest charm any woman ever possessed. She was always most sweet and kind to me."*[6]

The Grand Duchess had tried to ease the new Empress Alexandra's way into Russian society, offering friendly advice on manners and morals, aristocrats and activities forming elite life in St. Petersburg. Perhaps she also hoped to exercise some influence over the new Empress by winning her confidence, though her efforts seem to have been sincere. Countess Marie Kleinmichel recalled that the Grand Duchess was *"eager to guide her movements."*[7] The results, though, proved disastrous. Numerous figures later recalled how Alexandra rebuffed these overtures, insisting that – despite being newly arrived – she knew what was best for Russia and what was needed in an Empress.[8] Marie Pavlovna, her pride wounded, thereafter became one of the Empress's most dedicated enemies, and openly criticized her for abandoning her ceremonial duties. *"One ought to know one's job,"* the Grand Duchess once pointedly declared to an official, adding, *"You may pass that on to the Grand Court."*[9] *"She's the woman we ought to have had as Empress!"* a Russian official once commented.[10]

And Marie Pavlovna certainly knew how to entertain. It was her passion and gave her a purpose in life. The Grand Duchess, thought one contemporary, *"had an inherent, restless dread of being alone."*[11] Her niece Marie of Romania described the *"atmosphere of unlimited prosperity"* that surrounded her. *"She was the undisputed center of her world; her very aspect invited attention."*[12] Marie Pavlovna, said one writer, was the only Romanov *"who gives life and brilliancy to society, keeping it in continual movement. This has become so usual that when a party is being talked of the question is generally asked, 'Will Marie Pavlovna be there?' Her presence adds luster to the festival and gives it the requisite style. None but a very foolish hostess would think of neglecting to invite the Grand Duchess, whose presence would ensure the success of her party. Dinner parties graced by Her Imperial Highness are always extremely luxurious. Only people of ample means can afford the pleasure of inviting her to their hospitable board."*[13]

Marie Pavlovna opened up the exquisite rooms of her palace to millionaires, intellectuals, artists, and even visiting Americans. Anyone who was amusing, had money, and could entertain her seemed to meet with the Grand Duchess's approval.[14] Sir George Buchanan added: *"Her entertainments, no matter what form they took, were never dull, and no one was ever bored. At her dinners and receptions one met many of the younger members of*

the Imperial family and the elite of Russian society, more especially the smart set, as well as a sprinkling of the official and artistic worlds."*[15]

Inevitably this led to criticism. The prolific writer Princess Catherine Radziwill, who lavishly praised the Grand Duchess in one book only to fault her in another, once decried her *"disastrous influence over Russian society,"* insisting that she surrounded herself by questionable elements and thus, *"more than anyone, helped to bring about the laxity in morals which prevailed in the Russian capital during the last few years....She was the first member of the Imperial Family to number amongst her friends divorced people, and for this innovation she was bitterly reproached by the few remaining persons who had been born and bred under the old Regime. No member of the real old Russian aristocracy frequented the Grand Duchess Marie Pavlovna's salon, but one met there a number of nouveax riches, or people who had never before succeeded in breaking down the very effective barriers which up to that time had protected the exclusive circle from those who hovered on the outer edge."*[16]

Grand Duchess Marie Pavlovna Sr.

Perhaps there was reason for some criticism, yet as Meriel Buchanan aptly pointed out, much of this talk was simply inspired by the Grand Duchess's success in her role, and by spite: *"It was inevitable that anybody with her vivid personality should have enemies in a society like that of St. Petersburg, and it was perhaps natural that aspersions should have*

Grand Duke Alexei Alexandrovich.

been cast upon both her moral and her public character by censorious busybodies, for she was fearless and of too strong a character ever to be ignored or thrust into the background. Her vigorous mentality could not but deplore the attitude of the young Empress, but though she took a keen interest in both foreign and international politics, she was never guilty of an anti-Russian intrigue, and never anything but dignified, regal, and gracious in public."[17]

In 1908 Marie Pavlovna finally converted to Orthodoxy. Nicholas II announced the conversion in a Manifesto dated April 10, 1908: *"Our Beloved Aunt, Grand Duchess Maria Pavlovna, by the inclination of her soul, has wished to unite herself to Us in the Faith and in the communion of prayers and sacraments. Today, to Our great joy, she has received Our Faith and been anointed. Announcing this greatly desired event to Our Subjects, We command that Her Imperial Highness henceforth be styled as Orthodox Grand Duchess."*[18]

Although Marie Pavlovna's decision to retain her Lutheran faith on marrying distressed her husband, it followed both precedent and law. Article 184 of the Fundamental State Laws of the Russian Empire allowed, at the Emperor's discretion, marriages between *"members of the Imperial House"* and *"persons of other denominations."* Alexander II used this provision to approve Vladimir and Marie Pavlovna's marriage, just as his son Alexander III applied it to the 1884 unions of his brother Grand Duke Sergei Alexandrovich and Elisabeth of Hesse, and that of his cousin Grand Duke Konstantin Konstantinovich to Elisabeth of Saxe-Altenburg. The Emperor always had the final word.

With the 1908 death of Grand Duke Alexei Alexandrovich, Grand Duke Michael Alexandrovich's ongoing liaison with a woman deemed unsuitable for marriage into the House of Romanov, and the illness of Tsesarevich Alexei, critics assumed, Marie Pavlovna was simply attempting to retroactively cover her bases on behalf of any claims her sons might make. Kirill now stood fourth in line to the throne, after Alexei, Michael, and his father Grand Duke Vladimir. Given the passions that raged around the Vladimirs, and the animosity that existed against them at Tsarskoye Selo, it is not surprising that a few courtiers and cynical enemies ascribed the Grand Duchess's conversion to ambition.

Whether this was true or not – and given the Grand Duchess she might well have harbored such thoughts – the sentiment was irrelevant. According to Article 128 of the Fundamental Laws of the Russian Empire, only the issue of an Orthodox mother could succeed to the throne. Later critics, like head of Nicholas II's Court Chancery Alexander Spiridovich, insisted that a judicial investigation determined that, as

Marie Pavlovna had not converted prior to Kirill's birth, he was therefore ineligible for the throne. But the three Vladimirovichi sons already possessed succession rights precisely because Article 128 specified that only the eldest son of the Emperor, and the eldest son in first generational descent from an emperor, were to be considered direct heirs to the throne and thus subject to the rules regarding an Orthodox mother. Alexander II precisely spelled out four provisions for Vladimir's possible inheritance of the throne: he could not accede until his wife converted to Orthodoxy; if Marie Pavlovna had not converted by the time Vladimir succeeded, his rights to the throne would be considered renounced; if Marie Pavlovna died before converting and Vladimir then succeeded, his rights to the throne were valid; and if Vladimir died before his wife converted, their children *"born of this union still retain full rights of succession and are Members of the Imperial House."* Alexander II signed the decree, and it was passed by the Imperial Senate.[19]

Grand Duke Vladimir Alexandrovich.

From this, it is clear that there was thus no reason for Marie Pavlovna to simply convert to cement succession rights for her sons. Alexander II had decided the issue, declaring that they owned succession rights no matter their mother's religion. With Kirill now so close to the throne, the decision was undoubtedly an astute political one, perhaps designed to ease any worries, but it was unnecessary to obtain for him a right he had possessed since birth.

Grand Duke Vladimir died in 1909, and his wife succeeded him as president of the Imperial Academy of Fine Arts. Although increasingly stout, the Grand Duchess still cut a formidable figure with her regal bearing, lavish jewels, and exquisite gowns. Increasingly, she spent time in Paris, where she the brightest star in a circle of Vanderbilts, Astors, and other wealthy Americans on extended holidays.[20] American heiress Elizabeth Drexel Lehr called her *"naturally charming and gay, with a flair for saying precisely the right thing at the right time."*[21]

When World War I erupted in 1914, Marie Pavlovna temporarily abandoned her pleasures, and spent her days organizing military hospitals and ambulance trains. Despite her German origins, Marie Pavlovna was ardently pro-Russian: *"My forty years' residence in Russia, all the happiness I have known here, all the dreams that have come to me, all the affection and kindness I have received,"* she declared, *"has given me a wholly Russian soul."* She established a workshop in the Vladimir Palace, and her dinner invitations now came with a caveat: any guest was welcome as long as they spent time rolling bandages or made themselves useful in the war effort.[23]

Grand Duchess Marie Pavlovna Sr.

Much has been made of the hostility that existed between the Vladimirovichi and Empress Alexandra; it is useless to deny it, though perhaps it has been overstated with the passage of time. In the summer of 1915, Marie Pavlovna told her son Andrei of a perplexing conversation she'd had with Alexandra. "Alix," the Grand Duke recorded in his diary, *"looks on things exactly as we do, and everything that she said was clear, affirmative, and true. This episode in our family life is important, in that it gave us the possibility of understanding Alix. Almost the whole of her life in our country has been veiled in a shadowy incomprehensible aura. Nobody really*

From the left, standing: Grand Duchesses Victoria Feodorovna and Olga Nikolaievna, Grand Duke Kirill Vladimirovich, Princesses Elisabeth and Olga of Greece, Grand Duchess Anastasia Nikolaievna, and Princess Marina of Greece. Seated, same order: Grand Duchess Marie Pavlovna Sr., Empress Alexandra Feodorovna, Tsar Nicholas II, and Grand Duchess Elena Vladimirovna.

knew her, in fact, or understood her, and the guesses or suppositions that were made, became in time an array of the most varied legends. But in any case that conversation was important. We saw her in a new light, and realized that many of the legends are false, and that she is on the right path."[24]

This certainly sounds conciliatory, yet the Grand Duke made clear that the conversation revolved around the actions of the two former Montenegrin Grand Duchesses, Militsa and Anastasia, and their behavior. Marie Pavlovna apparently agreed that the two sisters were unscrupulous, and perhaps allowed that they had negatively influenced her perceptions of the Empress. But this didn't signal any significant rapprochement, or suggest a change in the Grand Duchess's thinking. On learning that Nicholas II was relieving Grand Duke Nicholas Nikolaievich of his post as Supreme Commander and assuming the position himself, Marie Pavlovna sobbed, *"It is quite disastrous!"*[25] To French Ambassador Maurice Paleologue, Marie Pavlovna confessed, *"I'm always easy in my mind when the Emperor is away from the Empress. It is she who makes him go wrong."*[26]

Grand Duke Kirill Vladimirovich.

Grand Duke Kirill Vladimirovich, Grand Duchess Victoria Feodorovna, and Princesses Maria and Kira Kirillovna

Born at Tsarskoye Selo on September 30, 1876, Grand Duke Kirill Vladimirovich was the eldest surviving son of Grand Duke Vladimir and his wife Marie Pavlovna. In his later memoirs, he wrote of having learned the importance of the *"management and the ability to maneuver in all the possible and seemingly impossible situations"* that, as a naval officer, the sea might throw at him; the words, though, also summed up the Grand Duke's tumultuous life and his capacity to weather its sudden storms.[27]

A listless looking young man, with watery blue eyes and a thin mustache, his early years and youth had been largely happy and uneventful. Raised by an English nanny and a series of tutors, Kirill was a less boorish clone of his father. *"He tipped lavishly,"* recalled Grand Duke Alexander Mikhailovich, *"he traveled often, he danced well."* Describing Kirill as *"kind-hearted and gay,"* Alexander Mikhailovich deemed him *"the idol of all women and friend of most of the men"* in fashionable St. Petersburg circles.[28]

Kirill completed his education and trained with the Sea Cadet Corps of the Imperial Navy, graduating from the Nikolaiev Naval Academy. In 1896 he was promoted to the rank of Midshipman and undertook a yearlong voyage that took him to the Far East, Japan, and America. After serving on the battleship *Rostislav*, he was promoted a lieutenant and held posts on the battleship *Peresvet* and then on the cruiser *Admiral Nakhimov*. At the beginning of 1904, Nicholas II promoted his cousin to Chief of Staff in the Russian Pacific Fleet; just a month later, the Russo-Japanese War erupted.

After several months of disastrous setbacks, the Russian outpost of Port Arthur in Manchuria was under constant siege. Kirill was then appointed First Officer on the battleship *Petropavlovsk*, a dreadnought that served as Admiral Stepan Makarov's flagship of the 1st Pacific Squadron. On March 31, 1904, as the vessel returned to the outer harbor at Port Arthur after briefly pursing a group of Japanese destroyers, she struck a mine that blew off the bow and ignited the forward magazine. Kirill had been on the bridge with Makarov when a ball of fire engulfed the vessel; the Grand Duke barely managed to slip down to the deck before the boilers exploded. Thousands of pieces of metal, glass, and wood shot through the air, scarring the Grand Duke's back and blowing him into the sea. In all, 631 sailors and officers, including Makarov, perished.[29]

Rescue from the frigid water took several hours; Kirill had suffered numerous burns, injuries from flying shrapnel, and permanent damage to his back. During his stay in hospital, he was found to be suffering from shell shock, and sent back to St. Petersburg. Although he eventually recovered from his wounds, the sinking had left the Grand Duke shaken and his nerves shattered.[30] Having barely escaped death, he was now determined to live his life to the fullest – a desire that quickly brought him into conflict with Nicholas II when he insisted on marrying their mutual cousin Victoria Melita.

A visit to Darmstatd in 1894. Standing, from the left: Tsesarevich Nicholas Alexandrovich, Princess Alix of Hesse and by Rhine, Princess Victoria of Battenberg, and Grand Duke Ernst Ludwig of Hesse and by Rhine. Seated, same order: Princess Irene of Prussia, Grand Duchess Elisabeth Feodorovna, Grand Duchess Victoria Melita of Hesse and by Rhine, and Grand Duke Sergei Alexandrovich.

"Ducky," as Victoria Melita was called, was the second daughter of Prince Alfred, Duke of Edinburgh – Queen Victoria's second son – and of his wife Grand Duchess Marie Alexandrovna, only surviving daughter of Emperor Alexander II. Born November 25 (New Style), 1876, while her father was stationed with the Royal Navy in Malta, she had always been known for her somewhat difficult, straightforward temperament. Her sister Marie of Romania described her as *"austere, more unbending than I was…the one who would tolerate no nonsense, who admonished or cautioned,"* with *"a steely rectitude about her which commanded respect."*[31] Although her aunt the Empress Friedrich called her *"such a dear and so sympathetic, unaffected, gentle and ladylike,"* many others deemed her rather spoilt, brittle, and headstrong.[32] Sharp faced, tall, and dark, Victoria Melita was handsome rather than beautiful: that honor went to her sister Missy, the future Queen Marie of Romania.

No one could ignore Victoria Melita's troubled marital history. In April 1894, she had married her first cousin Grand Duke Ernst Ludwig of Hesse and By Rhine, and was thus Empress Alexandra's sister-in-law – indeed, it was at their wedding that Alix of Hesse had finally accepted Nicholas's proposal. No great romance, the union had come about through family pressure: Queen Victoria was convinced that these two grandchildren belonged together. In her quest to marry them, she ignored their shared immaturity, selfishness, dedication to pleasure, and completely different personalities. Victoria Melita caved to family pressure, but the emotionally volatile Ernst Ludwig, alternating between manic fits of exuberance and deep depression, tried desperately to escape the union. He first objected by raising concerns that in marrying his first cousin they risked genetic damage to any children; Queen Victoria brushed this aside. He tried again, saying he worried about being *"an adequate husband"* and wondered if he was capable of fathering children. Once again, the Queen dismissed his objections, unaware of what lay behind them.

It took no longer than her wedding night for Victoria Melita to discover that she and her new husband were *"sexually incompatible."* At seventeen, she had no understanding of what lay behind her husband's reticence. Her mother Grand Duchess Marie Alexandrovna, the Duchess of Edinburgh and of Saxe-Coburg and Gotha, told her daughter that it was a blessing that Ernie had so little interest in *"sensual"* pleasures, but Victoria Melita felt that something was wrong.[33]

Grand Duchess Victoria Melita and her daughter Elisabeth.

Still, Ernst Ludwig did his duty and in 1895 Victoria Melita gave birth to a daughter, Elisabeth. Ernst Ludwig indulged her while Victoria Melita ignored her. Soon loud arguments echoed through the palace in Darmstadt; the sound of breaking mirrors and china was commonplace. Ernst Ludwig threw himself into the arts, championing the art nouveau movement and transforming his capital into a renowned artists' colony. But the more he ignored her the more Victoria Melita rebelled. She neglected less pleasant ceremonial duties in favor of house parties, entertaining amusements, and endless riding on her fiery stallion Bogdan.[34]

Not until later did Victoria Melita apparently discover Ernst Ludwig's secret, when she supposedly found him in bed with another man. *"No boy,"* she told her niece Princess Ileana of Romania, *"was safe; from the stable hands to the kitchen help, he slept quite openly with them all."*[35] Humiliated, she locked herself in her room for three days. Her mother Marie Alexandrovna soon let it be known that Ernst Ludwig *"is no man,"* while Kaiser Wilhelm II scolded the Grand Duke for his *"unnatural"* desires.[36]

According to Victoria Melita, Ernst Ludwig proposed a quiet arrangement, *"which would have assured a life of perfect happiness and care to me…but which my dignity and self-respect could never have allowed me to accept."*[37] This presumably would have allowed both husband and wife to embark on their own, discreet affairs, but Victoria Melita was too proud to consider such an arrangement.

Everyone knew that the couple was unhappy, but Queen Victoria refused to hear of any divorce. She did, though, finally admit that she had forced the union, saying sadly, *"I will never try to marry anyone again."*[38] After her death in 1901, the obstacles fell away, and on December 21 of that year the Supreme Court of Hesse dissolved the marriage on the rather extraordinary grounds of *"invincible mutual antipathy."*[39] The tragic 1903 death of Elisabeth from typhoid while staying with Nicholas and Alexandra in Poland forever severed Victoria Melita's last links to her former life.

As the divorced former Grand Duchess of Hesse, Victoria Melita found herself largely ostracized by members of her extended family. She behaved honorably, keeping her ex-husband's alleged

Grand Duchess Victoria Feodorovna.

A fun visit to Schloß Wolfsgarten, near Darmstadt. From the left: Empress Alexandra Feodorovna, Grand Duke Boris Vladimirovich, Tsar Nicholas II, Grand Duchess Victoria Melita, Prince Nicholas of Greece, Grand Duke Ernst Ludwig, Grand Duke Andrei Vladimirovich, and Grand Duke Kirill Vladimirovich.

homosexuality to herself rather than use it to justify the divorce, but the conventions of the time largely demonized the woman in such proceedings and Victoria Melita was made to suffer from the marital failure. Empress Alexandra, likely aware of her brother's true inclinations, insisted on lies, while her husband callously thought it would be better for everyone had the troublesome husband and wife died rather than forcing their families to endure *"the general disgrace of divorce."*[40]

The situation garnered attention in Russia because many were aware that Grand Duke Kirill harbored romantic interests in the former Grand Duchess of Hesse. Although first cousins, they had apparently taken real notice of each other only in 1891, when Victoria Melita traveled to Russia with her mother for the funeral of Grand Duchess Alexandra, wife of her uncle Grand Duke Paul Alexandrovich. Kirill and Victoria Melita seemed immediately attracted to each other, but her mother warned against any romance. Romanov Grand Dukes, she insisted, were usually drunken louts who kept mistresses and made terrible husbands.[41] Then, too, Kirill and Victoria Melita were first cousins – and the Russian Orthodox Church forbid such marriages.

Kirill and Victoria Melita frequently met again: at Nicholas II's coronation in 1896, where she notably flirted with him, and at other royal celebrations throughout the years.[42] In 1900, Kirill spent three weeks at Wolfsgarten, hunting lodge of the Grand Duke of Hesse, where he lavished Victoria Melita with attention. Those three weeks, Kirill later wrote, *"were decisive for the whole of my life."*[43]

After her divorce, Victoria Melita was quite open about the attraction between herself and Kirill. *"As to Kirill's attachment to me,"* she confided to her uncle Grand Duke Sergei Alexandrovich in 1902, *"Ernie was by no means ignorant of it, as we talked upon this subject together and I have hidden nothing from him."*[44] Now, according to Grand Duchess Xenia Alexandrovna, Kirill wandered around St. Petersburg *"with a languid expression of persecuted innocence."* The only honorable thing for him to do, she believed, was to *"marry Ducky and take the corresponding punishment."*[45]

Kirill refused to conceal his feelings. His mother suggested that he simply take Victoria Melita as his mistress and marry someone else, but he insisted that this was dishonorable. *"To those over whom* the shadow of death has passed," he later wrote, "life has a new meaning. It is like daylight. And I was now within visible reach of fulfillment of the dream of my life. Nothing would cheat me of it now. I had gone through much. Now, at last, the future lay radiant before me."[46] He sought out Father Ioann Yanishev, Personal Confessor the Nicholas and Alexandra, and asked if the Russian Orthodox Church really did have established laws forbidding the marriage of first cousins. Yanishev – rather confusingly in light of the Church's stance on the issue – soon reported that, *"from the point of canon law,"* there was no impediment to such a union.[47] The Grand Duke next approached Nicholas II, laying out the issue and his desire to marry. According to Kirill's account, Nicholas never gave any indication of opposition to the proposed match; indeed, he assured Kirill that it was *"his sincere hope that things could be straightened out."*[48]

Grand Duke Kirill Vladimirovich and Grand Duchess Victoria Feodorovna with his mother, Grand Duchess Marie Pavlovna Sr.

This may well have been yet another example of Nicholas II's scrupulous avoidance of uncomfortable personal situations, as he attempted to placate and please everyone. This time, though, the signals were mixed, and Nicholas even let his cousin go off to Europe to join Victoria Melita in Germany in the spring of 1905. Princess Daisy of Pless recorded: *"Two nights ago, Grand Duchess Anastasia* [Mikhailovna] *gave an evening party for Grand Duchess Cecilie, who leaves soon for Germany.*

There were crowds of people. The Grand Duchess of Hesse and her unmarried sister came with Grand Duke Kirill in his motor. They are coming here this afternoon to spend the night. The Grand Duchess and the Grand Duke are certain to marry although he will probably have to give up most of his fortune and live abroad."[49]

Kirill apparently took the Emperor's vague statement as permission. Events suddenly seemed to conspire in Kirill's favor. In 1904 Tsesarevich Alexei's hemophilia was as yet unsuspected and Kirill, now third in line for throne after the boy and Grand Duke Michael Alexandrovich, had little reason to believe that he would ever be called upon to shoulder the burden. Then, in February of 1905, Ernst Ludwig had remarried, with Empress Alexandra's blessing. These two events apparently convinced Kirill to act. As he later admitted, *"I considered it would be easier for the Emperor to make a decision if he were to be confronted with a* fait accompli.*"*[50] On September 25/October 8, 1905, Kirill and Victoria Melita were finally married at a villa on the Tegernsee near Munich. They wed in an Orthodox service, conducted by Father Smirnov, confessor to Victoria Melita's mother Grand Duchess Marie Alexandrovna. Though the wedding was secret, it was not a morganatic one, as Victoria Melita was descended both from Alexander II and Queen Victoria. Having been performed by an Orthodox priest, it was also religiously valid.

One sticking point remained, something that critics to this day attempt to use against the marriage. Much has been made of the Orthodox Church's prohibition against marriages between first cousins. The simple fact is that exceptions had often been made in the past: Grand Duchess Catherine Pavlovna, for example, had been allowed to wed her first cousin, as had Nicholas Nikolaievich Sr. when he wed Alexandra of Oldenburg. The same Orthodox rules also forbade marriage between second and third cousins, though this had not stopped the unions of Nicholas I to Charlotte of Prussia; Grand Duchess Elena Vladimirovna to Prince Nicholas of Greece; Grand Duke Alexander Mikhailovich to Grand Duchess Xenia Alexandrovna; Grand Duke Sergei Alexandrovich to Elisabeth of Hesse; Grand Duke Paul Alexandrovich to Alexandra of Greece; Grand Duke George Mikhailovich to Marie of Greece; or even second cousins Nicholas II and Empress Alexandra. In July 1904, the Holy Synod had even allowed marriages between first cousins under special circumstances.

The real problem with the marriage was that it was conducted without the Emperor's approval and knowledge, as required by Article 183 of the Fundamental Laws of the Empire. It was thus deemed illegal. Kirill quickly learned what the repercussions of his action would be when he returned to St. Petersburg and confessed all. This was what his parents Vladimir and Marie Pavlovna

Grand Duke Kirill Vladimirovich.

thought best; Nicholas would chastise his cousin but would forgive him. Yet Nicholas did not relent; late one night, he dispatched a courtier to Kirill, informing him that he must leave Russia at once and would never be allowed to set foot in the country again. Nicholas illegally stripped him of his Grand Ducal title, his military commissions, and his incomes.[51]

The next day, an infuriated Grand Duke Vladimir stormed into his nephew's study, ripped the medals from his chest, threw them down on the Emperor's desk, and resigned all of his military commissions in protest.[52] Vladimir and his wife were absolutely convinced that Empress Alexandra was behind the unexpectedly harsh punishment, believing that she was taking revenge through Kirill on the woman who had divorced her beloved brother. A British visitor to the Vladimir Palace noted that *"the language used"* about the Emperor and Empress there *"is most violent."* [53] *"The blind vindictiveness and rage of the young Empress,"* Marie Pavlovna insisted, *"has, for sheer malice, exceeded anything the wildest imagination could conceive. She stormed and raged like a lunatic, dragging her weak husband along with her until he lent her his power and so made it possible to revenge herself on her ex-sister-in-law."*[54] Certainly the Empress was infuriated, insisting that she would never receive Victoria Melita and condemning her as *"a woman who had behaved so disgracefully."*[55]

Kirill confessed himself *"dumbfounded by the severity"* of Nicholas II's punishment, *"as the Emperor had at no time indicated or even vaguely hinted at such drastic steps."*[56] Consistency was never Nicholas II's strong suit: under pressure from the Vladimirs, as well as his mother, he soon relented and within a few weeks restored Kirill's title. *"I wonder whether it was wise to punish a man so publicly,"* he wrote to his mother, *"and to such an extent, especially when his family was against it."*[57] He did, though, insist that Kirill remain in exile, without access to his fortune.

Kirill and Victoria Melita duly took up residence in Paris, purchasing a house with money provided by their parents.[58] After nearly two years, the Emperor relented again: on July 15, 1907, Nicholas II issued a ukase recognizing the validity of the marriage and granting retroactive approval. This was the end of the issue: Nicholas II was not only the arbiter of how the Fundamental Laws were applied but also the Supreme Head of the Russian Orthodox Church. Victoria Melita was given the new title and name of Grand Duchess Victoria Feodorovna, she converted to Russian Orthodoxy, and their children were to be members of the Imperial House, with full succession rights. They were allowed to return to Russia.

Nicholas allowed Kirill to resume his naval career: the Grand Duke served as a captain of the cruiser *Oleg* and, in 1913, joined the *Garde Equipage*. But

Grand Duchess Victoria Feodorovna with her daughters Princesses Maria Kirillovna and Kira Kirillovna.

his experience aboard *Petropavlovsk* had left Kirill incapable of naval service: several times he boarded vessels only to flee when he felt their engines rumble to life beneath his feet.[59] Kirill purchased a small mansion at No. 13 Nikolskaya (now Glinka) Street in St. Petersburg. "Ducky," said her sister Crown Princess Marie of Romania, *"had perfect taste and the same passion as I have for arranging her rooms in a rather unusual and uncommon way."*[60] Invited to take tea with the Grand Duchess, Princess Cantacuzene *"found her in informal dress in her small sitting room; there was the usual beauty and comfort in all the arrangements of her palace, which kept more an air of home than any other in the city. With its books and knitting, soft chairs and lights, and all its treasures in marbles and collections so disposed as to be merely harmonious parts of the general scheme of decoration it was wonderfully attractive. She herself looked older, seemed grown taller, and was all in black. As we smoked and drank tea, and talked, I heard with joy her calm, fair judgment of people and things; and I was won by the uncomplaining way she had of accepting a situation which upset her life so thoroughly."*[61]

Two children, both girls, arrived during their parents' exile in Europe: Princess Maria was born February 2 (New Style), 1907, while Kira was born May 9 (New Style), 1909. They were, said Crown Princess Marie, both *"splendid children, well-grown, solid, with lovely hair and perfect skin and*

Grand Duchess Victoria Feodorovna with her daughters Maria and Kira, c. 1911.

as superlatively groomed as English ponies. They had everything on earth of which human children could dream and were flatteringly glad to have me in their midst.[62] Grand Duchess Victoria Feodorovna made herself extremely popular in St. Petersburg society, entertaining lavishly and befriending the most influential figures of the day. She had a particular passion for motorcars, and organized several distance races; in the summer of 1914, she and Kirill even participated, driving a course laid out between Pskov and Riga.[63]

Victoria Feodorovna, noted one contemporary, *"achieved the difficult feat of remaining on very good terms with her mother-in-law Grand Duchess Vladimir."*[64] Relations with Nicholas and especially Alexandra, remained ostensibly cordial but uncomfortably cool.[65] Hostility from Tsarskoye Selo, though – along with the cold Russian winters – eventually led to extended stays abroad on the Riviera or with Victoria Feodorovna's mother in Germany, where the couple could live more openly and without the Empress's opprobrium.

On the outbreak of the Great War, Kirill became Commander of the *Garde Equipage*, though he had to confine his duties to land as he was still suffering from what would now be called post-traumatic stress disorder as a result of his experience during the Russo-Japanese War. Victoria Feodorovna, more practically minded than her mother-in-law, trained as a Red Cross nurse, funded an ambulance train, and organized a motorcar ambulance unit. She frequently visited the front, and several times came under enemy fire. Previously Victoria Feodorovna had managed the difficult task of maintaining good relations with her powerful mother-in-law; as she complained to her sister-in-law Elena, though, she now felt that Marie Pavlovna was selfishly attempting to claim laurels that did not belong to her. She also developed an active dislike of the Grand Duchess's rather fast social circle, deriding them as *"such awful people."*[66] Perhaps not surprisingly, Empress Alexandra agreed. Writing to Nicholas on March 8, 1915, she praised her former sister-in-law, saying *"she really does a lot with her unit, and is really under fire. Miechen promenades with her decorations to all exhibitions, etc."* Victoria Feodorovna, she added, should be given the St. George Cross as she *"deserves it certainly."*[67]

Grand Duke Boris Vladimirovich

Born on November 12, 1877, Grand Duke Boris, the second Vladimir son, was a charming reprobate who, despite his misadventures, was his mother's favorite. A contemporary wrote that he *"seemed to have been born for the express purpose of getting into scrapes — and disreputable ones at that. He was a handsome fellow, but absolutely unscrupulous."*[68] *"Gay or sulky by turns,"* said his cousin Marie of Romania, *"he had an attractive, rather husky voice, kind eyes, and a humorous smile, which crinkled his forehead into unexpected lines. Not exactly handsome, he had nevertheless great charm, and a slight lisp added a certain quaintness to his speech."*[69]

After completing his education Boris entered the Nikolaievsky Cavalry School, graduating with the rank of coronet in 1896 and joining the Life Guards Hussar Regiment, though his dedication to the military was always second to his pursuit of pleasure. Having openly flirted with his cousin Crown Princess Marie of Romania at Nicholas II's coronation in 1896, he visited her the following year in Bucharest; there were even rumors that he had fathered one of her children.

In one of his alcohol-fueled forays he seduced a certain Mademoiselle Demidov; in the resulting furor her fiancé broke off his engagement, and all St. Petersburg was abuzz with the scandal. Boris, wrote a contemporary, was *the terror of jealous husbands as well as of watchful mothers, who were always anxious when he invited one of their daughters to dance."*[70] He challenged men to duels and even once publicly struck a woman who rebuffed his advances.[71] His drinking and profligate nature only escalated: in one year, he reportedly spent 25,000 rubles on food and 8,000 on motorcars, while giving 46 rubles to the church. His mother was often forced to step in and pay his debts.[72]

Grand Duke Boris Vladimirovich in his regiment's uniform.

In 1901, Boris had a liaison with a Frenchwoman named Jeanne Aumont-Lacroix, who gave birth to his bastard son the following year. Although Boris did not recognize the son, also named Boris, he often saw him while visiting France and also provided substantial payments to his mother.[73] For the Grand Duke, the endless liaisons soon blended one into another. He complained to his brother Kirill: *"After a while, every woman is the same, nothing is new except the face."*[74]

Hoping to prevent further scandals, his parents sent Boris on a world tour in January 1902. He visited Egypt, India, and Japan before continuing on to America, where at first he won laurels for his impeccable English and easy-going manner. But, far from reforming the Grand Duke's wayward tastes, the freedom of the tour only afforded more opportunities for misadventure. In Chicago, he made headlines by flirting with chorus girls, tipping them with $20 bills, and drinking champagne out of their satin slippers.[75] A slight diplomatic scandal ensued when Boris called on President Theodore Roosevelt at his Long Island estate, Sagamore Hill. Owing to the Grand Duke's less than stellar reputation, the President decided his wife Edith should absent herself from the luncheon. The press still complained, infuriated that the President had received *"a personage whose presence would stain the moral repute of his abode."*[76]

In 1904, when the Russo-Japanese War erupted, Boris went to Manchuria to join in the fighting. A story, apparently apocryphal, quickly spread in St. Petersburg that he had smuggled a dozen prostitutes, dressed as Red Cross nurses, aboard his train to keep him entertained.[77] When Kaiser Wilhelm II heard of this, he insisted that Boris *"is not a fit person to shake hands with."*[78] Grand Duke Nicholas Nikolaievich once condemned Boris, commenting that although *"he is a nice, sweet boy…wherever he goes he leaves a stinking trail behind him."*[79]

Perhaps surprising, Boris managed to acquit himself well during the Russo-Japanese War. He served at the headquarters of Russian Commander-in-Chief Alexei Kuropatkin and participated in several dangerous battles. In December 1904 Nicholas II rewarded Boris for his bravery in action and promoting him to Staff Captain.[80]

Though Boris lacked the temperament or inclination to settle down, he made a half-hearted proposal to Princess Victoria Eugenie of Battenberg in 1905. As she was only seventeen, she put him off, and Boris's interest soon waned. He filled his days with official duties, eventually rising to the rank of colonel, and his nights with pleasure. Although he had a palace on St. Petersburg's English Embankment, Boris threw himself into the creation of Wolf Garden, his English-style palace at Tsarskoye Selo, whose bourgeois interiors were designed and furnished by Maples Department Store in London.[81] Guests at Wolf Garden were usually stunned to find themselves assaulted by Auguste, the Grand Duke's pet pig, *"who used to trot round after his master like a dog, begging for tidbits from the table."*[82]

Grand Duke Boris Vladimirovich getting off his horse.

With the outbreak of World War I, Nicholas II gave Boris commanded of a regiment of Ataman Cossacks. The Grand Duke, though, was not particularly keen in his duties, and he openly disliked his military role at headquarters, which kept him from the lavish entertainments and dissolute pleasures he so enjoyed. He managed to drunkenly cause offense by excoriating Great Britain in the presence of the British Military Mission. British Ambassador Sir George Buchanan made a formal complaint, and Nicholas sent Boris a written reprimand, demanding that he make an apology.[83] But despite the apology, French Ambassador Maurice Paleologue thought that nothing would change: *"Boris Vladimirovich will calmly continue his life of pleasure and idleness. What has he been doing since the war began? Nothing. He has held vague commands and inspectorships that occasionally take him to the Front, but these have been simply an excuse for him to vary the round of his pleasures – from Moscow to Kiev, Warsaw to Odessa, the Caucasus to the Crimea."*[84]

Boris got around his boredom by seducing Zenaida Rachevskaya, a pretty young woman nearly twenty years his junior, and making her pregnant. Since Boris couldn't marry her, he paid a military officer to do so and conceal the pregnancy. As it was, the child died shortly after birth.[85] Despite his obvious shortcomings, Boris remained his mother's favorite. In 1916, Grand Duchess Marie Pavlovna even astutely suggested that he might propose to Nicholas and Alexandra's daughter Olga, something that would cement the family's powerful position and influence. Empress Alexandra was appalled. *"The more often I think about Boris,"* she complaining to her husband in a letter of February 13, *"the more I realize what an awful set his wife would be dragged into, his and Miechen's friends, rich French people, Russian bankers, the society...and all such types, intrigues without end – fast manners and conversations....To give over a well-used, half-worn*

out, blasé young man to pure, fresh girl eighteen years his junior, and to live in a house in which many a woman has 'shared' his life....An inexperienced girl would suffer terribly, to have her husband 4th or 5th hand, or more."[86]

Grand Duke Andrei Vladimirovich before the monarchy's fall.

Grand Duke Andrei Vladimirovich

Grand Duke Andrei, the third Vladimir son, was born May 2, 1879 at Tsarskoye Selo. He was the quietest of the couple's children, a shy, intellectual, studious man, tall and thin, with a receding hairline and a small cavalry mustache. Although he had little taste for military life, it was the expected course of action for a Grand Duke, and after graduating from the Mikhailovsky Artillery School Andrei duly joined the Imperial Horse Guards Regiment; eventually, he rose to command the Horse Guards Artillery. His true passion, though, was law. Shortly after the turn of the century, he began studying at the Alexandrovsky Judicial Academy, focused on criminal and military investigations.

Yet even Andrei was not above scandal. In 1900 his brothers invited him to a dinner party given by Nicholas II's former mistress, ballerina Mathilde

Kschessinska. Kschessinska was pretty, talented, charming, and possessed an enormous ego. After successfully bedding the future Nicholas II, she found herself cast aside when he became engaged to Alix of Hesse. But Nicholas did not forget her, asking his cousin Grand Duke Sergei Mikhailovich to look after her. Soon she and Sergei were lovers, a condition that apparently did not interfere with her romance with Andrei Vladimirovich. For a time, she shared the affections, and the beds, of both men. *"You should be proud to have two Grand Dukes at your feet,"* a prince once told her. *"What's surprising about that?"* she haughtily answered. *"I have two feet!"*[87] This bold and flamboyant manner did not appeal to everyone. Vladimir Teliakovsky, Director of the Imperial Theatres, called Kschessinska a *"morally impudent, cynical and brazen"* woman, *"living simultaneously with two Grand Dukes, and not only not concealing the fact but, on the contrary, weaving this 'art' into her stinking, cynical wreath of human offal and vice."*[88]

Kschessinska was nothing if not ambitious. Sergei Mikhailovich was less attractive, poorer, less influential, and much further down the line of succession to the throne than was Andrei, who could shower her with expensive jewels and sparkling holidays on the Riviera. She cast aside the slavishly loyal Sergei in favor of the wealthier, more

prominent Andrei.[89] Still, no one was absolutely certain who fathered her bastard son Vladimir in June 1902. Kschessinska, who later married Andrei in exile, wrote of *"our son,"* yet Vladimir carried the patronymic *"Sergeievich,"* and his birth certificate listed Grand Duke Sergei as his father.[90] Vladimir later confessed that he actually had no idea which Grand Duke had been his father.[91]

Andrei had never enjoyed military life. He went through the motions expected of a Grand Duke with little enthusiasm and even less interest. But he knew his patriotic duty when the Great War began, joining the staff of the Northern Front, where he commanded first the Horse Guards Artillery Brigade and then the 130th Kherson Infantry Regiment. His duties were largely ceremonial, but they

Grand Duke Andrei Vladimirovich with Mathilde Kschessinska and their son Vladimir while traveling outside Russia.

had one unforeseen benefit: they kept him away from Kschessinska, whose wartime activities were to cause an immense scandal.

By the autumn of 1916, the Vladimirs had become thoroughly disillusioned with Nicholas II and his stubborn consort. In a letter to her mother, Victoria Feodorovna complained of Rasputin: *"We are passing through bad times here because of all the priest and prophet stories….It is all much more serious than one is allowed to mention."* It was as if, she wrote, *"some terrible aberration"* held Nicholas and Alexandra in its grip."[92]

Steeling herself for what she must have known would be an unpleasant interview, Victoria Feodorovna called on her former sister-in-law Empress Alexandra at Tsarskoye Selo that December. She began by speaking in generalities, decrying the government's disintegration without ever mentioning Rasputin's name. The Grand Duchess tried to convince Alexandra that her entrenched attitudes and interference in political affairs was alienating public opinion and leading toward disaster. Alexandra cut her off: *"All of this discontent so widely discussed,"* she insisted, *"is simply Petrograd gossip. Russia is absolutely quiet and content."*[93] Nor was Alexandra receptive to any suggested changes. Firmness, she insisted, was needed, and she refused *"to let the Emperor yield any more."* There was no discontent: the army was loyal to a man, and the peasants fully supported the autocracy.[94] Such talk stemmed only from those who *"want to tear to pieces all the fabric of traditional autocracy in Russia and then throw the power of the throne to a lot of howling, disloyal liberals."* When Victoria Feodorovna protested that it wasn't just liberals who worried about the state of affairs, Alexandra cut her off, saying that she knew better and that *"the country has never been more satisfied than now or had more confidence in the government."*[95]

Mathilde Kschessinska and her son Vladimir Andreievich.

People now openly talked of conspiracy. Grand Duchess Vladimir even carelessly spoke of the need to *"annihilate"* the Empress.[96] Duke Alexander of Leuchtenberg told a friend in 1916 that Kirill, Boris, and Andrei had asked him *"whether I would lead my Cossack regiments in a planned revolt against the Government. I answered that I would take no sides in all this mess, so I resigned my command."*[97]

Such talk clearly reflected the growing frustration among members of the Romanov Family. Perhaps it is not surprising that the ambitious Vladimirovichi might lend their support to such an idea, yet it would be wrong to solely characterize their actions as selfish, for the plan was to apparently storm the Alexander Palace, force Nicholas to abdicate, and have Alexei proclaimed Emperor, with Grand Duke Nicholas Nikolaievich as Regent.[98] Nicholas Nikolaievich would wield the power, not Kirill, Boris, or Andrei. Like many members of the dynasty, they seemed more concerned with saving what they saw as a doomed throne than with personal advancement. But by February 1917, the situation had gone too far for any Romanov to save the Imperial Throne.

Chapter V

The Junior Alexandrovich Line: Grand Duchess Elisabeth Feodorovna, Grand Duke Paul Alexandrovich & Grand Duke Dimitri Pavlovich

Grand Duchess Elisabeth Feodorovna

During the Tercentenary Celebrations of 1913, one figure invariably stood out amongst the Romanovs: Grand Duchess Elisabeth Feodorovna. In previous years, she had been accustomed to the attention. *"Her eyes, her lips, her smile, her hands, the way she looked at you, the way she talked, the way she moved,"* recalled her niece Marie of Romania, *"all was exquisite beyond words."*[1] Everyone seemed charmed by her grace, beauty, and gentleness. In 1913, though, the widowed Grand Duchess was most notable for her attire: a nun's robe of soft gray baize, with white cambric wimple and a white wool veil. Thus gowned, the Grand Duchess – as the Dowager Empress once bitterly commented – presented herself as *a theatrical martyr, relishing the attention"* drawn by her exotic costume.[2]

Grand Duchess Elisabeth Feodorovna.

Born November 1 (New Style), 1864, Princess Elisabeth of Hesse, called "Ella" within the family, was the second child of Princess Alice and her husband Ludwig, the future Grand Duke of Hesse. With an uncanny sense of predestination, her mother named her after a distant ancestor, St. Elisabeth of Hungary. Beautiful and refined, graceful and elegant, she had spurned the attentions of her cousin the future Kaiser Wilhelm II. Grand Duke Alexander Mikhailovich later rhapsodized about her *"ravishing beauty, rare intelligence, delightful sense of humor, infinite patience, hospitality of thought, and generous heart."*[3]

Elisabeth surprised everyone by marrying the strange Grand Duke Sergei Alexandrovich, fifth son of Alexander II. Queen Victoria opposed the match, complaining of Russia's *"very bad state of society and its total want of principle from the Grand Dukes down."*[4] Sergei was tall and thin, intelligent and regal, coldly handsome with his piercing eyes and closely cropped beard. Yet he was aloof, self-conscious, and seemed forever to wear a barely disguised sneer of disdain. People thought he was an arrogant despot, quarrelsome and prone to bursts of anger. *"Try as I will,"* said Grand Duke Alexander Mikhailovich, *"I cannot find a single redeeming feature in his character."*[5] Even his sister Grand Duchess Marie Alexandrovna found her brother Sergei odd: he was, she complained, *"strange," "stubborn,"* and *"a spoilt Mama's boy"* with *"the tastes of a young girl."*[6]

Elisabeth and Sergei wed in the Cathedral of the Winter Palace on June 3, 1884, and took up residence in the former Belosselsky-Belozersky Palace on the Nevsky Prospekt; in the summer, they retreated to Ilinskoye, Sergei's country estate outside of Moscow. Sergei and Elisabeth's marriage confounded everyone. He controlled every aspect of Elisabeth's

Standing in the back, from the left: Hereditary Grand Duke Ernst Ludwig of Hesse and by Rhine, Prince Louis of Battenberg, and Princess Alix of Hesse and by Rhine. Seated, same order: Princess Irene Hesse and by Rhine, Grand Duchess Elisabeth Feodorovna, Princess Alice and Princess Victoria of Battenberg, Grand Duke Sergei Alexandrovich, and Grand Duke Ludwig IV of Hesse and by Rhine.

life, selecting her dresses, reading her correspondence, and picking out the books she was allowed to read. She was his possession, and he treated her like a child, often delighting in openly criticizing her *"in the harshest of language and most brutal of terms"* and apparently priding himself on humiliating her before others.[7]

"Their relations toward each other were distinguished by a strained fondness," said a relative. *"They never seemed very intimate and avoided being alone together."*[8] Sergei, said his cousin Grand Duke Alexander Mikhailovich, *"flaunted his many peculiarities in the face of the nation. His private behavior gave the regime's enemies inexhaustible material for libel."*[9] Within two years of their marriage, noted a contemporary, there was *"already a lot of chatter in the salons of Petersburg, spread by malicious people, about different rumors"* concerning Sergei and Elisabeth's marriage.[10]

Sergei was widely believed to be homosexual, *"a wretched fellow in the fullest sense of the word,"* said State Senator A. A. Polovtsov, a man who indulged in *"unmentionable vices enjoyed by the Ancient Greeks,"* as one author so delicately phrased it.[11] *"His private life was the talk of the town,"* commented Alexander Mossolov, Head of Nicholas II's Court Chancellery.[12] The stories, if true, perhaps explain Sergei's otherwise enigmatic character. There is no doubt that he was deeply religious, having inherited his mother's almost extreme piety; if the Grand Duke was indeed homosexual, it is likely that his life was an agonizing struggle to reconcile desire and Orthodox teaching.

Royal wives of the period didn't complain or confess the secrets of their bedrooms, but many suspected the worst. Elisabeth dismissed the *"abominable lies"* surrounding her marriage, protesting that she was supremely happy and that *"people will intrigue and lie as long as the world exists,"* but few were convinced by her repeated denials of unhappiness.[13] Recognizing that he wouldn't father any children, Sergei changed his will, leaving everything to his brother Paul Alexandrovich's two children Dimitri Pavlovich and Marie Pavlovna. According to rumor, he even told Elisabeth that she was free to take a lover from their entourage as long as she was discreet. Much later, after her brutal death, most of Elisabeth's royal relatives stumbled over themselves in painting her as the most pure, virtuous and dedicated of humanitarians, but popular sentiment during her own life was somewhat more realistic. More than one critic thought that the Grand Duchess used the popular perceptions of her unhappy married life to win personal acclaim. The inimitable Princess Catherine Radziwill even suggested that she posed *"as a victim of circumstance"* in an effort to gain sympathy.[14]

Grand Duchess Elisabeth Feodorovna, Grand Duke Sergei Alexandrovich, and Grand Duke Paul Alexandrovich.

This is perhaps a bit too harsh, but there is no doubt that Elisabeth harbored a different, determined side that contrasted with the aura of saintly sweetness and light. She constantly defended Sergei, decrying the sordid stories about her husband as malicious gossip. But she apparently couldn't ignore the gossip that erupted sometime in 1890. Sergei, it is said, had surrounded himself in St. Petersburg with a group of young guards officers and male actors; some homosexual scandal ensued, and twenty of the guards were instantly dismissed from their regiments.[15] And, on the heels of this, at least according to Kaiser Wilhelm II, Sergei was caught having sex with a handsome young priest who had been appointed to his household.[16] The incident was hushed up, and Alexander III decided to appoint his brother as Governor-General of Moscow, perhaps in the hope that removing him to the former capital would help ease the scandal. On arriving in Moscow Sergei promptly vented his frustrations on the city's Jews. Jews, Sergei insisted, *"ought to be crucified!"* Some 20,000 were expelled; young girls who remained had to register as prostitutes.[17]

Elisabeth finally broke, and she converted to Orthodoxy with a passion that her husband found incomprehensible. Questions have always surrounded her decision, and Elisabeth's contemporaries were often cynical in their appraisals. Her cousin Kaiser Wilhelm, who admittedly bore a grudge after she had rejected his romantic advances, suggested that she converted from *"an inordinate pursuit of popularity, a desire to improve her position at court, a great lack of intelligence, and also a true want of religiousness and patriotic feeling."*[18] Marie Feodorovna was equally suspicious of her sister-in-law's motivations, apparently believing that Elisabeth had converted merely to use her new faith as a weapon in her ongoing effort to convince her sister Alix to do likewise and thus accept Tsesarevich Nicholas's proposal – something that Elisabeth indeed confirmed had been a factor when writing to her family. The Grand Duke had received his appointment to Moscow on February 26, 1891; Elisabeth had converted to Orthodoxy on April 14. This timeline led French Ambassador Maurice Paleologue to suggest that she only converted because, as the newly appointed Governor-General, Sergei thought it impolitic to take up his position in Moscow without an Orthodox spouse at his side – again something that Elisabeth strongly hinted at in letters to her family. Whatever the initial motivations, Elisabeth certainly seemed sincere in her religious quest, and her subsequent life revealed the depth of her profound faith.

Grand Duke Sergei Alexandrovich.

Elisabeth did her share of manipulation and outright lying when it came to the romance between Nicholas and her sister, openly deceiving Alexander III and Marie Feodorovna as to his eventual chances of her winning her hand. Once Alix had married Nicholas, Elisabeth seems to have considered herself as something of the power behind the throne. In the first decade of her brother-in-law's reign, she constantly intruded with unsolicited political opinions and advice that echoed the deeply reactionary, conservative views of her husband. Her outspoken efforts caused tension and laid the groundwork for an eventual break with her sister over the issue of Rasputin.

In 1902, when his brother Paul Alexandrovich was exiled from Russia for contracting a morganatic marriage, Sergei and Elisabeth took in the two children from his first marriage, Grand Duke Dimitri Pavlovich and Grand Duchess Marie Pavlovna. Sergei was stern and demanding, but he doted on the children, perhaps a little too much, and both Dimitri and Marie developed an unhealthy emotional dependence on each other; their traumatic childhoods resulted in later depression and alcoholism. Elisabeth seemed to resent the two children. She was, Marie recalled, cold and aloof toward them, and angry that the husband who denied her any affection so lavishly showered it on these children.

Although both Elisabeth and Sergei had not been shy about trying to influence Nicholas II to more conservative policies, by the beginning of 1905 – with the Russo-Japanese War eroding public support and unrest pushing the Emperor to make half-hearted illusory concessions – the Grand Duke recognized that his former power was on the wane, and he resigned his post as Governor-General. Sergei, though, remained in Moscow as Commander of the Military District. Owing to unrest in the former capital he – along with Elisabeth, Dimitri Pavlovich, and Marie Pavlovna – moved into the Nicholas Palace in the Kremlin, which offered more protection.

On the afternoon of February 17, Socialist-Revolutionary Ivan Kalyayev hurled a bomb at Sergei's carriage as the Grand Duke left the Kremlin. The resulting explosion literally blew Sergei to pieces: one of his fingers, with ring still attached, was later found on a roof several hundred yards away. Elisabeth rushed out onto the crimson-stained snow, gathering the charred and bloody clumps of flesh into the folds of her dress. Few mourned his death. Elisabeth, Marie Pavlovna saw, was stoic, *"her face white, but there were no tears."* Only after the funeral did she collapse in sobs.[19]

Grand Duchess Elisabeth Feodorovna.

Once Sergei was entombed, Elisabeth did something unthinkable, visiting the assassin in prison and praying for him, though stories that she offered to intercede with the Emperor for his life are apocryphal. The death of her husband closed one chapter in the Grand Duchess's life and opened another. After essentially forcing young Marie

Pavlovna into a loveless marriage, Elisabeth turned to God, though, like her sister Alexandra, she did so in her own peculiar way, charting a previously unknown course that caused scandal and suggested feelings of superiority. According to Marie Pavlovna, Sergei Alexandrovich had *"regarded with anxiety his wife's increasing absorption in things spiritual, and ended by regarding it as immoderate."*[20]

This apparent taste for flamboyance took visible expression in her decision to found an order of nursing sisters. This, in itself, was not so extraordinary: other Romanov women had, at times throughout the Dynasty's history, abandoned court life and disappeared into nunneries or monasteries, devoting themselves to the care of the poor. What made Elisabeth's decision different is that she refused to go quietly, insisting instead that religious laws be bent, abandoned, and changed to accommodate her desire for a larger, more prominent role.

Elisabeth insisted that her nursing sisters be granted the title of deaconess, and that the Holy Synod recognize her as Abbess. The Synod erupted in protest: clerical ranks were given only to men. The matter became so heated that several bishops tried to intervene with the Emperor against his sister-in-law. After two years of a very public battle, though,

Elisabeth won. In April 1910 she announced the foundation of the Order of St. Mary and St. Martha in Moscow. Having sold her possessions, she used the money to purchase land and build a church and hospital. In so doing, Elisabeth was careful to maintain a sense of elegant style. Fashionable painter Michael Nesterov not only embellished her new church, a fusion of ancient Muscovite architecture and art nouveau trends, but also designed her monastic robes. As a final nod to her luxurious tastes, the Grand Duchess actually commissioned her habit from Parisian hâute couture house Paquin.[21] Nor did she entirely abandon comfort within. A visitor was somewhat surprised to find the Abbess's own rooms filled with *"many books bound in the lapis blue which seems to be the Grand Duchess's favorite color; a few pictures, mostly of the Madonna and Child; some small tables, one with Stephen Graham's book,* The House of Mary and Martha, *held open upon it by a piece of embroidery carelessly dropped. There were easy chairs of English willow with blue cushions, and a businesslike little desk crammed with papers. Everywhere, in the window, on tables and the desk, were bowls and vases of flowers. Every room in the place, in fact, was filled with flowers."*[22]

For the rest of her life Elisabeth devoted herself to

The four Hessian sisters. From the left: Princess Irene of Prussia, Empress Alexandra Feodorovna, Grand Duchess Elisabeth Feodorovna, and Princess Victoria of Battenberg.

helping the poor and suffering. *"I am as if bidding goodbye to the past,"* the Grand Duchess wrote to Nicholas II on taking up her vows, *"its faults and sins and with the hope of a higher goal and purer existence. Pray for me, deary...my taking of vows is even more serious than if a young girl marries. I am espousing Christ and His cause. I am giving all I can to Him and our neighbors, I am going deeper into our Orthodox Church and becoming like a missionary of Christian faith and charity work and, oh dear, I am so unworthy of it all and I do so want blessings and prayers."*[23]

The sisters of the Order of St. Mary and St. Martha, like their mistress, did not remain cloistered, but freely moved through the worst Moscow slums, providing food and medical attention to the destitute. The Grand Duchess also established a free hospital, a pharmacy, and an orphanage as she sought to relieve the lives of the Emperor's impoverished subjects and provide them with spiritual counseling.

By 1913, Elisabeth again found herself in religious conflict, this time with her sister over the issue of Rasputin. More practical and even-minded than Alexandra, she could not understand her sister's reliance on and devotion to the infamous peasant. She seems to have genuinely believed that Rasputin was a charlatan and that his influence was destroying the throne. Unfortunately, she freely associated with many of Rasputin's more vocal opponents, which in turn led Alexandra to suspect her of betrayal. In a letter to Nicholas II, the Grand Duchess once lamented, *"I fear you think I am proud and self satisfied, that I interiorly puff myself up with the satisfaction of creating something grand....I know Alix images I allow people to call me a saint – she said so."*[24]

From the left: Tsar Nicholas II, Grand Duchess Elisabeth Feodorovna, Grand Duchesses Maria, Grand Duchess Anastasia, Grand Duchess Olga, Grand Duchess Tatiana, and Empress Alexandra Feodorovna.

The ever naïve, ever loyal Anna Vyrubova echoed what must have been Alexandra's thoughts when she later wrote of the Grand Duchess's *"coolness"* and *"chilly refusal to listen to her sister's denial of preposterous tales of the political influence exerted by Rasputin."* Of course, Rasputin's political involvement was real; in 1911 Nicholas and Alexandra had even asked him to interview prospective candidates for high office. Vyrubova, though – as did Alexandra – painted the situation as *"a plot"* against the Imperial couple. The gulf between Elisabeth and Alexandra grew *"wider and deeper, until their association was robbed of most of its old intimacy."*[25] By 1915, Alexandra was railing against *"Ella's not good, very bigoted clique"* of Moscow friends in letters to Nicholas.[26]

Elisabeth increased her charity work when World War I erupted. But, like her sister, she was frequently – and erroneously – suspected of secretly harboring pro-German sympathies. In May 1915, a Moscow mob accused her of hiding her brother Grand Duke Ernst Ludwig of Hesse inside her convent and demanded her arrest. The riot was eventually put down, but the depth of suspicious anger was an ugly hint of things to come.

In early December 1916, Grand Duchess Elisabeth Feodorovna came by train from Moscow to see her sister at Tsarskoye Selo. She begged Alexandra to have Rasputin sent away, warned of growing hatred against the dynasty, and even dared hint at a coming revolution – *"Remember the fate of Louis XVI and Marie Antoinette!"* she supposedly said.[27] The Empress was unmoved, and finally cut her sister off. *"Perhaps it would have been better if I had not come,"* the Grand Duchess said quietly. *"Yes,"* the Empress agreed.[28] *"She drove me away like a dog!"* Elisabeth later bitterly complained.[29] The two sisters never met again.

Grand Duke Paul Alexandrovich

Born on September 21, 1860, Grand Duke Paul Alexandrovich was the youngest of Alexander II's sons. Deeply affected by his father's brutal assassination in 1881, he was a quiet, genial young man who followed custom and entered the army, rising to the rank of Commanding Officer of the Horse Guards Regiment and later of the Guard Corps.

The Grand Duke, recalled his valet Alexei Volkov, was a man of *"fairly even temperament,"* with *"moments of liveliness"* alternating with *"great benevolence…. He was never very talkative and kept a modest and confined life."*[30] Alexander Mikhailovich thought him *"the nicest"* of Nicholas II's four uncles, noting that he *"danced well"* and *"was greatly admired by women."*[31] There were a few early whispers about the Grand Duke, most suggesting that he was, in fact, in love with his sister-in-law Grand Duchess Elisabeth Feodorovna, wife of Grand Duke Sergei Alexandrovich, but for the most part, Paul attracted little attention.[32]

Indeed, the most striking thing about the young, thin Grand Duke with the sloped shoulders and closely cropped hair seemed to be his fragile health. Doctors suggested that, like his mother the late Empress Marie Alexandrovna, Paul might be suffering from tuberculosis. As a young man he was forced to lead a quiet life, often abroad where it was hoped warmer climates would improve his health.[33]

Grand Duke Paul Alexandrovich.

While attending the Silver Wedding Anniversary celebrations in Athens for King George I and Queen Olga of Greece, Paul met and fell in love with Princess Alexandra, the couple's eldest daughter. *"We were extremely fond of him,"* recalled Alexandra's sister Marie, *"as he was full of fun, a good sport, and not very much older than my eldest brothers."*[34] On June 4, 1889, when Alexandra was eighteen, she married Paul in the Cathedral of the Winter Palace. The following year, on April 6, a daughter, Marie Pavlovna (usually called "the Younger" to differentiate her from the Imperial Family's other Marie Pavlovna, Grand Duchess Vladimir), was born. Paul and Alexandra spent the summer of 1891 with his brother Sergei and his wife Elisabeth at their Moscow country estate, Ilinskoye. Alexandra was again expecting at the time. On the morning of September 6, she slipped while getting into a boat and fell, leading to an onset of premature labor. Carried back to the main house, Alexandra gave birth to a son, Dimitri, and quickly slipped into a coma probably caused by pre-eclampsia. By the time doctors arrived, nothing could be done, and she died without regaining consciousness six days later, at the age of twenty-one.[35]

At the funeral, remembered Marie of Romania, Paul's brother Sergei had to gently pull him away when he tried to protest the closing of the coffin lid.[36] He returned to his residence, the former Stieglitz Mansion on St. Petersburg's English Quay, and settled into despair. *"The black shadow of death, inconsolable pain, the fear over the fate of the baby – all this sadness would not permit Grand Duke Paul's aching soul to heal,"* recalled Volkov. The Grand Duke, he noted, *"had become a shadow of his former self,"* a widower with a young daughter and a premature son Dimitri whose health also seemed precarious.[37] As a father he was loving but distant and, as his daughter Marie Pavlovna remembered, *"never displayed towards us spontaneous tenderness, embracing us only when bidding us good morning or good night."*[38]

Sometime in 1895, Paul first met Madame Olga von Pistolkors, the wife of Erich von Pistolkors, an officer in the regiment that the Grand Duke commanded.[39] Born in 1865, Olga was *"a very pretty woman, with radiant brown eyes that have the power of being caressing or full of mirth at will,"* as one contemporary recorded.[40] She had three living children with her husband, whom she had married in 1884: Alexander, born in 1885; Olga, born in 1888; and Marianna, born in 1890. Paul and Olga soon began a liaison; on December 28, 1896, she gave birth to his son, Vladimir.

The long-suffering Erich von Pistolkors, knowing his place in the scheme of things, tolerated this situation, but it was an incident at an imperial ball sometime in 1901 or 1902 that finally brought the scandal to a head. Paul entered one of the Winter Palace halls with Madame von Pistolkors on his arm; around her neck she wore an immense diamond necklace that had u n m i s t a k a b l y belonged to Paul's mother Empress Marie Alexandrovna. Dowager Empress Marie Feodorovna recognized the piece and ran to her daughter-in-law in indignation. Alexandra summoned a chamberlain and gave him the disagreeable task of ordering Madame von Pistolkors from the palace.[41]

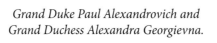

Grand Duke Paul Alexandrovich and Grand Duchess Alexandra Georgievna.

An irritated and embarrassed Erich von Pistolkors, in exchange for what was said to be *"generous financial consideration,"* agreed to divorce his wife and renounce all claims to paternity over young Vladimir.[42] When Paul talked about marrying his mistress, Nicholas II summoned his uncle and *"had a rather stern talk"* with him, *"warning him of all the consequences his proposed marriage would have for him,"* as the Emperor wrote to his mother. The Grand Duke was unmoved. *"How painful and distressing it all is,"* Nicholas continued, *"and how ashamed one feels for the sake of our family before the world.... In the end I fear a whole colony of members of the Russian Imperial Family will be established in Paris with their semi-legitimate and illegitimate wives! God alone knows what times we are living in, when undisguised selfishness stifles all feelings of conscience, duty, or even ordinary decency.*"[43] Nicholas even dispatched Alexander Mossolov, Head of the Court Chancery, to warn Olga that such a morganatic marriage was sure to result in severe punishments. She dismissed him, insisting that the Emperor would certainly not blame the Grand Duke for *"making legal a situation everyone knew already existed."*[44]

Olga was wrong. On September 27/October 10, 1902, Paul married her morganatically in an Orthodox church at the Italian resort of Livorno. An infuriated Nicholas II wrote to his mother: *"I have little doubt as to what is my duty in Uncle Paul's case. The nearer the relative who refuses to submit to our family statutes the graver must be his punishment."*[45] The Grand Duke's brother Vladimir was equally appalled: *"His behavior cannot be called anything but criminal,"* he wrote. *"And to her I said plainly that if she will become the wife of my brother I will turn my back on her and she will never in life see my face again. What will become of him? How will he be able to live the life of an outcast?"*[46]

Punishment was swift in coming. Nicholas II stripped his uncle of all of his military honors;

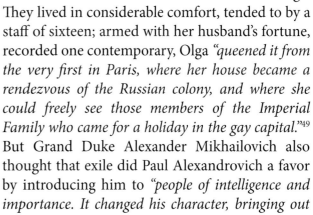

Grand Duchess Alexandra Georgievna.

confiscated his income and assets in Russia; seized control of the Grand Duke's two young children Marie Pavlovna and Dimitri Pavlovich and placed them in the care of Grand Duke Sergei Alexandrovich and his wife; and banished Paul from Russia.[47] Paul had no doubt that Empress Alexandra was the vindictive mover behind most of this – something that Alexander Mossolov later confirmed.[48]

Paul had cagily removed millions of rubles from Russia and deposited them in foreign banks before his marriage, ensuring that he had a considerable income on which to live. He and Olga purchased a large mansion on Avenue Victor Hugo in Boulogne-sur-Seine near Paris from the Yussoupov family and settled down to family life with their son Vladimir. On December 21 (New Style), 1903, they had a second child, Irina, and another daughter, Nathalia, was born on December 5 (New Style), 1905. In 1904, Prince Regent Luitpold of Bavaria bestowed the title of Countess Hohenfelsen on Olga. They lived in considerable comfort, tended to by a staff of sixteen; armed with her husband's fortune, recorded one contemporary, Olga *"queened it from the very first in Paris, where her house became a rendezvous of the Russian colony, and where she could freely see those members of the Imperial Family who came for a holiday in the gay capital."*[49] But Grand Duke Alexander Mikhailovich also thought that exile did Paul Alexandrovich a favor by introducing him to *"people of intelligence and importance. It changed his character, bringing out*

Clockwise from the top: Grand Duke Paul Alexandrovich, Princess Marie of Greece holding her niece Grand Duchess Marie Pavlovna Jr., Grand Duchess Elisabeth Feodorovna, and Grand Duke Sergei Alexandrovich.

human traits formerly hidden under a mask of nonsensical haughtiness."[50]

By 1905, and after the assassination of Paul's brother Grand Duke Sergei Alexandrovich, Nicholas II's attitude toward his uncle softened. Paul attended the funeral in Moscow and met the Emperor when he returned to Paris through St. Petersburg. Apparently things went well, for an encouraged Grand Duke happily wrote to his nephew, reminding him that *"you are no longer angry at me, that you understand me, and have forgiven me, that you yourself told me that I behaved honorably."*[51] Nicholas II told Paul that he was welcome to return to Russia. His income would be restored if he did so. The Countess of Hohenfelsen, though, was not included in this offer: Empress Alexandra insisted that she could not set foot in Russia. Eventually, the Grand Duke worked out an arrangement that kept him in voluntary exile but provided him with access to his fortune.[52]

The engagement and marriage of the Grand Duke's daughter Marie Pavlovna to Prince Wilhelm of Sweden in 1908 became yet another occasion for bitterness. Not only did Paul complain that the matter had been decided without his consultation but he resented the order that, while he could attend

Grand Duke Dimitri Pavlovich and his sister Grand Duchess Marie Pavlovna Jr.

the wedding at Tsarskoye Selo, his morganatic wife could not. *"I was willing to be understanding at the beginning and patiently endured everything,"* the Grand Duke angrily wrote to his nephew, *"but after five years of exemplary family life I have the right to expect a different attitude towards us both. Could you really think that I would leave my wife alone, she whom everyone here loves and respects, may God grant to everyone a position such as hers, while I myself participate in the wedding celebrations? I did not make the break and sacrifice everything to let her then be humiliated and insulted without reason."*[53]

Finally, in 1912, the Emperor relented: he recognized the marriage as legal, though morganatic, restored his uncle's lost honors, and allowed the couple to return to St. Petersburg.[54] They settled in Tsarskoye Selo, building a replica of their Parisian mansion, though relations with the Imperial couple remained strained. Empress Alexandra allowed that the Countess could meet members of her husband's family, though she managed to find a way that would inflict the most humiliation. Olga would be presented only in private, not through official channels as was done for aristocratic women. She was also not allowed to sign the guest book, as any other lady of the court did, but forced to instead leave her calling

Grand Duke Paul Alexandrovich and his second wife, Princess Paley.

card.[55] Such pettiness infuriated Paul, who publicly railed against the *"many insults at the hands of my Imperial relatives and their satellites, most men and women of social degeneracy."* He went so far as to refer to the Emperor as *"one of the principal persecutors of myself and my family,"* terming him *"a political imbecile."*[56]

World War I helped erase some of this lingering animosity. Always suspicious of her husband's family, Empress Alexandra soon found that Paul evinced absolute devotion to the throne and seemed to back Nicholas II's every move. *"He was very nice,"* Alexandra reported to her husband, *"and spoke honestly and simply, meaning well, not wishing to meddle with what does not concern him."*[57] Olga, too, behaved impeccably, never pushed herself forward, and was charming to everyone. When Olga established a relief operation in her palace, Empress Alexandra agreed to serve as patron, though she occasionally complained that the Grand Duke's wife *"bored with her way of saying how devoted she is."*[58]

In April 1915, Olga – believing herself on firm ground – dared to dispatch a letter to the Empress, in which she suggested that the best way to reward Paul's devotion was for Nicholas II to grant her and her children Russian titles and to raise them all to the rank of prince or princess. *"All can be alright in her wish,"* Alexandra wrote to her husband, *"excepting the 'Princess,' that is vulgar to ask for. You see it will sound well when one announces them together, almost as a Grand Duchess. Only what reason to Misha* [Grand Duke Michael Alexandrovich] *later – both had children before, whilst married to another man, though Misha's wife was already divorced."* She added that for Nicholas II to grant such titles would only underline the fact that Paul and Olga's son Vladimir had been conceived out of wedlock – *"for them, I don't mind, let them openly carry their sin, but the boy?"*[59] But Nicholas II was more forgiving than his wife: *"I think there's no difficulty about this question,"* he replied to Alexandra. *"A little goodwill on our side and the thing shall be done, and we shall have one less worry in life."*[60] The Emperor duly gave Olga the courtesy title of Princess Paley; her children with Paul were raised to the rank of Prince or Princess, with the style of Serene Highness.

Alexandra's comment about Paul's son Vladimir was one of the few generosities she felt toward the Romanovs, but then the young man was widely regarded as rather exceptional. He had graduated from the elite Corps des Pages in St. Petersburg and joined the Imperial Army; Empress Alexandra even attended an early morning service with the family and gave the young Prince an icon and a prayer book. He was, the Empress noted, *"good looking, and reminds one very much of the Princess."*[61]

Painter Leon Bakst once described Vladimir as *"the Prince Charming who is dreamt of in fairytales."* Extremely handsome, he threw himself into the war but his real talent lay in poetry. His half-sister Grand Duchess Marie Pavlovna called him *"an extraordinary being, a living instrument of rare sensitivity that could of itself produce sounds of startling melody and purity and create a world of bright images and harmonies. In years and experience he was still a child, but his spirit had penetrated into regions reached only by a few. He had genius."*[62]

"By temperament a dreamer," his proud mother later recorded, *"he observed everything and nothing escaped his subtle, watchful attention; neither nobility of feeling nor beauty nor ugliness nor, above all, the ridiculous. He loved nature ardently. He went into ecstasy over everything God had created. A moonbeam inspired him, the scent of a flower gave him an idea for a poem."*[63] When the first volume of his poetry was published in 1915, a copy went to Empress Alexandra, who had made Olga promise to provide her with all of his works. The Empress even described him as *"a marvelously gifted boy."*[64]

Prince Vladimir Paley.

At the start of World War I Nicholas gave his uncle command of the 1st Corps of the Imperial Guard. *"When I informed Paul of my intention,"* he wrote to Alexandra, *"he wept and nearly suffocated me – he wants so much to take part in the war."*[65] But the Grand Duke was plagued by constant health problems – a British official said *"he gave me the impression of being ill and nervous."*[66] In November 1915 prolonged trouble with his gall bladder kept Paul away from the action. *"I doubt his ever being able to take up his service,"* the Empress reported to Nicholas, *"to my mind it's a finished man; that does not mean he may not continue living with care, but not at the war, and I pity him deeply."*[67] A few days later, she reported that the Grand Duke had lost weight and *"at night screams from pain."*[68] Not surprisingly, she consulted Rasputin, who advised that any operation would kill him. Alexandra even suspected that the illness was divine retribution: *"The evening before he fell ill, he had a discussion with Georgi [Grand Duke George Mikhailovich] at Headquarters about Our Friend [Rasputin]. Georgi said the family call him a follower of Rasputin, whereupon Paul got furious and said some very strong things – and fell ill that night."* Rasputin, she reported to her husband, had assured her that *"no doubt God sent it to him because he ought to have stood up for a man you respect and his soul ought to have remembered that he received everything from you."*[69]

Paul gradually began to improve, though the process was slow and he was never again to enjoy good health. On November 24, 1915, he wrote to the Emperor: *"I cannot tell you personally how devastated*

Grand Duke Paul and his second family. From the left: Princess Paley, Princess Irene Paley, Prince Vladimir Paley, Princess Nathalia Paley, and Grand Duke Paul Alexandrovich.

I am that the doctors will not allow me to go to the Front. I was so elated with and proud of the command with which I have been entrusted. But about that, I beg you, don't count me out yet. God grant that by the end of this winter, I will be so much stronger that I will be able to serve you."[70] Not until May 1916 was the Grand Duke finally able to take up active command. With his health still uncertain, Nicholas named the Grand Duke Inspector General of the Imperial Guard and allowed him to live at Army Headquarters at Mogilev; Vladimir soon joined him.

In November 1916, Olga and her two daughters with the Grand Duke traveled to Mogilev for a brief reunion. Alexandra and her children also happened to be visiting the Emperor at Stavka, and one day she sent word that she would like to bring her family to the Grand Duke's little house for afternoon tea – a measure of just how friendly relations between them had become, although Alexandra still occasionally complained that the Princess was too obsequious – *"wish she would leave me in peace,"* she wrote to Nicholas in May 1916.[71] Nicholas II arrived pale and tired, but Alexandra, recalled Olga, was smiling and beautiful while Tsesarevich Alexei and the four Grand Duchesses were happy to be entertained by both Vladimir and by the Grand Duke's son from his first marriage, Dimitri Pavlovich. It was a last moment of joy before the darkness descended.

On the afternoon of December 3, 1916, Grand Duke Paul Alexandrovich arrived at the Alexander Palace. The Imperial Family had implored him to make one last attempt to convince Nicholas II to grant a responsible government. He spoke cautiously but candidly: anti-monarchist sentiment was on the rise, he warned. Morale in the army was low; the voices of the dissatisfied were becoming more pronounced with every passing day. The family, he explained, had asked him to convince the Emperor to grant a responsible ministry and prevent the government's disintegration. *"What you ask is impossible,"* Nicholas finally replied. *"At my coronation I took my oath to pass this inheritance intact to my son."* This wasn't true: Nicholas had taken no such oath during his coronation, but both he and Alexandra erroneously conflated the words of his prayers as a pledge to preserve the autocracy intact. Both ignored the fact that Nicholas II had ceased to be an autocrat in 1905. Sensing that his mission was failing, the Grand Duke dared mention Rasputin, speaking of his *"evil influence"* over some of the most important ministers. This time Nicholas remained silent while Alexandra fought back. Rasputin, she insisted, was *"merely a victim of the calumny and envy of those who wished to be in his place."* As such there could be no question of replacing any ministers. The Grand Duke eventually left, shaken and convinced that disaster was soon to come.[72]

Grand Duke Dimitri Pavlovich

While Grand Duke Paul's morganatic son Vladimir began to make a name for himself as a poet of some talent, his other son, Grand Duke Dimitri Pavlovich, was beginning to likewise attract attention, not all of it favorable. At the time of his premature birth on September 6, 1891, no one had expected the young boy to survive; he did, but remained weak and afflicted by tuberculosis. Dimitri, like his sister Marie Pavlovna, also struggled with deeper

Grand Duke Paul witm his children Grand Duke Dimitri Pavlovich and Grand Duchess Marie Pavlovna Jr.

demons. They had lost their mother in 1891; in 1902, they lost their father when he chose to marry Olga von Pistolkors. Brother and sister were inordinately close, emotionally dependent on one another, and brought up under peculiar circumstances by their guardian Grand Duke Sergei Alexandrovich and his wife Elisabeth, who resented their presence in the household. Both children, as Marie Pavlovna recalled, were thus *"deprived of a normal upbringing"* and *"enjoyed no real family life."*[73]

Life with Sergei and Elisabeth was at times difficult. The notoriously grim Sergei, as Marie Pavlovna

Grand Duke Dimitri Pavlovich and his sister Grand Duchess Marie Pavlovna Jr.

recalled, had welcomed them into the household by announcing, *"It is I who am now your father, and you are my children."*[74] She added: *"In his fashion he loved us deeply. He liked to have us near him, and gave us a good deal of his time. But he was always jealous of us. If he had known the full extent of our devotion to our father it would have maddened him."*[75]

After Grand Duke Sergei was assassinated in 1905, both Dimitri and his sister regularly spent time with Nicholas and Alexandra at Tsarskoye Selo. This provided some measure of the family life they had been denied. *"Then we were happiest,"* Marie Pavlovna recalled, *"for there we sensed ourselves in a real family atmosphere, tender, simple, and calm."*[76] Nicholas and Alexandra, in turn, treated Dimitri like a second son, and the Emperor in particular allowed him liberties that would have brought censure upon any other Romanovs. Nicholas appreciated his ribald sense of humor, and Dimitri made risqué jokes about his infatuation with the Empress: *"Tell her I so often think about her that I succumb to tears of powerless, useless passion. I hug my pillow thinking about her."* He referred to her as *"my illegal mother (sorry, I am her illegitimate son)."* As for Nicholas, he promised that he belonged to the Emperor *"heart, soul and body (except for arsehole)."* Another time, he apologized in advance for a long letter, advising Nicholas to *"take this message with you to shit. Time will be pleasant, ideal, and in extreme cases you can wipe your arse with it (mixing business with pleasure)."*[77]

There is no doubt that the lively Dimitri brought a certain welcome jocularity to the insulated inhabitants of the Alexander Palace. The four Grand Duchesses, in particular, appreciated his easy manner and elegant looks. In time, though, Dimitri increasingly found fault with the way in which the Imperial couple lived. He thought that Tsesarevich Alexei was a badly brought up, spoiled child, once confiding to his sister that he sincerely hoped that her son did not turn out to be anything like the young heir. He also thought that Alexandra was an idiot, enraptured with the notorious Rasputin to the detriment of the country.[78]

Like all Grand Dukes, Dimitri had been shuffled off to a military academy, though he had little taste for army life. He seems to have done the bare minimum to pass his examinations and drills, and nothing more, as in three years he never received a promotion in rank.[79] What Dimitri seemed most interested in was pleasure. *"Tall, slim, pale and delicate looking, he lacked the virile magnificence of some of his uncles and cousins,"* said a contemporary, *"but although he was still a little shy and uncertain of himself, he possessed all the Romanov charm."* No one could fail to note the dark circles habitually beneath his blue eyes, or the slightly dissipated look he carried with him, and he seemed to embody *"a lack of purpose, indecision, and an inherent weakness."* He avoided most balls,

Grand Duke Dimitri Pavlovich.

95

"on the pretext that his military duties were too strenuous to permit him to stay up late every night," Meriel Buchanan recalled, *"though he made it to all the smaller, more intimate and certainly more entertaining dances given by the young married women."* He enjoyed being *"pursued, made much of, and flattered."*[80]

No one was more vigorous in pursuit of the Grand Duke than Prince Felix Felixovich Yussoupov, heir to Russia's greatest private fortune. While Dimitri apparently carried on a number of affairs with women, it is his relationship with the effete, dilettantish Yussoupov that has always attracted the most attention. The handsome Felix made no secret of his taste for drugs, cross-dressing, and seducing young men. In his memoirs, he was certainly rapturous in describing the Grand Duke: *"Dimitri was extremely attractive: tall, elegant, well-bred, with deep thoughtful eyes, he recalled the portraits of his ancestors. He was all impulses and contradictions; he was both romantic and mystical, and his mind was far from shallow. At the same time, he was very gay and always ready for the wildest escapades. His charm won the hearts of all, but the weakness of his character made him dangerously easy to influence. As I was a few years his senior, I had a certain prestige in his eyes. He was to a certain extent familiar with my 'scandalous' life and considered me interesting,*

Grand Duke Dimitri Pavlovich.

and a trifle mysterious. He trusted me and valued my opinion, and he not only confided his innermost thoughts to me but used to tell me about everything that was happening around him….Almost every night we took a car and drove to St. Petersburg to have a gay time at restaurants and night clubs and with the gypsies. We would invite artists and musicians to supper with us in a private room; the well-known ballerina Anna Pavlova was often our guest. These wonderful evenings slipped by like dreams and we never went home until dawn."[81]

Rumors that the two young men may have been romantically involved have long persisted. The gossip certainly circulated in St. Petersburg, and Empress Alexandra seems to have learned of it and urged Nicholas to intercede. The Imperial couple forbade Dimitri to ever see Felix again, and charged police agents to shadow the two men to ensure that the orders were followed. This apparently only infuriated the Grand Duke, who decided it was time to take up residence in his own palace in St. Petersburg and live away from the insular world at Tsarskoye Selo. Thereafter, at least during 1912-1913, Dimitri and Felix were nearly inseparable.

Dimitri managed to fight the more scandalous stories about him with a true burst of spirit. In 1912, he joined the Russian Equestrian Team and participated in the Stockholm Olympics. He did

At far left is Grand Duke Dimitri Pavlovich, a talented equestrian, who competed in the Stockholm Olympic Games.

well under the circumstances, coming in seventh in show jumping. By 1913, as the Romanov Dynasty prepared to celebrate its Tercentenary, Dimitri seemingly stood poised for fame, but World War I cut short such pursuits. Although Dimitri joined his Horse Guards Regiment and, in autumn 1914 received the St. George Cross for rescuing a wounded solder while under fire, he was a less than enthusiastic participant in the fight. His father constantly complained that his son was being too diligent in the pursuit of pleasure to the detriment of serving his country; as the tensions grew, Dimitri began complaining of his stepmother, apparently blaming Princess Paley for Grand Duke Paul's attitude. He admitted that he saw as little as possible of the Princess and her *"honorable family,"* while Olga in turn repeatedly warned her husband, *"Don't trust Dimitri,"* saying, *"I myself was deceived by his damned tricks! I have rarely hated people as I hate him right now."*[82]

The problems stemmed from Dmitri's sybaritic style of life. He far preferred remaining in Petrograd, dancing, drinking, and haunting the various nightspots with his questionable friends to his military duties. This behavior resulted in a steady stream of letters in which Empress Alexandra begged her husband to intercede. Paul, she reported to Nicholas, *"is greatly shocked at the way the boy goes on in town."*[83] The young Grand Duke was ruining his life, *"as he has absolutely nothing to do and wastes his time."*[84] She derided Dimitri as *"without any character, and can be led by anybody,"* writing of his *"goings on in town during the war"* that were *"scandalizing"* Petrograd – *"town and woman are poison for him."*[85]

Nevertheless, it is clear that Alexandra continued to view Dimitri not merely as a wayward Grand Duke but also as a potential husband for her eldest daughter Olga Nikolaievna. Olga herself seems to have been less than enamored of the idea; with her high-minded approach to life, she was too disapproving of Dmitri's penchant for pleasure and tendency to float idly through life. But writing to Nicholas II in February 1916 on

Grand Duke Dimitri Pavlovich on his horse.

the subject of Grand Duke Boris Vladimirovich's half-hearted matrimonial overtures toward Olga, Alexandra reminded her husband that *"Dimitri therefore ought to be held tight in hand by you, and explained what married life means."*[86] Nothing came of the idea, but before the year was out the Grand Duke managed to obtain immortality, not through heroic deeds or personal accomplishment but by joining Felix Yussoupov in the notorious murder of Gregory Rasputin.

Dimitri undoubtedly acted out of misguided patriotism, thinking that Rasputin's murder would lessen Alexandra's influence and force the Emperor to change course. Nicholas II, though, saw it as an act of betrayal and sent Dimitri to his regiment in Persia as punishment. On December 29, members of the Romanov Family met at the Vladimir Palace to discuss the situation. They decided to address a petition to the Emperor, asking that leniency be granted to Grand Duke Dimitri Pavlovich; according to Grand Duke Alexander Mikhailovich, Queen Olga of Greece composed the document. He refused to sign it: *"It would have been difficult to write anything more stupid!"* he complained to his wife Xenia Alexandrovna.[87] The petition cited the Grand Duke's ill health and warned that the climate in Persia could lead to his death. Reminding Nicholas that Dimitri *"deeply loves you and this country"* and, *"from childhood had the joy of living in your house and loving you like a father,"* it implored the Emperor to rescind his punishment and *"turn your wrath into mercy."* Sixteen members of the family appended their names to the plea: Queen Olga of Greece; Grand Duchess Vladimir; Grand Duke Kirill Vladimirovich and his wife; Grand Dukes Boris and Andrei Vladimirovich; Grand Duke Paul Alexandrovich; Grand Duchess Marie Pavlovna; Grand Duchess Elisabeth Mavrikievna; Prince Ioann Konstantinovich and his wife Princess Elena; Princes Gabriel, Konstantin, and Igor Konstantinovich; and Grand Dukes Nicholas and Sergei Mikhailovich.[88]

The answer came two days later: *"No one,"* the Emperor had written across the top of the petition, *"has a right to kill. I know that many people are troubled by their own consciences, because Dimitri was not the only person involved. I am greatly surprised that you should have appealed to me."*[89] The break between Nicholas and Alexandra and the Romanov Family was complete.

Chapter VI

The Konstantinovich Line

The Konstantinovichi branch of the Romanov family descended from the second son of Emperor Nicholas I. Konstantin Nikolaievich was also his parents' fifth child, and, having a determined personality from a young age, he soon rebelled against a school room full of his sisters, and was appointed a tutor of his own at the age of five.

Nicholas I intended that Konstantin would be the Admiral General of the Russian Fleet, and so his education was directed towards the naval sciences and foreign languages. By his adulthood, he was proficient in mathematics, military history and strategy, and played the piano and cello. He was a consistent diarist and indefatigable in pursuit of his interests and passions. Perhaps surprisingly, he was liberal in outlook. Personally, he could be difficult among those who were more relaxed in their approach to life, and the most common complaint about him was that he was brash and rough-edged. He did not stand out in a family of tall, beautiful people; his sandy hair, gray eyes and large nose did not fit the stereotypical *"handsome prince,"* but in 1848 the lovely Princess Alexandra of Saxe-Altenburg did not object to his proposal of marriage.

Grand Duke Konstantin Nikolaievich, Grand Duchess Alexandra Josifovna and their daughter Grand Duchess Olga Konstantinovna.

Konstantin was ten days short of his twenty-first birthday and Alexandra was seventeen. For almost twenty years, the Konstantins were happy. But as Konstantin's brother Alexander II slowly drifted away from the liberalism that marked the first decade of his reign, the Grand Duke found his views – and soon enough himself – falling out of favor. The tragic end of Alexander II's reign brought to the throne an even more reactionary Emperor, and Konstantin's disfavor was cemented. He was sidelined politically and professionally, with little to do except turn to his personal life for satisfaction. Following a short liaison with a mistress that produced one illegitimate daughter, Konstantin turned away from Alexandra and towards a woman who would become his permanent mistress, ballerina Anna Vassilievna Kuznetsova.

The Marble Palace, St. Petersburg.

Alexandra remained in the family homes of the Marble Palace, Strelna, and Pavlovsk, and continued to raise the six children she and Konstantin had produced: Nicholas, born in 1850; Olga, born in 1851; Vera, born in 1854; Konstantin, born in 1858; Dimitri, born in 1860; and Vyacheslav, born in 1862 and who died before coming of age. These strong-willed, hard-working, artistic, temperamental and mostly admirable people were known collectively as "the Konstantinovichi."

Grand Duke Nicholas Konstantinovich

Konstantin and Alexandra's eldest son was the source of most of their parental problems. His name was Nicholas and he was born on February 2, 1850. Nicholas, like his father, was intended for a career in the Imperial Navy, and received a high-quality liberal education under the tutelage of some of the best minds the Grand Ducal couple could find. Much to his father's disappointment, Nicholas soon left the Navy, enrolling in the Academy of the General Staff and taking a commission with the Hussars Life Guards Regiment.

Nicholas took to republican ideas with a surprising vigor, given his Imperial background. He developed a certain disdain for the trappings and ceremonies of the Imperial Family, extending that distaste towards his mother, whom he found to be cold and shallow, concerned with little more than gossip, jewelry and her social position.

Though gifted intellectually, the young Grand Duke was emotionally and psychologically stunted. Today, his behavior would be met with serious concern, especially the episodes which included cruelty towards smaller children and animals. But within the Imperial Family, Nicholas's behavior only drew attention when his sociological interests took him into the capital, where he mingled with not only members of the *demimonde*, but also with criminal elements rumored to include the future revolutionary Sophia Perovskaya, who would shortly help assassinate Alexander II.[1]

As he entered his twenties, the Grand Duke began an affair with one of his mother's ladies-in-waiting, which led to the young woman's ruin and dismissal from court. Nicholas was unconcerned; while nursing a growing social conscience towards those less fortunate than himself, he cared little for those of his own class, and used them shamefully in the pursuit of personal pleasure. Tall and handsome, rich almost beyond his ability to spend, the world was Nicholas's oyster, and he exploited it. His parents' massive Marble Palace was the scene of orgies with hired prostitutes and other underworld characters. Not able to effectively discipline the Grand Duke, his minders could only chastise and dismiss from service those charged with attempting to control Nicholas as he allowed events to spin out of control.

Grand Duke Nicholas Konstantinovich.

The most famous of Nicholas's escapades caused an international incident with the United States, and a romantic scandal only matched in royal circles some seventy years later when Edward VIII abdicated his throne for Mrs. Simpson. In December 1871, at a masquerade ball at the Mariinsky Theater, Grand Duke Nicholas Konstantinovich met a young American woman by the name of Harriet Ely Blackford. Sparks flew and soon the couple was in a whirlwind romance. This was not a good thing for Nicholas, for Harriet Blackford was not only an unconnected, untitled American, she was also a known adventuress, and a woman who had already outstayed her welcome in the United States, in the United Kingdom, and in France. Russia was the end of the line for her, and many believed that she set her hat at the Grand Duke in order to make her fortune, one way or the other.

But the Grand Duke seemed to be genuinely smitten with Mrs. Blackford, and Harriet played the part of a woman in love. She was available whenever Nicholas was able to break away from his duties, and they were seen at social gatherings, dances, and on sleigh rides across the capital. Not being limited by decorum or social rules, Harriet was free to go about with Nicholas and to associate with all of his connections, even the less than savory ones. She infiltrated even his military barracks, disguised as a soldier, and he lavished her with expensive gifts far beyond what was reasonable for an Imperial mistress. Sensing that their liaison was trying the limits of even an Imperial Family in which the Emperor and his brothers indulged in fairly public and well-known affairs, Nicholas decided to take Harriet on a European trip, during which they visited his surprised but poised sister the Queen of the Hellenes. In January 1874, when

Grand Duchess Alexandra Josifovna and her son Grand Duke Nicholas Konstantinovich.

Grand Duke Konstantin Nikolaevich surrounded by his children: Nicholas Konstantinovich, Olga Konstantinovna, and Dimitri, Konstantin, and Vyatcheslav Konstantinovich.

Grand Duchess Marie Alexandrovna married Queen Victoria's son Prince Alfred, the Duke of Edinburgh, Nicholas indulged Harriet by providing a pass to watch the ceremony in the Winter Palace. Afterwards, Harriet sat behind a pillar and ate cake and ice cream brought to her from the wedding feast by an amenable servant.

The scandal soon exploded. Out of control, Nicholas took Harriet and one of his friends, a Lieutenant Savin, to the Marble Palace where, in Grand Duchess Alexandra's absence, they had a party in her bedroom. After downing the contents of several bottles of champagne, Nicholas, Harriet and Savin had sex on Alexandra's bed. A little later, still well under the influence, Nicholas himself pried several large jewels from an icon hanging over his mother's bed, an icon given personally by Emperor Nicholas I to Alexandra on the occasion of her marriage to Grand Duke Konstantin.

It took a few days for the absence of the jewels to be noticed. Servants were questioned before the shocking truth came to light. Harriet was arrested and imprisoned; forced to return most of Nicholas's gifts, she was banished from Russia. As for Nicholas, he was sent into internal exile by order of Alexander II: the Romanovs decided it was better to declare him hopelessly insane than to admit that he was a thief.[2] Nicholas was stripped of his military ranks and incomes, though he did not lose his Grand Ducal title or his place in the Imperial House. At first, he lived at his parents' lavish estate of Oreanda in the Crimea but after he began an affair with Alexandra Abaza Demidova, the estranged wife of a minor official who in 1877 bore the Grand Duke a daughter, Olga Volinsky, Nicholas Konstantinovich was sent to Uman. Demidova followed, and a year later gave birth to the Grand Duke's son, Nicholas Volinsky.[3]

Harriet Blackford.

Grand Duke Nicholas Konstantinovich.

Alexander II had the wayward Grand Duke exiled to Orenburg. Here, in 1882, he married Nadezhda Alexandrovich von Dreyer, the divorced daughter of the Orenburg Chief of Police. While not an equal marriage, it was certainly a respectable one, and the Emperor extended to any children of the marriage the right to the title of Prince or Princess Iskander. In the course of time, two sons were born to Nicholas and Nadezhda, Prince Artemi, in 1883, who was later killed in the Russian Civil War, and Prince Alexander, in 1887.[4] These sons were educated in the same fashion as other Romanov Princes, and attended school in St. Petersburg, housed and cared for by their father's brother, Grand Duke Konstantin Konstantinovich.[5] Through Prince Alexander's first marriage, Grand Duke Nicholas became a grandfather to Kirill, born in 1914, and Nathalia, born in 1917.

Tired of his cousin's misadventures, Alexander III banished Nicholas Konstantinovich to Tashkent in Central Asia, where he would spend the rest of his life. Here the Grand Duke found purpose. He invested his money and time and effort into improving the lives of the people. Nicholas had become a competent engineer and under his supervision, a large canal project was completed, leading to the regular and reliable irrigation of approximately 33,000 acres farmed by European and Slavic immigrants. He also built two small towns to house the workers from his irrigation projects; one was called Stary Iskander, and the other Novy Iskander. Inside the city of Tashkent, the Grand Duke was a patron of the arts, establishing in his own palace an immense and valuable collection of art, including paintings, sculpture and other *objets*, which today form the central collection of the State Museum of Arts of Uzbekistan. The grounds of the Grand Duke's palace also housed a small zoo, the proceeds of which were used to support his wife, mistresses and various children.[6]

Nicholas Konstantinovich's personal life remained unusual. The Grand Duke conducted affairs with the daughters of several local dignitaries, and even bigamously married a sixteen-year-old girl he had bought from a local Cossack, who gave him three more children.[7] As he aged, he developed a sort of personal honor by which he assumed responsibility for the numerous bastards he fathered. A true character, he made himself beloved in Tashkent, openly living his scandalous life without regard to his Grand Ducal title.

Grand Duke Konstantin Konstantinovich and Grand Duchess Elisabeth Mavrikievna

Grand Duke Konstantin Konstantinovich was born August 10, 1858. His father enrolled him in the Imperial Navy, but the young Grand Duke soon transferred his interest to the army, serving in the Izmailovsky Life Guards Regiment and then the Tiflis Grenadier Life Guards Regiment, during the Russo-Turkish War. *"In appearance he resembles his father,"* wrote one contemporary, *"though he has a much finer and more delicate countenance."*[8] Tall and elegant, with a closely cropped beard and blue eyes, Konstantin was a perfect officer and, on the surface, a model Romanov Grand Duke.

On April 15, 1884, Konstantin married his second cousin Princess Elisabeth of Saxe-Altenburg. Born January 25 (New Style), 1865, she was dark-haired,

Grand Duke Konstantin Konstantinovich (KR).

serious, and morally rigid, especially when it came to religion. Having been raised a Lutheran, Elisabeth refused to convert to Orthodoxy, much to her intended's distress. *"I pledge to you,"* she assured Konstantin, *"that I will do nothing to hurt or anger you because of our different religions."*[9] On wedding the Grand Duke, she received the name Elisabeth Mavrikievna, but was known in the family as "Mavra."

Konstantin and Elisabeth were parents to nine children – the largest of modern Romanov families. In June 1886, Elisabeth gave birth to a son, Ioann Konstantinovich. Nine days after his birth, Alexander III issued a ukase restricting the titles of Grand Duke and Grand Duchess to children and grandchildren descended in the male from an Emperor. Ioann, who was born a Grand Duke, thus became the first Imperial Prince of the Imperial Blood. Both Konstantin and Elisabeth were upset by what they perceived as a slight. Declaring that she no longer "burned" with loyalty toward Alexander III, the Grand Duchess even asked to examine her marriage contract to see if she had any legal recourse, fearing that children reduced to mere "Prince" or "Princess" would be treated as morganatic descendants. Only after being assured that her children were deemed full members of the Imperial House with succession rights did the Grand Duchess reluctantly abandon her fight.[10] Ioann was thus of the Imperial Blood, as were his siblings: Gabriel, born in 1887; Tatiana,

The children of KR and Elisabeth Mavrikievna: Ioann, Gabriel, Tatiana, Konstantin, Oleg, Igor, George, and Vera.

born in 1890; Konstantin, born in 1891; Oleg, born in 1892; Igor, born in 1894; George, born in 1903; Nathalia, born and died in 1905; and Vera, born in 1906. The family lived in St. Petersburg's magnificent Marble Palace and in the exquisite Pavlovsk Palace near to Tsarskoye Selo.

Grand Duke Konstantin Konstantinovich served as President of the Russian Academy of Sciences and Chief Inspector of Military Training Institutes, earning a reputation as a much honored and revered member of the Imperial Family. He spent his life in service of the Imperial House, devoting himself to such liberal causes as improving the conditions of Russia's soldiers and working towards providing compulsory education for girls throughout the Empire.

The Grand Duke also made a name for himself in the arts. A gifted pianist, he had befriended Tchaikovsky and was one his most ardent supporters. The Grand Duke, said the composer, was "*not only talented and intelligent, but also surprisingly modest, full of*

From the left: Tatiana Konstantinovna and her brothers Konstantin, Gabriel and Ioann Konstantinovich.

105

Grand Duchess Elisabeth Mavrikievna.

selfless devotion to art and of the noble ambition to distinguish himself...in the artistic sphere."[11] In 1892 the Grand Duke became Chairman of the Russian Musical Society, carrying on the tradition started by his parents.

Konstantin had begun writing poetry at an early age, a pursuit that flourished and gave him purpose throughout his life. In 1886 he published his first collection of poetry under the pseudonym "KR" (for "Konstantin Romanov") and won immediate praise: indeed, Tchaikovsky was so taken with several of the pieces that he set them to music. The Grand Duke did not stop at poetry, translating the works of Schiller, Goethe, and Shakespeare into Russian. In 1900 he produced a Russian translation of *Hamlet* and himself starred in the title role when the play was performed for the Imperial Family at the Hermitage Theatre in the Winter Palace. Enjoying theatrical life, the Grand Duke wrote and performed numerous plays. He also appeared as Joseph of Arimathea in a production of his play *The King of Judea*, put on amidst some controversy when the Holy Synod objected to the staging of such a sacred story.[12]

On the surface Grand Duke Konstantin Konstantinovich was all probity; with his wife Elisabeth and family of nine children, everything seemed sober and upright. Konstantin Konstantinovich, recorded a contemporary, *"is generally esteemed for his high moral character, and during his whole life has carefully abstained from taking any part in or even expressing an opinion on politics or any subject concerning them.*"[13] Another friend recalled his *"extraordinarily attractive graciousness and the sympathetic intuition that endeared him to all who the privilege of coming into intimate contact with him. Here, indeed, was a precious and priceless quality, the gift of unfailing tact and exceptional intuition, the power always to say the right thing at the right moment, and to enter warmly and cordially into the thoughts and feelings of others.*"[14]

The Grand Duke and his wife were among the very few members of the Romanov Family who enjoyed Nicholas and Alexandra's confidence: they respected

Clockwise from the right: Prince Gabriel Konstantinovich, Prince Oleg Konstantinovich, Prince Konstantin Konstantinovich, Prince Igor Konstantinovich, Prince Ioann Konstantinovich, and Princess Tatiana Konstantinovna.

his family life, considering it a model of morality when compared to other hedonistic Grand Dukes. Elisabeth Mavrikievna never made a fuss or indulged in scandal, qualities that endeared her to the Empress. The Grand Duchess was careful to cultivate the relationship, to the point that members of the extended Romanov Family privately warned each other to exercise caution when speaking with her. Elisabeth Mavrikievna could be reliably counted on to carry back to Alexandra anything she heard in the way of gossip or information regarding plots and plans fomenting among the uncles and cousins.[15]

Yet a secret lurked beneath the Grand Duke's careful veneer of respectability. Like all

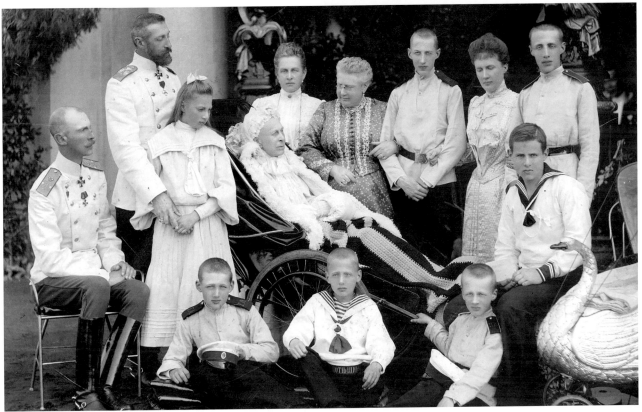

The Konstantinovich at Strelna.
From the left: Grand Duke Dimitri Konstantinovich, KR with Princess Tatiana Konstantinovna, Grand Duchess Alexandra Josifovna, Queen Olga of Greece, Grand Duchess Vera Konstantinovna, Prince Ioann Konstantinovich, Prince Gabriel Konstantinovich, and Prince Christoper of Greece. On the foreground: Princes Konstantin, Igor, and Oleg Konstantinovich.

Romanovs he had been taught to keep a diary, though Konstantin was unique in filling his not with entries on the weather or lists of his dinner guests – as were so common amongst his relatives – but rather with detailed descriptions of important events, philosophical ruminations, and worries over Nicholas II's political naiveté. He also filled them with a tortured chronicle of his battle against his sexuality. Despite having a long, fruitful and successful marriage with Grand Duchess Elisabeth Mavrikievna, Konstantin was homosexual.

Genuinely devoted to the Orthodox Church, Konstantin was haunted by his homosexual desires. His diary became not a place of refuge but his private confessional, as he described attractions to various men, recorded his "sin" in agonizing detail, and wrote of how he struggled and failed to resist temptation. He had married to fulfill convention and out of love for Elisabeth, but he admitted that he had no sexual desire toward any woman.[16] His wife suspected nothing, although at times the Grand Duke was undoubtedly reckless, haunting St. Petersburg bathhouses and picking up young soldiers for sexual encounters. Inevitably this led to near disaster: in 1905 one man threatened the Grand Duke with blackmail: terrified that his greatest secret would be exposed Konstantin had no alternative but to pay for the man's silence.

In the summer of 1914 the Grand Duke and Grand Duchess were in Germany with their two

KR and Grand Duchess Elisabeth Mavrikievna.

youngest children when World War I erupted. They tried to immediately return to Russia, but German authorities seized them as political prisoners. Only after Elisabeth Mavrikievna sent a personal appeal to Empress Augusta Viktoria did the German Government relent and allow the family to return home, though not without a bit of discomforting humiliation. Konstantin, who was not well, was forced to walk with his wife and two children the several miles between train stations at the resort town of Wildungen; by the time they finally reached the Russian line, the Grand Duke was exhausted.[17]

Konstantin Konstantinovich would never recover his health. In the summer of 1914, Nicholas, Alexandra, and their children came to Pavlovsk and listened as the Grand Duke recited the "Nunc Dimittis" from his *King of Judea*. "It was," recorded a courtier, "*a moving and admirable piece of poetry and its author, then already a sick man, with his fine features bearing the stamp of the many emotions of a sensitive spirit, his hair and beard streaked with gray, looked like an inspired patriarch taking leave of the world....It was the final farewell to his work, the last legacy of a true poet.*"[18]

Five of the Grand Duke's sons, as well as his son-in-law, joined the fight against Germany and Austria-Hungary but the conflict soon took a devastating toll. In October 1914, Prince Oleg, the Grand Duke's favorite son, was mortally wounded during a battle. This death broke the Grand Duke's spirit. There were no more visits to bathhouses and no more secret trysts, although the Grand Duke did find temporary pleasure in taking Grand Duke Paul's young son by his morganatic marriage, the extremely handsome Prince Vladimir Paley, under his wing and advising him on his poetry.

On the afternoon of June 2, 1915, Grand Duke Konstantin Konstantinovich was reclining on a chair in his study when he started to gasp for breath. His young daughter Vera immediately ran for help, but it was too late. The Grand Duke, patriarch of the Konstantinovichi, was dead of a heart attack at the age of fifty-six. His funeral was the last state occasion in Imperial Russia. During the reading of his will, his widow was stunned to find that her husband had placed his extensive – and compromising – diaries under quarantine. She was forbidden to read them, and they were not to be opened until a hundred years after his death.

Prince Ioann Konstantinovich and Princess Elena Petrovna of Serbia.

Prince Ioann Konstantinovich and His Family

Prince Ioann Konstantinvich was born June 23, 1886, and became the first member of the Dynasty to be christened as a Prince of the Imperial Blood, with the style of His Highness; among his godparents were Emperor Alexander

III, the Queens of Württemberg and the Hellenes, and his grandfathers, Grand Duke Konstantin Nikolaievich of Russia and the Duke of Saxe-Altenburg. The impressive list of godparents was assembled no doubt to assuage the worries of the Konstantinovichi regarding his reduced status.

Known in the family as "Ioannchik," the Prince was a shy child, given to fears and uncontrollable bouts of crying. Konstantin was a very affectionate father, and insisted that his children visit him in his office at the palace every day. For the very young Ioann, this was an ordeal as he was terrified at the sight of the bearskin rug on the floor. Konstantin was not sensitive to this fear, and teased his son mercilessly about it, even into adulthood.

Ioann's education followed that of his father and uncles in liberal breadth, but he was never intended for the sea. The Prince did well at his schooling; he grew up an extremely pious and religious young man, often thinking out loud about setting aside his Imperial title and becoming a monk. Perhaps wanting to give their son time to consider all his options, Konstantin and Elisabeth allowed Ioann an extra two years in his education before he took his oath to the Emperor and joined the Chevalier Life Guards Regiment. Although he was dutiful and regular in the performance of his job, it was thought that perhaps Ioann was better fitted for the religious life. A rather plain young man, notable only for his great height and exceptional thinness,

Prince Ioann Konstantinovich.

Princess Elena Petrovna.

he did not stand out as a catch on the marriage market.[19]

In 1911, Grand Duchess Elisabeth Mavrikievna arranged for her son to meet the dynamic, attractive, modern young Princess Elena Petrovna of Serbia. Born November 4 (New Style), 1884, Elena was the daughter of future King Peter I of Sebia and his wife Princess Zorka (née Montenegro). Like her aunts Militsa and Anastasia, she had been educated at St. Petersburg's Smolny Institute, possibly with an eye toward a future Russian marriage. In a case of opposites attracting, Ioann and Elena agreed that a marriage between her desire for a career in nursing and his love for his family's ancient religion was something that could work and, to the surprise of many, they were engaged. *"How did you like Ioannchik's engagement to the daughter of the King of Serbia?"* Nicholas II wrote to his mother. *"It happened like a flash of lightning! I should think it must be a risky thing to marry Ioannchik, he ought* to become a monk, which he himself talked of doing."[20] The Emperor's four daughters found the idea equally absurd. *"How funny if they might have children,"* wrote Grand Duchess Tatiana Nikolaievna to her aunt Grand Duchess Olga Alexandrovna, *"can they be kissing? What foul, fie!"*[21] Despite the general mirth the engagement caused, the couple was married on August 21, 1911 at Peterhof.

True to her desire, Elena studied medicine at the University of St. Petersburg, but was forced to abandon her quest when, on January 7, 1914, she gave birth to a son, Prince Vsevelod Ioannovich. Both Ioann and Elena had dedicated themselves to the war effort. The Prince joined his regiment and won laurels for his bravery fighting at the front

In exile, King Nicholas of Montenegro with his great-grandchildren
Princess Catherine Ioannovna and Prince Vsevelod Ioannovich.

before joining Nicholas II as an adjutant at Stavka, while Elena put her medical training to use and, with Grand Duchess Marie Pavlovna the Younger, joined a hospital train in Poland, a pursuit that had to be abandoned when a second pregnancy was diagnosed. On June 30, 1915, Elena gave birth to a daughter, Catherine Ioannovna, at Pavlovsk – the last member of the Imperial Family born during the sunset days of Russian Empire.

Prince Gabriel Konstantinovich

Prince Gabriel Konstantinovich.

Prince Gabriel Konstantinovich was born on July 2, 1887 at Pavlovsk. Like his brother Ioann, Gabriel was often ill in childhood. The two spent a good deal of time in each other's company in the Crimea, where they were sent for their health, and as a result they were extremely close. Health was not allowed to interfere with education. In contrast to the other branches of the Imperial Family, the Konstantinovichi children, as their mother proudly recalled, were taught to speak pure Russian, without recourse to more convenient words of phrases being borrowed from other languages.[22]

Gabriel was single-minded in his ambition: he wanted nothing more than to be an officer in the army and to go to the Nikolaievsky Cavalry School. By 1908, he had attained both of his goals, and the tall, thin young man took his oath of allegiance to the Emperor in January of that year. Once ensconced in his regiment, Gabriel proved himself to be much more interested in an active social life than had any member of his family since Grand Duke Nicholas Konstantinovich. But Gabriel did not become particularly wild in context of his circle, although he had a mistress in the form of ballerina Antonina Nesterovskaya, whom he had first met during a party given by Mathilde Kschessinska. Gabriel bought her a house in St. Petersburg that she shared with her mother, and they traveled together throughout Europe. Deeply in love, Gabriel wanted to marry Antonina but, despite the intercession of his aunt Queen Olga of Greece, the Emperor refused to consider such a union.[23]

Gabriel remained devoted to his ballerina and was determined to marry her in the future.[24] The romance continued until World War I temporarily separated the couple when Gabriel went off to fight with his regiment. By 1915, though, the Prince was back in Petrograd, studying at a military academy, which allowed him to resume his liaison.

Princess Tatiana Konstantinovna.

112

Wedding of Princess Tatiana Konstantinovna and Prince Konstantin Bagration-Mukhransky.

Princess Tatiana Konstantinovna

Princess Tatiana Konstantinovna was born January 11, 1890 in the Marble Palace. She grew up to become a lovely young woman, with dark hair and vividly blue eyes, vivacious and full of energy. It seemed as if her possibilities were endless, but in 1910 she stunned her parents by declaring that she wished to marry a Georgian Prince, Konstantin Bagration-Mukhransky.

Born March 2, 1889 in Tiflis, Prince Konstantin was an officer in the Chevalier Life Guards Regiment, a man *"as handsome as a Greek God,"* insisted a contemporary.[25] His family had ruled the Kingdom of Georgia until 1801, when it was absorbed into the Russian Empire – and therein was the problem for Tatiana's parents. The Prince was the scion of a non-ruling house; Grand Duke Konstantin Konstantinovich worried that, if Tatiana married him, the union would be morganatic by virtue of Article 188 of the Fundamental Laws of the Russian Empire, which specified that members of the Imperial House must contract equal unions. Tatiana was a strong-willed girl who went on a modified hunger strike, conceived to convince her father of the unfairness of having to conform to Grand Ducal laws without the benefit of having herself a Grand Ducal title.

Deeply fond of his daughter – and no doubt seeing her point – Konstantin approached the Emperor

Princess Tatiana Konstantinovna and her son Prince Teymuraz Konstantinovich Bagration-Mukhransky.

on her behalf. After some thought, Nicholas and Alexandra summoned Elisabeth Mavrikievna to tea at Tsarskoye Selo on November 30, 1910 to discuss the issue. According to the Grand Duke's diary, his wife *"told me that the Empress had reacted with more leniency than the Emperor about Tatiana's intentions. They both told my wife that they would not look on her wedding with Bagration as morganatic in view of the fact that he, like the members of the House of Orléans, is a descendant of a once-ruling dynasty. The Emperor even said that Tatiana would not lose her annual stipend."*[26]

A bit of legal wrangling followed, during which Nicholas II issued a number of ukases and changes to the Fundamental Laws that have since become fodder in arguments about the modern succession to the non-existent throne. Tatiana was allowed to marry Bagration-Mukhransky, but was required to sign a renunciation of her dynastic rights as a member of the Imperial House. An addendum of June 14, 1911 to Article 188 specified such an action if a member of the Imperial House entered into an unequal union or if they married a member of a foreign ruling or formerly ruling house. It also allowed that the Prince or Princess of the Imperial Blood entering such a union *"shall personally retain the title and privileges which are theirs by birth."* This is what happened when, on August 21, 1911, Tatiana married Bagration at Pavlovsk, in the presence of Nicholas and Alexandra. But the Imperial couple had previously insisted that the union would not be deemed morganatic. Indeed, within the Konstantinovich family it was said that Nicholas II asked Bagration to sign the marriage register as a Prince of Georgia, thus formally recognizing his equality with the Princess. The issue was never resolved: Tatiana retained her title of Highness and became Princess Tatiana Konstantinovna, Princess Bagration-Mukhransky.

Tatiana Konstantinovna and Konstantin Bagration-Mukhransky had two children, a son, Prince Teymuraz, born on August 21, 1912 – his parents' first wedding anniversary – and a daughter, Princess Nathalia, born on April 19, 1914. Following the outbreak of World War I, Konstantin Bagration-Mukhransky went to the front. He had been in a cavalry regiment, but he wanted to volunteer for much more dangerous infantry duty on the front lines where hundreds of men were lost every day. Tatiana was unhappy with this development but eventually agreed when Konstantin transferred to the Erivan Life Guards Grenadier Regiment. While he was away at the front, Tatiana lived with her parents at Pavlovsk along with her children.[27]

On May 19, 1915, while serving with the Russian Army in Galicia, Konstantin was fatally shot during a skirmish. Prince Gabriel Konstantinovich recalled receiving a letter from his mother with the news: *"General Brusilov, Commander-in-*

Prince Konstantin Konstantinovich.

Chief of the South Western Front, wired my father that Bagration was the Commander-in-Chief of a company and died a hero's death in his first action near Lvov....When I came to Tatiana, she was sitting quietly in the Pilaster Hall. Thanks Lord, she believed so much in God and accepted this hard blow with Christian humility. She did not even wear a black dress but only white, henceforth stressing her grief even more."[28]

The evening of May 20, 1915, there was a prayer service in the Pavlovsk Palace Church, at which the Emperor, Empress and their four daughters joined the grieving Konstantinovich family. Shortly after this, Tatiana, accompanied by her brother Igor, left by train for the Caucasus, where Prince Konstantin was to be buried following his funeral at the Svetitskhoveli Cathedral in Georgia's ancient capital city of Mtskheta. Georgian newspapers reported that Tatiana and Igor ordered all the flowers available in Tiflis to be loaded onto their train as they passed through so that they could take them to the funeral on May 31.[29]

Tragically, two days after her husband's funeral, Tatiana received a telegram from her mother informing her of her father's death. The young widow found consolation and strength in spending time with Grand Duchess Elisabeth Feodorovna at her Convent of St. Mary and St. Martha in Moscow. The Grand Duchess herself knew about losing a husband suddenly and violently. She was

Prince Konstantin Konstantinovich in a theater costume.

able to counsel Tatiana and reassure her that she would be reunited with her loved ones in Heaven.[30] The widowed Tatiana returned to Pavlovsk to bury her father; she remained at the Palace with her two young children.

Prince Konstantin Konstantinovich

Prince Konstantin Konstantinovich was born on December 20, 1891 at the Marble Palace. Called "Kostia" in the family, he was the quietest of all the Konstantinovichi children, shy and modest, though conversely he professed a love of acting and even appeared on stage alongside his father in the Grand Duke's plays. Like his brothers, Konstantin was tall, thin, and pallid – scarcely qualities to win him romantic conquest. In 1911, though, and in rapid succession, the Prince twice professed himself hopelessly in love. He developed a crush on Grand Duchess Olga Nikolaievna, Nicholas II's sixteen-year-old daughter. When it became apparent that this would lead to nothing, Konstantin transferred his interest to Princess Elisabeth, daughter of Crown Prince Ferdinand and Crown Princess Marie of Romania. Elisabeth's grandmother Grand Duchess Marie Alexandrovna, Duchess of Saxe-Coburg and Gotha, even interceded with her daughter on the issue but – as with Olga Nikolaievna – nothing came of the suggestion.[31]

After attending school at the Corps des Pages, the Prince became an officer in the Izmailovsky Regiment, where he served with distinction during the war, being noted for his heroic behavior in battle. He was, recalled a comrade, *"much beloved by his officers and soldiers alike: along with them he was a brave soldier who distinguished himself....I personally remember seeing him in the trenches among the soldiers, risking his life."*[32]

Prince Oleg Konstantinovich

Prince Oleg Konstantinovich was the fourth son and fifth child of Grand Duke Konstantin and

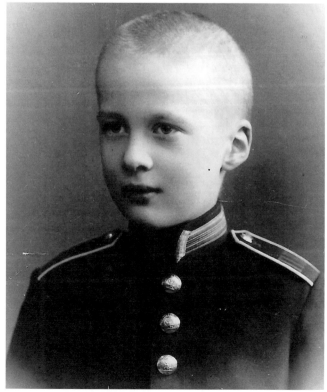

Prince Oleg Konstantinovich.

Grand Duchess Elisabeth. He was born on the afternoon of November 15, 1892, at the Marble Palace in St. Petersburg while his father was playing billiards downstairs. His godparents included his grandmother Grand Duchess Alexandra Iosifovna, Empress Marie Feodorovna, the future Emperor Nicholas II, and a slew of German Princes and Princesses.[33]

The Prince, more than the other children, was his father's son. Not only was he handsome, talented, sensitive and thoughtful, but Oleg also meshed well with his father. They shared many interests, including music, poetry, art and architecture. Far and away the most intelligent of the Konstantinovichi children of this generation, Oleg was assigned by his father a course of education unique in the Romanov family. Rather than receive a military education preparing him for a career in the armed forces of the Empire, the Prince was enrolled in the Alexander Lyceum where he pursued a course of university education and simultaneously, as a sop to the Imperial Family's military traditions, as an external student at the Polotsk Military Academy.

Prince Oleg Konstantinovich in a theater costume.

Oleg excelled at both courses of study, much to the consternation of several of his brothers who felt, not unreasonably, that their father was favoring Oleg. But Oleg went further than even his father expected: after performing at a level neither school could accommodate, the Prince entered a private, one-on-one independent course of study under the supervision of Major-General N. Ermolinsky. As a result of this independent study, Oleg produced an outstanding piece of work covering the judicial ideas of Feofan Prokopovich, Bishop of Pskov, for which he won the Pushkin Prize, which was awarded to the Russian who had achieved the highest standard of literary excellence for each year. This triumph silenced his brothers' objections, and sealed the Grand Duke's admiration for his fourth son.[34]

Prince Oleg and his brother Prince George Konstantinovich.

Oleg fell in love with a distant cousin, Princess Nadezhda Petrovna, the younger daughter of Grand Duke Peter Nikolaievich and his wife Militsa. Ironically, given that she arrived in Russia from a small, largely rural country and had attended a regular school rather than receiving an education in the royal schoolroom, Militsa did not think Oleg was her daughter's social equal, and protested any proposed marriage. Family opinion, however, over-rode the Grand Duchess's snobbery, and the young couple was unofficially engaged when World War I began.

In the first weeks of the war, Oleg joined his brother Ioann in the Horse Guards Regiment. *"We are five brothers,"* Oleg wrote, *"and are all going to the war. This fact pleases me immensely, for it proves that at trying moments the Imperial Family knows how to rise to the occasion."*[35] At the Battle of Kauschen in August, the Russians met the overwhelming power of the German

Prince Oleg Konstantinovich before the outbreak of the Great War.

reserves. Of the twenty-four officers of the regiment, sixteen were killed; both Oleg and Ioann came through safely.[36] Six weeks later, Oleg was not so lucky when he was involved in a cavalry attack near the village of Pilviski in Poland. Chasing a retreating German battalion, Oleg was shot; his horse reared up, and he fell to the ground, where he lay until rescued.[37]

At first, it was believed that the wound was minor, but as Oleg was transferred to a Red Cross field hospital in Vitebsk, it became evident that his case was much worse. On arrival at the hospital, the Prince was rushed into surgery, and his parents were informed of his injury in battle. In the course of the surgery, it was discovered that the bullet had hit Oleg at hip-level, and had traversed his body, striking the right sciatic prominence, cutting through his rectum and lodging in the left sciatic prominence. Fearing blood poisoning from infection, the surgeon allowed Oleg's wounds to remain as open as possible to allow drainage, but even this course of action was not without danger in 1914. In the end, Oleg succumbed to blood poisoning, but fortunately his parents arrived in time to be with their son when he died on September 29. In his final hours, Oleg's father presented to him, on behalf of Nicholas II, the very Cross of the Order of St. George that had been awarded to Oleg's grandfather, Grand Duke Konstantin Nikolaievich fifty years previously.[38] *"I am happy to die,"* Oleg had insisted. *"It will be good for the troops to know that the Imperial House does not fear to shed its blood."*[39]

Grand Duke Konstantin and Grand Duchess Elisabeth agreed that Oleg would be buried not in the Grand Ducal vault, but at their country estate of Ostashevo near Moscow, where Oleg had always enjoyed reading and writing under the trees on

Princes Igor and Oleg Konstantinovich.

the bluff above the Ruza River.[40] The family began to gather at Ostashevo, including Ioann and his wife Elena; Gabriel; Konstantin; Igor; George; Tatiana; Grand Duke Dimitri Konstantinovich; the Queen of Greece; and Grand Duchess Elisabeth Feodorovna. Only eight-year-old Princess Vera was missing; her parents thought she was too young to attend the funeral of her favorite brother. Even years later, as an old woman, this remained one of the few issues on which Vera would mildly criticize her parents.[41] More than a thousand peasants stood with bared and bowed heads as the funeral cortege passed them, led by representatives from the Corps des Pages from Petrograd, from the Assembly of the Nobility, the Russian Zemstvo Union, the Moscow Province Zemstvo, and the City of Moscow Government.[42]

In the aftermath of Oleg's death and burial, his parents authorized a short biographical book on their son in order to protect and preserve his memory. It was simply called *Prince Oleg*. It constituted a collection of essays written by those who had known him; photographs from his personal albums, and several excerpts from Oleg's own diary. Proceeds went to a charity named after the Prince; the copies given to members of the Imperial Family uniquely included two original watercolors executed by Prince Oleg during his life.[43] Among the most poignant – and prescient – of the diary entries was Oleg's own rumination on the specter of death, written in 1908: *"I sometimes to imagine what would happen in my own immediate circle if I were to die."* He envisioned *"the steps of my catafalque,"* his mother's expression, *"people thinking of me so regretfully,"* and his obituary, wondering *"which photograph of me they will publish. All this gives me extraordinary satisfaction."* But, he added, *"I don't want to die without fame, without having done anything, without deserving to be remembered by anybody."*[44]

Prince Igor Konstantinovich

Prince Igor Konstantinovich was born on May 29, 1894. Igor was a pleasant, aimless young man who drifted through his education at the Corps des Pages with little interest. Friends called him "Baby Boy," a nickname

Prince Igor Konstantinovich.

Prince George Konstantinovich.

indicative of his immaturity. If Igor was known for anything it was for his boisterous manner. He seemed to go through life always shouting at the top of his lungs and playing pranks on those around him. Ballerina Lydia Kyasht remembered him as *"the most irresponsible man I have ever known."*[45]

At the start of World War I, Igor was serving as a captain in the Izmailovsky Life Guards Regiment. It was then that his failing health became apparent. The Prince frequently complained of exhaustion, suffered from shortness of breath, and coughed up blood. After doctors diagnosed pleurisy, Nicholas II decided to remove the Prince from danger, and appointed him a personal adjutant assigned to Stavka.[46]

Prince George Konstantinovich

Prince George Konstantinovich, the youngest son of Grand Duke Konstantin and Grand Duchess Elisabeth, was born April 23, 1903 at the Marble Palace in St. Petersburg. The baby had no fewer than nine godparents, including his oldest brother Ioann and sister Tatiana, along with Empress Alexandra Feodorovna. The Empress's own son, Tsesarevich Alexei, born only fifteen months later, became one of George's childhood playmates, and the boys met frequently both at the Alexander Palace and also at the Konstantinovichi's neighboring suburban palace of Pavlovsk. As the home to nine creative and boisterous children, Pavlovsk was equipped with an extensive play area watched over by numerous nannies and dyadkas, the sailor-attendants drawn from the Imperial Navy. This degree of supervision meant that Pavlovsk was one of the few places Alexandra could relax and allow her son to play normally. Strangely prescient, George once played a game of chauffeurs with Alexei, confiding in his cousin that when he grew up, he was going to be a chauffeur in New York City; Alexei was charmed with this idea, and promised to be his assistant driver.[47]

In 1914, four years after a visit to Russia by Robert Baden-Powell, the first ever Boy Scout campfire was lit in the woods at Pavlovsk. At this campfire, George and Alexei had the honor of becoming the first Boy Scouts in Russia, an event commemorated by a special song. At the start of World War I, George was still in the schoolroom and a member of the Orlovsky Cadet Corps.[48]

Princess Vera Konstantinovna

The youngest child of Grand Duke Konstantin and Grand Duchess Elisabeth, Princess Vera was born at Pavlovsk on April 11, 1906. The parents wanted to call her Marianne, after Elisabeth Mavrikievna's sister Princess Marie Anne of Saxe-Altenburg. Before the christening, though, her paternal aunt Grand Duchess Vera Konstantinovna asked that the baby be named after her.[49]

Very close to her father, Vera was educated at home under his supervision. As a child she was a favorite of Nicholas and Alexandra's four daughters. Vera later remembered how she would lunch with Olga, Tatiana, Marie and Anastasia, and how they would stuff her with her favorite chocolate pudding. On one occasion, Grand Duke Konstantin Konstantinovich gave her a note to deliver to the Emperor. Vera decided that she would ride

Princess Vera Konstantinovna.

her pony – a gift from her Uncle Dimitri – the three miles from Pavlovsk to the Alexander Palace at Tsarskoye Selo. In her imagination, she was delivering a note to a captive Emperor, riding under great peril – a circumstance that would soon come to pass.[50]

Vera was eight years old when the war broke out, and, despite her gilded life and tender years, she had to grow up quickly. In quick succession she lost her beloved brother Oleg, her brother-in-law Prince Konstantin Bagration-Mukhransky and, devastatingly, her father Grand Duke Konstantin Konstantinovich. Unfortunately, the worst losses were still to come.

From the left: Grand Dukes Dimitri Konstantinovich, Vyacheslav Konstantinovich, KR, and their sister Grand Duchess Vera Konstantinovna.

Grand Duke Dimitri Konstantinovich

Grand Duke Dimitri Konstantinovich was born June 1, 1860 at the palace of Strelna, the third son of Grand Duke Konstantin Nikolaievich and his wife Grand Duchess Alexandra Iosifovna. He was christened in the Cathedral of the Winter Palace, with Emperor Alexander II among his godparents. At the christening, the baby Grand Duke was created an Honorary Colonel-in-Chief of the Migrelia Grenadier Life Guards Regiment, and was enrolled as an honorary member of the Izmailovsky Life Guards as well as the Horse Guards Regiment. A month later, he became a member of the *Garde Equipage* and the Imperial Family's 4th Rifle Battalion Life Guards Infantry Regiment.

As a child, Dimitri was a shy and retiring personality; as he grew, it became evident that he preferred reading to any other activities, and he disliked attention or being in the spotlight. His education at home was a typical round of history, geography, mathematics, naval science and languages; Dimitri was fluent in Russian, French, German and English, which was the language of the Imperial nurseries and schoolrooms. He also had a beautiful singing voice, and loved music, having studied violin and piano with tutors from the Imperial Conservatory.

Having been disappointed in the careers of his two older sons, Grand Duke Konstantin Nikolaievich intended that Dimitri would have follow him and go to sea. At the age of fifteen, Dimitri set sail on the tender *Kadetski* for a working cruise in the Gulf of Finland. He lived among the other sea cadets, took his turn at watch and, as future commander, learned how to drill the cadets. The time aboard ship, though, failed to cement in Dimitri a love of the sea. In 1877, when he was seventeen, the young Grand Duke was expected to assume his place in the Imperial Navy; he used a temporary illness to beg his father to release him from Naval service and allow him to join the Army. Grand Duchess Alexandra Iosifovna added her voice to the pleas, and once again, Grand Duke Konstantin was denied the pleasure of seeing a son follow in his seafaring footsteps.

In late 1880, having completed his infantry training, Dimitri was gazetted to the Horse Guards Regiment with the rank of Lieutenant. On Sunday, March 1, 1881, he was scheduled to deliver his first report as an Imperial Adjutant during a review by the Emperor. That morning, the secret police warned Alexander II to avoid public appearances due the possibility of terrorist activity. When Grand Duchess Alexandra Iosifovna heard these worries, she reminded the Emperor that her son was looking forward to making his first report that afternoon. Not wanting to disappoint the young officer, Alexander II set off for the parade ground. As Dimitri delivered his report, the Imperial Family looked on with pride; less than two hours later, the Emperor would be dead, killed by a Nihilist bomb.

In 1892, the Grand Duke was raised to the rank of a senior officer, and, in due course, he was promoted to Commander. Exceptionally tall, Dimitri Konstantinovich shared his brother Grand Duke Konstantin Konstantinovich's light brown hair and blue eyes, although he was not considered as handsome or elegant.

Grand Duke Dimitri Konstantinovich.

He never married. In the aftermath of Nicholas Konstantinovich's scandalous liaison and exile, Grand Duchess Alexandra Iosifovna had gathered her three youngest sons and made them swear that they would abstain from drinking and avoid self-indulgence. Dimitri took the vow seriously. Perhaps it was his brother's romantic indiscretions that drove Dimitri's misogyny: *"Beware of skirts!"* he would warn younger Romanovs – advice that the Grand Duke scrupulously followed throughout his life.[51]

Throughout the balance of his military career, Dimitri proved himself an involved and intelligent officer, caring more than most about the conditions of his men. He did what he could to improve their circumstances, but as a rather straight-laced individual, he despaired of the alcohol use and abuse that happened in the barracks. His own cousins and father disgusted him because of their mistresses and unwholesome lifestyles. Many people remembered Dimitri as a religious man, and indeed, he turned his attention in this direction and spent a good deal of his free time and money in refurbishing and supporting churches as and when he could. *"One day,"* recalled Alexander Mossolov, Head of Nicholas II's Court Chancellery, *"he turned over to me a very considerable sum for the maintenance of a little village church. 'If you make gifts everywhere on this scale,' I said, 'your revenues will not last.'"* But the Grand Duke insisted that the Romanov fortune was *"not intended to enable us to live as sybarites; this money is put into our hands in order that we may augment the prestige of the Imperial Family."*[52]

Perhaps it was this devotion to duty and the absence of scandal that led Nicholas II to reward this most upright and supportive member of his extended family with the post of Director General of the Imperial Stud in 1896. The Grand Duke was thrilled, loving nothing in his life more than horses, and this job meant that he was able to travel far and wide in search of horseflesh. But by 1904, Dimitri was beginning to lose his eyesight. Recognizing that he was no longer fit for service in the Horse Guards, he retired, donating his dacha at Krasnoye Selo to the Horse Guards Regiment for use by the officers. The following year, he also gave up his position as Director General of the Imperial Stud, although in retirement Dimitri continued to pursue his love for horses, establishing a famous stud farm, the Dubrovsky, in Poltava, complete with a school of equine veterinary medicine and a training facility for racecourse jockeys. The Grand Duke spent time breeding Orlov Trotters and crossing them with local Rostopchin and English Thoroughbreds. Visiting family could always find him in the barn, where he would enthusiastically show them his latest crop of beautiful yearlings.

Dimitri Konstantinovich had always predicted World War I. *"War with Germany is imminent!"* he would assure relatives. When it finally came in 1914, though, the Grand Duke was nearly blind. Unable to serve in the conflict he had so long hoped for, Dimitri Konstantinovich was reduced to a ceremonial role, supervising the training of cavalry regiments destined for the fight.[53]

Grand Duke Dimitri Konstantinovich.

Chapter VII

The Junior Nikolaievich Line

Grand Duke Nicholas Nikolaievich, Jr. & Grand Duke Peter Nikolaievich

Born on November 6, 1856, Grand Duke Nicholas Nikolaievich was the eldest son of Grand Duke Nicholas Nikolaievich and his wife Princess Alexandra of Oldenburg; to distinguish father and son, the elder Grand Duke was known as Nicholas Nikolaievich Sr., while his junior son was more commonly called "Nikolasha" within the Imperial Family. His unhappily married parents did little to provide a comforting home: his sensual father was wildly unfaithful and carried on a long term liaison with his ballerina mistress, who bore him a number of bastard children, while his plain, pious mother gave way to religious exaltation and whiled away her time with priests and questionable holy men. In 1879 the elder Nicholas Nikolaievich ejected his hated wife from their St. Petersburg palace, publicly accusing her of infidelity with her confessor Vassili Lebedev; she eventually settled in Kiev where, in 1889,

Grand Duke Nicholas Nikolaievich Jr.

she founded the Pokrovsky Monastery and took religious vows as an Orthodox nun.

The two sons born of the marriage, Nicholas and Peter, sided with their absent mother. Alexander II had indulged his brother's affair; Alexander III did not and exiled the elder Nicholas Nikolaievich to the Crimea. Insanity marked his last years: officially he died of oral cancer in 1891, although it has been suggested that he in fact succumbed to the effects of syphilis. Alexandra refused to attend her husband's funeral, and it was left to Nicholas to sort out his father's tangled estate. Both sons were horrified to learn that their father had squandered nearly all of his immense wealth on his ballerina and their illegitimate children; even his magnificent Nikolaievich Palace on St. Petersburg's Annunciation Square was heavily mortgaged. To settle their father's debts the sons had to sell the palace.[1]

This peculiar and tangled childhood left the younger Nicholas aloof and reserved: he concealed all emotion and protected his own inner thoughts.

As a Grand Duke, the younger Nicholas was brought up to be a soldier. He was educated first by tutors and then at the Nikolaievsky Military Engineering Academy and finally the Academy of the General Staff. In 1872, he was promoted to the Imperial Army. In 1877, during the Russo-Turkish War, he joined the staff of his father, who had been sent by his brother Emperor Alexander II to oversee military operations along the Danube. Young Nicholas proved himself an adept officer, and quickly rose through the ranks: in 1884, he became commander of the Imperial Life Guard Hussars Regiment; eleven years later, he was promoted Inspector-General of the Cavalry, with general charge of all cavalry training in the country. In 1905, he was appointed Commander-in-Chief of the St. Petersburg Military District, a post he would keep nearly a decade. Nicholas had little practical experience on the field of battle: his was more an intuitive style of command, and he seemed to favor men of humble origins to aristocrats when it came to military promotions.

The Grand Duke evoked his Romanov ancestors: standing six-feet-seven-inches, he towered over his relatives. With his lean figure, closely cropped beard and hair, and clear blue eyes, he resembled his grandfather, Emperor Nicholas I. *"He was*

Grand Duke Nicholas Nikolaievich Sr.

every inch the well-groomed soldier," remembered Princess Cantacuzene, who added that *"one felt the strength and power"* in his penetrating gaze.[2] French Ambassador Maurice Paleologue recalled his *"fierce energy...incisive, measured speech, flashing eyes and quick, nervous movements."* Beneath the imposing exterior, he thought he detected *"something irascible, despotic and implacable"* that linked the Grand Duke to his Muscovite ancestors.[3]

Few agreed about his character. Dowager Empress Marie Feodorovna once said, *"One cannot call the Grand Duke mad. Neither can one call him completely normal."*[4] *"One could not describe him as being particularly brilliant,"* recalled Grand Duchess George, *"nor was he very popular while he commanded the Guards before the war, because he was terribly severe and rather hard."*[5] He seemed to delight in humiliating his men on the training field, and was known to use *"such language that all the ladies present blushed"* when he barked his reprimands.[6]

Yet Princess Cantacuzene, whose husband was appointed to the Grand Duke's staff, had nothing but praise for Nicholas Nikolaievich:

"It was marvelous how he kept free of traps and

intrigues. Foreign diplomats made up to him at the club, the military looked up to him as to some one very sure, the Imperial Family counted on him when in trouble, though many members tried to undermine his influence with the Emperor, at other times, this in a wish to tear him down and replace him themselves. Avoiding all but the most official entertainments still, keeping his warm intimate circle closely about him, throwing himself into his work with all his heart, by degrees outgrowing the exploits which in old times had been told in lowered voices, the Grand Duke became a larger and more luminous star with each year in the constellation of the Russian capital…. The Grand Duke had a sunny charm, which won immediate allegiance, and he knew the secret of true friendship and companionship, without ever lacking dignity. He seemed to consider his position with others depended, not on the accident of birth and fortune, but only on the superiority of his capacities, if he made good. So he proceeded to do this in every line of his work or pleasure, carrying his success with utmost modesty and simplicity. There existed a legend, which was handed about, as to the Grand Duke's violent temper; but in the ten or more years I knew him, it was certainly under perfect control, and I never heard of a case in which he lost

it. He had severe words and just punishment for officers under him, who neglected their duty to their country or their men; and he had no use for any one not honest and courageous; but he was always full of understanding, ever helpful and generous to those in trouble, and as loyal to those below as to the Sovereign over him, ready to assume responsibility and to uphold any lost cause, if he thought it a right one. While not a man to turn many compliments nor to carry on empty conversation if he could avoid it, he was neither taciturn nor inert at a party, and he had a trick of voice and manner and of smile, which made those about him feel individually flattered by what seemed to be his entire attention."[7]

Grand Duke Nicholas Nikolaievich Jr. in his youth.

The Grand Duke had a marked distaste for most imperial and society entertainments. Although he had a small palace in St. Petersburg, he preferred to spend time on his country estate at Perchina in Tula Province, where he kept a costumed dwarf as a novelty and devoted himself to his true passions: hunting and collecting. As a hunter, the Grand Duke was renowned, and was said to be one of the best shots in the Empire. As a collector, he had two main interests: borzois and fine porcelain. He carefully nurtured his pet dogs to join him on wolf hunts, and became famous for his kennels,

Grand Duke Peter Nikolaievich.

though this did not prevent him from once horrifying his dinner guests by slicing a howling dog in half to demonstrate that his was the sharpest sword in the empire. It was a hint of the brutality soldiers under his command often experienced. Yet his taste for exquisitely delicate plates and china statuary also reveled his artistic side, a side he kept carefully concealed from most people.[8]

For a time, Nicholas Nikolaievich had shown little inclination to wed. He was secretly engaged to Baroness Nina Pilar, a member of Empress Marie Alexandrovna's suite; when he was refused permission to marry her, he arranged one last meeting in Switzerland, during which the pair sadly tossed their engagement rings into an Alpine lake.[9] Next he fell in love with Sophie Burenina, daughter of St. Petersburg's mayor. He carried on an affair with her for several years, and Sophie quietly gave birth to two of his children. Finally, Nicholas Nikolaievich worked up the courage to ask Alexander III if he could marry her, saying that his father fully approved. The Emperor apparently agreed, provided that it was recognized as a morganatic union, with no titles or succession rights for the Grand Duke's wife or their children. But when Alexander III investigated, he learned that the Grand Duke Nicholas Nikolaievich Sr. had never given his consent to such a union. The Emperor quickly withdrew his support and Nicholas Nikolaievich reluctantly ended the liaison.[10]

By this time, Nicholas Nikolaievich's brother Peter had married. Born on January 10, 1864, Peter Nikolaievich had been educated by tutors, and served in the Imperial Army, rising to become a Lieutenant-General in Her Majesty's Life Guards Lancer Imperial Regiment and an Adjutant-General to the Emperor. But the two brothers were quite different in both appearance and in character. Peter was shorter than the towering Nicholas, with his mother's rather broad, plain face, while Nicholas Nikolaievich was all sharp angles. Sergei Witte deemed him *"a very nice young man of limited ability,"* incapable of *"performing any useful function."*[11] Peter was also exceptionally shy and quiet, and suffered from bouts of frequent pneumonia and later tuberculosis.[12]

On July 26, 1889, Peter had married Princess Militsa, daughter of the future King Nicholas I of Montenegro. Born July 14 (New Style), 1866, Militsa had come to St. Petersburg with her younger sister Anastasia, born June 4 (New Style), 1868, to be educated at the famous Smolny Institute for Noble Young Ladies at the expense of Alexander III.[13] Both sisters were darkly beautiful, serious-minded, and charming, with an interest in religion and philosophy, and as Orthodox princesses, they seemed admirable brides for lesser

Romanovs. A few weeks later, Anastasia wed widowed Romanov relative Prince George Maximilianovich, who became 6th Duke of Leuchtenberg in 1901.

Peter and Militsa were fortunate in their marriage. The couple had four children: Princess Marina, born March 11, 1892; Prince Roman, born October 17, 1896; Princess Nadezhda, born March 3, 1898; and her twin, Princess Sophie, who lived only a few hours after her birth. The couple seemed genuinely happy, and Militsa flung herself into intellectual pursuits. She spoke five languages; could read ancient Persian texts; and studied mysticism and the occult. Those who later derided her as a vain, ambitious, and dilettantish woman were driven by motives of personal animosity, not fact.

But if Militsa found happiness, Anastasia did not. George of Leuchtenberg had lost his first wife, by whom he had a son, Alexander. At first, he seemed to care for his new wife, who bore him two children, Sergei in 1890, and Elena, in 1892, but soon his Romanov heritage revealed itself in barely disguised

Grand Duchess Militsa Nikolaievna.

liaisons, unrepentant gambling, and nights spent drinking. Shortly after the turn of the century, he had simply abandoned his second wife and children, and lived openly with his latest mistress at Biarritz.[14] Anastasia's humiliation and suffering did not go unnoticed, especially at Tsarskoye Selo.

Shortly after 1900, Militsa and Anastasia cemented a place in Empress Alexandra's rarely extended affections. How and why this came about has been the subject of debate. Sergei Witte, who hated the sisters, believed that they *"were the only ones to bow before her as before an Empress, and to flaunt a most abject admiration and infinite love for her"* that simply appealed to Alexandra's admittedly strong vanity.[15] Yet it must be said that Alexandra had her own reasons for gravitating to the sisters. With Militsa, she discovered a shared passion for philosophy and religious exploration, while Anastasia's unhappy married life undoubtedly played on her sympathies.[16]

In time, this friendship between the three women took on a more sinister tone, with the two Montenegrin sisters painted as malevolent schemers who preyed on an unstable Empress and introduced her to a parade of questionable mystics. Such ideas have little merit: Alexandra was as much of a religious seeker as either Militsa or Anastasia, and welcomed such introductions, especially when they promised the son that God had, as of yet, denied to her. Hopeful naiveté soon led to various self-described seers and holy men, including the rather infamous Philippe Nazier-Vachot, a French mystic who claimed varied spiritual powers. No one knows precisely how he first came to the attention of the Montenegrins, though it is likely that they met him sometime before 1901 during visits to France. When Nicholas and Alexandra paid a visit to the country later that year, they arranged to meet Nazier-Vachot, and were so impressed that he followed them back to Russia.

Nazier-Vachot was a quack of the highest order, a man who claimed the power to control the sex of an unborn fetus. He had previously been arrested multiple times for practicing medicine without a license, but such formalities never stopped him, nor do Nicholas and Alexandra seem to have questioned his claims. Nicholas II personally ordered that he be awarded a doctor's diploma, and for a time Nazier-Vachot held the Imperial couple in thrall. Their frequent meetings took place at Znamenka, Nicholas Nikolaievich's country estate on the Gulf of Finland, usually with the Grand Duke and his brother Peter, as well as Militsa and Anastasia, in attendance as well.

It didn't take long for stories about these goings on, which allegedly ranged from séances to bizarre rituals, to leak out, and most of the blame fell on the two Montenegrin sisters. Alexandra, in particular, was said to have fallen under the spell of the man she now called, *"Our Friend."* Those already predisposed to suspect the Montenegrins of undisguised ambition saw in these meetings further evidence of their intentions. Previously, they had been known among St. Petersburg society as *"the Black Pearls,"* a name befitting both their dark coloring and their place of ancestry. Critics now twisted this into the more ominous *"Black Perils."*[17] Nazier-Vachot lasted three years before he was duly sent back to his native Lyons. The mystical void was filled by another man, this time with far more devastating results. His name was Gregory Rasputin.

History has always blamed Militsa and Anastasia for Rasputin's introduction to the Imperial couple; certainly, they played a part, but many of Nicholas and Alexandra's trusted, high-ranking Orthodox religious advisors also promoted the peasant who, it must be said, was a very different man in 1905 to the figure of infamy he would later become. It is true that Militsa and Anastasia were careful to control the unpredictable Rasputin in these early years, limiting his contact with the Imperial couple – or attempting to do so, for the peasant, craftier than the two sisters, actually circumvented them and used them to attain his own goals.[18]

Grand Duchess Anastasia Nikolaievna.

Nor, despite claims in a few recent revisionist efforts overtly favorable to the peasant, did the two sisters actively undermine Rasputin and attempt to destroy his reputation – at least not before 1909.

Throughout this period, Nicholas Nikolaievich drew closer to his unhappy sister-in-law Anastasia. Any thoughts of possible romance, though, were pushed aside by the 1905 Revolution. For the first decade of Nicholas II's reign, Grand Duke Nicholas Nikolaievich was in the background, quietly going about his military obligations. Then in October 1905, he took center stage as the Empire's greatest drama played itself out. Faced with the loss of the Russo-Japanese War, Bloody Sunday, political assassinations, widespread strikes, and growing unrest, Nicholas II pondered two resolutions. One would be to follow the advice of Sergei Witte and grant a constitution and a parliament, a Duma, with real legislative authority; the other was to name a military dictator to ruthlessly crush the revolt. Determined to hold on to his autocratic power, Nicholas II favored the latter, and let it be known that he was considering naming Grand Duke Nicholas Nikolaievich to the post. When the Grand Duke got wind of this, he was furious, storming into the palace, brandishing a revolver, and shouting, *"If the Emperor does not accept the Witte program, if he wants to force me to become dictator, I shall kill myself!"*[19] In the end, the Emperor granted the concessions, but he seems to have harbored some resentment over the Grand Duke's actions, believing that his melodramatic threat had forced his hand. Later, Empress Alexandra would become even more pronounced in her denunciation of the Grand Duke, hysterically deeming him an enemy, yet Nicholas Nikolaievich was nothing if not loyal and would never have dreamed of undermining the Emperor. *"To my mind,"* he once explained, *"the Emperor is not a mere human being, but rather a being intermediate between man and God."*[20]

But in the months following 1905, Alexandra was still favorably enough disposed toward Nicholas Nikolaievich to indulge Anastasia's feelings for him. After so many years of unhappy marriage, Alexandra decided that Anastasia had suffered enough. Knowing that she had fallen in love with Grand Duke Nicholas Nikolaievich, Alexandra pressed the Emperor to allow a divorce between the Leuchtenberg couple in November 1906.[21] Six months later, Nicholas II agreed that the Grand Duke could marry the divorced Princess. To his mother, Nicholas explained that the Holy Synod had no issue with the marriage, and that he was personally *"delighted"* at the outcome. *"You would hardly know him now,"* he added of the Grand Duke, *"so happy he is, and so lightly does he bear the burden of his service."*[22] Most of the Romanovs were against the union: the Dowager Empress, who claimed to be so upset that she had to take tranquilizers to calm herself, complained about it to her son, while Grand Duchess Xenia Alexandrovna was equally furious.[23] The wedding took place in April 1907 in the Crimea.

Nicholas Nikolaievich and Anastasia had no children of their own, but she continued to raise the son and daughter from her previous marriage.

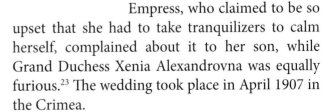

Grand Duke Nicholas Nikolaievich Jr.

Princess Marina Petrovna, oldest daughter of Peter and Militsa.

The couple lived quietly in St. Petersburg, at Znameka, and at Tchair, their Crimean estate. According to Princess Cantacuzene, Anastasia *"venerated her husband, and he seemed to find great comfort in her sympathy and companionship through all the years to follow. She cared as little for society as he and his old friends sufficed her."* She remembered Anastasia once confiding, *"When any one has been as unhappy as I, she is glad to have a home with a kind husband, and to be quiet; and neither the Grand Duke nor I need amusement or noise; also, we dislike greatly going out."*[24] Perhaps the worst that could be said of Anastasia was that she increasingly influenced her husband in his pro-Slavophile views, and was later vociferous in promoting the idea of Russia going to war in support of the ever-troubled Balkans.

Tuberculosis, and the need for a warmer climate than the chilly halls of the St. Petersburg apartment he rented in the former Von Dervitz mansion, eventually drove Peter to resign his post as Inspector General of the Military Engineering Department in 1909 and he permanently relocated his family to the Crimea. Here, he and Militsa had commissioned architect Nicholas Krasnov to build a magnificent Moorish-style palace, Dulber. They lived quietly with their growing children. In 1911 Prince Roman enrolled as a cadet at a Kiev military academy, while Marina studied painting at a Yalta academy. But by 1913, the two Grand Dukes and their wives had all but disappeared from life at court. Disagreements over Rasputin's increasing power led to the break between the sisters and Alexandra. Both Militsa and Anastasia soon saw that the peasant was a cunning charlatan, who was using and abusing his influence over the Imperial couple. No amount of pleading, though, could convince the Empress that her trust had been misplaced and that her judgment was faulty. Thereafter, relations cooled to the point of muted hostility, although Nicholas II – never as enamored of the peasant as his wife – continued to rely on the imposing Nicholas Nikolaievich for guidance. That he bore no ill will later became apparent when he named the Grand Duke Supreme Commander of the Russian Army when the Great War erupted.

The imposing Nicholas Nikolaievich seemed an obvious choice to lead the Russian Army. His father had served as Commander-in-Chief during the Russo-Turkish War, and Nicholas Nikolaievich was a career soldier, completely dedicated to the military. Yet the Grand Duke had no practical experience in supervising battle plans or military strategy; he was so overwhelmed by the appointment, according to rumor, that he actually broke down in tears.

Although the Emperor favored the Grand Duke with the position of Commander-in-Chief, he refused to allow Nicholas Nikolaievich to name his own chief of staff. The Grand Duke was saddled with General Nicholas Yanushkevich, whose practical experience amounted to three months' service in the General Staff. Despite his misgivings, Nicholas Nikolaievich moved to Baranovichi, where General Headquarters had been established. Here he lived simply on a train whose compartments were filled with bearskins and Turkish carpets. Princess Cantacuzene, whose husband Michael served on the Grand Duke's staff, recalled:

Princess Nadezhda Petrovna, Peter and Militsa's youngest child.

"Life at headquarters under the Grand Duke was of the simplest. The Chief rose early, and spent a busy day at his worktable, or in the military council chamber. Those who were on duty were immensely occupied, those off duty greatly bored, for no amusements were furnished them....Those whose energies were employed in the offices, lived near-by, in temporary buildings of the cheapest construction. The table fare was plain in the extreme, and so was the service, even when the Emperor, or a foreign mission, came to headquarters. The Grand Duke never took a day off, nor left Baranovichi, except for occasional and sudden trips of inspection to the front....He took no rest or recreation, save a short walk daily near his carriage....His behavior, according to universal report, was always even, quiet and courteous; and in the severe strain and tension to which he was subjected, though often his face went gray from anxiety, his self-control never failed him for a moment. Gambling and cards were forbidden; and the younger members of the staff and foreign attaches thought it very dull at Baranovichi, and the Chief much too austere; though they all added that at meal hours, when they met him, he was altogether charming."[25]

The Grand Duke's first strategic efforts, worked out in cooperation with the General Staff and the Minister of War, proved disastrous. Russian efforts in East Prussia resulted in humiliating defeat. The Russian campaign against Austria-Hungary in Galicia was more successful, but lack of artillery and ammunition crippled the army. Visiting Stavka in January 1915, Nicholas II reported to Alexandra of the Grand Duke: *"I must say that, when he is alone and in a good humor, he is sound – I mean to say, he judges correctly. Everybody has noticed a great change in him since the beginning of the war. Life in this isolated place, which he calls his Hermitage, and after the sense of crushing responsibility that rests on his shoulders, must have made a deep impression upon his soul."*[26]

Successes in early 1915 faded by summer. The Grand Duke made no secret of the fact that he blamed Minister of War Vladimir Sukhomlinov for the setbacks. Nicholas Nikolaievich had long hated Sukhomlinov – in 1908 he had actually resigned most of his military positions, saying that he could no longer work with him. The Grand Duke seized on the growing rumors that Sukhomlinov was corrupt and guilty of espionage – rumors that eventually led to the Minister of War's dismissal in June 1915 and subsequent trumped up charges of treason.

Sukhomlinov's ouster did nothing to alter the Russian military's spiral toward disaster: when Warsaw fell and the Russians retreated, the Grand Duke was beside himself. Anastasia recalled: *"Often the Grand Duke writes me how he wishes he might go out and under fire take part in the unfair battle, where the cream of our nation is being slaughtered. It breaks his heart to remain inactive, and to face the telegrams, with news of the retreat, which pour in daily, yet he has done everything human brain can devise to obtain ammunition. Nothing has helped, and he feels now he must shoulder the responsibility and let even his soldiers believe he has not worked for them, but has allowed them to be sacrificed, when he loves them as his children. The power against him is too great, and after many months he is in despair, and awaits his own fate quite calmly with his conscience at rest."*[27]

That fate was not long in coming. For many months Empress Alexandra had been assailing her husband

Grand Duke Nicholas Nikolaievich and Grand Duke George Mikhailovich

with demands that he replace the Grand Duke and himself assume Supreme Command. Nicholas II had long wished to do so, but the Imperial couple's motives differed. Nicholas felt that it was his duty to lead his army, while Alexandra despised the Grand Duke as Rasputin's enemy. When Rasputin offered to come to headquarters to bless the troops, the Grand Duke had threatened to hang him.[28] Nicholas Nikolaievich, the Empress warned her husband, was *"Our Friend's enemy, and that brings bad luck."*[29] She also resented the Grand Duke's popularity, blamed him for having coerced Nicholas into granting the Duma, and viewed him as a rival to her husband.

Although Nicholas II's decision to replace his cousin as Supreme Commander was later painted as an unmitigated disaster that horrified nearly everyone, the Romanovs themselves were divided on the question. The Dowager Empress begged her son not to remove the Grand Duke, but Nicholas insisted that it was his duty and that he had to *"save Russia."*[30] But both Grand Dukes Boris Vladimirovich and Alexander Mikhailovich believed that the move was for the best. For his part, Boris *"was quite certain that it would have a good effect, that the morale would be improved, and that the news would be received with great enthusiasm."*[31] And Alexander Mikhailovich insisted that *"nothing short of the Emperor himself assuming nominal command could have inspired new courage in the army."*[32]

No matter his personal feelings, Nicholas Nikolaievich behaved admirably on receiving the news. *"God be praised!"* he exclaimed. *"The Emperor releases me from a task that was wearing me out."*[33] Nicholas II could have eased concerns by keeping the Grand Duke at headquarters, but instead he gave in to Alexandra's paranoia and sent Nicholas Nikolaievich to the Caucasus, far away from the centers of power. The Grand Duke was named Commander-in-Chief of the Southern Army, directing Russia's efforts against the Ottoman

Grand Duke Nicholas Nikolaievich and Tsar Nicholas II.

Empire. There were successes, as Russian troops moved against the Turks, capturing Erzurum and flowing into Armenia, but for the man who had previously been responsible for the Empire's entire military, it was a undoubtedly a demotion. Nicholas Nikolaievich languished in exile with Anastasia, his popularity and talents sacrificed to the Empress's obsessive distrust.

In 1916, Nicholas Nikolaievich's nephew, Prince Roman, joined his forces in the Caucasus, and served on the Turkish front. Weak-lungs kept Roman's father Peter largely sidelined, confined to a ceremonial military role. His daughter Marina soon joined her brother in Caucasus, acting as a Red Cross nurse, while their mother supervised relief trains. But the once proud Nikolaievichi had been pushed to the sidelines as Russia slid toward disaster.

By late 1916, talk of conspiracies against Nicholas II seeped unchecked through the powers that be. One group of government officials whispered of plans to seize the Emperor's train and force him to abdicate in favor of his son. Another approached Grand Duke Nicholas Nikolaievich in the Caucasus, asking if he would serve as Regent if a way could be found to make the Emperor renounce the throne. The Grand Duke refused to cooperate, but it says something about the despair sweeping through the Romanov Family that he did not alert the Emperor to these plans.[34]

Chapter VIII

The Mikhailovich Line

The Mikhailovichi Grand Dukes lived lives that largely left their talents unfulfilled. Perhaps they suffered from unimaginative childhoods in the Caucasus, where their father Grand Duke Michael Nikolaievich, fourth son of Nicholas I, served as Governor-General. Dedicated to military matters, he was a man of dull habits who believed in unswerving loyalty to the Imperial Throne, while his wife Olga Feodorovna, the former Princess Cecilie of Baden, imposed her own rigid standards of obedience on their household. Undoubtedly intelligent, Olga was rigid, humorless, and widely disliked: certain Romanovs joked about the Grand Duchess, hinting that she was actually the illegitimate daughter of a Jewish banker and calling her "Mother Haber" (after the surname of her alleged father) behind her back.[1] Although the accusations remain unproven, they did their damage in anti-Semitic Imperial Russia. Yet somehow this odd couple enjoyed a happy marriage, which produced six surviving children: Nicholas, born in 1859; Anastasia, born in 1860; Michael, born in 1861; George, born in 1863; Alexander, born in 1866; Sergei, born in 1869; and

Grand Duke Nicholas Mikhailovich.

Alexei, who died at sixteen. The children respected their father; they feared their mother who, recalled her son Alexander Mikhailovich, *"dedicated all her efforts to the ungrateful task of suppressing even the slightest exterior signs of tenderness or affection."*[2]

Grand Duke Nicholas Mikhailovich

It was no secret that Grand Duchess Olga Feodorovna favored her eldest son, Nicholas Mikhailovich. *"I have loved you more than my other children,"*[3] she once admitted to him. Born on April 14, 1859 and called "Bimbo" within the family, the Grand Duke mirrored his mother's intelligence; he also absorbed liberal ideas that would later make him suspect to many in the Imperial Family. Like all other Grand Dukes, he was expected to devote his life to the military, although Nicholas's own inclinations leaned toward historical research and butterflies. He duly entered the Academy of the General Staff and did well but in 1877, after joining the Caucasian Archers Regiment and fighting in the Russo-Turkish War, his views turned pacifist. He kept up his military career to please his mother, though he took little interest

Grand Duke Michael Nikolaievich.

in his various regiments: he only agreed to serve in the Chevalier Guards as a personal favor to its honorary commander-in-chief, Empress Marie Feodorovna.

Nicholas, like all of the Mikhailovichi sons, was tall, though in later years he grew somewhat stout; he also began to lose his hair at an early age, compensating with a short, neatly trimmed beard. He adored children, loved rather immature practical jokes, and had a biting sense of humor; he could also be acerbic and rather too free in his criticisms, which alienated many Romanovs. Alexander Mikhailovich once complained of his brother's *"intolerance of the opinions of others,"* while Nicholas Mikhailovich freely admitted, *"I have many vices and my tongue has no controls."*[4] Alexander Mossolov thought him *"very intelligent"* but lamented, *"He spun intrigues wherever he went. He was always criticizing but never did anything himself."*[5] The Grand Duke hated Grand Duchess Vladimir and her sons, disliked Nicholas Nikolaievich Jr., and was a thorn in the side of many other relatives: only Dowager Empress Marie Feodorovna seemed to appreciate his intellect and straightforward manner.

Grand Duchess Olga Feodorovna.

Beyond the Romanov Family, though, many found the Grand Duke fascinating. French Ambassador Maurice Paleologue, undoubtedly impressed by Nicholas Mikhailovich's Francophone sympathies, praised him: *"Although he has German blood in his veins through his mother, a Princess of Baden, he hated Germany, German ideas and the German spirit. His whole intellectual and moral make up and all his sympathies and tastes incline him towards France. His intense interest in Napoleon I, which he puts to such a noble purpose in his historical work, is only one form of his admiration of the French genius....His open hearted talk and the outbursts of confidence and enthusiasm by which he satisfies the selfless needs of his impetuous nature have almost at once a reaction which expresses itself in cynicism, disparagement and jealous egotism. It is then that deep down within him one catches a glimpse of a great open sore, his pride, and one suspects the uneasy presence of ambitious dreams and hopes unfulfilled."*[6] And British Ambassador Sir George Buchanan deemed him *"a liberal-minded and cultured man."*[7]

Nicholas prided himself on his liberal views: his comrades in the Chevalier Guards nicknamed him "Philippe Egalité" after the French king's notoriously republican brother the Duc d'Orléans. The Grand Duke was a walking contradiction: while clinging zealously to all the privileges of his class, he espoused socialist ideas and entertained radicals. He came into early conflict with Nicholas II in the wake of the Khodynka disaster during the coronation in Moscow in 1896.

Supported by the Dowager Empress, he was vocal in warning the young Emperor against attending the ball given by the French Ambassador. *"You cannot revive the dead,"* he advised, *"but you must show your sympathy with their families. Do not let the enemies of the regime say that the young Tsar danced while his murdered subjects were taken to the Potter's Field."*[8] When Nicholas II rejected this view, the Grand Duke made no secret of his displeasure – and in so doing made an enemy of Empress Alexandra. The Revolution of 1905 horrified the Grand Duke: *"I suffer all the more from my silence,"* he confided to writer Leo Tolstoy, *"because every one of the government's flaws is so blindingly clear to me and I see no remedy except in a radical change from everything that now exists. But my aged father is still alive and, out of respect for him, I must be careful not to offend him by my views or my behavior."*[9]

The Grand Duke never married, although he is said to have fathered several children.[10] In his youth he had fallen in love with his cousin Princess Victoria of Baden. *"She is charming,"* he wrote, *"and pleases one immediately. She kisses you and makes you say a thousand things."*[11] He

Grand Dukes Nicholas and Michael Mikhailovich.

wanted to marry her but the idea was doomed by the Russian Orthodox Church's prohibition against such a close union. He later pursued Princess Amélie of Orléans, the eldest daughter of Prince Philippe, the Count of Paris, but this, too, was doomed – she was a Catholic and her family refused to allow her to convert.

Grand Duke Michael Nikolaievich died in 1909; as his eldest son, Nicholas Mikhailovich inherited his immense estate. There was the Novo-Mikhailovskii Palace on St. Petersburg's Palace Embankment, a building so large that he could easily share it with his brothers George and Sergei, who regularly rode bicycles through its corridors; the estate of Mikhailovskoye outside the capital; Borjomi, an estate in Georgia; and the Ukrainian estate of Grushovka. His inherited fortune – believed to be the largest among the Romanov Grand Dukes – allowed him the luxury of pursuing his own inclinations, chief among them research and writing.

Having resigned his army commission in 1903, Nicholas Mikhailovich published a ten-volume study of butterflies; books on hunting; a history of Russo-French diplomatic relations during the reign of Alexander I; and a number of historical biographies of his Romanov ancestors, including his monumental life of Alexander I. He served as President of the Russian Geographic Society and the Imperial Historical Society; was made a member of the French Academy; and received honorary doctorates in history and philosophy from the Universities of Moscow and Berlin. Not everyone was pleased at his literary endeavors. Countess Marie Kleinmichel called him *"a scandal-monger, who ransacked history for the*

The Mikhailovichi. Standing: George Mikhailovich, Sergei Mikhailovich, and Alexander Mikhailovich. In the middle: Michael Nikolaievich and Olga Feodorovna. On the ground: Alexei Mikhailovich and Nicholas Mikhailovich.

sake of gossip. The Eighteenth Century was his happy hunting ground, but he did not neglect the Nineteenth or the Twentieth Centuries. He felt very happy, for instance, when he discovered that his great-aunt Elisabeth Alexeievna, wife of Alexander I, who Russia revered as a saint, had had a lover, and he publishing with loving care every item of information he could find concerning the young officer."[12]

For all of his achievements, the Grand Duke limped through life, deeply wounded that he was unable to influence events. "He knows his personal worth, which is above the ordinary, and thinks there is no role he is not competent to fill," noted Maurice Paleologue. *"At the same time, he feels himself slighted and looked down upon, useless and impotent, and an object of suspicion to his sovereign and his caste."*[13] His brother Alexander Mikhailovich later summarized Nicholas Mikhailovich as *"condemned to political inactivity by persons who could not forgive him his talents and who would not forget his contempt for their ignorance. From the point of view, his life should be considered wasted."*[14]

During World War I, Nicholas Mikhailovich took a minor supervisory position in Galicia as the Russian Army advanced toward Austro-Hungarian troops; having no taste for military life, he spent his days visiting wounded soldiers, an experience that left him distraught. *"I have seen such suffering,"* he wrote, adding that the *"horrible spectacle"* of war *"tears my heart."*[15] By spring of 1916, he was so worried about the state of affairs in Russia that he wrote a startlingly frank letter on May 11 to Nicholas II questioning his haphazard way of running the government: "So long as your method of selecting ministers was known to a limited circle only, affairs went on somehow but as soon as this method was known, it became impossible to govern Russia in this way. You have often told me that you trust no one, that you are being deceived. If this is true then the same must be true of your wife who, through she loves you dearly, is led astray by the evil circle surrounding her. You trust Alexandra Feodorovna, which is natural, but what comes out of her mouth is the result of clever lies and not the truth. If you are not strong enough to separate her from these influences, at least guard yourself against this steady interference by those who act through your beloved wife." He urged the Emperor, *"of your own free will, to grant a Ministry that would be responsible to you and to constitutional legislative institutions."*[16] Nicholas didn't bother to reply; instead, he sent the letter to Alexandra, who quickly denounced the Grand Duke as yet another of her enemies: *"He has always hated and spoken badly of me,"* she insisted, adding that *"he is the reincarnation of all that's evil."*[17]

On November 6, 1916, Grand Duke Nicholas Nikolaievich called on the Emperor at Stavka. He spoke of the country's disintegration and growing unrest, but Nicholas II *"just sat there and shrugged his shoulders."*

The Grand Duke could no longer contain himself. *"I would be more pleased if you swore at me,"* he told the Emperor, *"struck me, kicked me out, than at your silence. Can't you see that you are losing your crown? Collect yourself while it's not too late. Give a responsible ministry. As long ago as last June I spoke to you about this. You just procrastinate. For the moment there is still time but soon it will be too late."* Nicholas II said nothing.[18]

In January 1917, Nicholas II was so suspicious of the Grand Duke that he ordered him to leave Petrograd. At first Nicholas Mikhailovich thought that there must be some mistake, as he was busily at work on a committee for a coming celebration. *"Perhaps I have already lost your confidence,"* the Grand Duke wrote, *"which would grieve me very much since I flattered myself that I enjoyed your affection in spite of all the possible indiscreet slips of my tongue."* The Emperor replied swiftly: *"I request that you follow this order....Your involvement with and work on the committee is no longer needed."*[19]

Grand Duke Michael Mikhailovich

Grand Duke Michael Mikhailovich, second son of Michael Nikolaievich and his wife Olga Feodorovna, was born on October 4, 1861. From an early age his family called him "Miche-Miche." According to his brother Alexander Mikhailovich, he *"had none of Nicholas Mikhailovich's talents."*[20]

Grand Duke Michael Mikhailovich.

His mother in particular seems to have regarded him as a disappointment, openly calling him *"stupid."*[21] Early on the young Grand Duke turned to the military for solace, serving in the Russo-Turkish War and entering the Egersky Life Guards Regiment. Tall, slim, and handsome, he proved particularly popular in St. Petersburg society: if he didn't sparkle intellectually, Michael Mikhailovich could boast of his dancing skills, his entertaining talk, and his charming manner.

In 1881, on turning twenty, Michael Mikhailovich decided to build a palace in St. Petersburg for himself and his future wife – not that he had any particular spouse in mind. He lavished money on a magnificent mansion on Admiralty Embankment, but the Grand Duke's efforts at finding a wife proved spectacularly unsuccessful. Overtures to Princess May of Teck and Princess Irene of Hesse were met with horror. Of the latter idea, Queen Victoria complained to her granddaughter Princess Victoria of Battenberg that she would *"never forgive it, if she also is to go to that horrid, corrupt country!"*[22] In 1887 he proposed to Louise, eldest daughter of the Prince and Princess of Wales: not surprisingly, after confessing he could never really love her, she, too, turned the Grand Duke down.[23]

The Grand Duke next declared himself hopelessly in love with Countess Catherine Ignatiev, daughter of a former State Secretary. *"Just think of it!"* his

Grand Duke Michael Mikhailovich with his wife and their three children:
Countess Zia (Anastasia), Countess Nada (Nadejda), and Count Michael de Torby.

mother cried on hearing the news. *"Misha has taken it into his head to marry young Katia Ignatiev! He announced it to us formally. He, who falls in love with a new girl every week!"* Unwilling to wait for parental approval, the Grand Duke raced off to see Alexander III. Initially the Emperor seemed agreeable – *if Michael Mikhailovich's father approved* – but within a day Grand Duchess Olga had run to Empress Marie Feodorovna, begging her to slam the door on any matrimonial hopes. *"Today it is the pretty little Ignatiev girl,"* Olga insisted. *"Tomorrow it may be the daughter of a business man, and the day after that it may be a fairly well educated servant girl. In this manner the Imperial Family must lose all its prestige."*[24] After what his brother Alexander remembered as *"painful scenes"* between the Grand Duke and his parents, the frustrated couple sent Michael Mikhailovich off to Europe to remove him from danger.[25]

Grand Duke Michael Mikhailovich and Countess de Torby.

This proved spectacularly disastrous, at least from the parents' point-of-view, for while at Nice the Grand Duke met twenty-three-year-old Countess Sophie von Merenberg. She was the daughter of Prince Nikolaus Wilhelm of Nassau and his morganatic wife Nathalia Pushkin, granddaughter of the famous poet Alexander Pushkin, while the previous year her uncle Adolphe had become reigning Grand Duke of Luxembourg. Sophie might be pretty but, as the descendant of an unequal marriage, she fell far short of Romanov standards. But after a whirlwind romance of six weeks, Michael Mikhailovich took her off to San Remo and, on February 26/March 10, 1891, married Sophie.

The Grand Duke's marriage was not only morganatic but it was also illegal, as Michael Mikhailovich had not received Alexander III's permission to wed, as required by the Fundamental Laws of the Russian Empire. On learning of this nuptial coup, Alexander III immediately stripped the Grand Duke of his military ranks and exiled him from Russia. When his mother heard the news, she collapsed in shock and set off by train to the Crimea; already in poor health, she suffered a heart attack on the journey and after an agonizing week died at the age of fifty-one. His father blamed Michael Mikhailovich for Olga Feodorovna's death, and the wayward Grand Duke was forbidden to return to Russia to attend her funeral.[26]

Feeling sorry for his niece, Grand Duke Adolphe granted her the courtesy title Countess de Torby, despite warnings from Alexander III not to do so. The disgraced couple first settled in Germany then moved to Cannes. Throughout his exile, Michael Mikhailovich was able to support himself in comfort due to a healthy income derived from a mineral-water bottling factory that he owned. This factory was located in Borjomi, Georgia, and the income flowed regularly and relatively richly,

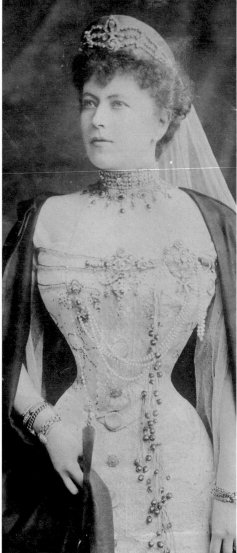

Top left: Countess Anastasia Mikhailovna de Torby (1892-1977), eldest child of Grand Duke Michael Mikhailovich and Sophie, married Sir Harold Wernher, a wealthy financier. The Wernhers were a very prominent couple in London financial circles and enjoyed close contacts with Buckingham Palace.

Above: Countess Sophie von Merenberg (1868-1927), eldest daughter of Prince Nikolaus of Nassau and his morganatic wife Nathalia Alexandrovna Pushkina.

Left: Countess Nadejda Mikhailovna de Torby (1896-1963), second daughter of Grand Duke Michael Mikhailovich and Sophie, married Prince George of Battenberg during the Great War. He was the nephew of Empress Alexandra Feodorovna.

though it is known that Michael occasionally applied to Nicholas II for supplemental amounts of money.[27]

This fortune allowed the couple to live in comfort with their children, Anastasia, born in 1892; Nadejda, born in 1896; and Michael, born in 1898. Michael Mikhailovich became a fixture on the Riviera, gambling in Monte Carlo, hosting golfing parties in Cannes, and presiding over his wife's elaborate entertainments for fashionable visitors. Family wounds eventually healed. Although the Grand Duke frequently saw his sister Anastasia, who also had a villa at Cannes, it was not until 1903 that he was reconciled with his father. After Michael Nikolaievich had a stroke, doctors sent him to Cannes to recuperate, and the

While King Edward VII was fond of Michael Mikhailovich and Sophie, Tsar Nicholas II found the couple a tiresome burden.

aged Grand Duke found himself quickly won over by his morganatic daughter-in-law's charm and beauty. Thereafter, Michael Mikhailovich's brothers began visiting him, as did most Romanovs passing through Cannes.

In 1901 the Grand Duke moved his family to England, where they rented Keele Hall in Staffordshire; it was so near the coalmines at Newcastle, recalled Agnes de Stoeckl, whose husband Alexander served as the Grand Duke's equerry, that *"if one touched a leaf"* in the garden *"one's hands were black."*[28] Michael's exile had

begun at a time when the long-term residence of a disgraced Russian Grand Duke was an object of interest and fascination rather than a point of political concern, and he was able to establish a firm foothold in British society, joining in the round of receptions, balls and hunting parties with enthusiasm. The couple quickly found themselves embraced by English aristocratic society, and King Edward VII – who in summer 1901 came to stay at Keele Hall – even appointed the Grand Duke an Honorary Knight Grand Cross in the Royal Victorian Order. The Grand Duke, in turn, was named Lord High Steward of Newcastle-under-Lyme, and became an important figure in local Staffordshire country life.[29] But the Grand Duke had something of a reputation both a gossip and a man who gave free expression to his *"nasty"* opinions about everyone, as Princess Daisy of Pless recalled.[30]

In 1908, the Grand Duke found ample opportunity to indulge both vices when he did the unthinkable and published a turgid book entitled *Never Say Die*. Although *Never Say Die* was a novel set among the aristocratic family of the fictitious German Prince Adolph of Donnerwetter, no one was fooled into thinking that it was anything other than autobiographical. The Grand Duke vented freely, if under the fictitious cover of a character named Prince Franz, about all of the injustices he

Kenwood House, the English home of Grand Duke Michael Mikhailovich.

felt he had suffered. Prince Donnerwetter, like Michael Nikolaievich, had six sons and one daughter. The eldest son hated the military and devoted himself to his study of butterflies. All of his children adored their father; *"with their mother, however, it was quite another thing. They did not love her at all, and they were terribly afraid of her."* Thus did the book present Olga Feodorovna under the guise of Princess Louise. As for Michael Mikhailovich's literary doppelganger Prince Franz, he was *"the handsomest of all the children, and was fortunate in possessing a charming character."* A sad, thwarted romance with an aristocratic girl eventually gave way to a hasty morganatic marriage, much against his family's wishes, with Ursula, the niece of British aristocrat Lady Ballington. Having made his courageous decision of love above duty, Franz and Ursula thus lived happily ever after.[31]

No one in the Romanov Family was amused. *"I read Misha's idiotic book,"* Grand Duchess Xenia Alexandrovna wrote in her diary. *"It's unbelievable and disgusting how he describes his life before his marriage."*[32] The Grand Duke got his revenge, but his novel was neither the financial boon he had once imagined nor did his indiscretion help erase the lingering animosity against him at the Russian Court. The usually reserved Nicholas II once dismissed him as *"as ass."*[33]

In 1910, Michael Mikhailovich moved his family to London, taking the lease on Kenwood, a magnificent mansion designed by Robert Adam that straddled the top edge of Hampstead Heath. This allowed Sophie even greater opportunities for entertaining, and the couple regularly lunched at Buckingham Palace and Windsor Castle with the King and Queen.[34] A visiting Prince Felix Yussoupov found the Countess *"a most delightful woman, very popular in London society. Her husband's cantankerous nature was a great trial to her; he never ceased thundering out abuse against his Russian family. Owing to his odd temperament, the Grand Duke could not be held responsible for his actions, but everyone was sorry for his wife."[35]*

Countess Sophie, constantly aware of her morganatic status, and unwilling to forgive her husband's extended family for their exile, began campaigning for her husband to ask his cousin King George V to bestow a British title on her. She sought security from the legitimacy that this title could have given her in terms of her continued position in society; the stamp of approval from the King became very important to her. George exchanged a flurry of mail with Nicholas II on this subject; Nicholas did not oppose – or even care – if Michael's wife received a title from George, but George knew that this gift was beyond his right.[36]

Michael Mikhailovich, too, was a jealous man, and a stickler for protocol and the manner in which he believed he should be treated. He was embittered against the family who had shamed and rejected him, and continued to blame him for his mother's

Grand Duke Alexander Mikhailovich.

heart attack and death. Perhaps this made him so sensitive to his status and position in society. When his cousin, the Emperor's brother Grand Duke Michael Alexandrovich, was exiled for his morganatic marriage, and chose to reside in Great Britain, Michael Mikhailovich never received him at home and never visited him. Michael Alexandrovich was the more senior Grand Duke, and Michael Mikhailovich could not risk being outranked and upstaged by this younger cousin.

Only in 1912 was Michael Mikhailovich finally allowed to briefly return to Russia, to participate in the Centenary of the Battle of Borodino. He remained in England during World War I, despite his plea that he be allowed to return and serve in the Russian Army; the continued[37] exile undoubtedly saved his life. As President of the Anglo-Russian Committee, he raised relief funds and attempted to win loans from France, and the Grand Duke offered Kenwood as a hospital for wounded soldiers, but the Grand Duke played little role in the conflict.

Grand Duke Alexander Mikhailovich, Grand Duchess Xenia Alexandrovna, Princess Irina Alexandrovna, and Princes Andrei, Feodor, Nikita, Dmitri, Rostislav, and Vassili Alexandrovich

Grand Duke Alexander Mikhailovich was born April 1, 1866 in Tiflis while his father Michael Nikolaievich was serving as Governor-General of Georgia. Called "Sandro" within the family, he made a career in the Imperial Navy, serving as an officer with the Black Sea Fleet and traveling around the world. He lost his virginity in a Hong Kong brothel, kept a longtime mistress while he was posted in Nagasaki, and visited Brazil and America, taking in the world beyond the Russian Empire. Standing six-feet-three-inches, with fine features and a closely trimmed beard, the Grand Duke, wrote one contemporary, was *"one of the handsomest and most elegant men in Russia. When he enters a room he attracts notice by his superior height and shapely figure, and he rivets attention by his peculiar charm of manner and great affability."*[38] American Gilded Age heiress Elizabeth Drexel Lehr called him *"the most human, the most natural, and the kindest of all the members of the Imperial Family."*[39] Believing himself particularly intelligent and gifted – two qualities he actually lacked – he was self-important, and ambitious enough to seek the hand of his first cousin Alexander III's eldest daughter Grand Duchess Xenia Alexandrovna.

Tsesarevich Nicholas Alexandrovich and his sister Grand Duchess Xenia Alexandrovna.

Born March 25, 1875, Xenia Alexandrovna was just eighteen when her father's cousin began showering her with attentions. Xenia was her mother's daughter, petite, dark-haired, pretty and elegant, though she had little of Marie Feodorovna's vivacity or love of pleasure. Prince Felix Yussoupov,

her future son-in-law, recalled her *"rare, delicate charm"* and her *"wonderful gray eyes"* that hinted at *"her grace, modesty, and kindness of heart."*[40] Having kept up a correspondence with the dashing Alexander Mikhailovich, she let romance carry her away, though both faced the obstacle of convincing Xenia's mother to allow the union. Marie Feodorovna openly accused the Grand Duke of *"trying to break her happiness"* and *"steal her daughter."*[41] *"My mother,"* recalled youngest daughter Olga Alexandrovna, *"just did not want to lose all control over Xenia. She meant her to stay on as a companion to herself."*[42]

After the engagement was finally announced in January 1894, the Empress complained to her mother Queen Louise of Denmark that the Grand Duke *"shows me no feeling at all and is as dry as a stick, which is more than ungrateful after all the courtesy I have shown him."* Alexander Mikhailovich, she decided, had *"a bad upbringing"* and lacked tact and polished manners.[43] The engaged couple managed to put others off with their constant displays of affection. Xenia's brother George complained of the *"gymnastic, sucking, sniffing and similar activities which these two persons indulge in all day. They almost broke the ottoman and generally behaved in the most inappropriate way; for instance, they would lie down on top of each other, even in my presence, in what you might call an attempt to play Papa and Mama."*[44]

Top left: Prince Andreas and Princess Marie of Greece, Grand Duchess Xenia Alexandrovna, and Grand Duke Alexander Mikhailovich.

Above: Grand Duchess Xenia Alexandrovna, who married her father's first cousin the same year of Tsar Alexander III's death.

Left: Several members of the Imperial Family were musically talented. In the case of Alexander Mikhailovich and Xenia Alexandrovna, the couple were very fond of Russian folk music and thus became avid balalaika players. In this image we can see them in their Petersburg palace with members of their court, all donning the uniquely Russian instrument. On the floor are their two oldest children, Princess Irina Alexandrovna and Prince Andrei Alexandrovich.

Grand Duchess Olga Alexandrovna, the Dowager Empress, Grand Duke Michael Alexandrovich, and Grand Duchess Xenia Alexandrovna. Inside the pram are Xenia's children: Irina Alexandrovna and Andrei Alexandrovich.

Alexander Mikhailovich and Xenia Alexandrovna married on July 25, 1894; their wedding at Peterhof was destined to become one of Alexander III's last public appearances. Within five months he was dead, and Xenia's brother Nicholas was Emperor. As Nicholas II's brother-in-law, Alexander Mikhailovich was one of the few Grand Dukes with any influence in the first years of the Emperor's reign. Early on Xenia had befriended Alexandra and encouraged her to marry Nicholas, and for a time the two couples were exceptionally close.

The situation, though, changed as Alexandra, desperate for a son, watched her sister-in-law give birth to one prince after another. A daughter, Irina, had been born July 3, 1895; but the rest of Xenia and Alexander's children were sons: Andrei, born January 12, 1897; Feodor, on December 11, 1898; Nikita, on January 3, 1900; Dimitri, on August 2, 1901; Rostislav, on October 20, 1902; and Vassili, on June 25, 1907. Although they were the grandchildren of an emperor, they were not immediate descendants in the direct male line, and thus received the titles of Princess and Princes of Russia. The Empress also resented the fact that Dowager Empress Marie Feodorovna seemed to favor Xenia's children over her own. By 1905, the relationship had cooled considerably; after the Revolution Xenia openly complained of Alexandra, *"That woman turned my brother into a dishrag!"*

As for Alexander Mikhailovich, he continued his naval career: in 1900 he was given command of the Black Sea Fleet's battleship Rostislav while heading the Empire's burgeoning merchant marine. But true to his reputation, he was never far from intrigues. State Senator A. A. Polovtsov called him *"a dangerous busybody, and a child without any understanding, which is all the more dangerous."*[45] Yet he also possessed some insights that might have proved immensely valuable to Nicholas II. He carefully studied the foreign navies of the world, and as early as 1896 he was warning that Russia needed a strong Pacific Fleet, as in less than a decade he fully expected that the country would be at war with Japan. No one took him seriously.[46]

Grand Duchess Xenia Alexandrovna.

After the turn of the century, Alexander Mikhailovich got himself involved in Russia's Far Eastern misadventure promoting the questionable Yalu Timber Company that allowed Nicholas II to move disguised soldiers into Manchuria and ultimately led to the Russo-Japanese War. After this disaster and the 1905 Revolution, the Grand Duke essentially fled Russia, spending long periods of time in Biarritz, where he mixed with wealthy Americans and increasingly questionable members of Riviera society.

It was while staying at Biarritz that the Grand Duke eagerly followed a newspaper account of an airplane flight over the English Channel. Alexander Mikhailovich immediately sensed that airplanes might be used in warfare and obtained the Emperor's permission to found Russia's first aviation academy outside of Sevastopol in 1909.[47] It quickly became one of the Grand Duke's most ardent passions.

Princess Irina Alexandrovna.

Another passion appeared in the Grand Duke's life at this time. By June 1907, when Xenia gave birth to their seventh child, Vassili, the marriage had broken down and Alexander Mikhailovich began a long affair with a woman of Spanish-Italian ancestry named Marie Ivanova. *"I let go,"* he later admitted. *"I was prepared to taste bitter poison at the bottom of that cup and I welcomed it. I compared my feelings toward Xenia with those I experienced toward this new woman: the parallel baffled me. I did not know which one of the two I needed more. One stood for all that was best in my character; another promised a possibility of tearing away from the strain and terror of the past."*[48]

Prince Andrei Alexandrovich.

Eventually the Grand Duke went to his wife and confessed all. *"She say very quiet,"* he recalled, *"then she commenced to cry. I cried, too. She behaved like an angel. Her heart was broken but awful as the truth was she preferred it to lies."*[49] He asked for a divorce but Xenia refused: the idea was too scandalous. And so they reached an agreement: they would remain married but each was allowed to pursue happiness outside of their union. Within a year Xenia had her own lover, an Englishman named Fane, and she and Alexander Mikhailovich even jointly arranged their schedules to accommodate meetings

Prince Feodor Alexandrovich of Russia.

Prince Nikita Alexandrovich with Prince Andreas and Prince Christopher of Greece, and Grand Duchess Elena Vladimirovna.

with their respective paramours.[50] This rather extraordinary arrangement didn't remain a secret for long: "*The Grand Duke and his wife,*" reported Princess Catherine Radziwill in 1913, "*live in circumstances unfettered by the exigencies of etiquette, which, although giving rise to no open scandal, nevertheless afford much food for gossip.*"[51]

Amidst this scandal, the couple's only daughter Princess Irina made her own peculiar decision. Beautiful in a quiet way, shy and contemplative, she stunned everyone by announcing that she wanted to marry Prince Felix Yussoupov, sole heir to the country's largest private fortune. It was a most peculiar choice. At twelve Felix had taken to dressing in his mother's gowns and jewels and haunting St. Petersburg's fashionable nightspots, flirting with handsome young officers; when caught, Felix enjoyed his scandalous reputation. Everyone agreed that he was "the most beautiful youth" in all of Russia, a young man of epicene qualities who knew no boundaries: there were rumors of opium and cocaine, whispered affairs with men – among them supposedly Grand Duke Dimitri Pavlovich – and any number of sordid tales that kept St. Petersburg gossips endlessly amused.

As the Emperor's only Russian niece, Irina was indeed a prized catch, an attractive young woman with unparalleled social standing. "*I married my wife out of snobbery,*" Felix later candidly said, "*and she married me for my money.*" The engagement, announced in October 1913, was just as suddenly broken when Irina's parents heard of Felix's sexual adventures. "*I have been very upset all this time by the rumors about Felix's reputation,*" Alexander Mikhailovich confided to his wife, "*but it's impossible to ignore it. I shall have to talk to him….If we start hearing things about again the wedding might have to be cancelled. I will tell you everything I have heard: at one point I thought he should not be allowed to see Irina at all….I did not believe anything that was being said, I don't want to believe, but there must be something as opinion about him is too steadfast.*"[52] Rumors even reached

From the left: Prince Nikita Alexandrovich, Prince Dimitri Alexandrovich, Princess Irina Alexandrovna, Prince Rostislav Alexandrovich, Prince Feodor Alexandrovich, Prince Andrei Alexandrovich, and Prince Vassili Alexandrovich.

At right: Grand Duke Alexander Mikhailovich.

Below: Grand Duchess Olga Alexandrovna and Grand Duchess Xenia Alexandrovna.

the Dowager Empress, and Felix was forced to assuage fears by both rejecting the tales circulating about him while at the same time repenting and swearing that his wild behavior was all in the past. And so, on February 9, 1914, Irina – wearing Marie Antoinette's lace wedding veil and an imposing Cartier tiara studded with diamonds – married Felix in the chapel of her grandmother's Anichkov Palace. Although Felix never abandoned his own flaunted affairs, he loved his wife and she him.

During World War I Alexander Mikhailovich hurled himself into his fledgling Russian Air Corps, stationed at Kiev, while his estranged wife Grand Duchess Xenia Alexandrovna funded ambulance trains and opened a hospital for the wounded in her palace on the Moika Canal. Instinctively, Xenia sensed that the war was dangerous to Russia's stability, feelings exacerbated after her brother Nicholas II took over Supreme Command of the Imperial Army despite her attempts to dissuade him from doing so. Her eldest sons joined the futile effort. Prince Andrei served in the Chevalier Guards, while Feodor and Nikita were both enrolled in the Corps des Pages, training to become officers.

In March 1915, Alexander Mikhailovich and Xenia Alexandrovna became grandparents when Princess Irina gave birth to a daughter, also named

Grand Duke Alexander Mikhailovich and Grand Duchess Xenia Alexandrovna.

Irina but called Bébé in the family. Princess Yussoupov did her part, working with her husband Felix to establish a hospital for wounded soldiers in his parents' Moika Palace, though the wayward Prince used his status as an only-surviving son to escape military duties. Pressure eventually forced him to enroll in a training course at the Corps des Pages with his young brothers-in-law. But in 1916 he won his place in history by murdering Gregory Rasputin; as punishment, Nicholas II exiled Yussoupov to one of his family's estates.

In January 1917 Grand Duke Alexander Mikhailovich appeared at Tsarskoye Selo. The Grand Duke didn't mince words: unrest was widespread, and the country was on the verge of revolution. Nicholas sat in silence, smoking, but Empress Alexandra interrupted her brother-in-law: *"It's not true!"* she insisted. *"The nation is still loyal to him – only the treacherous Duma and St. Petersburg society are my and his enemies."* The Grand Duke was unbowed. *"Nobody knows better than I your love and devotion for Nicky,"* he said, *"and yet I must confess that your interference with affairs of state is causing harm both to Nicky's prestige and to the popular conception of a sovereign. I have been your faithful friend, Alix, for twenty-four years. I am still your faithful friend, and as a friend I point out to you that all classes of the population are opposed to your policies. You have a beautiful family of children, why can you not concentrate on matters promising peace and harmony? Please, Alix, leave the cares of state to your husband.*" Hearing this the Empress blushed, but when the Grand Duke suggested that the Emperor grant a responsible ministry, she again erupted in anger. *"All this talk of yours is ridiculous! Nicky is an autocrat. How could he share his divine rights with a parliament?"* The Grand Duke dared point out that Nicholas had ceased to be an autocrat since granting the Duma in 1905. The interview achieved nothing and ended badly, with the Grand Duke shouting at the Empress: *"I realize that you are willing to perish and that your husband feels the same way, but what about us? Must we all suffer for your blind stubbornness? No, Alix, you have no right to drag your relatives with you down a precipice! You are incredibly selfish!"*[53]

Nicholas was unmoved. By this time, he was so suspicious that he was having secret agents spy on members of his own family: he even had their private correspondence, including letters by his sister Xenia and by his mother, intercepted and their contents reported to him.[54]

Grand Duke George Mikhailovich.

Grand Duke George Mikhailovich, Grand Duchess Marie Georgievna, and Princesses Nina and Xenia Georgievna

Grand Duke George Mikhailovich, third son of

Grand Duke Michael Nikolaievich and his wife, was born August 11, 1863 in Tiflis while his father was serving as Governor-General of the Caucasus. From an early age he had a talent for art and enjoyed painting; when he once told his parents of his interest during a dinner, they ordered that he not be served the dessert of cherry and vanilla ice cream as punishment for voicing such independent ideas.[55] Michael Nikolaievich wanted his sons to enter the army and be good soldiers, not become artists. And so the quiet, good-natured George – called "Gogi" in the family – duly enrolled in the Horse Guards Artillery Regiment. This, as his brother Alexander Mikhailovich, *"proved fatal to his colorful personality."* He *"lost all individuality, and began living in an atmosphere of riding schools, race horses, and cavalry officers."*[56]

Like his eldest brother Nicholas, George Mikhailovich grew up tall and, in his youth, slim; he also shared Bimbo's premature baldness. Aside from the army, his interests were limited to art and to numismatics. In 1895, Nicholas II appointed him director of the new Alexander III Museum in St. Petersburg, which was devoted to promoting Russian art. His invaluable coin collection, begun when just a boy and chronicled in nearly a dozen monographs written by the Grand Duke, was eventually donated to the museum.

At the age of thirty-three, and after a succession

Standing in the back: Prince Nicholas, Crown Princess Sophie and Crown Prince Constantine, Prince Andreas, and their sister Grand Duchess Marie Georgievna. Seated: Prince George, Grand Duke Michael Nikolaievich, Queen Olga and King George, and Grand Duke George Mikhailovich. Prince Alexander is on the foreground.

of thwarted romances, George fell in love with twenty-year-old Princess Marie of Greece, youngest daughter of King George I. Born March 3 (New Style), 1876, she was dark and diminutive, known in the family as "Greek Minny" to distinguish her from her aunt Dowager Empress Marie Feodorovna. She was also less than enthusiastic about the Grand Duke, being in love with a commoner she could not marry, and also being wooed by Prince Alexander of Serbia. Deciding that it was best to seize the opportunity to wed a Grand Duke who at least represented her mother's country and promised wealth and stability, she finally agreed to George's proposal as they were playing billiards: the Grand Duke was so overjoyed that he rushed to kiss her but Marie was not interested, and her lovesick fiancé ended up futilely chasing her around the table.[57]

Just as soon as she had agreed to the proposal, though, Marie had second thoughts: she wasn't in love with the Grand Duke, and at least once it seems the engagement was formally broken. George was not deterred: over the next four years he kept proposing and begging Marie to take him back. *"He could think and talk of nothing else but his love and the virtues of Princess Marie,"* recalled Agnes de Stoeckl. Finally, Nicholas II apparently summoned the Grand Duke to an audience: the situation had made George Mikhailovich a laughing stock amongst Europe's royal families. The Emperor ordered him to go to Greece and again ask for the Princess's hand: if Marie refused to commit to him, the Grand Duke was to abandon the idea once and for all. Even though Marie was Nicholas's first cousin, he insisted that he could not *allow a Russian Grand Duke to be made a puppet by the Princess of a smaller country."*[58]

George Mikhailovich made his final attempt, and Marie once again agreed to marry him, though she accompanied this news with some unwelcome bitter truths. She told the Grand Duke that she was not in love with him, and that she *"couldn't stand him,"* as the Dowager Empress confided to her sister Alexandra, Princess of Wales; even after telling George Mikhailovich that her feelings were unlikely to change, the Grand Duke was still willing to proceed.[59] On April 30 (New Style), 1900, he married Marie in Corfu.

Marie had made sure that everyone knew that she was marrying George for dynastic reasons. Although she admitted that he was *"known for his kindness of heart and his sound judgment,"* she had no love for him.[60] Nor did Marie ever adapt to life in her mother's country. George and his wife had an apartment in the immense Novo-Mikhailovskii Palace in St. Petersburg, where they lived with his brothers Nicholas and Sergei, but Marie's *"exceedingly sharp tongue,"* as Crown Princess Marie of Romania recalled, won her few friends within the Imperial Family.[61] Two daughters arrived, the darkly beautiful Princess Nina, born on June 20, 1901 and the blonde and delicate Princess Xenia born on August 22, 1903, but their births did little to bring the couple together. Finally, thinking that Marie's cool demeanor might thaw in another, less pressurized atmosphere, George made plans to build a large house in the Crimea near Yalta. Marie was horrified when she first visited: *"I must*

Engagement image of Grand Duke George Mikhailovich and Princess Marie of Greece.

Prince Nicholas and King George I of Greece, Grand Duchess Marie Georgievna, Grand Duchess Helen Vladimirovna, and Grand Duke George Mikhailovich.

157

Grand Duchess Xenia Georgievna with her daughters Princess Nina Georgievna and Princess Xenia Georgievna.

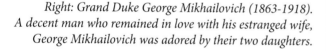

Right: Grand Duke George Mikhailovich (1863-1918). A decent man who remained in love with his estranged wife, George Mikhailovich was adored by their two daughters.

honestly confess that when my husband took my brother and me to show us the place, I sat on a rock and cried with despair at the thought of having to live there."[62] The couple asked architect Nicholas Krasnov to design and build a large house in the English style, which they called Harax: it soon became their favorite residence, and a place of refuge for the unhappy Grand Duchess. "We lived entirely a country life in the Crimea," she recalled, "*taking long walks, drives and rides. We spent a lot of time arranging the garden, where every tree and flower had become a personal friend. The children were really happy there, as they were out most of the day, free to do what they liked.*"[63]

After a decade the marriage had settled into an uneasy détente. George had never given up hope that, one day, his wife might come to share the romantic feelings he harbored for her. "She seemed touched by his devotion and the fortune he laid at her feet dazzled," recalled Marie's lady-in-waiting Agnes de Stoeckl. "*But through all this seeming bliss the Grand Duke was not happy. He felt all was not as well as he had hoped time would make. The Grand Duchess, for her part, seemed to feel more and more that nothing could bring that peace which she had known from the first would never exist in her married life.*"[64]

Neither husband nor wife proved especially sympathetic or tactful. Marie made no secret of the fact that she disliked Russia, while George was known to ruin otherwise pleasant evenings with his unpredictable temper. "*I began to think Grand Duke George was quite mad,*" Princess Daisy of Pless recorded after one such encounter. "*He shouted at everyone while we were playing bridge after dinner, denounced Germans and the English, and generally behaved in an astounding fashion.*"[65]

After a heart attack in 1905, Marie took to extensive European holidays to escape Russia and her husband's company. In June 1914, she was in England with her two daughters; ostensibly they went to Harrogate so that the sickly Princess Xenia could rest and recover her strength. In fact, it seems that Marie had gone pondering a possible separation: by this time, as Agnes de Stoeckl recalled, the Grand Duchess was *"more than indifferent"* about her marriage.[66] When World War I erupted a month later, the Grand Duchess used the hostilities to avoid returning to Russia. Neither she nor her daughters ever saw Grand Duke George Mikhailovich again.

For the first time, in Marie's absence, George did something that he had never done before: he sought out female companionship in the shape of the ballerina Mathilde Kschessinska. At this time, Kschessinska was involved with both George's brother Sergei and his cousin Andrei Vladimirovich, so it is possible that this was a platonic and conversational relationship – but Kschessinska does not seem to have been opposed to multiple partners, and her memoirs are silent on the point.[67]

Having suffered an earlier injury affecting his leg, Grand Duke George Mikhailovich took a position during World War I as adjutant at Stavka to Nicholas II, who in 1915 appointed him Chief of the 4th Kouban Cossack Battalion. The Emperor also tasked him with supervising general operations at the Front, in which capacity he reported on problems of corruption and disorganization. He undertook several foreign missions to the Far East and to Romania but by 1916 George, like many of the Romanovs, sensed that a revolution was imminent. That autumn he called on the Emperor, urging him to make concessions to save the country for impending revolution. *"Anyone who wants a responsible ministry is a fool!"* Empress Alexandra declared, dismissing the Grand Duke.[68]

Grand Duke Sergei Mikhailovich.

Grand Duke Sergei Mikhailovich

Born on September 25, 1869, Grand Duke Sergei Mikhailovich was Michael Nikolaievich's fifth son. He was his father's son when it came to the military. He graduated from the Mikhailovskii Artillery School and entered the Artillery Life Guard Cavalry Regiment. Training and exercises at Krasnoye Selo, the military camp outside of St. Petersburg, brought Sergei into close contact with Tsesarevich Nicholas, who was also stationed there with his regiment, and the two became friendly. When, in 1894, Nicholas broke his affair with ballerina Mathilde Kschessinska, he asked Sergei to look after her.

At six-feet-three-inches, Sergei was tall, thin, blonde, and the only blue-eyed Mikhailovichi scion, but no one called him handsome. Indeed, his sister-in-law Grand Duchess George once asked him, with her characteristic tactlessness, why, in a family of handsome men, he was so ugly. Not to shamed, Sergei answered good naturedly, *"It's my charm."*[69]

Although Sergei was lavish in his worship of the ballerina, Kschessinska never *"felt for him anything approaching my love"* for Nicholas, as she later recalled. He bought her a dacha at Strelna and, as President of the Imperial Theatrical Society, used his connections to ensure that Kschessinska always got the best roles on stage. Her description of the Grand Duke as faithful, affectionate and devoted suggests the inequity in the relationship: Sergei was like a temporary pet, a diversion to be used and enjoyed until such time as something better came along.[70]

That something better arrived in 1900 in the person of Grand Duke Andrei Vladimirovich. For a time, Kschessinska juggled both men as the meek Sergei willingly endured this humiliating turn of events: for a time both men shared not only the dacha Sergei had provided for the dancer, but also her bed, carefully avoiding each other. Sergei even gallantly recognized Mathilde's son Vladimir, born in 1902, as his own, even if no one was really certain which Grand Duke had been the father. *"He loved me,"* the dancer later wrote, *"and had become so attached to me that he forgave me everything. Whatever happened, he told me, he would stand by me as a faithful friend, feeling that I needed his devotion and protection."*[71]

In time, the Grand Duke turned his amorous attentions to the widowed Countess Varvara Vorontsov-Dashkov. In 1908, while staying in Switzerland, she gave birth to a son, Alexander, who was later adopted by a friend. It is believed that Sergei was the father. In these years Sergei pursued his military career, rising to the rank of Major-General in the Horse Guards Artillery Regiment in 1904; a year later, much to his father's delight, he replaced Michael Nikolaievich as Inspector General of the Artillery.

Of all the Mikhailovich Grand Dukes, it was Sergei who held the most responsible position during the war. As Inspector General of Artillery, he was in charge of the Russian Army's munitions. When it came to munitions, the Grand Duke, commented British Major-General Sir Alfred Knox, *"like a man who still loves a woman, though he knows all the time that she is bad."* After a few months of conflict, it became apparent that the Empire had not sufficiently armed itself. There were perpetual shortages and bullets and bombs had to be rationed. Sergei Mikhailovich, said Knox, was *"inspired only by patriotic motives,"* but was blind to the shortage problems and ignored warnings from French and English critics.[73]

Accusations of stupidity took a sinister turn when it was learned that the Grand Duke was allowing his former lover Mathilde Kschessinska to arrange munitions contracts with French artillery firms in exchange for bribes.[74] The rumors reached Empress Alexandra, who several times complained to her husband of the *"unclean stories"* about the ballerina's schemes.[75] In January 1916, amid an ongoing investigation into corruption, Michael Rodzianko, President of the Duma, called on the Grand Duke and flatly said, *"Unless you resign I will have you exposed in the Duma."*[76] Unwilling to risk public censure, the Grand Duke duly submitted his resignation. But Nicholas II, not willing to see Sergei Mikhailovich disgraced, simply named him Field Inspector General of the Artillery attached to Stavka, a position that deprived the Grand Duke of any real power but left him in illusory charge of operations at headquarters.

Chapter IX

The Grand Duchesses Abroad

In times prior to Catherine I, the daughters and granddaughters of Russia's rulers were born to a life of seclusion and only rarely married. But Peter the Great, recognizing the depth and breadth of his second wife's political intelligence, created a situation at the end of his life that enabled Catherine and her coterie of supporters to seize the throne from the hands of more dynastically legitimate claimants. Catherine I ushered in some tumultuous times in Russia's history, but it was also the first of three female reigns spanning almost forty years of the Eighteenth Century, which served to open up possibilities for ladies in the Romanov family.

Olga Konstantinovna, Queen of the Hellenes

Grand Duchess Olga Konstantinovna was born on August 22, 1851, daughter of Grand Duke Konstantin Nikolaievich and his wife, the former Princess Alexandra of Saxe-Altenburg. She spent her first years at Pavlovsk outside of the Imperial

Queen Olga.

capital and at the Marble Palace in St. Petersburg. She was closest to her brother Nicholas, a handsome but disturbed young man with a troubling tendency to dissipation and taste for questionable ladies. Olga's mother Grand Duchess Alexandra Iosifovna, known as "Aunt Sanny" within the Imperial Family, was elegant, refined, vain, and a stickler for protocol. She provided little warmth in the household, and the rather plain, somewhat plump Olga spent most of her time with nannies and tutors. Shy and sensitive, she was known to erupt into tears when asked questions during her lessons.[1]

In 1862, Alexander II appointed his brother Grand Duke Konstantin Nikolaievich Viceroy of Poland, and the family was uprooted to Warsaw. The Emperor had hoped that the presence of his brother would help tamp down Polish nationalism; instead, opposition to Russian rule increased, and the day after his arrival the Grand Duke was nearly assassinated by a patriotic sect. Konstantin Nikolaievich was known as a reformer: he had helped rebuild and revolutionize the

Left, top: Clockwise from top: Crown Prince Constantine, Princess Alexandra, King George I, Prince Andreas, Queen Olga, Princess Marie, Prince Nicholas, and Prince George.

Above: Queen Olga with Prince Andreas and Prince Christopher.

Left, bottom: Standing: Princess Maud of Wales, Princess Marie of Greece, Queen Louise of Denmark. Seated: Grand Duchess Xenia, Prince Andreas, Queen Olga, Princess Louise of Denmark, and Princess Victoria of Wales.

Imperial Navy after the disastrous Crimean War, and been instrumental in persuading his brother to free the serfs. In Poland, though he reinstated the native language and attempted political overtures, he failed to win the support of the more radical elements and after a year was finally forced to return to St. Petersburg.

As Olga matured into a pretty girl of fifteen in the schoolroom, plans were afoot to marry her off, set in motion by Marie Feodorovna, wife of Alexander II's heir Tsesarevich Alexander. In 1863, Marie Feodorovna's brother Wilhelm of Denmark had accepted an invitation to become King of Greece; now, as King George I of the Hellenes, he needed a suitable consort. In 1867, he visited his sister in St. Petersburg and Marie Feodorovna plotted and schemed to steer him toward the then fifteen-year-old Olga Konstantinovna. She was, after all, Orthodox, of Imperial descent, and would add luster to the relatively new Greek kingdom. Konstantin and Alexandra initially opposed the idea: Olga was too young, and the Greek throne too new and perilous to consider the idea of a match truly attractive, but George persisted and gradually her parents agreed, with the proviso that no marriage take place until Olga had completed her education and reached the age of sixteen. Olga had no say over the issue: after being told of her engagement, she spent her nights crying at the thought of having to leave her family and Russia.[2]

The marriage of Olga Konstantinovna to King George I took place in the Cathedral of the Winter Palace on October 15, 1867. The King was twenty-one; his bride had just turned sixteen. The spark of attraction was stronger on George's side: still immature, Olga faced a new, uncertain life in a foreign country. After a brief honeymoon, the pair traveled to Athens, Olga sobbing along the way and protectively clutching a case containing her favorite dolls.[3] She donned a dress in the blue and white national colors to greet her new subjects, and received thunderous ovations in approval, but Olga was stunned by Athens: the capital seemed squalid, dirty, and backward compared to glittering, refined St. Petersburg. The Royal Palace, her new home, seemed to be an apparently imposing structure yet many of its rooms were cold, dark, and it had only one bathroom.

Initially Olga, who spoke no Greek, felt herself isolated and alone. With the passing years, though, she adapted. She learned both Greek and English and gradually carved out a place for herself in Athenian society. Olga focused much of her early work on charities, founding a prison for young offenders to separate and protect them from older inmates, as well as several modern hospitals equipped with the latest technologies. Despite her efforts, many felt that their Queen

Queen Olga and her daughter Alexandra Georgievna.

Queen Olga with her son Prince Nicholas of Greece and his wife Grand Duchess Elena Vladimirovna.

163

remained too pro-Russian, and critics leaped at any perceived shortcoming. When Queen Olga tried to sponsor a new translation of the Gospels into everyday Greek, conservatives rebelled, claiming that it was a Slavic plot and demanding that anyone involved in the idea – the Queen included – be excommunicated. Riots in the streets left eight dead and more than sixty wounded before the Queen was forced to withdraw her support.

Despite her new country's democratic traditions, Olga remained decidedly autocratic in her outlook. Her son Nicholas described her as *"a staunch monarchist."* When he once suggested that the people must have a say in their own government, she replied, *"I would rather be governed by a well-born lion than by four hundred of my own species!"*[4] She existed, said her granddaughter Grand Duchess Marie Pavlovna the Younger, in her own world where *"the vulgar or equivocal sides of life"* played no part.[5] But despite her reputation as *"a kind hearted, benevolent woman, deeply religious and interested in all good works,"* one contemporary wrote, the Queen was *"deficient in tact"* and never managed to overcome suspicions that she remained too Russian in sentiment. *"While respecting her deep love for her own country, her subjects think that it goes too far."*[6]

Olga was fortunate in her private life. If her

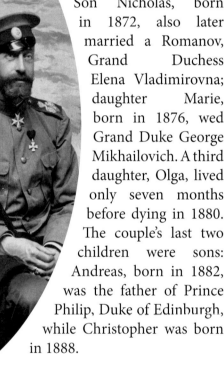

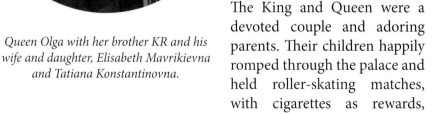

Queen Olga with her brother KR and his wife and daughter, Elisabeth Mavrikievna and Tatiana Konstantinovna.

marriage had been an arranged one, she grew in time to love her husband – *"I fell in love with the man, and not the King,"* she told her daughter Marie.[7] In 1868, Olga gave birth to a son, Crown Prince Constantine, known as "Tino." In 1889, Constantine married Kaiser Wilhelm II's sister Sophie. Of Olga and George's other children, George followed in 1869 then in 1870 came Alexandra, who later married Grand Duke Paul Alexandrovich of Russia and died in 1891 at the age of twenty-one. Son Nicholas, born in 1872, also later married a Romanov, Grand Duchess Elena Vladimirovna; daughter Marie, born in 1876, wed Grand Duke George Mikhailovich. A third daughter, Olga, lived only seven months before dying in 1880. The couple's last two children were sons: Andreas, born in 1882, was the father of Prince Philip, Duke of Edinburgh, while Christopher was born in 1888.

The King and Queen were a devoted couple and adoring parents. Their children happily romped through the palace and held roller-skating matches, with cigarettes as rewards, against their father in the ballroom. Each spring, the family journeyed to Mon Repos on Corfu, or to Tatoi, the country estate George had built for his wife to replicate the Farmhouse Palace at Alexandria, Peterhof; summers were spent with his family at Bernstorff in Denmark, where visiting Russian and English cousins swelled the walls until princes had to be put up in gardener's huts. Here etiquette was banished as relatives chased each other through the garden, turned summersaults on drawing room sofas, and pelted each other with bread across the dinner table. Empress Friedrich, visiting in 1889, wrote of *"the noise they all made, and the wild romps they had....It was certainly a very novel and original sight, very absurd sometimes, and they seemed happier and to enjoy themselves more thoroughly than children of five or six....I only wonder no arms or legs were broken. The Queen of Denmark's furniture must be unusually strong."*[8]

These holidays provided respite from Greece's increasingly chaotic political life. Although 1896 brought a moment of triumph when the Royal Family inaugurated the first Olympic games of the modern age, Greece stumbled from one disastrous misadventure to another. There seemed to be near-constant rebellions in the provinces. A war against the Ottoman Empire in 1897 ended in humiliating defeat. The following year, Prince George was named High Commissioner of Crete, renowned as a hotbed of anti-monarchist sentiment, and eventually political unrest forced him out. In 1898, King George had narrowly missed being killed as he and Olga drove in an open carriage and an anarchist fired six shots at them. Naval forces revolted, governments of the day fell, and the King's sons were forced to resign their commissions to avoid civil war.

A little more than ten years of uneasy peace ended with the Balkan Wars. Greece was successful in the first war, defeating the Ottoman Empire and winning a vast amount of Turkish territory, but the coalition of Greeks, Serbs, Bulgarians, and Montenegrins soon unraveled, with each country attempting to undercut their former allies. Hoping to quell dissent and reinforce Greece's supremacy of recently conquered Macedonia, King George took up temporary residence at Salonika in March 1913. Officials warned that it was too dangerous for the King to take his daily stroll, but George dismissed them with a smile. *"I am a fatalist,"* he declared. *"When my hour comes it will be no use."*[9]

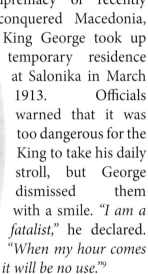

Queen Olga with her mother Grand Duchess Alexandra Josifovna.

On the afternoon of March 18 (New Style), King George left his villa for his usual walk. An anarchist shadowed him and, without warning pulled a pistol and fired at the King's back. The bullet shattered George's spine and pierced his heart. Queen Olga had been traveling when the telegram announcing her husband's death reached her; she and her family rushed to Salonika to accompany the body aboard the royal yacht *Amphitrite* back to Athens and later burial at Tatoi. *"It is the will of God,"* was her sad verdict on the tragedy.[10]

Her son was now King Constantine I, and Olga,

From the left: Queen Alexandra of Great Britain, the Dowager Empress Marie Feodorovna, and Queen Olga.

Queen Dowager. Yet her ties to Russia were stronger than to Greece, and she increasingly spent time back in her native country, staying with her brother Grand Duke Konstantin Konstantinovich at Pavlovsk. She lived quietly, raising funds for charities; increasingly shortsighted, she could often been seen presiding over meetings, an ivory lorgnette clutched tightly in her hand as she attempted to survey faces. In her old age, she had, ironically, become the perfect reincarnation of her coldly austere, regal mother.

With the outbreak of World War I, Olga funded several military hospitals and relief trains. Ever astute, she was horrified at the Empire's political disintegration under Nicholas II. Like most of the Romanovs, she blamed Empress Alexandra – and her notorious peasant healer Gregory Rasputin – for all of the misfortunes. In the autumn of 1916, Olga left Pavlovsk and went to nearby Tsarskoye Selo, hoping to confront Alexandra and convince her that the situation was nearing revolution. The Empress dismissed her concerns, later deriding Olga for having given way to hysterics. Any last ties were broken when Olga lent her name to a letter pleading for leniency on behalf of Grand Duke Dimitri Pavlovich over his role in Rasputin's murder. Nicholas and Alexandra were astonished that any member of their family was anything but horrified over the crime; neither understood just how united against them the Romanov Family had become.

Grand Duchess Marie Alexandrovna, Duchess of Edinburgh and of Saxe-Coburg-Gotha

Grand Duchess Marie Alexandrovna was born October 5, 1853 at Tsarskoye Selo. She was the only surviving daughter of the future Tsar Alexander II and his wife Marie Alexandrovna, formerly Princess Marie of Hesse and By Rhine. She was said to be Alexander II's favorite child, and she was indulged. She would flee lessons in the classroom and run to her father's study, where no tutor dared intrude.

Recognizing that the girl would need to achieve some consistent education, her parents appointed a governess, Countess Alexandrine Tolstoy, to curtail some of this wayward nature.[11]

Marie was known as warm-hearted, intelligent, and perceptive, though she concealed the first asset behind a steely demeanor. She was a fine musician and spoke Russian, English, and German, but preferred French, *"declaring that it was by far the most elegant language,"* recalled her daughter Marie, *"and that a beautiful letter could only be written in French."*[12] Contemporaries considered her to be the *"cleverest member of her family."*[13] As the Tsar's only daughter she was spoiled, and when her mother became increasingly withdrawn after the death of her eldest son Tsesarevich Nicholas, it was Marie who often acted as her father's hostess. She also began, at her father's request, to read through his papers and letters and offer advice on certain matters.[14] Marie Alexandrovna, said her father, *"never caused us anything but joy."*[15]

Grand Duchess Marie Alexandrovna.

In appearance Grand Duchess Marie Alexandrovna was somewhat plain and plump, with a broad face, dark hair and blue eyes; she had no illusions about her looks, and even mocked her appearance as unattractive. Few thought that she fit any definition of beauty. *"The expression of her features is not pleasant,"* recorded one contemporary, *"as it gives one an impression both of sulkiness, bad temper, and arrogance."*[16] As much as Marie tried to brush her appearance aside, though, it is likely that a good deal of her gruff and haughty behavior stemmed from insecurity. It was her misfortune to be intelligent and capable but condemned by her sex to a life of marriage and childbearing. She actually cared little for parties, gowns, jewels, and children. Her personality was more fitted to that of a Grand Duke than a Grand Duchess.

Although there had been some careless talk about marrying Marie Alexandrovna off to the homosexual King Ludwig II of Bavaria, nothing came of the efforts. Then, at eighteen, she fell in love with her father's adjutant, Prince Galitzine; when Alexander II learned of the burgeoning romance he had Galitzine

Grand Duke Alexei Alexandrovich, Tsar Alexander II, Grand Duchess Marie Alexandrovna, and Prince Alfred, Duke of Edinburgh.

shipped off to a posting far away from St. Petersburg.[17] It seemed as though Marie, hamstrung by her constitutional and physical inability to be the perfectly beautiful, flirtatious and intellectually vapid princess then so desirable at European courts, would have a difficult time finding a suitable husband. Marie's mother further complicated things by admitting that she really wanted her daughter to find a prince willing to uproot himself and live with her in Russia.

In 1868, while accompanying her mother Empress Marie Alexandrovna on a family holiday back to her native Hesse, the young Grand Duchess had met Prince Alfred of Edinburgh, Queen Victoria's second son. Apparently Princess Alice, the Queen's second daughter (and mother of Empress Alexandra), promoted the idea of a match between her brother, known as "Affie," and the Grand Duchess – at least this is what the Queen believed. Born in 1844, Alfred was a career officer in the Royal Navy and notoriously hedonistic. The two met again at Schloss Heiligenberg in the summer of 1871; they shared a love of music and seemed attracted to each other. The idea of a union between the two was startling: just twenty years had passed since the Crimean War, and Queen Victoria always suspected Russia of nefarious political ambitions. "The principles in Russia," she complained, *"are very loose: this Emperor's sons, sisters and brothers are no exception to this rule."*[18]

For a time, as the Queen noted, the Emperor and Empress also opposed the match as *"they wish to keep her in Russia."*[19] But whatever the parents might wish, the couple proved headstrong and in July 1873 they were engaged. *"I need not say that I can rejoice as if it was a match I much wished for,"* the Queen wrote to her daughter Louise, *"and I see many difficulties."* The only saving grace, as she saw it, was the hope that Marie *"may have a good effect on his character, which would be a blessing."*[20]

On January 11, 1874, Marie and Alfred were married in the Cathedral of the Winter Palace in St. Petersburg. They spent their wedding night at the Alexander Palace in Tsarskoye Selo, in the same bedroom that would later be used by Nicholas II and Empress Alexandra. *"How happy I am to belong to him,"* Marie wrote. *"I feel that my love for him is growing daily. I have a feeling of peace and inexpressible happiness."*[21]

The couple arrived in England on March 7 (New Style), 1874, and went to Windsor Castle where Queen Victoria waited to receive them. The Queen was pleased with her new daughter-in-law: *"I have formed a high opinion of her,"* she wrote, noting her *"wonderfully even, cheerful, satisfied temper, her kind and indulgent disposition, free from bigotry and intolerance, and her serious, intelligent mind, so entirely free from everything fast and so full of occupation and interest in everything."*[22]

The Duke and Duchess of Edinburgh.

The beginnings indeed seemed promising. Marie Alexandrovna, one newspaper rapturously declared, *"has burst upon the court like golden sunshine in a fusty, dusty room."* The paper dared hope that her vivacious presence would help lead the Queen *"out of mourning, heading a country dance on the lawn of Buckingham Palace with some gay gallant."*[23] Such hopes were futile, and Marie

Alexandrovna quickly found herself at odds with her powerful mother-in-law.

Marie Alexandrovna, recalled her daughter, *"never really felt completely happy in England."*[24] The Queen first insisted that Marie was to cede precedence not only to herself and to her daughter-in-law Alexandra, Princess of Wales, but also to Victoria's unmarried daughters. Marie rebelled. As the daughter of an Emperor, she insisted that she be styled as Her Imperial and Royal Highness, in that order, and given precedence over her sister-in-law Alexandra, who was the daughter of a mere king. Queen Victoria refused, though she eventually relented and allowed that Marie could take precedence immediately after Alexandra but before her own daughters.

Clarence House in London became the Duke and Duchess's home; here Marie installed an Orthodox Chapel, for she refused to abandon her faith, and the Russian priest she had brought with her from St. Petersburg. They also had a country estate, Eastwell Park, in Kent, which Marie much preferred, perhaps merely because it was away from London. Marie disliked the English climate, the soot that seemed to cover everything, the incessant fogs, the uninspiring food (she literally spat out her first serving of English food, much to the amused horror of her dinner guests), and the almost chilly aristocracy, so unlike the vivacious Russians.[25] With Queen Victoria in perpetual mourning, the Royal Court was but a shadow of its former glory; most attention centered on the Prince of Wales and his famous Marlborough House set, but Marie Alexandrovna never really liked the man known as "Bertie" or his wife Alexandra.

Queen Victoria expected subservience in all things. Accustomed to passing the chilly winters in the heated comfort of the Winter Palace, Marie Alexandrovna found the Queen's preference for open windows and bracing breezes agony. Once, shivering at Balmoral, she had a fire built only for the Queen to order it put out: fires, Victoria insisted, were *a form of degeneracy and she would not tolerate them.*[26] But Marie was not the kind of woman to disappear quietly. At times she clashed with the Queen and proved that she could be just as imperious as her mother-in-law. Marie took particular pride in her magnificent collection

Hereditary Prince Alfred of Saxe-Coburg and Gotha.

of jewelry: parures that had belonged to Catherine the Great, ropes of diamonds and pearls, and tiaras studded with rubies and sapphires. Marie liked to wear them not only to sartorial effect but also as a form of revenge. She had the habit of appearing bejeweled at every possible occasion, far outshining the Queen with her necklaces, tiaras, brooches and bracelets. Not that Victoria didn't express her displeasure: she would stare at her daughter-in-law *"like a bird whose plumage has been ruffled, drawing down the corners of her mouth in an expression those around her had grown to dread."*[27]

Alfred had undoubtedly found the most attractive thing about Marie to be the 2 million ruble dowry and considerable annual stipend his wife brought into the marriage.[28] A bluff and dedicated naval officer, the Duke was known for his rich and often startling vocabulary; his love of drinking and smoking; and his passion for music. Believing himself particularly adept, he often drove captive audiences of courtiers to despair by playing the violin for them for hours on end. His violent temper was famous, and he was regarded as having little tact.[29] As the years went by, he also became persistently unfaithful: Marie later

The Duke of Edinburgh and his brothers, the Prince of Wales and the Duke of Connaught.

The ducal family at Schloß Rosenau, near Coburg. From the left: Hereditary Princess Alexandra of Hohenlohe-Langenburg, Princess Beatrice of Edinburgh, Duke Alfred of Edinburgh and Saxe-Coburg and Gotha, Crown Princess Marie of Romania, and Grand Duchess Victoria Melita of Hesse and by Rhine.

admitted that the affairs were *"simply degrading,"* saying that she was merely Alfred's *"legitimate mistress."*[30]

Marie Alexandrovna remained a proud and stubborn enigma. *"Outwardly,"* recalled her daughter Marie, *"she may have appeared haughty, a stickler for form and proud of her rank, but inwardly she was humble, always tormenting herself, tortured by the idea that she had never lived up to the ideal set for herself by her parents."*[31] Prince Nicholas of Greece remembered that, as a child, he was *"always a little afraid"* of the Grand Duchess, who appeared *"rather austere"* and disapproving of any youthful boisterousness.[32] Yet her niece Grand Duchess Marie Pavlovna recalled her *"as a person of high spirits and of a sense of humor a little ironic."* [33]

In 1881 Alexander II was assassinated. Although there had been several previous attempts on her father's life, Marie Alexandrovna was stunned at his death, and she felt that her native country had somehow forever changed. Thwarted in her life, Marie Alexandrovna poured all of her energy and ambition onto her children. In October 1874 she gave birth to a son, Alfred, known as "Young Affie;" Marie, called "Missy," was born in 1875; Victoria Melita, called "Ducky," was born in 1876; Alexandra, called "Sandra," was born in 1878; and Beatrice, called "Baby Bee," was born in 1884. A stillborn son was born in 1879. All were raised to admire Germany and Russia, and echo their mother mother's dislike of England. Tutors and governesses played on Marie Alexandrovna's anti-English sentiments when raising the children. In turn, she gave them a free hand over her children, a move that proved particularly disastrous for her only son, who endured a strict and often brutal educational regime.

Marie Alexandrovna was extremely ambitious for her children, and her four daughters were largely considered to be amongst the most beautiful and charming of European princesses. *"Her whole life was given up to her children,"* remembered her daughter Marie. *"We were the supreme and central interest of her existence, but she had her own ideas about education and she never admitted any mixing of generations; she was never comrade nor companion, but always very definitely the parent."*[34] Where her daughters were concerned, the Grand Duchess insisted that they should all marry by the age of twenty. *"When they are over twenty,"* Marie Alexandrovna declared, *"they begin to think too much and to have too many ideas of their own."*[35]

The first to fall victim to her mother's machinations was the beautiful Marie. Known as "Missy," she attracted much attention, and her cousin the future King George V wanted to marry her, but Marie Alexandrovna's anti-English sentiments refused to let her consider the match, much to her husband's anger. Instead, in January 1893 Marie was abruptly married off

Crown Princess Marie of Romania and Grand Duchess Victoria Melita of Hesse and by Rhine in fancy dress costumes.

to Crown Prince Ferdinand of Romania, heir to King Carol. This was scarcely a love match, and the restless Marie would spend the rest of her life searching for happiness.

In 1887, the family moved to Coburg: by previous arrangement Alfred was to inherit the Duchy on the death of his uncle Ernst, Duke of Saxe-Coburg and Gotha. In the 1870s, aware that one day the family would have to live in Coburg, Marie Alexandrovna had built a new residence, the Palais Edinburgh, which gave her an independent stage on which to act, though often alone. Alfred continued serving in the Royal Navy. Having previously commanded the Mediterranean Fleet, he relocated to Devonport but Marie Alexandrovna did not follow, and only rarely visited despised England.

On August 23, 1893, Ernst, Duke of Saxe-Coburg-Gotha, died and the throne passed to Alfred. Marie Alexandrovna now became Duchess and for the first time was able to enjoy the freedom of having her own court. *"For Uncle Alfred,"* wrote Empress Friedrich to her daughter Crown Princess Sophie of Greece, *"this is a difficult time; he will have to give up dear old London for good and devote himself* to his German home and his new duties." But, she added, "*Aunt Marie will love being No. 1 and reigning Duchess, I am sure.*"[36] Marie Alexandrovna reluctantly abandoned the Palais Edinburgh for Schloss Ehrenburg, the official residence of the reigning Duke, but she far preferred summer holidays at Schloss Rosenau, the little Gothic villa outside of town where Prince Albert had been brought up.

In 1894, Marie Alexandrovna – this time together with Queen Victoria – essentially pushed her second daughter Victoria Melita into a marriage with her first cousin Grand Duke Ernst Ludwig of Hesse, another loveless union that ended in divorce. In 1895, Marie Alexandrovna arranged her daughter Alexandra's marriage to Prince Ernst of Hohenlohe-Langenburg, over the objections of both Alfred, who complained that his future son-in-law was not important enough, and of Queen Victoria, who thought that the bride was too young.

Hereditary Prince Alfred of Saxe-Coburg and Gotha.

was fleeced by gamblers, slipped heavily into debt, and lost both his reputation and his health."[37]

Empress Friedrich cautiously wrote to her daughter that "Young Affie" was "*giddy and wild, as many young men alas are, and that he contracted an illness, of which I know next to nothing, as I have never asked or heard anything about it, one dislikes thinking about it, and still more speaking or writing about it. This was neglected, and the poor boy led a dissipated life besides. Potsdam! — That was not the place for him. He was too inexperienced and heedless and giddy to resist temptations, bad examples, etc.*"[38]

In fact, the young Prince almost certainly contracted syphilis. Attempts to marry him off to an eligible princess had failed (a daughter of Grand Duchess Vera Konstantinovna), and his latest affair with a young woman caused a great deal of worry. During celebrations for his parents' twenty-fifth wedding anniversary, he allegedly shot himself. The bullet gravely injured him, but he did not die. Critics of Marie Alexandrovna have claimed that, distraught and embarrassed, she ignored the advice of doctors and had her only son bundled onto a train and sent away in an attempt to hush up the scandal; two weeks later, though, on February 6 (New Style), he died at Meran.[39] Feeling responsible, Marie Alexandrovna gave vent to her emotions at the funeral, sobbing openly in an uncharacteristic display of her grief. The other

Worse scandal came in 1899. "*Young Affie*" had become increasingly dissipated and wild. At the Kaiser's insistence, he had been sent off to Berlin to be educated. "*Once having Alfred there,*" wrote one historian, "*he placed him in a military circle and forgot him. No motherly or fatherly control was exercised by the Imperial couple, and being left entirely to his own devices he got into bad company,*

A royal gathering in Coburg, 1896. At front: Grand Duchess Marie Alexandrovna, Hereditary Princess Charlotte of Saxe-Meiningen, Fürstin Leopoldine of Hohenlohe-Langenburg. First row, from the left: Kaiserin Augusta Viktoria, Fürst Hermann of Hohenlohe-Langenburg, Grand Duchess Marie Pavlovna Sr., Princess Elise Reuß, the Duchess of York, Hereditary Princess Feodora of Leiningen, Grand Duchess Victoria Melita of Hesse and by Rhine, and Princess Beatrice of Edinburgh. Second row, same order: Princess Feodore of Saxe-Meiningen, Princess Louise of Saxe-Coburg and Gotha, Hereditary Prince Alfred of Saxe-Coburg and Gotha, Crown Princess Marie of Romania, Prince Max of Baden, the Duke of York, and Grand Duke Ernst Ludwig of Hesse and by Rhine. Third row: Hereditary Prince Bernhard of Saxe-Meiningen, Hereditary Prince Emich of Leiningen, Prince Philipp of Saxe-Coburg and Gotha, Crown Prince Ferdinand of Romania, Kaiser Wilhelm II, the Duke of Edinburgh and Saxe-Coburg and Gotha, and Grand Duke Paul Alexandrovich.

story, one that perhaps is closer to the truth, is that her son's physical condition was undermined by the spread of the venereal disease. Little could be done to stop its spread. Sending him to Meran, a course of action recommended by the ducal doctors, was en effort to assist in his recovery as the location had much better weather than frigid Coburg. The patient did not respond well to his treatment and death, therefore, ensued. It was a terrible tragedy, and one from which the family never recovered. Somehow, Marie Alexandrovna's critics appear to have won the day by accusing her of such callousness that she was more intent on saving her reputation, than the life of her only son. Based on her devotion to her children, one can safely argue, that nothing could be farther from the truth.

Duke Alfred was devastated by the death of his only son, and his drinking, already a worrisome problem, increased. In the spring of 1900 he fell ill; doctors found he was suffering from incurable cancer of the larynx, but the news was kept from his wife until the end was near. Despite their marital difficulties, Marie Alexandrovna was genuinely distressed. *"I had great anguish at heart the whole time, and the feeling besides that one could be of no use to him,"* she admitted.[40] Alfred died on July 30, 1900 at Schloss Rosenau. The throne passed to a nephew, Prince Karl Edward, Duke of Albany. Empress Friedrich met Marie Alexandrovna shortly after Alfred's death and wrote: *"She was*

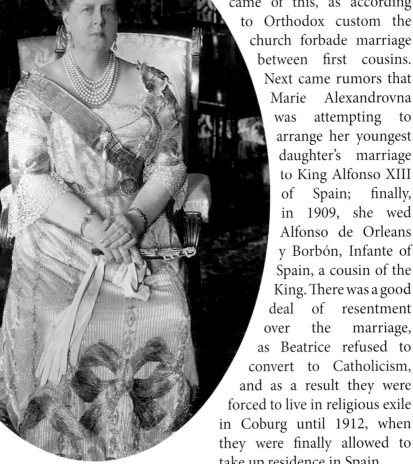

Grand Duchess Marie Alexandrovna.

very nice and kind…though she hates showing her feelings in general, she did not conceal from me how much she suffered."[41]

In 1902 Marie Alexandrovna's youngest daughter Beatrice became involved in a fleeting romance with her cousin Grand Duke Michael Alexandrovich of Russia, brother of Tsar Nicholas II. Nothing came of this, as according to Orthodox custom the church forbade marriage between first cousins. Next came rumors that Marie Alexandrovna was attempting to arrange her youngest daughter's marriage to King Alfonso XIII of Spain; finally, in 1909, she wed Alfonso de Orleans y Borbón, Infante of Spain, a cousin of the King. There was a good deal of resentment over the marriage, as Beatrice refused to convert to Catholicism, and as a result they were forced to live in religious exile in Coburg until 1912, when they were finally allowed to take up residence in Spain.

Marie Alexandrovna continued to live in Coburg as the Dowager Duchess, but she also regularly spent time at Château de Fabron in Nice and a villa on the Tegernsee in Bavaria. The one place she did not visit was Russia. Marie Alexandrovna was dismayed by her nephew Nicholas II and especially by his wife Empress Alexandra. She simply could not understand how they could abandon their ceremonial duties and live in isolation – something for which she entirely blamed Alexandra. To her daughter Marie of Romania, she once confessed that she felt herself *"completely set aside and cannot risk it in my dignity, as the only Russian aunt of Nicky's, to be treated as she treats every other member of the family there."*[42]

The Great War, when it came, left Marie Alexandrovna distressed. Her natural sympathies lay with Russia, but events during Nicholas II's reign had left her feeling alienated from the Imperial Court. Rather than return to her homeland, she decided to remain in Germany, living with her daughter Alexandra and her son-in-law Fürst Ernst of Hohenlohe-Langenburg in Coburg. She would never set foot in Russia again.

Grand Duchess Elena Vladimirovna.

Duchess Elena Vladimirovna, Princess Nicholas of Greece

Grand Duchess Elena Vladimirovna of Russia, the only daughter of Grand Duke Vladimir and his wife Marie Pavlovna, was born January 17, 1882. Raised in the immense Vladimir Palace in St. Petersburg, Elena was indulged and spoiled from birth. As an only daughter, she received a good deal of parental attention. She was, recalled Meriel Buchanan, *"adored and worshipped by her father,"* and was *"able to twist the big, powerful man round her little finger, to coax him out of his occasional bursts of temper*

with her winning smile, or if that failed, with tears brimming over in her big, dark eyes."[43] An English nanny taught her, and she thus learned English along with Russian as her principal languages. Elena could be headstrong and willful: there is a story that, at the age of four, she once threatened an artist with a knife. Even the Dowager Empress agreed that Elena, although *"she is really quite sweet,"* could be *"vain and pretty grandiose."*[44] She once described her priorities in life as *"God first, then the Russian Grand Dukes, and then the rest."*[45]

Elena was darkly beautiful, with abundant hair and *"the loveliest eyes imaginable,"* as Prince Felix Yussoupov recorded. *"Everyone fell under their charm."*[46] Princess Daisy of Pless thought her *"handsome and delightful,"* while Baroness Sophie Buxhoeveden recalled her as *"the idol of all the young folk,"* noting that, *"a great deal of entertainment was given in her honor."*[47] Meriel Buchanan thought that she possessed *"a fascination and a charm which are hard to describe. Many men thought that their hearts were broken because she was unobtainable."*[48]

As the granddaughter of Alexander II and the daughter of perhaps the two most important and powerful figures at the Imperial Court aside from the Emperor, Elena grew up headstrong and privileged. Being brought up with three brothers

Above left: Grand Duchess Elena Vladimirovna.

*Above right; Grand Duchess Elena Vladimirovna,
Grand Duchess Marie Pavlovna Sr., and
Grand Duke Boris Vladimirovich.*

*Right: Prince Nicholas of Greece and
Grand Duchess Elena Vladimirovna.*

*Below: Empress Alexandra Feodorovna and
Grand Duchess Elena Vladimirovna.*

undoubtedly hardened her character; she was brave, disliked being challenged, and had the same imperious air that surrounded both of her parents. Ambitious for her only daughter, Grand Duchess Vladimir suggested several possible husbands. Much attention centered on Prince Max of Baden. He was not only a great-grandson of Nicholas I, but would also likely one day inherit the Grand Ducal throne in Baden. Ironically, a decade earlier, he had suddenly appeared in Darmstadt and unsuccessfully asked for Princess Alix of Hesse's hand, only to be turned down. Now, somewhat reluctantly he asked Elena to marry him in 1900 and then suddenly changed his mind. This rejection was a humiliating insult. Prince Max never gave his reasons, and nasty inferences were drawn. For a Prince to break off an engagement with a royal lady certainly suggested something dishonorable about her. Elena was left deeply embarrassed, with her future marital prospects in danger.

Grand Duchess Marie Pavlovna, in distress, began to look about Europe for another similarly eligible prince. Grand Duke Konstantin Konstantinovich wrote: *"I heard from Minny about Maria Pavlovna's efforts to marry off her daughter Elena. After the failure with Max, they are desperate to find another husband. Their choice fell on Albert of Belgium, but he did not seem particularly keen. Marie Pavlovna then wrote to the Emperor, asking him to invite the*

King of Belgium to Peterhof for the summer, while Elena wrote to the young Empress, declaring her whole future depended on this invitation. At this point Albert of Belgium announced his engagement to a Bavarian princess, and Miechen telegraphed the Emperor that there was no longer any need to invite the King."[49]

Elena soon recovered. For a year, one prince in particular had been paying close attention to her: Nicholas of Greece, third son of King George and his wife Queen Olga, herself a former Russian Grand Duchess. Known in the family as "Greek Nicky" to differentiate him from his cousin Nicholas II of Russia, Nicholas was a decade older than Elena, tall, handsome, and just as important, apparently very interested in her.

The Vladimirovichi – Grand Duke Andrei, Grand Duke Vladimir, Grand Duchess Elena, Grand Duke Kirill, Grand Duke Boris, and Grand Duchess Marie.

He later recalled her as *"lovely and fascinating."*[50] When she learned of this attraction, Marie Pavlovna was distressed and told Nicholas *"not to count on Elena because, as the third son of a King, he was not a suitable match for her."*[51] Elena, though, was nothing if not her mother's daughter, proud, stubborn, and equally determined to get her own way. She had fallen in love with Nicholas, and although Marie Pavlovna tried to find another eligible suitor, her results failed. The couple was engaged in June 1902, and on August 29, they were married in the Cathedral of the Catherine Palace at Tsarskoye Selo.

After their honeymoon, Elena and Nicholas moved to Athens. *"When we entered the harbor,"* Nicholas remembered, *"we found the whole town in festive attire to receive us. My father and all the family, in full dress, came to meet us. Everyone was touched to see the new Princess dressed in blue and white* [the Greek national colors] *to make her first appearance in her new country."*[52] Elena and her husband had three children, all daughters: Princess Olga, born in 1903 (later Princess Paul of Yugoslavia); Princess Elisabeth (later Countess zu Toerring-Jettenbach), born in 1904; and Princess Marina, born in 1906 (later the Duchess of Kent). Although happy in her marriage, Elena apparently found life in Athens somewhat dull compared to the glamorous Russian Court. The palaces were shabby compared to those in St. Petersburg; Nicholas II solved this problem by having a mansion built for the couple in Athens, complete with central heating and numerous bathrooms – a feature notably lacking in the main Royal Palace.[53] Society was almost non-existent. There were frictions with her new family as well, particularly with her sister-in-law Alice, wife of Prince Andreas and mother of the present Duke of Edinburgh, and the couple increasingly took holidays to various spas in Germany and Switzerland.

Every year, Elena and her family tried to return to Russia for several months, staying with her mother at the Vladimir Palace in St. Petersburg or

Prince Nicholas of Greece and his daughters: Elisabeth, Marina, and Olga.

at her mansion at Tsarskoye Selo. Meriel Buchanan saw them frequently, and was captivated by the couple's three daughters, who were *"growing more enchanting every year. It was difficult when they were so small to know which was the prettiest although perhaps Princess Olga had the most classical features while Elisabeth, who because of her masses of dark curling hair was always called Wooley, had inherited her mother's eyes. But there was something even then about little Princess Marina that caught at one's heart: her rather crooked smile, the serenity and sweetness of her face, the sadness which one could sometimes glimpse beneath the laughter in her eyes. Often during the winter months I used to see the three little Princesses driving in an open sledge, their faces rosy with the cold, framed in fur trimmed velvet bonnets."* Marie Pavlovna made no secret of the fact that she preferred her youngest granddaughter: *"Marina is the most unselfish,"* she would declare. *"She has the sweetest nature. Marina is the most affectionate."*[54]

Elena and Nicholas happened to be in Russia when World War I erupted. They attended the *Te Deum* at the Winter Palace that followed the declaration of war, and witnessed the Emperor step out onto the balcony to the great acclaim of the gathered crowd. They returned to an increasingly chaotic Greece: in the wake of George I's assassination, King Constantine often found himself at war with the government of Prime

Grand Duchess Marie Pavlovna Jr.

Minister Eleftherios Venizelos, a situation that would eventually drive the Greek Royal Family into exile.

Grand Duchess Marie Pavlovna, Princess Wilhelm of Sweden

Grand Duchess Marie Pavlovna was born in St. Petersburg on April 6, 1890, the first child of Grand Duke Paul Alexandrovich, youngest brother of Emperor Alexander III, and his wife the former Princess Alexandra Georgievna, daughter of King George I and Queen Olga. Less than two years later, Grand Duchess Alexandra died after giving birth to a son, Grand Duke Dimitri Pavlovich. She spent her first years living in her father's palace in St. Petersburg, although several months each summer were often spent at Ilinskoye, the estate of her uncle Grand Duke Sergei Alexandrovich and his wife Grand Duchess Elisabeth Feodorovna, outside of Moscow. Following the vogue for everything English among the country's aristocracy, a British nanny tended to Marie and she did not actually speak a word of Russian until she was six.

Paul was a loving father, yet he was often kept busy by his imperial and military obligations, and after his wife's death he was less than attentive to his young children. As a result, Marie early on developed an intense emotional attachment to her brother Dimitri. He became the one constant in her life, and the person to whom she was most devoted. Those ties increasingly became important as her father's interests passed to a new romantic affair with Olga Pistolkhors. For several years, the affair continued without attracting too much attention or controversy but in 1902, Paul illegally married Olga during a trip to Italy. *"How could my father do this?"* Marie Pavlovna recalled thinking on hearing the news, *"he who lacked nothing, who led so agreeable a life; who had us, both of us, alone to himself?"*[55]

Infuriated, Nicholas II responded by exiling his uncle from Russia. The loss of their father left Marie and Dimitri essentially orphaned in Russia. In a letter to Dowager Empress Marie Feodorovna, they wrote: *"We are so sad and so grieved that that our dear Papa cannot come back."*[56] The Emperor refused, however, and sent Marie and Dimitri to live under the guardianship of Grand Duke Sergei and his wife, who had no children of their own. *"Towards Dimitri and me he displayed a tenderness almost feminine,"* Marie wrote of her uncle Sergei. *"Despite which he demanded of us, as of all his household or following, exact and immediate obedience."*[57]

Marie's relationship with her aunt Elisabeth, though, was not as comforting, and she found her oddly cold and even hostile. When she once complimented her aunt's beauty, Elisabeth coldly turned to Marie's nanny and said, *"You must really teach her not to make personal remarks."* When she tried to hug her, Elisabeth angrily pulled away.[58] Elisabeth was apparently jealous of her husband's devotion to this niece and nephew and took out her frustrations on Marie. This, at least, is the picture Marie portrayed in her memoirs. It is difficult to completely discount her portrait of Elisabeth, which was published during her brother's lifetime.

Grand Duchess Elisabeth Feodorovna.

Dimitri. Somewhat emotionally immature, she found it difficult to empathize with others; at times she was cynical and at others she was amusing, the result of her conflicted childhood. This caused difficulties, for Marie was naturally intelligent and yet insecure. She apparently never blamed her father for her predicament, instead holding Sergei and Elisabeth accountable for the unhappiness and unstable childhood she experienced. In time she came to believe that her uncle and aunt were actually keeping her from her father who, in fact, was not allowed to return to Russia.

In February 1905, a revolutionary hurled a bomb at Grand Duke Sergei's carriage as he was leaving the Kremlin in Moscow. The explosion tore the vehicle apart and eviscerated the Grand Duke into hundreds of bloody pieces. Hearing the explosion, fifteen-year-old Marie rushed through the palace and found her aunt kneeling beside what remained of her husband, the carnage thankfully concealed by a blanket. *"I did not dare look at her,"* Marie wrote. *"Her face was white, her features terrible in their stricken rigidity. She did not weep, but the expression of her eyes made an impression on me I will never forget as long as I live."* When she and Dimitri ran to embrace Elisabeth, the Grand Duchess looked at them and said, *"He loved you so, he loved you so."*[59]

Marie grew up balanced on the outside, full of spirit and always eager for excitement, but her difficult childhood and its conflicting influences also left her somewhat selfish and occasionally temperamental. She had learned to keep her feelings inside; her fragile emotions and the damaged legacy of her childhood left Marie confused, feeling out of place, and seeking affection and comfort. She had no real family, no sense of belonging to anyone except to

In the wake of this trauma, Paul was allowed to

Grand Duchess Marie Pavlovna Jr. with her mother Alexandra Georgievna.

briefly return to Russia for the funeral, but Elisabeth continued to act as guardian for Marie and Dimitri. But Elisabeth's life changed now: intensely, overtly religious, she flung herself into the pursuit of a single goal: founding and heading an order of nuns. Marie's continued presence was undoubtedly something of a hindrance to this quest, and so Elisabeth quickly arranged a marriage. Marie was an attractive young lady, *"full of life and very jolly,"* said Grand Duchess George, *"but inclined to be self-willed and selfish, and rather difficult to deal with."*[60] Another contemporary called her *"A charming woman, not exactly pretty, but with a clever, interesting face and a slender figure, graceful and straight as a dart."*[61]

At least on paper Marie Pavlovna seemed full of promise to be an admirable wife. Unfortunately, Elisabeth selected a man completely unsuited to her niece, Prince Wilhelm, second son of King Gustav V of Sweden. Six years older than Marie, Wilhelm was tall, thin, and pale, and nearly a complete stranger to her. Marie recalled: *"The Prince came to Moscow for Christmas. The holidays, spent from morning till night side by side, proved difficult. We really had nothing to say to each other. It seemed that my fiancé had become to me a stranger – a stranger, however, to whom I was bound. Soon I regarded him almost with hostility. His rare caresses were disagreeable to me. The situation was becoming intolerable. I shivered to contemplate this impasse into which I had been led. Preparations for the marriage took their course without my being able to feel any pleasure or interest in them."* To Marie, it felt as if *"I was offering him a heart almost empty, and was using him, in a sense, only to obtain my freedom."* At the time, Ella had to undergo a serious operation and Marie took advantage of her illness to try to break off the engagement, writing Wilhelm a letter suggesting that it would be best for them both to go their own ways. Wilhelm replied with a "charming" letter, asking Marie to *"think carefully before making a decision which would cause him great pain."*[62]

"The genuine sincerity of feeling that animated his letter moved me deeply," Marie wrote, *"but failed to alter my decision."* Just as she was determined to tell Elisabeth of her intent, though, a third party entered the picture. This was Princess Irene of Prussia, Elisabeth's sister who,

Grand Duchess Marie Pavlovna Jr.

having learned of Marie's intent, now insisted that it was impossible to break the engagement. To do so would have serious political consequences, she argued, and the scandal would be immense. Finally, and with a flair for the theatrical, Irene insisted that Marie's proposed breaking of the engagement would kill her aunt. If she insisted on going ahead, Irene warned, Elisabeth might die and the fault would rest solely with Marie. *"The whole thing was too much for me,"* Marie recalled, *"and I had no one competent to help me. My aunt Ella, whose condition was satisfactory, was nevertheless still weak; the shock, for all I knew, might really prove fatal. What could I do? I gave in."*[63]

Emotionally blackmailed into an untenable situation and a loveless marriage, Marie apparently tried to make the best of this *fait accompli*. *"I was tired of the ordered existence, dull and tranquil, which we then were undergoing,"* she admitted, adding that she *"longed for movement, noise, excitement, release, for any change."* [64]She now wrote letters to her fiancé, suggesting that she anticipated her marriage and the freedom it offered to her. The letters are less than convincing, as if Marie was attempting to find some silver lining in her impending union and talk herself into the marriage. More letters, dictated by her Aunt Elisabeth, went to Grand Duke Paul, in which Marie Pavlovna insisted that she was *"madly in love"* with Prince Wilhelm." But privately she complained about *"that old fool,"* as she described

Grand Duchess Marie Pavlovna Jr. and her grandfather King George I of the Hellenes.

Elisabeth. *"She, and only she, has made my last years the unhappiest of my life. She is a rat!"*[65]

Grand Duke Paul was furious when he learned of the engagement, and railed that Elisabeth had shown a *"complete lack of common sense and humane feeling"* in pushing for the union.[66] He felt that his daughter was being forced into a loveless marriage. *"As for the Swedish prince, what can I say about him?"* he bitterly wrote to the Emperor. *"As the children are wards, the father doesn't have the opportunity of either meeting the fiancé or pronouncing himself for or against, or expressing his opinion that a girl of seventeen is too young to be given away in marriage. The wardship has decided so many questions without me that in reality the children have been distanced from me to the utmost possible degree."*[67]

The Grand Duke was allowed to return to Russia for the ceremony itself, which took place on April 20, 1908, in the cathedral of the Catherine Palace at Tsarskoye Selo. Mathilde Kschessinska happened to be traveling on the same train that carried the newlyweds away to Sweden. *"In spite of having been married the day before,"* she recalled, *"the Grand Duchess looked sad and rather preoccupied. Her husband did not appear any happier."*[68]

Marie used her dowry to purchase a large house in Stockholm, Oak Hill, and settled down to life

Grand Duchess Marie Pavlovna Jr. and Prince Wilhelm of Sweden.

at Gustav V's court. Her father-in-law quickly took to her, and Marie actually won the acclaim of many by undertaking numerous royal duties and apparently enjoying her role in Stockholm.[69] Yet appearances were deceptive. The reserved Swedish court found Marie bold, brash, and too brittle for their tastes. She had hoped for freedom: it was, indeed, the only promise that had made her go through with the unwanted marriage. The rigidity of life at the rather dull Swedish court soon proved a bore, and there were difficulties with her mother-in-law Queen Victoria as well, who did not share her husband's appreciation for Marie's *"effervescence, charm, and unconventionality."*[70]

On May 8 (New Style), 1909, Marie gave birth to a son, Lennart. Unfortunately Marie lacked any real maternal instinct. Having been deprived of a mother at an early age, and of any semblance of real maternal affection or warmth throughout her troubled childhood, she was unable to overcome the emotional distance she felt. The relationship with Lennart would always be strained and distant.

Even more troublesome was Marie's increasingly bad relationship with her husband. It is unlikely that the couple had ever been in love; many royal marriages were arranged and many succeeded on their own terms, but Marie felt trapped and despised living what she thought to be a lie. Marie and Wilhelm had both been young and emotionally immature when they wed. They were completely opposite in character: she was intelligent and headstrong, while Wilhelm was concerned only with his naval career and seemed compliant.

Marie apparently complained that her husband was cold and shy. He seemed to be largely uninterested in any intimacy with her, and never overcame the almost bumbling manner with which he apparently approached her. When Marie tried to talk to him and share her feelings of neglect and rejection, Wilhelm either avoided the conversation or broke into tears.[71] There have always been suggestions that Wilhelm was homosexual. As Grant Menzies noted, *"There must have been plenty of indications to those making the arrangements on the Swedish side"* that the Prince was *"no more suited to marriage"* than had been Grand Duke Sergei Alexandrovich. *"And one has to wonder: Had Ella, intentionally or no, perversely attempted to replicate her own strange marriage in brokering Marie's with the Swedish prince?"*[72] There are stories that Marie went to her father-in-law and implored him to allow a divorce but the King refused. Gustav V had his own secrets to conceal: his marriage to Victoria hid his own sexual indiscretions, including what was apparently a long-term affair with a Swedish man named Kurt Haijby.

In this oppressive atmosphere Marie began to suffer from apparent depression. During a 1912 visit to Siam, she openly flirted with several men, and a terrified Swedish Court tried to intervene by attempting to exile the Grand Duchess to Capri, on the excuse that she was suffering from some unspecified kidney disease. Marie apparently alleged that Axel Munthe, the physician who treated her, was guilty of sexually assaulting her, and temporarily fled the country.

By 1913, Marie had had enough, and she finally told her husband that she wanted a divorce. Her father Paul came to her rescue and took her to live with him and his morganatic wife and children in Paris. In a letter to his nephew Nicholas II, Paul wrote: *"If only you could see what the poor girl looked like when she arrived to us! She was fainting every minute, she was white as a sheet, she could not eat or sleep, she was coughing dreadfully, and she still complains about her kidneys. She is only beginning to recover under the influence of*

A multigenerational photograph: Grand Duchess Marie Pavlovna Jr., her grandmother Queen Olga of Greece, great-grandmother Alexandra Josifovna, and son Prince Lennart of Sweden.

our love and caress. It is unthinkable that she should return to Sweden and I beg your permission for us to begin negotiating a divorce."[73] Nicholas reluctantly agreed. As part of the decision, Marie agreed to the Swedish Court's demand that she leave her son Lennart in Sweden, to be raised by her husband and his parents; he was, after all, a Swedish Prince, and even had she wished to do so it would have been unlikely that Marie would have been allowed to take him from the country when she returned to Russia. By the terms of the agreement, she would only be allowed to see him on certain occasions.

Marie was free of her husband and adopted country, but fell victim to guilt over having to abandon her son. A lifelong battle with depression began, though World War I offered temporary respite from her personal troubles. Marie enrolled in Red Cross courses and trained as a nurse, working in a hospital barracks in Petrograd before joining Queen Olga of Greece's hospital train at the Front along with Princess Elena of Serbia. The Grand Duchess, commented a contemporary, *"had to endure no end of hardships, for to work under such circumstances was difficult indeed. The close vicinity of strong forces of the enemy, uncertainty as to what might happen from hour to hour, the daily appearances of Zeppelins dropping bombs in the region of the hospital, and the continual increase of war victims required strength of will, self-abnegation and indefatigable labor.*[75]

The hardships were real enough. Witnessing her first death, that of a wounded soldier she had been treating, left Marie shaken as she stumbled from the room. Yet she found a sense of purpose previously missing in her life; indeed, she admitted, *"My happiness was so great that I was at times remorseful at experiencing such ecstasy in the midst of all this pain."*[76] Her bravery won accolades: even Empress Alexandra praised the Grand Duchess, writing to Nicholas II that she thought Marie Pavlovna deserved to be awarded the medal of the Order of St. George for her bravery.

Grand Duchess Anastasia Mikhailovna of Mecklenburg-Schwerin

Grand Duchess Anastasia Mikhailovna was born July 12, 1860, the second of Grand Duke Michael Nikolaievich and his wife Grand Duchess Olga Feodorovna's children. She was the first Romanov to bear the name Anastasia since the wife of Ivan the Terrible. Her life was unusual for a Grand Duchess: when she was two, her father was appointed Viceroy of the Caucasus by his brother Alexander II, and the entire family moved to Tiflis in Georgia. Although they returned to their palace in St. Petersburg

Grand Duchess Anastasia Mikhailovina and her brother Grand Duke Alexander Mikhailovich.

every year, or to their estate on the Gulf of Finland, this meant that the Mikhailovichi children, as they were known, were brought up quite apart from most other members of the Imperial Family, and remained enigmas to many. They seemed somehow exotic, living in the Caucasus, and it was much easier for stories to circulate about them in St. Petersburg, where they were largely unknown.

Anastasia, called "Stassie" in the family, had an unusual position: as the only daughter among six brothers, she was isolated and indulged – at least by her father and by her tutors. She took lessons away from her brothers, and lived in a more comfortable wing of the palace: only on Sundays did the entire family reunite.[77] Separation, in this case, only strengthened ties, and Anastasia was especially close to her eldest brother Nicholas. Like him, she had an artistic flair and a multitude of interests. She grew into a tall and quiet beauty, with dark hair and green eyes.

In 1878, Grand Duchess Olga and Grand Duchess Vladimir conspired to marry Anastasia to Friedrich Franz, Hereditary Grand Duke of Mecklenburg-Schwerin in northern Germany. He was twenty-seven to Anastasia's seventeen, wealthy, and a future ruler: he also happened to be Marie Pavlovna's beloved brother, and she was ever watchful for opportunities to advance her family's power and influence. Anastasia, Marie Pavlovna wrote to her father, was *"enchantingly dear in both her character and her appearance. I do not doubt for a moment that she will fill her place and her new position to perfection now, and will be equal to the future. In her movements, her carriage and her speech she will remind you of Queen Olly* [Queen Olga of Greece] *though she has big, clear expressive eyes, that promise much. To the outward appearance, her figure is still very slim and childlike, but when she speaks this impression is wholly dispelled. She is very well educated and carefully raised."*[78]

Anastasia knew nothing of these plans until Friedrich Franz arrived in Tiflis one day and abruptly asked Anastasia to marry him. He was jovial and not unattractive; he was also a semi-invalid, suffering from asthma and heart troubles, and was rumored to be homosexual.[79] Anastasia's brothers quickly noted that he often had an unbecoming case of eczema as well.[80] Anastasia did not know him, but her feelings played no part in the issue: a determined Olga insisted, and the engagement was announced. The couple was married the following January 12, 1879, in the Winter Palace.

Anastasia soon found life in Mecklenburg-Schwerin

Grand Duchess Anastasia Mikhailovna.

Above: Grand Duchess Anastasia Mikhailovna and her daughter Duchess Alexandrine of Mecklenburg-Schwerin.

Left: Hereditary Grand Duke Franz Friedrich III of Mecklenburg-Schwerin and Grand Duchess Anastasia Mikhailovna.

Below: Grand Duchess Anastasia Mikhailovna and her daughter Duchess Cecilie of Mecklenburg-Schwerin.

unbearable. Her father-in-law, the reigning Grand Duke Friedrich Franz II, gave the couple the Marie Palais, but Anastasia was forbidden to decorate her rooms as she wished. The court seemed oppressive, especially compared to the relative freedom Anastasia had enjoyed in the Caucasus, and she found herself unable to adjust to her new position. Ladies attached to the court openly disapproved of Anastasia's free and easy manner, and soon condemned her as *"fast."*[81] Luckily her husband's fragile health meant that the couple had to travel often to various resorts in France and Italy, which allowed Anastasia to escape Schwerin with some regularity.

In 1879 Anastasia gave birth to a daughter, Alexandrine; three years later, another child, Friedrich Franz, was born while the couple was staying at Palermo. Then, on April 15 (New Style), 1883, word came that Grand Duke Friedrich Franz II had died. Anastasia and her husband had to return to the Grand Duchy. Taking the throne as Grand Duke Friedrich Franz III, Anastasia's husband now faced the unwelcome task of living in his realm, with its chill winters. At first, the couple tried to make a go of it, moving into the beautiful Schloss Schwerin and presiding over the small court, but soon enough Anastasia again felt trapped. The regular holidays began again, which caused much resentment and criticism of the Grand Duchess's apparent wanderlust. Finally, to appease his subjects, Friedrich Franz agreed that they would live in Schwerin for five months each year and spend the other seven months traveling so that he could cater to his health. Any future children, by this agreement, were to be born in Schwerin.[82]

Anastasia complied with these conditions, and was in Schwerin for the birth of her daughter Cecilie in 1886. She built a hunting lodge near the Baltic Sea as an escape, but her dislike for Schwerin was too intense, and finally in 1889 her husband built her a house, Villa Wenden, overlooking Cannes, where they could live from November until May each year.[83] Here, Anastasia regularly entertained visiting relatives who had come to the Riviera to gamble at Monte Carlo and enjoy the sunshine at Cannes. Anastasia seems to have been relatively happy in her marriage, and unlike her own mother, had a warm relationship with her children, attempting to bring them up simply and unaffected

Grand Duke Friedrich Franz III.

Grand Duchess Anastasia Mikhailovna.

***Grand Duchess Anastasia Mikhailovna and her sister-in-law Grand Duchess
Marie Pavlovna Sr. at the Coronation of Tsar Nicholas II, Moscow, May 1896.***

Duchess Alexandrine of Mecklenburg-Schwerin and her groom Prince Christian of Denmark.

by their positions. During her stays at Villa Weden, Anastasia followed the precedent of many of her Romanov relatives, haunting the Casino at Monte Carlo, smoking and drinking. Her luck was never good, and she is said to have lost considerable money at the gaming tables.[84]

After eighteen years of marriage, though, Friedrich Franz's health continued to deteriorate. Medical worries may have led to depression; there are also persistent rumors that the Grand Duke was homosexual and feared exposure, or that he felt humiliated by his wife's alleged affairs.[85] In April of 1897, the couple was staying at Villa Weden. On the morning of April 10, servants found him unconscious in the garden. Carried to the villa, he died later that day. Although officially it was announced that he had suffered a heart attack and fallen from the terrace, it was whispered that the Grand Duke had deliberately hurled himself over the terrace in an effort to end his life; certainly stories of his suicide circulated widely in aristocratic circles.[86]

Anastasia's fifteen-year-old son became Grand Duke Friedrich Franz IV, ruling under the regency of his uncle until he came of age in 1901. Her husband's unfortunate death, if anything, made Anastasia even more unpopular in Schwerin: there were even rumors that she had had him killed.[87] Not surprisingly, she preferred to spend as little time as possible in her son's Grand Duchy, instead retreating to Villa Weden or to her hunting lodge on the Baltic. The year after her husband's death, her eldest daughter Alexandrine married Prince Christian of Denmark, eldest son of Crown Prince Frederick and future King of Denmark.

Only thirty-six when she was widowed, Anastasia flung herself into a life of pleasures. She frequently visited Russia, and spent even more time in Paris or Monte Carlo, gambling and attending parties. She soon began an affair with Vladimir Paltov, her secretary and a man

Grand Duke Friedrich Franz IV of Mecklenburg-Schwerin and his bride Princess Alexandra of Hannover.

fourteen-years her junior, and became pregnant by him. Her condition was first disguised as a tumor and then as a case of the chickenpox, for which she insisted she had to be quarantined. It was during this official period of quarantine that, in December 1902, she allegedly gave birth to Paltov's illegitimate son Alexei in Nice. He was later given the name Count de Wenden, after Anastasia's villa in Cannes.[88]

In 1904 Anastasia's son Friedrich Franz IV married Princess Alexandra of Hannover, and the following year her daughter Cecilie married Crown Prince Wilhelm, eldest son of Kaiser Wilhelm II. The Kaiser only reluctantly allowed her to attend the wedding in Berlin, advising that – given her reputation – it would be best if in the future she kept her distance from her daughter. At the wedding on June 6 (New Style), 1905, said Princess Daisy of Pless, Anastasia *"looked handsome, cold, and proud – and no wonder, after what the papers have said about her....I felt so sorry for her."*[89]

Crown Prince Wilhelm and Crown Princess Cecilie with their firstborn son Prince Wilhelm of Prussia.

Magic City with all comers till two in the morning and associates with the scum of the aerodromes.[91] Prince Felix Yussoupov met her that year in Paris, and described her as *"kind and affectionate,"* though also *"eccentric and despotic."* She would go out to the theatre in the evening only to inevitably fall asleep in the first act; waking with a start, she would then loudly declare that the performance *"was stupid"* and demanded to go someplace else, often changing her choice of entertainment venue two or three times each night. When midnight came, she would insist on going dancing at some seedy club, where she remained until dawn.[92]

The outbreak of World War I brought an end to such pursuits. Like most other Grand Duchesses who had married abroad, Anastasia's heart belonged to Russia but her son was a reigning German Grand Duke and her daughter had married the Kaiser's heir. In the end she decided to remain abroad, though in neutral Switzerland, where she lived in a hotel and, true to her heritage as a Romanov Grand Duchess, gradually fell back into a diverting round of pleasures.

Anastasia, said one acquaintance, was *"completely indifferent to anything but her own desires,"* and she continued to live much as she had done before, devoting herself to parties and gambling.[90] By 1913, according to one diplomat, she was living *"openly with an Argentinean blackguard, dances at*

Chapter X

The Leuchtenberg, Oldenburg, and Mecklenburg-Strelitz Families

Leuchtenberg

Three distinguished families, descendants of Romanov ancestors, occupied illustrious positions at court and in society before the Revolution. The Leuchtenberg family traced its descent to Grand Duchess Marie Nikolaievna, eldest daughter of Nicholas I and his wife Empress Alexandra Feodorovna. In 1839, she had married Maximilian de Beauharnais, 3rd Duke of Leuchtenberg, Empress Josephine's grandson. The union was not a particularly brilliant one for the Emperor's eldest daughter: Maximilian, as a minor Bavarian royal, was a mere Serene Highness, his father having been ennobled by King Maximilian I Josef of Bavaria, but his two sisters, Josephine and Amelie, had married, respectively, King Oscar I of Sweden and Norway and Emperor Pedro I of Brazil, while his brother August became consort to Queen Maria II of Portugal. But the headstrong

Grand Duchess Marie Nikolaievna, Duchess of Leuchtenberg.

Marie Nikolaievna insisted, and her father agreed to the marriage on the condition that she not leave Russia. To sweeten the deal, he gave Maximilian the style of Imperial Highness, along with a magnificent residence in St. Petersburg, the Mariinsky Palace, and a country estate, Sergievka, west of Peterhof on the Gulf of Finland.

The couple had seven children; they technically bore the surname de Beauharnais, the Leuchtenberg titles of Duke or Duchess and the Russian titles of Prince or Princess Romanovsky, with the style of Imperial Highness. The eldest daughter, Alexandra, was born in 1840 but died at the age of three. Marie was born in 1841 while Nicholas, the eldest son, was born in 1843. Princess Eugenie followed in 1845; Prince Eugene in 1847; Prince Sergei in 1849; and Prince George in 1852. In 1863, Marie married Prince Wilhelm, younger son of Leopold, Grand Duke of Baden, and lived outside of Russia until her death in 1897: their youngest son was Prince Maximilian of Baden, the last German Imperial Chancellor. Coincidentally, after breaking his engagement to Grand Duchess Elena Vladimirovna, Maximilian married Princess Marie Louise of Hannover, older sister of Alexandra, Anastasia Mikhailovna's daughter-in-law.

Born July 23, 1853, Nicholas Maximilianovich was the eldest son of Grand Duchess Maria Nikolaievna and Duke Maximilian. On his father's death in 1852, he became 4th Duke of Leuchtenberg. In 1868 he made a morganatic marriage with Nadezhda Annenkova, who was already expecting at the time. She gave birth to their two sons, Duke Nicholas Nikolaievich on October 17, 1868, and Duke George Nikolaievich on December 10, 1872. Nicholas Maximilianovich spent much of his life outside of Russia, and he died in Paris on December 25, 1891. Duke Nicholas Nikolaievich married Countess Maria von Grabbe in 1894, and had seven children but as descendants of a morganatic union they did not inherit rights of succession or the style Imperial Highness; they were collateral Romanov relatives but not members of the Imperial House. The same provisions applied to the family of his brother George Nikolaievich, who married Princess Olga Repnina in 1895. The couple spent most of their time in southeastern Bavaria, where they lived in Kloster Seeon, a converted abbey near the Austrian border. They had six children:

Grand Duchess Marie Pavlovna Sr. and her friend Zenaide Skobeleva, Duchess of Leuchtenberg.

Duchess Elena, born in 1896; Duke Dmitri, born in 1898; Duchess Nathalia, born in 1898; Duchess Tamara, born in 1901; Duke Andrei, born in 1903; and Duke Konstantin, born in 1905.

Eugene Maximilianovich, the second of Grand Duchess Maria Nikolaievna's sons, was born January 25, 1847. He contracted a morganatic marriage with a woman named Darya Opotchinina in 1869. She died a year later, on March 7, 1870, while giving birth to a daughter, whom her husband named Darya in her honor. Eight years later, Eugene made another morganatic marriage, this time with Zenaide Skobeleva, who was created Her Serene Highness Duchess of Leuchtenberg in 1889. Zenaide was a famous beauty – Grand Duke Alexander Mikhailovich later insisted that it was impossible *"even remotely to convey the physical attributes of that woman. I have never seen anyone like her in all my travels."*[1] That beauty inevitably attracted attention, especially from Alexander III's brother Grand Duke Alexei Alexandrovich, who made no secret of his amorous interests. One night, so the gossip went, Eugene returned home and went to his wife's room only to find the door locked. After repeated knocking, it was finally opened by a somewhat disheveled Grand Duke Alexei Alexandrovich, who beat the husband over the head, and kicked him down the staircase to

Duke Nicholas of Leuchtenberg.

Duke Eugene of Leuchtenberg.

Duke Sergei of Leuchtenberg.

Duke George of Leuchtenberg.

Marie Leuchtenberg and her children, Marie and Maximilian.

Eugenie Leuchtenberg, Duchess of Oldenburg.

sleep in his study. The next day Eugene ran to Alexander III complaining of his humiliation, but the Emperor sent him away with the warning that if he couldn't make his wife behave he should not expect that someone else – even the monarch – could. Thereafter, Eugene regularly slept on a sofa in his study and left his bedroom to the Grand Duke and an unrepentant Zenaide.[2]

In 1891, on the death of his brother Nicholas Maximilianovich, Eugene became 5th Duke of Leuchtenberg. Zenaide died June 16, 1899, while Eugene died on August 18, 1901. Eugene's daughter Darya de Beauharnais, known as Dolly, was something of a scandalous figure during Nicholas II's reign. Although, as a morganatic descendant, she was not a member of the Imperial House, her misadventures were freely associated with the Dynasty. In 1893 she had wed wealthy Prince Lev Kotchoubey but soon found that married life did not hold any appeal. The restless Darya left Russia and went to Paris, where she studied at the Sorbonne. In 1911 she finally divorced Kotchoubey; on February 9, 1911, she married naval officer Baron Waldemar von Grävenitz, who having spotted Darya on a passing ship through his binoculars had ordered his own vessel turned around to pursue her. According to rumor, Nicholas II was so infuriated by the Baron's actions that he ordered him to be court-martialed, at least until he learned the circumstances. Being with the wayward Darya, he decided, was a punishment in itself, and he let the matter drop. But as late as 1916 the Emperor was still complaining about her escapades. On September 15, he confided to Alexandra that Darya had suddenly appeared at Stavka demanding the title of Duchess of Leuchtenberg: *"after that,"* he added, *"you may be sure she will demand money from the districts, to which she has no shadow of right."*[3]

Sergei Maximilianovich, the third of Grand Duchess Marie Nikolaievna's sons, was killed in action in the Russo-Turkish War, while George, the youngest son, was to play a rather prominent

*The wedding of Duke
George Maximilianovich of
Leuchtenberg and Princess
Anastasia of Montenegro*

role during Nicholas II's reign. From his birth on February 29, 1852, there were persistent rumors that George's actual father was not Duke Maximilian but rather Count Gregory Stroganov, with whom Grand Duchess Maria Nikolaievna was said to be on intimate terms and whom she married after Maximilian's death. On May 12, 1879, George Maximilianovich married Duchess Theresa Petrovna of Oldenburg, whose grandfather had wed Grand Duchess Catherine Pavlovna, daughter of Emperor Paul, and whose brother Duke Alexander Petrovich had wed George's sister Eugenie in 1868. On November 1, 1881, Theresa gave birth to their son Alexander but her health was fragile and she died on April 7, 1883. On August 16, 1889, George wed a second time. His wife, Princess Anastasia, was a daughter of Prince Nicholas of Montenegro and sister to Militsa, who would wed Grand Duke Peter Nikolaievich. They had two children, Duke Sergei, born July 4, 1890, and Duchess Elena, born January 3, 1892.

Duke Alexander Georgievich of Leuchtenberg.

George Maximilianovich became 6th Duke of Leuchtenberg on the death of his brother Eugene in 1901. Together with her sister Militsa, Anastasia made herself indispensable to Empress Alexandra, showering her with devoted attentions while cultivating a friendship based on mutual interests in spiritual matters. The two Montenegrin sisters introduced a number of questionable "holy men" to Nicholas and Alexandra, and were among Rasputin's early promoters. Anastasia also won Alexandra's sympathy as her marriage to Duke George Leuchtenberg quickly disintegrated. Within a few years of his second marriage, he was already spending much of his time on the Riviera, openly living with his mistress and, Alexander III commented angrily, *"washing his filthy body in the waves of the ocean."*[4] After a miserable decade, and through Alexandra's intervention, Anastasia was finally able to divorce George on November 15, 1906; the next year she married Grand Duke Nicholas Nikolaievich, Junior.

Duke Sergei Georgievich of Leuchtenberg.

Duke George never did much with himself. For a time, was briefly considered as a possible successor to the murdered King Alexander I of Serbia, though nothing ever came of the idea. When he died in Paris on May 3, 1912, the Leuchtenberg dukedom passed to his eldest son Alexander. A rather unremarkable young man and a career officer in the Life Guards Hussars Regiment, Alexander served as an adjutant to Nicholas II and was on friendly terms with his family. In 1909 there were rumors that Alexander wanted to marry American Gilded Age heiress Marjorie Gould, but his father's apparent insistence that she come armed with a suitably impressive dowry brought an end to the speculation.[5] By this time the Goulds had already lost a considerable fortune through the disastrous marriage of Marjorie's aunt Anna to French Count Boni de Castellane, and were reluctant to grant yet another European aristocrat access to their much loved bank accounts.

Duke Alexander Petrovich of Oldenburg and his wife Princess Eugenie Maximilianovna of Leuchtenberg.

Oldenburg

Princess Eugenie Maximilianovna, Grand Duchess Maria Nikolaievna's youngest daughter, remained in Russia. Born March 20, 1845, she had been brought up in the Mariinsky Palace, and inherited her mother's artistic eye as well as her father's scientific interests. Most people agreed that she was the most remarkable of the Grand Duchess's children, *"the most cultured and amiable woman that could be met,"* recorded a contemporary, and a great favorite of St. Petersburg society.[6] Yet, as her future daughter-in-law Grand Duchess Olga Alexandrovna recalled, she had a *"tongue like a scorpion"* and was often given to spiteful outbursts.[7]

There was much talk of potential husbands, including proposed matches with Umberto, the Italian crown Prince, and Prince Ludwig of Bavaria, but Eugenie surprised everyone when, on January 7, 1868 at the age of twenty-two, she married Duke Alexander of Oldenburg. Born June 21, 1844, Alexander – despite his German title – was himself a Romanov descendant through Grand Duchess Catherine Pavlovna, Emperor Paul's daughter, who in 1809 had married Duke Georg of Oldenburg. Alexander and his siblings, grandchildren of the Grand Duchess, had been brought up in Russia and were regarded as members of the Imperial Family. One sister, Alexandra, had married Grand Duke Nicholas Nikolaievich Sr., while his younger sister Theresa later became the first wife of Duke George Maximilianovich of Leuchtenberg.

Alexander inherited the bulk of the family fortune, while the dowry Eugenie brought to the marriage dramatically increased the Oldenburg coffers. The newly married couple lived in considerable comfort in an immense palace in St. Petersburg, and also had a country estate in southwestern

Grand Duke Paul Alexandrovich, Prince Georg of Schaumburg-Lippe, Empress Alexandra Feodorovna, Grand Duke Sergei Mikhailovich, Tsar Nicholas II, Duke George of Leuchtenberg, Grand Duchess Marie Pavlovna Sr., Duchess Eugenie of Oldenburg, Duchess Anastasia of Leuchtenberg, Grand Duke Sergei Alexansdrovich, and Grand Duke Vladimir Alexandrovich.

Russia, a gothic mansion called Ramon. They had only one child, a son named Peter, who was born in November 1868.

Eugenie was a prominent figure in St. Petersburg society, and her salon was known for its cultivation of literary, scientific, and philanthropic ideas. Alexander commanded a regiment of the Imperial Guard and served as Adjutant-General to Alexander III, who appreciated his loyalty and avoidance of scandal. According to Grand Duke Alexander Mikhailovich, Alexander had something of an unfortunate reputation among his troops: *"His severity verged on insanity,"* the Grand Duke insisted. *"The news of his approaching inspection produced nervous breakdowns among the officers and caused a panic among the soldiers. He could not keep quiet for a second, jumping from town to town and pyramiding rows in the manner suggestive of a provincial actor engaged for the role of Frederick the Great."*[8] Both Olga Alexandrovna and Empress Alexandra later attested to Alexander's frenetic and ferocious temper, while Queen Marie of Romania complained that he was *"a mighty terror to all those working under him, whom he rules with a rod of iron."*[9]

In 1886, Alexander's close ties to the Russian Throne almost won him a crown of his own. After forcing the abdication of Alexander Battenberg as reigning Prince of Bulgaria, the Russians suggested Duke Alexander of Oldenburg as a suitable –and loyally sympathetic – replacement. The idea horrified German Chancellor Otto von Bismarck, who had no wish to see Russian influence so overtly extended into the Balkans. In the end, Bismarck had his way, and Prince Ferdinand of Saxe-Coburg-Gotha took the Bulgarian throne.

Eugenie helped establish the Red Cross in Russia and, together with her husband, founded a number of hospitals, schools, and philanthropic institutions. The couple enjoyed widespread reputations as among the most generous members of the extended Romanov family, providing for their various concerns from their own funds, although this seems not to have been entirely true. They certainly gave freely of their private fortune, but as Count Sergei Witte recalled, the Duke was ruthless in repeatedly demanding government funds to provide for their widespread endeavors.[10]

By the turn of the century, the couple's son Peter, known as "Petya," was still unmarried. Born November 9, 1868, Peter was thin, pale, and prematurely balding, a shy, unimaginative army officer whose only real asset was his family's proud lineage. Peter also had a taste for pleasure: he liked nothing better than drinking and gambling at his club, and seems to have rapidly

Duchess Eugenie of Oldenburg and her son Duke Peter Alexandrovich.

and indiscreetly made his way through a substantial portion of his family's fortune. Apparently hoping to rectify the situation, Eugenie hatched a plan. She had always been friendly with Dowager Empress Marie Feodorovna, and the two mothers seem to have conspired to marry Peter off to young Grand Duchess Olga Alexandrovna.

Born on June 1, 1882, Grand Duchess Olga Alexandrovna was the youngest daughter of Alexander III and Marie Feodorovna. She was brought up at Gatchina, enjoying the vast park and frequent walks with her adored father. Relations with her mother were more distant. *"Going to her rooms,"* Olga later said, *"was a duty laid on me....I never felt at my ease. I tried to be on my best behavior. I could never bring myself to speak naturally. She had a horror of anything beyond the bounds of etiquette and propriety."*[11]

Dark clouds soon enveloped Olga. In 1888 she was traveling aboard the Imperial Train with her family when it went off to rails at Borki, killing nearly two-dozen people. In 1894, when she was just twelve,

Grand Duchess Olga Alexandrovna.

her father fell ill and died and her brother took the throne as Nicholas II. Then in 1899 came word that her brother George had perished while living at his home in the Caucasus. Life under her mother's roof, too, was becoming a strain: naturally boisterous, hating the etiquette and ceremony surrounding her position, Olga later admitted that she felt *"as though I were an animal in a cage."*[12]

Although the Dowager Empress had always favored her sons, she at least indulged her eldest daughter Xenia, who most resembled her in stature and in dark beauty. Olga was different. No one thought she was beautiful – *"she is not pretty by any means,"* insisted one contemporary, *"but is pleasant, clever, amiable, good-natured, and very much in love with gaiety in any shape or form."*[13] First Lord of the British Admiralty Sir Jackie Fisher called her *"a peculiarly sweet creature,"* so well liked, it was said, that *"if you walked about with her you would not get bombed by an anarchist."*[14] Another chronicler admired

Dowager Empress Marie Feodorovna and her daughter Grand Duchess Olga Alexandrovna.

her *"natural, unaffected way,"* and *"delightful way of speaking to everybody, no matter what his or social position."*[15] Caring nothing about court life, Olga threw herself into painting, gaining an impressive mastery at an early age. Along with religion, painting would always be Olga's preferred means to escape the unpleasantness of life.

In 1901, and presumably at his mother's prompting, Peter of Oldenburg began circling around Olga Alexandrovna. Some fourteen years, along with any hint of shared interests or outlook on life, separated them, but this did nothing to stop what Olga later described as a plot cooked up by the two mothers. *"I was just tricked into it,"* Olga said. She was so surprised when he proposed, she insisted, *"that all I could say was 'Thank you.'"*[16] Eugenie, for her part, was no doubt delighted to have the Emperor's sister as a daughter-in-law, while Peter was believed to have welcomed both the social prestige and Olga's fortune.

Duke Peter Alexandrovich of Oldenburg.

are children no more! I am sure you won't believe what happened. Olga is engaged to Petya and both are very happy. I had to consent, but it was all done so quickly and unexpectedly that I still cannot believe it."* Nicholas II, too, was somewhat incredulous at the news: *"I cannot believe,"* he replied to his mother, *"Olga is actually* engaged *to Petya. They were probably both drunk."*[17]

Had Olga made her own choice? Despite her later memoirs, she apparently cultivated the romance with Peter, not out of love but as a means by which to escape her mother's control. Perhaps Olga feared that Marie Feodorovna would try to force her into an unwelcome, subservient role. Olga knew the tendency ran in her mother's family: the Dowager Empress's sister Queen Alexandra had deliberately kept her daughter Victoria unmarried so that she could act as a constant companion, and treated her as a kind of glorified maid. Even if Peter wasn't handsome or charming, a union with him offered Olga her freedom. Love so seldom played any real role in royal marriages; the young Grand Duchess apparently decided to cut her mother's apron strings before she lost the opportunity. And so, on July 27, 1901, she wed Peter of Oldenburg, thinking that at least she had carved out an independent future for herself.

This, at least, is the version of events Olga later presented to history. But considerable evidence suggests that the Grand Duchess was engaged in a fair bit of revisionism. In fact, she seems to have made the decision independent of her mother, who professed herself stunned at word of the engagement. In a letter to Nicholas II, the Dowager Empress wrote: *"Children*

Disillusion was not long in coming. Olga spent her wedding night alone, in tears, while her husband took to his club to gamble. According to Olga, the marriage was never consummated: *"I shared his roof for nearly fifteen years,"* she later said, *"and never once we were husband and wife."*[18] Olga didn't know what most of aristocratic St. Petersburg did: Peter of Oldenburg, it was widely believed, was homosexual.[19] One contemporary hinted that he suffered from *"a chronic disease, which left little hope of ever being cured,"* without mentioning the specifics, but his inclinations were scarcely a secret.[20]

Olga and Peter soon moved into a 200-room palace on Sergievskaya Street in St. Petersburg, where they kept separate bedrooms in wings at the building's opposite ends.[21] Peter had no interest in his wife, though he did make good use of her money: in the first year of marriage he reportedly gambled away nearly all of her $1 million dowry.[22] Unhappy, Olga suffered a nervous breakdown: her hair fell out and she spent her days alone. Then, one April day in 1903, she met a man who would change her life.

Tall and handsome, twenty-one-year-old Nicholas Kulikovsky, scion of a wealthy family of Ukrainian landowners, was an officer in Grand Duke Michael Alexandrovich's Life Guards Cuirassier Regiment.

Duke Peter of Oldenburg and Grand Duchess Olga Alexandrovna.

Olga spotted him while attending a review of her brother's regiment at Pavlovsk; she asked Michael to seat Kulikovsky next to her at luncheon and within days Olga was smitten – *"I learned that love at first sight does exist,"* she later declared.[23]

Never one to stand on etiquette, Olga decided that truth was her best ally: she went to Peter and asked for a divorce. Peter, though, was unwilling to shoulder the scandal of a failed marriage to the Emperor's sister, though he did promise her that he would reconsider in seven years if she still felt the same way.[24] In 1906, though, he did make an unusual concession to his wife, appointing Kulikovsky as his adjutant, which allowed him to live at the Sergeievskaya Street palace. It did not take long before gossip-hungry St. Petersburg learned of this unorthodox arrangement. The ménage à trois kept the capital entertained. In 1914, Princess Catherine Radziwill, using the pseudonym of Count Paul Vassili, dared mention the relationship in her book *Behind the Veil at the Russian Court*. The Emperor, she wrote, had refused any idea of a divorce, but the scandal had no effect on Olga's popularity, as most people believed she had been forced into her unhappy marriage.[25]

If Eugenie ever regretted her presumed role in the union between her son and the Grand Duchess, she never admitted it. She and Alexander went on with their philanthropic endeavors, though even their generous reputations could not spare them from the turmoil of Nicholas II's reign. In 1907, the couple attended the opening of their latest project, St. Petersburg School of Experimental Medicine. Without warning, a revolutionary burst forth from the crowd and opened fire; in the chaos, Eugenie thought that her husband was hit and she fainted. Only when she came to did she learn that Alexander was unhurt, although the bullets had claimed the life of a general standing next to him.[26]

In the summer of 1914, Duke Alexander of Oldenburg suffered serious injuries in a motorcar accident while in Germany. He was still recovering when, a few weeks later, World War I erupted. Despite his age and infirmities, Nicholas II named the Duke as Supreme Head of the Imperial Army and Navy Medical Services, given general charge of hospital and relief organizations during the conflict. But his famous temper caused difficulties: when Empress Alexandra sent an official to ask questions about a relief train, Alexander *"screamed at him and insulted him and understood everything wrong,"* she reported to Nicholas. *"He is so impossible, rushing about the room, giving others no time to speak and screaming at all."*[27]

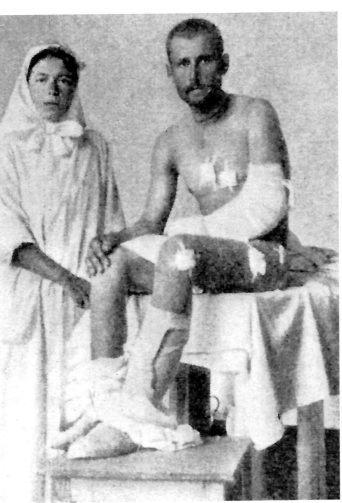

Grand Duchess Olga Alexandrovna served as a nurse during the Great War. Here she is attending to a wounded soldier.

Peter occupied himself with military duties, while Grand Duchess Olga Alexandrovna used the conflict to escape even further from her hated marriage, working as Red Cross nurse, first at Rovno near the Polish-Austrian border and then, when the army had to retreat, at Kiev. She quickly gained a reputation for her tireless devotion to the cause; wounded soldiers were stunned to find their Emperor's sister caring for them and dressing their wounds.[28] Empress Alexandra was full of admiration for her sister-in-law – *"she does work so bravely,"* she wrote to Nicholas on September 24, 1914, *"and how many grateful hearts will carry home pictures of her bright sweet being into the ranks again and others home into their villages, and her being your Sister will make the link yet stronger between you and the people."*[29]

But these charitable thoughts faded when Olga Alexandrovna began pressuring her brother for a divorce. The Grand Duchess's thoughts were never far from Kulikovsky, who had been sent to the Front with his regiment. In the summer of 1916, she begged her brother Nicholas II to transfer him to Kiev and the Emperor agreed. He was less agreeable to her constant pleas that she be allowed to divorce Peter and marry Kulikovsky. The divorce of the Tsar's sister would have caused a scandal, but Olga upped the ante by pushing for an annulment, explaining that her marriage had never been consummated. Empress Alexandra, in thrall to the notorious Rasputin and herself the subject of public scandal, railed against the idea. *"The moment when all minds are so unpatriotic and against the family,"* she warned Nicholas, *"it's hard she should think of such things; his part is unpardonable."*[30] A week later, she followed this with a stronger letter: *"I cannot tell you,"* she

Grand Duchess Olga Alexandrovna and Colonel Nicholas Kulikovsky and their sons Tikhon and Guri.

wrote to her husband, *"what bitter pain it causes me for you, your own sweet sister to do such a thing! I understand all and don't and can't grudge her longing first for liberty and then happiness, but she forces you to go against the family laws, when it touches one's own nearest it's far worse. She, an Emperor's daughter and sister! Before the country, at such a time when the dynasty is going through heavy trials and many counter-currents are at work is sad. The society's morals are falling to pieces and our family, Paul, Misha, and Olga show the example, not speaking of the yet worse behavior of Boris, Andrei and Sergei….It's wrong she puts you into this false position and it hurts me it's through her this new sorrow has been inflicted on you. What would your Father have said to all this? We have been far too weak and kind to the family."*[31]

Nicholas proved more understanding of his sister. *"Poor girl!"* he wrote to Alexandra in April 1916. *"It is only natural that she should suffer – she hid her feelings for so long that she had to give them vent at last. She aspires to real personal happiness, which she has never had."*[32] When Dowager Empress Marie Feodorovna finally interceded and announced that she supported her daughter's decision, the Emperor relented and, on October 16, 1916, the marriage between Olga and Peter was formally annulled.

Olga waited just thirty days before she wed Kulikovsky, in a small ceremony in Kiev attended only by a few officers, two nurses from her hospital, her brother-in-law Grand Duke Alexander Mikhailovich, and her mother Dowager Empress Marie Feodorovna. *"Something like new strength came to me,"* Olga recalled, *"and then and there, in that chapel, standing beside my beloved Kulikovsky, I resolved to face the future, whatever it brought. I was so deeply grateful to God for granting me such happiness."*[33] *"Olga was dressed in an old but lovely dress, like a Greek shirt,"* Alexander Mikhailovich reported to his wife Xenia Alexandrovna; *"it was white, and there were some orange flowers in her hair and round her waist."* The Grand Duchess, he thought, *"looked happy and so lovely; he [Kulikovsky] was radiant, too, and it was a joy to look at them."* Although he deemed the ceremonies "third-class," the Grand Duke thought they had been dignified. The Dowager Empress, he noted, *"was so happy that she had decided to attend the wedding."*[34] It must have been quite a task for the proud Dowager Empress to watch as her youngest daughter married a commoner.

Mecklenburg-Strelitz

The third of the families descended from the Romanovs, the Mecklenburgs, were much less prominent than the Leuchtenbergs and the Oldenburgs. The Mecklenburg-Strelitz family in Russia was a junior line of the German dynasty of Mecklenburg, descended from Grand Duchess Catherine Mikhailovna, granddaughter of Emperor Paul, and her husband Duke Georg August of Mecklenburg, who himself was a first cousin to Nicholas I's consort Empress Alexandra Feodorovna. Catherine and Georg had three surviving children: Elena, born in 1857; Georg Alexander, born in 1859; and Karl Michael, born in 1863, all considered members of the Imperial Family despite the fact that they were practicing Lutherans, not Russian Orthodox.

Born January 4, 1857, Duchess Elena was at one time considered as a bride for the ill-fated Prince Alexander of Battenberg, who lost his Bulgarian throne in 1886. Like all of Catherine and Georg's children, Elena was raised with a deep appreciation of music. Alexander Benois said that *"her voice is beautiful, full-sounding, precise.... She could easily have become one of the premier performers of Bach, but her*

Duke Georg August of Mecklenburg-Strelitz.

Duchess Elena Georgievna of Mecklenburg-Strelitz.

position and a natural self-consciousness did not allow her.[35] On December 1, 1891, she married the widowed Prince Albert of Saxe-Altenburg. For the first few years of their marriage, the couple divided their time between Berlin and St. Petersburg, but the Prince's strained relations with Kaiser Wilhelm II led them to abandon the German capital entirely. They spent some of each year at an estate in Schwerin and the rest in St. Petersburg. After Albert's death in 1902, Elena returned permanently to the Russian capital.

Duke Georg Alexander of Mecklenburg-Strelitz and his family.

Georg Alexander, the eldest son, was brought up in opulent surroundings: in the winter the family lived in St. Petersburg's Mikhailovskii Palace, and in the summers they resided at Oranienbaum on the Gulf of Finland. His grandmother Grand Duchess Elena Pavlovna instilled in him a love of music, and Georg Alexander became a skilled cellist, later organizing a private string quartet that performed to great acclaim across Europe.[36] After receiving an education at a military academy the Duke, as a German Prince, attended the Universities of Strasbourg and Leipzig, where he studied philosophy and the fine arts. On returning to Russia in 1881, he entered the Imperial Army and served as Commander of the Life Guards Dragoon Regiment.

In 1884, Georg Alexander fell in love with Nathalia Feodorovna Vanljarskaya, who served as one of his mother's ladies-in-waiting. Born in 1858, Nathalia shared Georg Alexander's love of music. At the time she was, noted a contemporary, *"past her first youth, was not pretty, and no one thought of any danger from that quarter; but she was clever and fascinating, and her charm of manner was attractive."*[37] Although a member of the minor nobility, she was not deemed of sufficiently grand birth to be an acceptable bride for a Romanov descendant. Grand Duchess Catherine was horrified on learning of her son's feelings and promptly dismissed Nathalia from her position. Georg Alexander, though, was determined. In the summer of 1889, he asked his uncle Grand Duke Friedrich Wilhelm of Mecklenburg-Strelitz, the German head of the family, for permission to marry Nathalia; the Grand Duke agreed on the condition that the union be recognized as morganatic. On February 14, 1890, and over his mother's objections, Georg Alexander and Nathalia were married in St. Petersburg.

Grand Duke Friedrich Wilhelm gave the new bride the morganatic title of Countess von Carlow, to be shared by any children the couple might have. Grand Duchess Catherine reluctantly welcomed her son and new daughter-in-law into an expansive apartment in her Mikhailovskii Palace, where they lived until 1895, when Nicholas II purchased it to house the new Alexander III Russian Museum. The couple then moved to a house at No. 46 Fontanka Canal, where they brought up their four children: Countess Catherine von Carlow, born in 1891; Countess Marie, born in 1893; Countess Nathalia, born in 1894; and Count Georg, born in 1899.

Georg Alexander and his family lived quietly. The Duke pursued his interest in music, forming the Mecklenburg String Quartet in 1896. Each Wednesday, they gave private performances for the Duke's invited guests. The Countess was careful and, in time, Grand Duchess Catherine forgave the marriage and embraced her daughter-in-law; when she died in 1894, she left Nathalia the largest part of her impressive jewelry collection. In December 1909, Georg Alexander died suddenly at the age of fifty. The following year, his widow and children all became naturalized Russian citizens. In 1913 Countess Catherine married Prince Vladimir Golitsyn; a few months later, her younger sister Nathalia died at the age of nineteen.

Karl Michael, the second of Grand Duchess Catherine's children, was born June 5, 1863, and become heir presumptive to the Grand Ducal throne of Mecklenburg-Strelitz on his brother's morganatic marriage. Like Georg Alexander, he attended the University of Strasbourg and served in the Imperial Army. When Georg Alexander died in 1909, Grand Duke Adolf Friedrich

Duke Karl Michael of Mecklenburg-Strelitz.

V of Mecklenburg-Strelitz named Michael as guardian for his nephew Count Georg. In the summer of 1914, Grand Duke Adolf Friedrich V died, and was succeeded by Adolf Friedrich VI; Duke Karl Michael decided to formally renounce his rights of succession. A week after World War I began Karl Michael became a naturalized Russian citizen and joined his regiment at the Front.

Epilogue

O n February 22, 1917, Nicholas II left Tsarskoye Selo aboard the Imperial train, headed for Stavka; that afternoon, workers at the Putilov Factory, Petrograd's largest steelworks, went on strike. Within a day, a general strike had paralyzed the capital, as some 200,000 demonstrators filled the streets demanding bread, peace, and an end to the monarchy.

In a letter to her husband, Empress Alexandra dismissed the *"hooligans"* protesting against the throne, while Alexander Protopopov, the incompetent Minister of the Interior, assured Nicholas that the situation was not serious. Both were wrong: over the following days shops were looted, buildings set aflame, and members of the Imperial Guards regiments deserted to join the burgeoning revolution. The President of the Duma sent Nicholas a cable warning that only a responsible ministry could save the situation. *"That fat Rodzianko,"* the Emperor declared, *"has again sent me more nonsense to which I shall not even bother to respond."*[1]

On learning of the mass desertions and the announcement of the Provisional Government under the authority of the Duma, Nicholas finally decided to return to the capital, but the Imperial train was blocked and forced to Northern Army Headquarters at Pskov. Over the next twenty-four hours, increasingly urgent telegrams warned the Emperor that the chaos could no longer be contained. Unwilling to share his authority and betray his understanding of autocracy, Nicholas offered a series of half-concessions that satisfied no one. By the morning of March 2, the Provisional Government and most of the generals in Nicholas's High Command demanded his abdication.

Nicholas was stunned. For twenty-two years, he'd been unable to escape the insistent voices and critical advice; even his wife was full of admonitions. Attempts to please everyone while ruling left him tired and depressed. Rather than risk plunging his country into civil war, the Emperor finally agreed to abdicate in favor of his son Alexei. Yet within a few hours he changed his mind, deciding to abdicate for himself and for his son, in favor of his brother Michael. The decision was illegal: the laws of the Russian Empire didn't allow the Emperor to renounce his son's rights. Nicholas framed it as an act of parental concern, wanting to keep the hemophiliac Alexei with him and safeguard his health, but it was also an act of vengeance against a government and a Romanov Family that had risen up against him. At 11:40 that night, Nicholas signed the abdication document, drafted by an official at Stavka; before going to bed, he wrote tersely in his diary: *"In order to save Russia and keep the army at the front quiet, such a step must be taken. I have*

agreed. I have a very heavy heart because of the things gone through. All around me there is treachery, cowardice, and deceit."²

Tsar Nicholas II and Tsesarevich Alexei Nikolaievich during the Great War.

Grand Duke Michael Alexandrovich learned of his brother's abdication the following morning while hiding in the Petrograd apartment of an aristocratic friend. Duma President Michael Rodzianko, along with the Provisional Government's new Minister of Justice Alexander Kerensky and several others, warned the Grand Duke that the unrest continued; further, there were serious legal questions as to whether

Above and left: Tsar Nicholas II and members of his retinue working in the garden and shoveling snow at the Alexander Palace.

Below: The Tsar's snowcar requisitioned by the revolutionaires during the February revolution.

Michael could accede to the throne in place of his nephew Tsesarevich Alexei. The Grand Duke decided not to risk it: he signed a manifesto announcing that he would take the throne only if called upon to do so by a future Constituent Assembly. This, of course, never happened. Rule of the 304-year-old Romanov Dynasty had come to an end.

Above: Tsar Nicholas II, Grand Duchess Tatiana, Grand Duchess Anastasia, Grand Duchess Marie, and Grand Duchess Olga.

The former Nicholas II returned to the Alexander Palace, where he and his family were arrested and kept under detention along with a hundred courtiers and servants who remained to loyally tend to their needs. Nicholas seemed, recalled Imperial tutor Pierre Gilliard, to accept his abdication *"with extraordinary serenity and moral grandeur. No word of reproach ever passed his lips."*[3] Yet he complained to Anna Vyrubova of his *"decadent, treacherous kinsmen and subjects,"* adding that *"even if all Russia now came to me on their knees I would never return."*[4] Alexandra was even less forgiving: Russia, she believed, had sinned against its monarch, and the disasters that followed were punishment for having turned its back on the Emperor.

Nicholas and Alexandra had hoped that they would be allowed to live at Livadia in the Crimea; barring this, they expected to go to England. But the new Provisional Government, after having initially gained an offer of British asylum, was surprised when word came that the invitation was rescinded. The idea of welcoming his cousins plagued King George V: public

Tsar Nicholas II in captivity at the Alexander Palace.

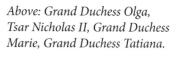

Above: Grand Duchess Olga, Tsar Nicholas II, Grand Duchess Marie, Grand Duchess Tatiana.

opinion viewed Nicholas II as a despotic and inept ruler, while Alexandra was seen as a hysterical and unbalanced woman whose belief in Rasputin had led Russia to ruin. France, too, rejected the Romanovs: they found themselves abandoned by former friends and allies, left to their uncertain fate in Russia.

Unable to send the former Imperial Family out of Russia, the Provisional Government's new leader Alexander Kerensky decided to send them away from the dangers surrounding Petrograd. On August 1, accompanied by nearly fifty retainers, over 300 specially selected soldiers, and two freight cars of luggage, they left Tsarskoye Selo. Their destination was Tobolsk, a small, isolated Siberian town, where the Romanovs lodged in the former Governor's House. Here, they would spend the winter under house arrest.

Members of the Imperial Family outside the Governor's Mansion in Tobolsk.

Life in Tobolsk wasn't uncomfortable. The townspeople, largely sympathetic to the former ruling family, bowed to the Governor's House, and sent gifts of fish, cakes, milk, eggs, and sugar. But the Bolshevik Revolution that autumn signaled a sharp change. Money grew scarce, and many of the soldiers guarding the prisoners gradually turned against them. There were petty incidents that underscored this new tone: soldiers objected to Nicholas wearing a ceremonial Circassian dagger and to the epaulets he and Alexei still sported; carved obscenities on the swing used by the Grand Duchesses; and refused to allow the Romanovs to attend church services after a priest inadvertently prayed for them at Christmas using their former titles. On February 22, 1918, the Bolshevik Government placed the prisoners on soldiers' rations, forcing them to dismiss a number of servants who had loyally accompanied them to Siberia.

Nicholas marked the anniversary of his abdication amidst this growing uncertainty. *"How much longer,"* he wrote in his diary, *"must our unfortunate homeland be torn and lacerated on the inside and outside by enemies?"*[5] The Treaty of Brest-Litovsk, by which the Bolsheviks concluded a humiliating separate peace that ceded Finland, the Baltic Provinces, Poland and the Ukraine to Germany, left the former Emperor horrified. It was, he complained, a *"disgrace"* and *"suicide"* for Russia.[6]

Empress Alexandra Feodorovna.

It was April 22, according to the Julian Calendar which the Bolsheviks had recently adopted, when a mysterious figured identified as Vassili Yakovlev arrived in Tobolsk at the head of an armed detachment with orders to bring the prisoners to Moscow. On learning that Alexei had suffered a serious attack of hemophilia and could not yet be moved, Yakovlev decided to transport Nicholas immediately, with his family to follow. Hearing this, Nicholas flatly refused to go. Yakovlev implored him to agree: if he failed, he warned, Moscow was likely to

Tsar Nicholas II and Tsesarevich Alexei Nikolaievich sawing wood in Tobolsk.

215

dispatch another, less sympathetic man. Promising that Nicholas could take with him anyone he liked, the commissar told the former Emperor that they would leave early the next morning.

The former Emperor was sure that the Bolsheviks wanted him to sign the Treaty of Brest-Litovsk, optimistically still believing that his name carried political cachet in the new Soviet regime. Alexandra agonized between remaining with her ill son or accompanying her husband. Finally, she decided to join Nicholas, commenting, *"If he is taken alone, he'll do something stupid, like he did before. Without me, they can force him to do whatever they want."*[7] This allusion to his abdication revealed just how little faith Alexandra had in her husband's judgment. And so, early the next morning, she joined Nicholas, their daughter Marie Nikolaievna, and a few attendants in a convoy of carts that sped away from Tobolsk and into the Siberian dawn.

Grand Duke Michael Alexandrovich and his secretary Nicholas Johnson.

Arriving at Tyumen, Yakovlev learned that Bolsheviks from the Ural Mountain city of Ekaterinburg planned to intercept his train and seize the prisoners. He tried a desperate gamble, heading first to Moscow then abruptly switching east in an attempt to outrun the rebels but his efforts failed. Outnumbered and outgunned, Yakovlev was forced to take the Romanovs to Ekaterinburg, where on April 30 they were imprisoned in an ornate little villa called the Ipatiev House. The

three Grand Duchess and the Tsesarevich arrived from Tobolsk on May 23 and joined their parents behind the tall wooden fences ringing the Ipatiev House. None of the Romanovs would leave their last prison alive.

By this time, Grand Duke Michael Alexandrovich had also arrived in the Urals. After declining to accept the throne, he had returned to Gatchina, living quietly with his wife Natasha and son George. In March 1918, the Petrograd Soviet arrested him and exiled him to the city of Perm. After a few days in jail, the Grand Duke was allowed substantial freedom: he took rooms in an elegant hotel for himself and the five servants who had accompanied him, including his private secretary Nicholas Johnson. After arranging for Danish diplomats to smuggle their young son George out of the country, Natasha traveled to the Urals to spend a week with her husband.

Russia was now in the midst of a civil war, as Bolsheviks faced the combined forces of the White Army and thousands who belonged to the Czech Legion. Advances by the counter-revolutionary forces across Siberia worried the Ural Bolsheviks, who feared that the imprisoned Romanovs might be freed. On the night of June 12, acting under the authority of the Ural Regional Soviet in Ekaterinburg, Perm Bolsheviks took Michael and

Johnson from their hotel, drove them out into a forest near the Motovilikkhi Factory, and shot them.[8]

The Ural Regional Soviet used the Grand Duke's murder to test Moscow's reaction. Authorities in Perm sent a telegram to Moscow saying that the Grand Duke had been kidnapped. Although the Soviet government made a half-hearted effort to investigate, their obvious lack of concern led the Ural Regional Soviet to anticipate a similar reaction if they killed the Romanovs in Ekaterinburg.

The former Nicholas II turned fifty in the Ipatiev House

The Ipatiev House, Ekaterinburg.

Nicholas II spent 78 days in the Ipatiev House: he turned 50 there on May 19, 1918 – *"it seems strange even to me,"* he wrote in his diary.[9] The Romanovs spent seventy-eight days in the Ipatiev House. For most of the Twentieth Century, history portrayed this as one long exercise in coarse cruelty and humiliation: Bolshevik guards who tormented the prisoners; spat at them; snatched food out of their hands; made the Grand Duchesses sing lewd songs; and sexually taunted the young women by following them to the bathroom. In fact, many of these tales were nothing but fabricated monarchist propaganda. Most of the guards treated the prisoners well and actually came to like Nicholas and his children; some even talked of helping them to escape. Alexandra alone failed to elicit any sympathy.

But if deliberate humiliation was lacking, a monotonous, terrible uncertainty reigned in the Ipatiev House. The prisoners could only wonder what their fate would be, especially after a series of smuggled letters promised a rescue that never came. The Romanovs had no idea that the Ural Regional Soviet had sent the letters to elicit favorable replies that they could then use to justify an eventual execution to authorities in Moscow. The local Bolsheviks took their first steps on this path with the murder of Grand Duke Michael Alexandrovich; at the beginning of July, they replaced most of the interior guards at the Ipatiev House, who had become too friendly and thus unreliable, with workers from local factories. There was also a new commandant, Yakov Yurovsky, appointed to tighten security at the Ipatiev House in anticipation of an eventual execution.

As the first week of July 1918 slipped into the second, the White and Czech forces were fast approaching Ekaterinburg; it was obvious that the Bolsheviks would soon have to flee the city. Deciding that the Romanovs presented a problem, the Ural Regional Soviet sent an emissary to Moscow to present the case for the prisoners' execution. But Moscow refused to sanction such action; the only apparent concession was agreement that the Ural Regional Soviet could execute the former Nicholas II should the circumstances demand it. On July 16, Ekaterinburg decided to act on its own authority and shoot the Romanovs and the four retainers imprisoned with them. To give themselves cover, they sent a late night telegram to Moscow, warning that if the Soviet Government had any objections it should reply at once; without waiting for an answer, the Ural Regional Soviet went ahead with the executions.

At half-past one on the morning of July 17, Yurovsky woke the sleeping prisoners and asked them to dress, explaining that they had to be moved immediately to avoid danger. An hour later, the commandant led the small group through the Ipatiev House and down to a small basement room. Nicholas carried Alexei, who was still unable to walk following his last hemophiliac episode in Tobolsk; Alexandra followed, leaning on a cane, trailed by her four daughters, Dr. Eugene Botkin, footman Alexei Trupp, cook Ivan Kharitanov, and maid Anna Demidova. Once in the room Alexandra asked for chairs; Yurovsky had two brought in, one for the Empress and one for the Tsesarevich, before briefly leaving, having closed the double doors behind him.

When Yurovsky returned he was no longer alone: nearly a dozen men crowded around him in the doorway, facing the prisoners. The commandant read from a piece of paper: *"The Executive Committee of the Soviet Workers', Peasants', and Soldiers' Deputies of the Urals have resolved to shoot you."* Confused, Nicholas asked him to read it

The "death" room in the basement of the Ipatiev House.

again, asking, *"What? What?"* In reply, Yurovsky and his men pulled out revolvers and began firing into the room. Nicholas fell first, shot repeatedly; Alexandra was knocked from her chair by a bullet to the head, and Trupp and Kharitanov also died in the initial volley. But smoke from the revolvers quickly filled the room, making it impossible for the assassins to see the other victims and leaving most of the prisoners still alive as bullets ricocheted around the cellar. Several of the executioners fled, horrified by the scene; when the others returned, they found a room of screaming would-be victims. One by one they eventually fell still, shot, stabbed and beaten into silence.

Less than twenty-four hours after the Ekaterinburg executions, the Ural Regional Soviet continued its bloody vengeance against five members of the Romanov Dynasty who had come to be imprisoned at the Siberian town of Alapayevsk. After the February Revolution, Grand Duke Sergei Mikhailovich had eventually returned to Petrograd, living with his brother Nicholas Mikhailovich at their immense palace on the Neva. The Bolshevik Revolution marked a downward turn: all male Romanovs had to report to register with the Cheka and were forbidden to leave Petrograd. In March of 1918, most of them were exiled to the Ural Mountain town of Vyatka. This included Sergei, his secretary Feodor Remez, and Princes Ioann, Konstantin, and Igor Konstantinovich, as well as Prince Vladimir Paley, son of Grand Duke Paul Alexandrovich's second, morganatic marriage.

At the beginning of May 1918, the Ural Regional Soviet moved the prisoners to Ekaterinburg, where they were kept under guard at a hotel a short distance from the Ipatiev House. A few days later, Grand Duchess Elisabeth Feodorovna arrived in the city, having been arrested in Moscow. With her came a nun of her nursing order, Sister Barbara. The Ural Regional Soviet transferred all of these prisoners some 120 miles west, to Alapayevsk, on May 18, confining them in the disused Napolnaya School on the edge of town.

Late on the evening of July 17, members of the Alapayevsk Cheka arrived at the school and told the prisoners that they were being transferred. It was after midnight when the convoy of horse-drawn carts arrived at an abandoned mineshaft deep in a nearby forest. The prisoners, who had been blindfolded and bound, were beaten over their heads and flung into the shaft; Sergei Mikhailovich, who at the last moment tried to run, was shot in the head before being tossed into

Grand Duchess Elisabeth Feodorovna.

the mine. His last words had been a plea: *"Tell me why?"* he begged. *"I have never been interested in politics."*[10]

Four more Romanovs fell victim to the Bolsheviks. For the first few months following the February

The Napolnaya School, Alapayevsk.

Revolution, Grand Duke Paul Alexandrovich and his family remained in their elaborate villa at Tsarskoye Selo. Bolsheviks raided the property after they came to power; arrested, the Grand Duke was held at Petrograd's Smolny Institute before his ill health won him release. In early 1918, with his assets confiscated, the Grand Duke moved his family to the nearby villa of his nephew Boris Vladimirovich. The same poor health that had won his release from the Smolny also prevented Paul Alexandrovich from joining his son Vladimir and the male members of the Romanov Family when they were exiled to Vyatka in the spring of 1918.

At the time of the Revolution Grand Duke Nicholas Mikhailovich had been living in remote rural exile, a punishment placed upon him by Nicholas II after the Grand Duke wrote unflattering letters about the Empress. After the Emperor's abdication, Grand Duke Nicholas Mikhailovich returned to his Petrograd palace, which he briefly – and oddly – shared with a contingent of Bolsheviks.[11]

Almost immediately following the fall of the monarchy, George Mikhailovich resigned his military post and applied to the Provincial Government for permission to leave Russia and join his estranged wife and daughters in England, where they had been living since the outbreak of World War I. While the Provisional Government was willing to allow George to leave Russia, the British Government was not prepared to accept him, or any Romanov Grand Duke. Instead, George was given permission to move to Finland, where he lived from June 1917 until the spring of 1918.[12]

Grand Duke Nicholas Mikhailovich.

George moved around in Finland, varying his residences from Helsingfors to country villas and villages; he was constantly alert for the opportunity to escape to Sweden, where he thought he could stay until joining his family. Unable to find any route out that did not require travel documents, George, always a stickler for protocol, decided in early 1918 to apply for a passport from the new Soviet Government. This proved to be a fatal miscalculation: on April 3 the Bolsheviks arrested George in Finland and brought him back to Petrograd, ordering him not to leave the city.[13]

In the spring of 1918, both brothers had been sent to Vologda, where Grand Duke Dimitri Konstantinovich soon joined them. When the Revolution exploded in Petrograd in February 1917, Grand Duke Dimitri Konstantinovich was living in his new mansion on the Petrogradsky Quay.[14] Almost completely blind by this time, Dimitri was dependent on his Adjutant,

Grand Duke Paul Alexandrovich.

Grand Duke Dimitri Konstantinovich.

Grand Duke George Mikhailovich.

Alexander Korotchenzov, for his daily existence. The Grand Duke's widowed niece, Princess Tatiana Konstantinovna, also lived in the house with her two children, helping to take care of her uncle.

In November 1917, following the Bolshevik Revolution, city newspapers published a notice summoning all Romanovs remaining in Petrograd to the offices of the Cheka. Princess Tatiana accompanied Dimitri to the Cheka, in the hope that her presence would ameliorate any pressure or abuse her uncle might be likely to receive at the hands of the revolutionaries. But in the end, this trip to the Cheka building was only to be registered, and Dimitri was allowed to return to his house, where he was ordered to remain until further notice – further notice meaning when the Bolsheviks had decided what they wanted to do with the Romanovs still remaining in Russia.

In the spring of 1918 the Petrograd Bolsheviks decided to send the male members of the Imperial Family not already imprisoned into internal exile. Interestingly, Dimitri Konstantinovich was asked to make a choice between Vologda, Olonets or Vyatka.[15] He chose Vologda, a city close to Petrograd, which was still in danger of being overrun by the German Army. Perhaps Dimitri made a purposefully strategic decision. On April 18, 1918, Dimitri Konstantinovich, Princess Tatiana, her two children, and Alexander Korotchenzov departed Petrograd for Vologda, joining Nicholas Mikhailovich and his brother George.

At first the Romanovs in Vologda enjoyed considerable freedom, walking around the town, shopping, taking coffee, and visiting each other freely. Their only requirement was to report to the Cheka office once a week. In the middle of May, Colonel Alexander von Leiming, one of Dimitri Konstantinovich's adjutants, arrived in Vologda with news that passage had been prepared to for the elderly Grand Duke to leave Russia for Finland; perhaps lulled by the peaceful and unthreatening life he led in Vologda, Dimitri Konstantinovich refused to leave his family.

On July 14, 1918, two days before the execution of the Imperial Family in Ekaterinburg, and three days before the execution of the Romanovs at Alapayevsk, the three Grand Dukes were taken to a small, walled garrison under guard. Grand Duke George wrote to his wife: "*We were each given a cell, and later on were joined by Dimitri. I saw him arriving through the iron bars of my window, and was struck by his sad expression. The first twenty-four hours were hard, but after that, they luckily allowed us to have our camp beds and also our clothes. There is no one in the prison but we three....They* [the Latvian guards] *treat us like comrades, and have not locked our cells after the second day, while they allow us to walk in the small garden.*"[16]

Prince Gabriel Konstantinovich.

The three Grand Dukes remained in their walled compound for only a few weeks. By the end of July, they were back in Petrograd, detained in the small jail at Cheka headquarters for questioning and interrogation by agents. Their next destination was Shpalernaya Prison, where each Grand Duke was assigned a cell to which he was restricted except for several times a day, when they were allowed to gather in the courtyard to smoke and exchange news.

A surprise awaited Dimitri Konstantinovich at Shpalernaya: his nephew Gabriel Konstantinovich, brother of Tatiana, who had been scooped up by the Cheka in Petrograd in the middle of July. Gabriel Konstantinovich had registered at the Cheka, along with the rest of the Romanov males in Petrograd in November 1917. But aside from that, Gabriel had been left alone by the authorities, and he had found a measure of freedom in his life post-Revolution that he had not imagined before. Like many Romanovs before him, Gabriel had a ballerina girlfriend, and he wanted to marry her – and here he was, with no Imperial command to say no. His mother, the Grand Duchess Elisabeth Mavrikievna, argued against it, but Gabriel set aside her opinion, and married his ballerina, Antonina Nesterovskaya, on April 9. On his way to the Church for his wedding, he passed two of his brothers, who had just watched Antonina go by in a wedding dress; it wasn't until later that they put it all together.[17]

When the Bolsheviks finally got around to arresting Gabriel, they were told that he was suffering from tuberculosis; this stalled matters until July, when he was taken to Shpalernaya. Before the end of the year, Gabriel, who really was sick by this time, was released from prison with the assistance of Maxim Gorky, whose wife was a close friend of Antonina. Still with Gorky's help, Prince Gabriel and Antonina were able to quickly leave Russia, setting up home in Paris by 1920.[18]

Grand Duke Paul Alexandrovich and his children Grand Duke Dimitri Pavlovich and Grand Duchess Marie Pavlovna Jr.

In August, Grand Duke Paul Alexandrovich, the last Grand Duke allowed his freedom, was also arrested and incarcerated at Shpalernaya. Owing to his ill health, he was taken to the prison hospital in December. Here he saw his wife for the last time. She brought the Grand Duke's two young daughters Irina and Nathalia to see him before sending them to Finland while she remained in Petrograd, pressuring Maxim Gorky to release her husband. A month later, her efforts apparently paid off: Gorky won from Lenin permission to have the four Grand Dukes imprisoned in Petrograd released.

But before he could deliver the news, the Petrograd Cheka took matters into their own hands. Early on the morning of January 28 the ailing Paul Alexandrovich was taken on a stretcher to the Fortress of St. Peter and St. Paul; soldiers soon brought Grand Dukes Nicholas and George Mikhailovich and Dimitri Konstantinovich into the courtyard. As they passed the Cathedral, the Grand Dukes crossed themselves. *"All of your mannerisms,"* a soldier mocked, *"do not change the fact that we are going to shoot you, and we are not going to bury you under slabs of marble, but under slabs of wood."* Nicholas Mikhailovich handed his pet cat to one of the guards, saying, *"Look after it, in memory of me."* The soldiers lined up the prisoners in front of a trench, which already contained a number of bodies, and opened fire. The two Mikhailovich brothers and Dimitri Konstantinovich tumbled into the grave, shot in the head. Paul Alexandrovich, too weak to stand, was killed on his stretcher before his body was tossed into the common grave. For their service, each executioner received a book and a loaf of bread; one of them also stole George's boots.[19]

A last glimpse of "Imperial" Russia – The wedding of Prince George of Battenberg and Countess Nadejda of Torby.

Colonel von Leiming, Dimitri Konstantinovich's adjutant, had been in the habit of sending food each day to Shpalernaya for the Grand Duke. On the morning of January 29, 1919, it was returned to him with a note stating that the Grand Duke had no further use for it. Von Leiming went in search of news, and was told of his Grand Duke's fate. It is said that von Leiming went to the place of execution and either bought or stole the body of Dimitri Konstantinovich, which he rolled in a rug and had carried from the Fortress to the garden of a certain address in Petrograd, where it was secretly buried until such time that it could be properly interred with full Imperial honors.[20] Perhaps it is possible that there is one last Romanov mystery to solve.

By this time, both of Paul Alexandrovich's children from his first marriage were safely outside of Russia. Grand Duchess Maria Pavlovna, after a lifetime of disillusion, finally found temporary happiness with Prince Sergei Putyatin, son of the former palace commandant at Tsarskoye Selo. On September 6, 1917, she married him at Pavlovsk and the couple quietly settled in Petrograd. In late June of the following summer, she gave birth to a son, Prince Roman. By now the situation in Russia was rapidly deteriorating, and Marie decided to flee with her husband: with the same lack of maternal instinct she had shown toward her first son Lennart, the Grand Duchess decided to leave her new baby with her husband's family. Eventually she made her to Odessa and to Romania at the invitation of her cousin Queen Marie. Grand Duke Dimitri Pavlovich remained in Persia, where he had been exiled after his part in Rasputin's murder, but left for Tehran shortly after the February Revolution. There he befriended the British Consul, who in 1918 was instrumental in winning the Foreign Office's permission for the Grand Duke to settle in England.

Several Romanovs, of course, were already in England. Grand Duke Michael Mikhailovich, living in his continued exile. His only son, also named Michael but called "Boy," completed his education at Eton in 1916 and began to pursue a career in art and design. He had a true talent and was much admired for his style, which was derivative of the Chinese porcelains which he collected, but his devotion to recreational drugs was beginning to gain him a bad reputation.[21]

In 1916 Grand Duke Michael Mikhailovich's youngest daughter Nadejda married Prince George of Battenberg, son of Prince Louis of Battenberg and his wife Victoria, Empress Alexandra's eldest sister, in a wedding attended by the King and Queen, Queen Alexandra, and many members of the Royal Family. In the summer of 1917, with anti-German feeling on the rise, King George V bestowed new, Anglicized names on many of his relatives living in England, including Nadejda and her husband, who now became Mountbattens.

That same summer, Michael and Sophie's eldest daughter Anastasia married the extremely wealthy Sir Harold Wernher. The wedding, on July 20, brought security to the stateless and formerly Imperial Mikhailovichi. By this time the Grand Duke's Russian incomes had disappeared, and Michael and Sophie had to alter their flamboyant way of life. They moved to a more modest house located near Regent's Park, helped by a gift of some $10,000 from King George V.[22] Sir Harold Wernher's wealth now came in extremely handy, and almost immediately he took on the task of supporting his in-laws through their financial difficulties.

The outbreak of World War I had found Grand Duchess George and her two daughters Princesses Nina and Xenia staying at Claridge's Hotel in London. The Grand Duchess chose not to undertake the arduous return trip to Russia across Europe, but instead moved her girls to Harrogate in Yorkshire, where she worked to establish four army hospitals, which she funded herself. Grand Duke George kept up a long and extensive correspondence with his daughter Xenia, with whom he was particularly close. Isolated and unhappy in Yorkshire, the Princesses began to resent their mother's Victorian ways and her control over their fate. They wanted to return to Russia: fortunately, though, their mother overruled them, thus likely saving their lives.[323]

Grand Duke Konstantin Konstantinovich (KR) with his brother Grand Duke Nicholas Konstantinovich and his wife Nadejda Dreyer.

The Revolution claimed four members of the Konstantinovichi Family, Princes Ioann, Konstantin, and Igor Konstantinovich, when the Bolsheviks killed them at Alapayevsk, and Dimitri Konstantinovich when he was shot in Petrograd in 1919. The first Konstantinovich to die, however, did not fall victim to the Bolsheviks. In distant Tashkent, the disgraced Grand Duke Nicholas Konstantinovich greeted news of the Revolution by dispatching a congratulatory telegram to Alexander Kerensky. On January 26, 1918, the Grand Duke died in Tashkent. For decades rumor insisted that the Bolsheviks had executed him; in fact, he died at home, from bronchitis, in the care of his daughter Darya. He had the singular distinction among the Romanov Family of being the only member of the former Dynasty to be given a full, state funeral by the Bolsheviks, attended by thousands in Tashkent, with a Guard-of-Honor of Red Army soldiers that surrounded his coffin as it lay in state in the Cathedral of St. George. The most decorated and fierce revolutionaries were picked to lower his body into a special vault. Thirty-five years after his funeral, in 1952, the Cathedral was torn down and the location of the Grand Duke's remains are unknown.[24]

In the early summer of 1917, the widowed Grand Duchess Elisabeth Mavrikievna was living in the central wing at Pavlovsk with her two youngest children, Prince George and Princess Vera. Until his arrest and exile, her son Ioann had also lived here with his wife Princess Elena Petrovna and their two children, Prince Vsevelod and Princess Catherine, as had Princess Tatiana and her two children. Elisabeth Mavrikievna's elderly sister-in-law Queen Olga of Greece had been living at Pavlovsk since returning

Grand Duchess Elisabeth Mavrikievna, Queen Olga, and Grand Duchess Marie Pavlovna Sr.

to Russia following her husband's assassination.

Tatiana was the first to leave Pavlovsk, moving to Petrograd to care for her Uncle Dimitri, who had recently arrived from the Crimea. The Princess had followed him when he was exiled to Vologda, but in July 1918 she heard rumors that Nicholas II had been executed in Ekaterinburg. Thoroughly shaken, she gathered up her children and caught the train to Petrograd, accompanied by Alexander Korochenzov. He found her a small apartment on Permskaya, and she lived there very quietly and unobtrusively, looking after her children and plotting their escape with Korochenzov. The resourceful Adjutant was able to finagle an appointment to an outpost in the Ukraine and, having obtained a Georgian passport for

Princess Tatiana Konstantinovna.

the Princess and the children from a man called Usov – not an entirely illegal idea, as Tatiana was a Georgian from her marriage to the late Prince Konstantin Bagration-Mukhransky – they fled the former Imperial capital for Kiev. Here, they were able to cross the border into Romania with the help of Queen Marie, finally arriving safely in Switzerland.[25]

In the summer of 1917, the Provisional Government sent a contingent to Pavlovsk, informing the family that they intended to catalogue its art and other contents in order to protect against looting. No longer feeling that this country palace was quite theirs, the remaining family, minus Queen Olga, who would not leave her childhood home, decamped for the Marble Palace in Petrograd; none of them ever saw Pavlovsk again. The elderly Queen soon faced the uncertainties of life in Russia alone, but still refused to leave. If Russia was in turmoil, so, too, was Greece. In June 1917 Prime Minister Eleftherios Venizelos forced King Constantine I into exile, the throne taken by Olga's grandson Alexander. More Russian than Greek, Olga decided to ride out the storm in her native country, amid increasing shortages of food and invasions of the palace by mobs of soldiers. After the Bolshevik Revolution, the Queen finally decided that the time had come to leave Russia, but it took many months of appeals to her late husband's family in Denmark before arrangements could be

made for Olga to travel to neutral Switzerland in 1919.

The rest of the Konstantinovichi remained in Petrograd. When the Bolsheviks sent Prince Ioann to the Urals, his adventurous wife Princess Elena followed. Unlike her husband she was not under arrest and could move freely. Leaving her two children, three-year-old Vsevelod and two-year-old Catherine, in Petrograd with Grand Duchess Elisabeth Mavrikievna, Elena spent several weeks with Ioann after his transfer to Alapayevsk. When Ioann read in the newspapers of the upheaval and disturbance in Petrograd, and concerned for his mother and his children, he asked Elena to travel back to the city and try to use her position as a foreign Princess to gain some sort of egress from the country for the remaining family.

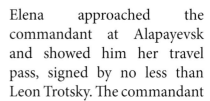
Queen Olga of Greece.

Elena approached the commandant at Alapayevsk and showed him her travel pass, signed by no less than Leon Trotsky. The commandant informed her that Trotsky had no power in the Urals and that she should go to Ekaterinburg to obtain travel orders from Alexander Beloborodov, the head of the Ural Regional Soviet, unaware of the trouble he was unleashing.[26] Arriving in Ekaterinburg, Elena began a two-pronged campaign. She divided her days between harassing Beloborodov for travel documents and for permission to visit the Imperial

Family then being held at the Ipatiev House, and harassing the British Consul Thomas Preston to place the Ural Romanovs under his protection and spirit them out of the country. Elena proved an admirably headstrong Princess, but she was slowly creating a situation in which her freedom was seriously jeopardized. One day, no doubt frustrated at the delays and refusals meeting her requests and demands, she marched up to the front door of the Ipatiev House, announced herself as the daughter of the Serbian King, and demanded to see the Emperor and his family. This was a serious miscalculation on her part, which was compounded by the simultaneous arrival of four men detailed to retrieve the Princess and bring her back to Petrograd. One of these men was her husband's Aide-de-Camp, Sergei Smirnov, and a second was a Serbian Army officer, dispatched by her father. Beloborodov, under great stress as the White Army approached Ekaterinburg, cut the Gordian knot and arrested and imprisoned Elena and all of her supporters in the Ekaterinburg City jail.

Princess Elena Petrovna.

After the executions in Ekaterinburg and Alapayevsk, and just a few days before the White Army captured the city from the Bolsheviks, Elena and her group were hurriedly taken from the jail, bundled onto a train, and sent to another prison, this one in the city of Perm.[27] Elena would remain there for five months, during which time she saw

the members of the household and suite who had survived their various passages to the Urals; among these were the ill-fated Countess Hendrikova and Mademoiselle Schneider.

In Petrograd, Grand Duchess Elisabeth Mavrikievna was slowly ceding territory in her own palace. The Bolsheviks pushed further and further into the Marble Palace until the Grand Duchess and the four children in her charge were relegated to a small apartment in the corner of the great edifice. The Grand Duchess had friends in Sweden and Belgium – where she and her husband had become great friends with both sets of Kings and Queens – who agitated for her release and safe passage from Russia. But she was determined not to leave the country while her sons remained in danger. She survived the last months of 1918 by selling off small pieces of art and jewelry, carefully entrusted to her remaining servants.

Princess Vera, twelve-years-old at the time, recalled that winter in later years, when she and her mother and brother were ordered out into the courtyard and street to shovel snow to clear a path for the Bolshevik automobiles.[28] Eventually, word reached Petrograd of the deaths of Ioann, Konstantin and Igor in the Urals. Princess Tatiana and her children had already fled the country, and Antonina Nesterovskaya had wangled Prince Gabriel's release from Shpalernaya Prison. There

Duchess Elena of Mecklenburg-Strelitz.

was nothing further the Grand Duchess could do in Russia, and so she accepted help from the Swedish Embassy, which arranged her passage from Russia aboard a ship crossing the Baltic. It took eight days for the *Angermanland* to reach Stockholm, during which time it was stopped and searched twice – once by the Bolsheviks and the second time by the Germans. Both parties sought the Grand Duchess's jewels, which she had thoughtfully entrusted to the diplomatic pouch, and so she arrived in Sweden with a reasonable amount of wealth in hand.[29]

The redoubtable Elena of Serbia, lost in Ural prisons for almost six months, was eventually transferred to Moscow, where she was held in an apartment in the Kremlin. Somehow, she managed to impress the fearsome Bolshevik Yakov Peters, who bought her food, books, clothes, perfumes and other luxuries. He also helped her gain an exit visa through the Norwegian Embassy, and even sent a large bouquet of flowers to her on the evening of her departure, apologizing for not being available to accompany her to the station. On arriving in Sweden, Elena was soon reunited with her children.[30]

Other members of the Imperial House also fled Russia in these years. Alexander, 7th Duke of Leuchtenberg, who in January 1917 had contracted a morganatic marriage, spent many months imploring British Ambassador Sir George Buchanan to intercede on behalf of Nicholas II and his family, but to no avail. Briefly arrested by the Bolsheviks in late 1917, Alexander eventually managed to flee across Siberia and escape Russia. Alexander of Oldenburg and his wife Princess Eugenie fled to Paris, as did their son Prince Peter. Duchess Elena of Mecklenburg-Strelitz escaped to Denmark in 1918, while her brother Karl Michael made his way out of the country through the Caucasus.

The Crimea saw the greatest concentration of Romanovs after the February Revolution: in all, fifteen members of the Imperial House lived in alternating states of freedom and arrest on the peninsula until April 1919. Dowager Empress Marie Feodorovna headed this contingent, which included her two daughters Xenia and Olga and their families; Grand Duke Nicholas Nikolaievich and his wife Anastasia, and Sergei and Elena, her two children by the 6th Duke of Leuchtenberg; and Grand Duke Peter Nikolaievich, his wife Militsa, and their three children Prince Roman and Princess Nadezhda and Marina. Marie Feodorovna lived with Xenia and her husband and children at Grand Duke Alexander Mikhailovich's estate of Ai-Todor on the Black Sea; Nicholas Nikolaievich and Anastasia took up residence at their villa, Tchair; and Peter, Militsa and their children lived at their immense Dulber Palace. Xenia's only daughter Princess Irina Yussoupov divided her time between her husband's family and a small villa she and Felix had built above the Black Sea.

As time went on tensions cemented. Xenia and Alexander were estranged, the Dowager Empress treated her son-in-law Nicholas Kulikovsky like an outcast, and Marie Feodorovna struggled to adjust to the immense changes brought about by revolution. *"My poor mother-in-law,"* Alexander Mikhailovich recalled, *"greatly grieved over the uncertainty surrounding the fate of her Imperial son, could not stand this new sobriquet added to our former titles. I tried in vain to explain to her the pitiless course of all revolutions....She could not comprehend why the family that had given Russia Peter the Great, Alexander I, and her own beloved husband, Alexander III, should be accused of being hostile to the Russian people."*[31]

In the first few months there were moments of joy, as Princess Nadezhda Petrovna married Prince Nicholas Orlov, and Duchess Elena of Leuchtenberg wed Count Stephan Tyshkevich. But early on the morning of May 8, mobs of pistol-brandishing soldiers from the Sevastopol Soviet raided Ai-Todor, Tchair, and Dulber, pillaging the residences, pilfering through papers, collecting anything

Grand Duchess Xenia Alexandrovna.

they deemed to be a weapon, and confiscating letters and diaries, and even the Dowager Empress's Bible. Marie Feodorovna, recalled her daughter Olga, berated the men with such language that they finally threatened to *"take the old hag"* with them; only Alexander Mikhailovich's quick thinking managed to save the situation.[32]

Soon an order came from the Provisional Government in Petrograd ordering the Romanovs placed under house arrest: only Princess Irina, who had renounced her dynastic rights on marrying Prince Felix Yussoupov, and Olga Alexandrovna, who had married a commoner, were exempted. A guard from the Sevastopol Soviet surrounded the estates. The Romanovs were now truly prisoners.

The overthrow of the Provisional Government by Lenin's Bolsheviks marked a downturn in the fortunes of the Crimean prisoners. One day a new commandant,

Grand Duchess Olga Alexandrovna.

Zadorozhny, appeared on behalf of the Sevastopol Soviet. The Yalta Soviet wanted to execute the prisoners, and Zadorozhny, *"a murderer but a charming man,"* as Olga Alexandrovna wittily called him, decided to move all of the Romanovs to Dulber, where he could better protect them from revolutionary vengeance.[33] Olga, who in August had given birth to a son, Tikhon, was again exempted from the order, as were Princess Irina and Princess Nadezhda, the latter then living in an apartment in Yalta.

Zadorozhny fully expected an armed confrontation between his men and a mob from the Yalta Soviet. For five uneasy months, the Romanovs at Dulber joined the Sevastopol Soviet in manning machine gun stations along the roof, awaiting an attack. In March 1918 the situation became critical after the Treaty of Brest-Litovsk was signed. With the invading German Army expected in the Crimea any day, the Yalta Soviet again clamored for the prisoners' executions and there were armed standoffs at Dulber.

Princess Irina Alexndrovna.

Alexander Mikhailovich, refused to reside with him and instead took up residence at Harax, the estate of Grand Duke George Mikhailovich, with her daughter Olga, her husband and her son. After selling Tchair, Nicholas Nikolaievich and his wife Anastasia remained at Dulber.

No one knew what to expect. Rumors of Nicholas II's execution at Ekaterinburg reached the Crimea but the Dowager Empress dismissed them; she also refused a constant stream of offers to leave the country for her own safety. But the fall of Imperial Germany in November 1918, and the subsequent departure of the Kaiser's troops, once again left the peninsula in chaos. In December, when a contingent of British naval vessels arrived, Alexander Mikhailovich took advantage of the situation to leave Russia, taking with him his son Andrei and the latter's pregnant wife Elisabeth. The Grand Duke hoped to travel to Versailles, to intercede with the victorious Allies and convince them to support the White Army in Russia's Civil War; his efforts came to nothing, as no one of importance would receive him and listen to his pleas. Olga Alexandrovna, by this time again pregnant, also decided to leave with Kulikovsky and their young son Tikhon, much to her mother's dismay.

The arrival of the Kaiser's soldiers at Dulber undoubtedly saved the prisoners' lives, though rescue by the Germans was a new humiliation for the Romanovs. Freed from house arrest by their former enemies, they once again scattered: Xenia Alexandrovna, her husband, and their sons eventually returned to Ai-Todor; the Dowager Empress, openly warring with her son-in-law

Although the Dowager Empress continued to refuse offers of rescue, and the remaining

On board HMS Nelson – Top, left: Grand Duke
Nicholas Nikolaievich Jr. Top, right: Princess Marina
Petrovna. In the middle: Prince Roman Petrovich;
Above: The Dowager Empress Marie Feodorovna;
Right: Grand Duchess Anastasia Nikolaievna.

Grand Duke Alexander Mikhailovich with his mother-in-law the Dowager Empress Marie Feodorovna behind him.

Romanovs felt obligated to remain in Russia, the decision was finally made for her when King George V sent several British naval vessels to the Crimea with orders to evacuate the prisoners no matter their own wishes. On April 11, 1919, the *HMS Marlborough*, a British Iron-Class Dreadnought, sailed away from Yalta, carrying Marie Feodorovna and the remaining Romanovs. They stood on deck, watching the shoreline recede, as sailors on a nearby vessel sung *God Save the Tsar* to the group of pathetic refugees.

Ironically, the last Romanovs to leave Russia belonged to the once mighty Vladimirovichi. As might be expected for the controversial family, their experiences were fraught with accusations of treason, high drama, and more than a little style. Grand Duke Kirill Vladimirovich would never quite escape the opprobrium surrounding his actions during the February Revolution, when he had pledged members of his *Garde Equipage* to the Duma. This was not, as his enemies later claimed, the act of a revolutionary but rather the desperate move of a man attempting to preserve the only legitimate ruling authority in Petrograd and thus save the throne. Nor, as has often been claimed, did the Grand Duke order his men to abandon their posts guarding the Alexander Palace at Tsarskoye Selo: several weeks before the Revolution the Government ordered the regiment back to Petrograd, replacing them with some reserves and troops from an infantry regiment, who later revolted under their commander Lieutenant Miasokdov-Ivanov and his subordinate Lieutenant Kouzmin.[34] The Grand Duke's only provocative move amidst the turmoil came when he raised a red flag over his house on Glinka Street, but even this was apparently an effort to spare it – and his family, including two young daughters and a then-pregnant Victoria Feodorovna – from the wrath of the revolutionary mob.[35]

Grand Duke Kirill Vladimirovich.

Concern for the pregnant Victoria Feodorovna led Kirill to flee Russia in the summer of 1917. Although Grand Duke Alexander Mikhailovich later painted a thrilling escape, with Kirill carrying his pregnant wife across the frozen Gulf of Finland as Bolshevik soldiers chased them, the couple in fact left Petrograd aboard a train in June.[36] They were safely in Finland when, in August, Victoria Feodorovna gave birth to a son, whom the couple called Wladimir after the Grand Duke's father. Eventually they made their way to Germany and later to France.

Following the February Revolution, Boris Vladimirovich was quickly arrested by the Provisional Government and confined to his dacha at Tsarskoye Selo, suspected of treason. He was freed in July, in time to join British agent Albert Stopford in sneaking into the

In exile – Standing: Grand Duke Andrei Vladimirovich, Grand Duke Boris Vladimirovich, and Grand Duke Kirill Vladimirovich. At front, seated: Grand Duchess Victoria Feodorovna, and Grand Duchess Elerna Vladimirovna.

Vladimir Palace in Petrograd to retrieve his mother's fabled collection of jewelry, which Stopford smuggled out of the country to England.[37] Fortune seemed to be with Boris: he left Petrograd before the Bolshevik Revolution, taking his mistress Zenaide Rachevskaya to the Caucasus, where his mother Grand Duchess Vladimir and his younger brother Grand Duke Andrei were living at the resort town of Kislovodsk. A year passed quietly before the Bolsheviks arrested the two brothers: they were saved

Grand Duchess Marie Pavlovna Sr. at Contrexéville in happier times. A ghost of her former self, Marie Pavlovna Sr. died there soon after safely escaping from Russia. She was buried in a small chapel in Contrexéville.

from a firing squad only because Boris had once assisted the Bolshevik commander in his previous life as a painter. Once freed, the brothers fled into the surrounding mountains, hiding until the White Army liberated the town in September 1918.

Like her sister-in-law, the proud Grand Duchess Vladimir refused to leave Russia, but sensing the inevitable, Boris had no such hesitations and fled with his mistress to the Crimea, where he tried in vain to obtain passage aboard a British naval vessel. Eventually the pair fled via Constantinople to Italy where, in July 1919, Boris married Zenaide.

Throughout the ever-dutiful Andrei remained at his mother's side, having been joined in Kislovodsk by Mathilde Kschessinska and her son Vladimir. When the Bolsheviks advanced on the town at the end of 1919, the Grand Duchess finally agreed to leave; Andrei, with Mathilde and Vladimir in tow, escorted her to Novorossiysk on the Black Sea, where they lived in a battered railway car.[38] But the Civil War was lost, and finally the Grand Duchess decided that there was no reason to remain in Russia. On March 3, 1920, accompanied by Andrei, his mistress Kschessinska, and her son Vladimir, Marie Pavlovna boarded an Italian liner bound for Venice.[39] Marie Pavlovna passed away at Contrexéville in Switzerland on September 6, 1920. The proud Grand Duchess had been the last Romanov to leave Russia; she was the first to die in exile, a symbol to the end of elegance, sophistication, and power.

Afterword

A Russian Exile: The Romanovs in the Urals and Siberia

by Katrina Warne

Perm

Perm lies on the western side of the Ural Mountains. It is this mountain chain that divides Europe from Asia. They are the oldest mountain range in the world and they have sunk making them little more than hills now. Perm is 891 miles from Moscow along the Trans-Siberian railway. Yegoshikha (as Perm was originally called) was founded on May 4, 1723.

In mid-July 1914 Grand Duchess Elisabeth Feodorovna arrived in Perm with her sister Princess Victoria of Battenberg and her niece Louise (later Queen of Sweden). Elisabeth Feodorovna said she wanted to go to Alapayevsk, but it

The former Korolev Rooms in Perm.

seems she didn't make it there as she had to return to St. Petersburg as World War I broke out on July 19, 1914 (OS) on the feast of St. Seraphim of Sarov. It was *"her destiny to go there later"* Father Stephen Lukanin said. Father John of Kronstadt is reported to have said that, *"there is a black cross above Perm district."* At that time Ekaterinburg and Alapayevsk belonged to Perm district. However, in her memoirs that were written in about 1942 Victoria Milford Haven (the former Princess Victoria of Battenberg) said that Elisabeth did go to Alapayevsk in 1914. Following her arrest in Moscow on 27 April 1918 Elisabeth Feodorovna would spend a few days in Perm again, this time staying in the Assumption Convent. On 1st May she left Perm for Ekaterinburg and her ultimate fate in Alapayevsk.

On March 19, 1918, Grand Duke Michael Alexandrovich arrived in Perm with his secretary Nicholas Johnson. At first Michael was confined in the medical unit of a prison. After a week he was released and allowed to live at the Korolev Rooms on Sibirskaya Street, which had been re-christened "Hotel No. 1." This building is still there, and it is now painted yellow and white. It is lived in by people who work at the opera house. Of course, the interior is no longer the same as when Michael stayed there,

The commemorative plaque to Grand Duke Michael outside the former Korolev Rooms in Perm.

but it is possible to identify which of the first-floor rooms were his from the outside. One of them had a balcony and that is still there. There are two plaques on the front of the house commemorating Michael's stay there. A black plaque with a lighted candle on it reads *"From this building Hotel Korolyovsky on 12 June 1918 secretly and deceitfully were abducted and taken away for execution Grand Duke Mikhail Alexandrovich Romanov and his secretary, English subject Brian Johnson. Eternally remembered innocently murdered!"* Another plaque with a relief of Michael reads *"In this building in 1918 lived Grand Duke Mikhail Alexandrovich Romanov (1878-1918)."* It is interesting to note that Johnson is described as an English subject, although this is not true. There is also some confusion over his Christian name as he is called Nicholas or Brian in various books.

Michael had to report to the local police once a day, but this left him with time to walk along the River Kama. Sometimes he sailed on the river. His wife Natasha joined him for a period and at Easter 1918 they both attended the service at the Peter & Paul Cathedral. Michael and Natasha looked at several properties in which they might live as a family if they had to live in Perm for the long term. In Michael's diary he mentions attending the opera. Michael made many friends within the local nobility.

Late in the evening of June 12, 1918, three men arrived at the Korolev Rooms and took both Grand Duke Michael and Johnson away. The usual story is that they were both driven some distance to the edge of the city and shot in the early hours of the morning. So far neither body has been recovered. On the outskirts of Perm a memorial church to Michael has been built. A local journalist who has researched the matter feels that there is a fifty-fifty chance that the church has been built on the location of the shooting. There are various theories as to how the bodies were disposed of. One is that they were burnt in a local industrial furnace. However, it is known that it wasn't working at the time. Another is that the bodies were thrown into the River Kama. A third theory is that some peasants found the bodies and buried them in a local cemetery in unmarked graves.

Tyumen and Tobolsk

Tyumen in Western Siberia is 1,332 miles east of Moscow and 430 miles from Perm. It was in Tyumen that the Imperial Family arrived from Tsarskoe Selo by train near midnight on August 17, 1917, leaving

Tyumen at six the following morning on a river boat called the "Rus" to travel to Tobolsk. In Tyumen, on the bank of the River Tura, they have built a memorial to the Imperial Family where they boarded the "Rus." There is a large Orthodox cross and a white stone plaque with a quotation from Nicholas' diary entry on it for August 4/17, 1917. This begins *"Crossing Urals, perceptibly cooler. Passed Ekaterinburg early morning"* and it is followed by the diary entry quoted in *"A Lifelong Passion"* – *"We advanced unbelievably slowly, in order to reach Tyumen late at night. There the train went right up to the jetty, so that we were able to get straight onto the steamer."*

Northeast from Tyumen towards Tobolsk and after about 55 miles away is the village of Pokrovskoe where Gregory Rasputin was born. Pokrovskoe is built on the bank of the River Tura and it is situated on the main road from Tyumen to Tobolsk on what was the Great Siberian highway. Rasputin's house was destroyed in the 1980s. The village street looks like it hasn't changed very much since Rasputin's time except for tarmac road down the middln

Tyumen - the bank of the River Tura, where the Imperial Family boarded the "Rus" om their way to Tobolsk.

Another 100 miles further northeast is Tobolsk, which was the capital of Siberia until 1894 when the capital was moved to Omsk as the Trans-Siberian Railway passed further to the south of the city. It was founded in 1587 on the steep right bank of the River Irtysk opposite the mouth of the River Tobol. Tobolsk is built on two levels. On the upper level is the modern city with a Kremlin, which overlooks the lower town. A lot of houses in the lower town aren't inhabited possibly because of regular flooding There is a very steep hill with a passage way down to the lower town via a ravine next to the Kremlin. This passage way and Tobolsk itself is described in detail by Baroness Buxhoevden in *"Left Behind."*

The vast white stone Kremlin replaced the former wooden Kremlin on the Trinity cape above the River Irtysk. The main cathedral in the Kremlin is called St Sophia and this was built in the 17th century. It was used only in the summer and in the winter, they used the nearby Cathedral of the Intercession of the Virgin. In the Cathedral of the Intercession is the coffin containing the body of St John of Tobolsk and the coffin containing the body of Archbishop Hermogen who was in Tobolsk at the same time as the Imperial Family. He had previously fallen out of favour with them because of his opposition to Rasputin. On 10 July 1891, the future Nicholas II visited Tobolsk on his return from his Far East tour. He visited the Kremlin and the cathedrals. The Museum of Fine Art near the Kremlin was also visited by Nicholas. It has a feather pen in it, which was used by Nicholas on his visit.

The Governor's Mansion, Tobolsk.

On August 18, 1917, the Imperial Family sailed past Pokrovskoe and arrived in Tobolsk on two days later. They had to stay on the boat until the Governor's House was made habitable for them. They moved into the white stoned two-storied house on 26 August. It is a substantial building, which is very well maintained. It stands in a large square and the house on the left-hand side of the square from it is where the family's retainers lived. This building was known as the Kornilov House. On the opposite side of the square to the Governor's House is a chapel built in honour of Alexander II. It was built by the same architect that constructed the Church on the Spilled Blood in St Petersburg after Alexander II's assassination. From looking at old photographs of the house taken in 1917 and 1918 a large part of what is now the square was fenced off to form the garden of the house and this included the area where Nicholas II was pictured sawing wood.

The Governor's House was restored as it was when the Imperial Family lived there, and it is now turned into a museum with more rooms restored to the way they looked in 1917-1918. In 1991, on the upper floor they recreated the Tsar's study in the corner room on the left-hand side overlooking the square. It looks very much like a photograph taken of the study when Nicholas used it, but the only furniture inside that was there in Nicholas' time are some wooden chairs. The walls are covered in deep blue wallpaper. There is a desk with photographs on it of Alexander III and Empress Alexandra. There is also an icon corner and a desk covered with various books published in Russian about the family.

On April 26, 1918, Nicholas, Alexandra and Marie left Tobolsk for Ekaterinburg. The next day they changed horses in Pokrovskoe right under the windows of Rasputin's house. They boarded a train at Tyumen for Ekaterinburg. On May 20, 1918, the other three Grand Duchesses and Alexei left Tobolsk by the "Rus" for Tyumen, where they too boarded a train for Ekaterinburg.

Ekaterinburg

Ekaterinburg is the capital of the Urals and it is 1,130 miles from Moscow. It is the fourth largest city in Russia. It was founded on November 18, 1723 and named after the Empress Catherine I. The Trans-Siberian railway arrived here in 1888. The name of the city was changed to Sverlovsk in 1924 and it was renamed Ekaterinburg in 1991.

Nicholas II, Empress Alexandra and Grand Duchess Marie arrived in Ekaterinburg on 30 April 1918 and the remaining members of the family arrived there a little over three weeks later, on 23 May. They were housed in the Ipatiev House on Vozenesensky Prospekt east of the River Iset. The Imperial Family were murdered in the early hours of July 17, 1918 in a semi basement room of the house. On July 27, 1977, Boris Yelstin destroyed the house on the instructions of Moscow. In fact, what he did was to level the house that was built into the side of a steep hill. Before the Cathedral on the Blood was built on the site of the Ipatiev House, archaeological excavations were carried out that revealed the site of the murder room or *"the shooting room"* as the guide book calls it.

The Cathedral on the Blood of all Saints, Ekaterinburg.

This now forms a corner chapel in the lower church of the cathedral. In this corner area the walls are plain white. There is an altar in the middle made of pink rhodonite. To the front, the area is surrounded by low gates, so that there is no access to the public. To the right of this area there are plaques to the family. The high ceiling of the chapel has a tent-like cover that is topped by a crown, which is visible in the upper church. The main iconostasis of the lower church has icons of the Imperial family members on it.

The full name of the cathedral is The Cathedral of the Blood in Honour of All the Saints Radiating in The Land of Russia. It is a white building with golden domes with gold crosses on top. There is a main dome surrounded by four smaller ones. The domes are covered in titanium nitrate rather than gold as this is cheaper. The base of the cathedral containing the lower church has brown bricks walls. The upper church is a more conventional orthodox church. It is very bright and light inside. At the front of the cathedral to the left of the entrance of the lower church is a statue of the seven members of the family grouped around a cross. At the lower level

Memorial cross to the Imperial Family, Ekaterinburg.

241

is Nicholas II carrying Alexei in his arms with Grand Duchess Olga on the left and Grand Duchess Tatiana on the right. Up some steps to the higher level of the upper church and at the back of the cross is Empress Alexandra with her right hand held up shielding her eyes. To the left is Grand Duchess Marie and to the right Grand Duchess Anastasia.

Lots of people attended the founding of the cathedral on September 23, 2000. The finished cathedral was consecrated on 16 July 2003. People gathered outside to listen on loud speakers as the capacity of the upper church is restricted to 1,000 people. On July 16-17, 2003 an all-night liturgy and vigil took place. This was followed by *"The March of the Cross"* to the site of the Four Brothers Mine

The Pig's Meadow burial site.

along the same road that the bodies had been carried 85 years before. These events now take place every year and are known as *"The Romanov Days."*

The Pig's Meadow burial site.

Next door to the cathedral is a small wooden chapel dedicated to Grand Duchess Elisabeth Feodorovna, which was built in the late 1980s. Near the chapel are a white cross and a metal cross on a marble plinth. These had originally been erected on the site of the Ipatiev House before the cathedral was built. There is also a stone slab that lists the names of the family and their retainers.

Eighteen miles along the road towards Koptyaki through silver birch and pine forests is the Four Brothers mine where the Bolsheviks first tried to dispose of the Imperial Family's bodies. It is known to the Russians as mine No 7 and it is at the centre of a complex known as the Monastery of St. Martyrs on Ganina Yama (Ganin's Pit). It was opened in 2000. There are seven churches (one for each member of the family) and a monastery.

The main church of the complex is called the Church of the Holy Royal Martyrs, which is in the immediate proximity of the mine. The church altar is decorated with a reliquary cross said to have belonged to the family and a ring that is said to have belonged to Grand Duchess Tatiana. The church of St. Nicholas the Miracle Worker contains an icon that is also said to have belonged to The Imperial Family, which they are reputed to have prayed to during their time in Ekaterinburg.

What is left of the mine shaft is out in the open and not contained within a church. It is quite a large area of sunken ground with wild flowers growing in it. It is surrounded by a covered wooden walkway so that one can walk around the area of the mine. There is a large wooden Orthodox cross on a stone plinth in front of the mine. Next to the entrance to the walkway is a sign in English that reads *"After July 17, 1918 near this mine No 7 the bodies of the Holy Royal Martyrs of Russia were burned with the use of petrol and then destroyed by sulphuric acid."* A stone memorial in Russian is nearby, the left-hand side of which says something similar *"Not far from this mine in July 1918 fire and sulphuric acid were used on the honest and upright bodies of the consecrated Royal Family Martyrs and their faithful servants."* On the right-hand side is a quote from Amos Chapter 2 verse 1. According to Empress Alexandra's diary Grand Duchess Tatiana had read to her from this book on the last day of her life. The entry in her diary for 3/16 July reads *"Tatiana stayed with me & we read: Bk. of the Pr. Amos and Pr. Obadiah."* In the eyes

Ganina Yama – the Four Brothers Mine.

of the Russian Orthodox Church, this is where the family were buried and not in the mass grave where most of their bodies were discovered in 1979.

In keeping with the description of the area in books the road has a railway line alongside it for part of the way and there was a level crossing not far from the entrance to the memorial site known as the *"Pig's Meadow."* There is a wooden gateway at the entrance with a sign across it saying – *"Memorial to the Romanovs."* The site is very simple. In a clearing in the middle of silver birch trees there is a large Orthodox cross at the head of the mass grave, which is covered with railway sleepers and surrounded by marigolds. The cross had a large red and white floral wreath on it. There was a smaller cross at the foot of the grave, which also had a floral tribute on it. A stone plaque says how the murderers tried to hide the bodies here; who found them and when; and, when they were taken away for burial. Another memorial plaque commemorates who was buried there. The remains of the Tsesarevich Alexei and Grand Duchess Marie were found in 2007 not far from the main grave.

There were other Romanov prisoners brought to Ekaterinburg during part of the time that the Imperial Family were there. On May 3, 1918, Grand Duke Sergei Mikhailovich, Princes Ioann,

The Holy Trinity cathedral – Alapayevsk.

Konstantin and Igor Konstantinovich and Prince Vladimir Paley arrived in the city along with Ioann's wife Elena Petrovna. They stayed at the Atamanov Hotel on Glavni Prospect. Shortly afterwards, Elisabeth Feodorovna arrived in Ekaterinburg with two nun companions – Barbara Yakovleva and Catherine Yanishevna.

The various books on Grand Duchess Elisabeth Feodorovna do not agree on where she stayed in Ekaterinburg in 1918. Some say that she stayed at the Atamanov Hotel with the other Romanovs and some say that she stayed at Novotikhvinsky Convent. This convent, which supplied food to the Ipatiev House, was revived in 1994.

In Alapayevsk, they have a copy of a document (the original of which is kept in archives in Ekaterinburg) dated May 19, 1918. All the Romanovs had to sign this document to say that they would all be at Ekaterinburg railway station on 20 May to be transported to Alapayevsk. Their signatures are in the following order going down – Grand Duchess Elisabeth Feodorovna, Prince Ioann, Princess Elena Petrovna, Prince Konstantin, Prince Igor, Prince Vladimir Paley and Grand Duke Sergei Mikhailovich. Locals report a conversation that took place in Ekaterinburg between Grand Duke Sergei Mikhailovich and a man called Kabanov, who was a member of the Cheka. Sergei Mikhailovitch asked, *"Where are you taking us?"* Kabanov replied that *"It's too hot for you in Ekaterinburg and so we are taking you to the Alapayevsk dachas."* Sergei Mikhailovitch answered *"I have visited all the facilities around Ekaterinburg and I can't recall any dachas in Alapayevsk."* This group of Romanov prisoners all left Ekaterinburg for Alapayevsk on May 20, 1918.

Alapayevsk

Alapayevsk is approximately 100 miles north of Ekaterinburg. It is a large town rather than a city with a population of about 55,000 people who live mostly in wooden houses. The town is very much a backwater.

The Romanov party (Grand Duke Sergei Mikhailovich, Princes Ioann, Konstantine and Igor Konstantinovich, Prince Vladimir Paley, Ioann's wife Princess Elena Petrovna, Grand Duchess Elisabeth Feodorovna and her two nun companions – Barbara Yakovleva and Katherine Yanishevna and some retainers) arrived in Alapayevsk on May 7/20, 1918. At Alapayevsk station armed revolutionaries met them and transported them away in a peasant's cart. They were taken to the Napolnaya School, which translates

The Napolnaya School, Alapayevsk.

as *"the school on the field."*

The Napolnaya School is still a working primary school. The single storey red brick building was constructed in 1915. Outside the school is a plaque saying - *"Memorial Rooms of The Blessed Grand Duchess Elisabeth Feodorovna."* Another underneath says that this is *"The Napolnaya School where the blessed Grand Duchess Elisabeth Feodorovna spent her final earthly months and that she had previously dwelt as a Sister of Charity at the Martha and Mary Convent."*

The school has a main corridor down the center with three large rooms off each side. The first room on the left from the front entrance was occupied by Grand Duke Sergei Mikhailovich and Prince Vladimir Paley, along with Sergei's secretary Feodor Remez and Vladimir's valet Ceslav Kronkovsky. The middle left room was occupied by Princes Konstantin and Igor Konstantinovich. Prince Ioann Konstantinovich and his wife Elena Petrovna lived in a room on the opposite side of the corridor. The far-left hand corner room was occupied by Grand Duchess Elisabeth Feodorovna and her companions Barbara

Memorial room to Grand Duchess Elisabeth Feodorovna – The Napolnaya School, Alapayevsk.

Memorial cross at the Sinyachikha Mine.

Yakovleva and Katherine Yanishevna. This room is now dedicated to The Grand Duchess. The room contains icons, photographs and mementoes of Grand Duchess Elisabeth Feodorovna and the other members of The Romanov Family that were imprisoned with her. It is a large room, which is very light as it has large windows on two sides of the room that are covered in floor length net curtains. The school is considered to be a holy place. The guide in the memorial room who appeared to be a lay sister began by saying *"The Lord Preserve this corner"* and added that *"The Lord preserved the places connected with the family."*

The guide told us about Grand Duchess Elisabeth Feodorovna's time at the school saying that *"St Elisabeth was praying and crying and getting ready to die bearing a cross given to her by God,"* which meant that *"Elisabeth would have cried for Russia not for herself."* The guide at the school told us that *"The locals sympathised by providing food to the prisoners. They respected most of all Grand Duchess Elisabeth Feodorovna as some of them had heard about what she had done in Moscow and they called her the "Mother of Russia."*

Many of the prisoner's belongings were given away, but some were later returned when the museum was opened. We also saw a copy of the funeral register, the original of which is kept in Ekaterinburg. This lists their names and ages at the time they died as follows:

Grand Duke Sergei Mikhailovich – 49
Grand Duke Ioann Konstaninovich – 32
Grand Duke Konstanin Konstaninovich – 28
Grand Duke Igor Konstaninovich – 24
Grand Duchess Elisabeta Feodorovna – 54
Prince Vladimir Paley – 23
Maid of Honour to Grand Duchess Elisabeta Feodorovna, Barbara Yakovleva
Feodor Remez – 40

No age is given for Sister Barbara and very little is known about her.

Originally, the Romanovs had been free to walk around the town and attend church services, but after Grand Duke Michel Alexandrovich's murder in Perm a far more rigorous regime was imposed in Alapayevsk. On June 20, Elena Petrovna left Alapayevsk to re-join her children. Most of the retainers were expelled on 21 June. The two nuns, Barbara Yakovleva and Katherine Yanishevna, were forced to leave Grand Duchess Elisabeth Feodorovna. They were both taken back to Ekaterinburg, both pleaded to be allowed to return to her, but only Barbara was allowed to return. Katherine Yanishevna disappears from the history books at this point and it is not known what happened to her.

The mine where the Romanovs, Sister Barbara and Feodor Remez were murdered is about 10 miles north of Alapayevsk near the village of Sinyachikha. The Romanovs and their retainers were taken to the mine by horse drawn carts with one person per cart during the night of July 17/18, 1918. The carts weren't able go right up to the mine, so they had to walk the last part of the way one by one, so the others didn't see what was happening to the person in front of them. It isn't known exactly what order they died in, although the order in which bodies were recovered perhaps

The Sinyachikha Mine.

indicates this. It is generally agreed that Grand Duchess Elisabeth was thrown in first and that Feodor Remez died last. Accounts as to exactly how they died differ, but most agree that they were all thrown in alive except for Grand Duke Sergei Mikhailovich, who was shot first as he resisted the assassins led by Vasily Ryabov.

The mine is now inside a walled monastery called the Novomuchenikov Monastery or the New Martyrs Monastery. The site was opened in 1992. There is a tall white gatehouse at the entrance to the site with bells in it and it is topped by a single gold onion dome. There is a large red brick-built church and a small white chapel topped by a single blue dome dedicated to Grand Duchess Elisabeth. The mine where they all died has collapsed. It is surrounded by pine trees and there is a large Orthodox cross for veneration by the mine. A large mound of earth is next to it, which presumably came out of the mine. The guide we had met at the Napolnaya School said that it was a coal mine and not an iron ore mine as it often written. She added that it had never been a working mine, but it had only been used to search for coal. No coal was in fact found there and so

Prince Vladimir Pavlovich Paley.

The coffins of Grand Duchess Elisabeth and Sister Barbara, Jerusalem.

it had been abandoned for fourteen years by 1918. It was about 60 metres deep and partly filled with water. She also told us that the shaft didn't go straight down, but that it descended in a step pattern. If what we were told is true, then this explains why a number reports of the murders at Alapayevsk talk about some of the Romanovs sitting on "ledges" after they were thrown down the shaft.

After their bodies were recovered from the mine shaft around October 8 to 11 (NS), their bodies were brought to the Holy Trinity Cathedral, where the Romanov prisoners had been allowed to walk to. A funeral service was held on October 5/18 and a burial service on October 6/19, 1918 when the coffins were placed in the crypt under the cathedral. The coffins were kept in the in the crypt from October until July 1919. Then as Alapayevsk was about to be re-taken by the Red Army, Father Seraphim Kuznetsov removed all the coffins from the crypt. He travelled with them as far as Beijing. In 1920, when Victoria Marchioness of Milford Haven heard that the body of her sister Grand Duchess Elisabeth Feodorovna was there along with that of her companion Sister Barbara, she arranged for Father Seraphim to take both coffins to Jerusalem where they now rest in the Russian Orthodox Church of St Mary Magdalene on the Mount of Olives. The rest of the coffins stayed in Beijing and it is not exactly clear what has become of them.

(*) Most of this afterword is taken from articles written after a tour of this region by the author, the publisher, and other Eurohistory subscribers in 2005. Apart from describing some of the places visited and some historical background, it also includes the opinions of Russian people that we met about The Romanovs and their fate. Obviously, this is just their opinions, but I feel that it is of interest to share what Russians themselves believe to be true about their own history.

The grave of Grand Duchess Elisabeth, Orthodox Church of St Mary Magdalene, Mount of Olives, Jerusalem.

Endnotes

Prologue

1. Cited in Lieven, page 167
2. King, *"Diaries of Grand Duke Andrei Vladimirovich,"* entry of March 8, 1917, page 50
3. Alexander Mikhailovich, *Once*, page 240
4. Infanta Eulalia of Spain, page 171
5. Vyrubova, page 99
6. Kokovtsov, page 168
7. Naryshkina-Kurakina, page 206
8. Wortman, pages 2:489-90
9. Elchaninov, pages 17-21, 28, 133
10. Cited, Lieven, pages 199-200
11. Sazonov, pages 201-02
12. Cantacuzene, *Revolutionary Days*, page 15

Chapter 1

1. Buxhoeveden, *Before the Storm*, page 317
2. Paleologue, *Ambassador's*, page 1:98
3. Mossolov, pages 6, 72; Lowe, page 322; Surguchev, pages 44-49
4. Witte, page 40
5. Bing, page 33
6. Ibid., page 36
7. Taylor, page 54
8. Witte, page 359
9. Shelayev, Shelayeva, and Semenov, page 12; Lieven, page 35; Warth, page 6; Wortman, page 2:312
10. Cited, Sorensen, page 114
11. Grand Duke Konstantin Konstantinovich, Diary entry of December 7, 1894, in GARF, F. 660, Op. 1, D. 41
12. Vorres, page 67
13. Tsesarevich Nicholas, Diary entry of December 21, 1891, in GARF, F. 601, Op. 1, D. 55
14. Witte, pages 124-25
15. Queen Marie of Romania, page 1:330
16. Gibbes, page 2
17. Mossolov, page 16
18. Izwolsky, page 264
19. Mossolov, page 7
20. Naryshkina-Kurakina, page 162
21. Tsesarevich Nicholas, Diary entry of May 31, 1884, in GARF, F. 601, Op. 1, D. 19
22. Marie Louise of Schleswig-Holstein, page 50
23. Queen Marie of Romania, page 1:332
24. Vacaresco, page 162
25. Tsesarevich Nicholas, Diary entry of April 1, 1892, in GARF, F. 601, Op. 1, D. 56

26. Grand Duke Sergei Alexandrovich to Tsesarevich Nicholas, letter of October 14, 1893, cited in Montefiore, page 479
27. Princess Alix of Hesse to Tsesarevich Nicholas, letter of November 8, 1893, in Maylunas and Mironenko, pages 32-33
28. Tsesarevich Nicholas to Princess Alix of Hesse, letter of December 17, 1893, in Maylunas and Mironenko, page 34
29. Princess Alix of Hesse to Grand Duchess Xenia Alexandrovna, letter of March 30, 1894, in Maylunas and Mironenko, page 45
30. Lee, *Empress Frederick*, page 169
31. Tsesarevich Nicholas, Diary entry of April 8, 1894, in GARF, F. 601, Op. 2, D. 33
32. Radziwill, *My Recollections*, pages 308-09
33. de Schelking, page 18
34. Witte, page 197
35. Princess Alix of Hesse, writing in Tsesarevich Nicholas's diary, entry of October 15, 1894, in GARF, F. 601, Op. 1, 33
36. Alexander Mikhailovich, *Once*, page 168
37. Gilliard, page 48
38. Hall, *Little Mother*, page 183
39. Gibbes, page 6
40. Cockfield, page 173
41. Vyrubova, page 34; Voyekov, page 208; Radziwill, *Secrets of Dethroned Royalty*, page 75; Vassili, pages 229-30; Cantacuzene, *My Life*, pages 224-26
42. Mossolov, page 91
43. Izwolsky, pages 245-47
44. Mossolov, pages 19-20
45. See Elchaninov, pages 17-29
46. Vyrubova, pages 55-56
47. Witte, page 190
48. Krasnii Arkhiv, Volume V, 1926, page 105; Kokovtsov, pages 166-68
49. *The Times of London*, February 2, 1905
50. Bing, page 188
51. Cited, Pipes, page 20
52. King, "Diaries of Grand Duke Andrei Vladimirovich," entry of March 8, 1917, page 51
53. Wortman, pages 2:394, 506-10; Verner, pages 239-41; Elchaninov, pages 123-27
54. Witte, pages 242-43; A. A. Polovtsov, "Dnevnik," in Krasnii Arkhiv, Volume 3, 1923, page 170
55. King, *"Diaries of Grand Duke Andrei Vladimirovich,"* entry of March 8, 1917, page 51
56. Gurko, page 90
57. Unpublished report to Kaiser Wilhelm II from Count Paul von Hintze, dated 1910, in authors' collection
58. King and Wilson, *Fate*, page 43
59. Nicholas II to Alexandra Feodorovna, September 22,

1914, in GARF, F. 540, Op. 1, D. 102

60. King, *"Diaries of Grand Duke Andrei Vladimirovich,"* entry of December 29, 1916, page 43

61. Buchanan, *Dissolution*, page 129

62. Alexandra Feodorovna to Nicholas II, August 22, 1915, in GARF, F. 601, Op. 1, D. 1149

63. Father George Shavelsky, statement in GARF, F. 640, Op. 1, D. 79

64. Alexandra Feodorovna to Nicholas II, August 22, 1915, in GARF, F. 601, Op. 1, D. 1149

65. Alexandra Feodorovna to Nicholas II, February 22, 1917, in GARF, F. 601, Op. 1, D. 1151

66. Buchanan, *Mission*, page 1:238

67. King, *"Diaries of Grand Duke Andrei Vladimirovich,"* entry of December 29, 1916, page 43

68. Nicholas II to Alexandra Feodorovna, September 9, 1916, in GARF, F. 640, Op. 1, D. 114

69. Nicholas II to Alexandra Feodorovna, November 10, 1916, in GARF, F. 640, Op. 1, D. 106

70. Nicholas II to Alexandra Feodorovna, December 4, 1916, in GARF, F. 640, Op. 1, D. 106

71. Alexandra Feodorovna to Nicholas II, September 23, 1916, in GARF, F. 601, Op. 1, D. 1151

72. Wilton, *Russia's Agony*, page 36

73. Marie Pavlovna, *Education*, pages 248-49

74. Alexandra Feodorovna to Nicholas II, December 17, 1916, in GARF, F. 601, Op. 1, D. 1151

75. Nicholas II to Alexandra Feodorovna, December 18, 1916, in GARF, F. 650 Op. D. 111

76. Nicholas II, Diary entry of December 21, 1916, in GARF, F. 601, Op. 1, D. 254

77. Hall, *Little Mother*, page 273

78. Francis Lindley to Foreign Office, January 15, 1917, in McKee, page 283

79. Kokovtsov, pages 40-02

80. Botkin, page 125

81. Paleologue, *Ambassador's*, pages 3:151-53

Chapter 2

1. Gilliard, page 76

2. Dehn, page 76

3. Vyrubova, page 77

4. Buxhoeveden, *Alexandra Feodorovna*, pages 158-59

5. Marie Pavlovna, *Education*, pages 14-15

6. Buxhoeveden, *Alexandra Feodorovna*, page 153

7. Gilliard, page 19; Dehn, page 75; Vyrubova, page 78

8. Buxhoeveden, *Alexandra Feodorovna*, pages 153-54

9. Eager, page 66

10. Botkin, page 27

11. Buxhoeveden, *Alexandra Feodorovna*, pages 153, 159; Vyrubova, page 78; Gibbes, in Wilton, *Last Days*, page 54

12. Gilliard, page 20

13. Buxhoeveden, *Alexandra Feodorovna*, page 154;

Vyrubova, page 79; Gilliard, page 20; Dehn, page 76

14. Vyrubova, page 79

15. Buxhoeveden, *Alexandra Feodorovna*, page 154; Vyrubova, page 79; Gilliard, page 75

16. Nicholas II to Alexandra Feodorovna, May 29, 1916, in GARF. F. 640, Op. D. 110

17. Buxhoeveden, *Alexandra Feodorovna*, page 154

18. Gilliard, page 75

19. Buxhoeveden, *Alexandra Feodorovna*, page 92

20. Ibid., page 155; Gilliard, page 75; Dehn, page 78; Vyrubova, page 78

21. Gilliard, page 75

22. Dehn, page 78

23. Eagar, page 39

24. King Edward VII to Nicholas II, June 19, 1901, in Royal Archives, RA, VIC W60/125/A, cited in McKee pages 160-61

25. Buxhoeveden, *Alexandra Feodorovna*, pages 155-56; Dehn, page 78; Gilliard, page 75

26. Grabbe and Grabbe, page 69

27. Gilliard, page 78

28. Gilliard, pages 72, 78-79; Buxhoeveden, *Alexandra Feodorovna*, page 155

29. Gilliard, page 72

30. Nicholas II, Diary entry of July 30, 1904, in GARF, F. 601, Op. 1, D. 247

31. Mossolov, page 28

32. Cited in Rappaport, page 18

33. Voyekov, pages 182-83

34. Gilliard, page 40; Buxhoeveden, *Alexandra Feodorovna*, pages 150-51

35. Vyrubova, pages 81-82

36. Gilliard, page 40

37. Gibbes, page 4

38. Buxhoeveden, *Alexandra Feodorovna*, pages 150-51

39. Gilliard, pages 39-40

40. Gibbes, page 5

41. Gilliard, page 39

42. Information from Princess Vera Konstantinovna to Penny Wilson

43. Vassili, page 396

44. Gibbes, page 6

45. Anatole Mordvinov, Na voenno-pridvornoi sluzhbe, in GARF, F. 5811, Op. 2, D. 512

46. Father George Shavelsky, statement in GARF, F. 640, Op. 1, D. 79

47. Grand Duke Konstantin Konstantinovich, Diary entry of March 10, 1912, in GARF, F. 660, Op. 2, D. 53

48. Gilliard, page 93

49. Queen Marie of Romania, page 1:574

50. Maylunas and Mironenko, page 320

51. Cited, King and Wilson, *Fate*, page 47

52. Alexandra Feodorovna to Nicholas II, March 13, 1916, in GARF, F. 601, Op. 1, D. 1150

53. Maylunas and Mironenko, page 320

54. Ibid., page 334

55. Alexandra Feodorovna to Nicholas II, March 13, 1916, in GARF, F. 601, Op. 1, D. 1150

56. Buxhoeveden, *Alexandra Feodorovna*, page 155

57. Gilliard, page 79

58. Vyrubova, page 79

59. Naryshkina-Kurakina, page 195; Mossolov, page 247

60. Maylunas and Mironenko, page 330

61. Radzinsky, pages 129-30; Vyrubova, pages 62-65

62. Vyrubova, page 93; Buxhoeveden, *Alexandra Feodorovna*, page 132

63. Spiridovich, page 2:288; Mossolov, pages 150-51

64. See Bing, page 271; Gilliard, page 28; Buxhoeveden, *Alexandra Feodorovna*, page 131; Vyrubova, page 90; Spiridovich, pages 2:272-285

65. Vyrubova, page 94

66. Vorres, page 112

67. Hall, *Little Mother*, page 247; Buxhoeveden, *Alexandra Feodorovna*, page 181

68. Queen Marie of Romania, pages 1:575-76

69. Gilliard, page 94

70. Buxhoeveden, *Alexandra Feodorovna*, page 180

71. Maylunas and Mironenko, page 432

72. Alexandra Feodorovna to Nicholas II, October 31, 1915, in GARF, F. 601, Op. 1, D. 1149

73. Nicholas II to Alexandra Feodorovna, October 6, 1915, in GARF, F. 640, Op. 1, D. 106

74. Nicholas II to Alexandra Feodorovna, November 12, 1915, in GARF. F. 640, Op. 1, D. 106

75. Gilliard, pages 149-52

76. Maylunas and Mironenko, page 507

Chapter 3

1. Chavchavadze, *Grand Dukes*, page 93

2. Lerche and Mandal, page 173

3. Krog et al, pages 140-41

4. Ibid., pages 141-42

5. Buchanan, *Mission*, page 1:175

6. Grand Duchess George, page 81

7. Intimacies, page 155

8. Buchanan, *Victorian Gallery*, page 160

9. Prince Christopher of Greece, page 37; de Fontenoy, page 263

10. Lerche and Mandal, page 185

11. Lee, *Empress Frederick*, pages 179-80

12. Queen Victoria to Princess Victoria of Battenberg, December 29, 1890, in Hough, page 110

13. Vorres, page 60

14. Naryshkina-Kurakina, page 179

15. Vorres, page 82

16. King, *Court*, page 89

17. Intimacies, page 164

18. Bing, page 83

19. Ibid., page 158

20. Paleologue, *Ambassador*, page 2:65

21. Kudrina, page 47

22. Bing, pages 88-89

23. Ular, pages 244, 257-58; Cantacuzene, *Revolutionary Days*, page 132

24. Kokovtsov, pages 295-96

25. Hall, *Little Mother*, page 218

26. Cantacuzene, *Revolutionary Days*, page 57

27. Ibid., pages 55-56

28. Buchanan, *Victorian Gallery*, pages 172-73

29. Grand Duke Andrei Vladimirovich, diary entry of August 24, 1915, in GARF, F. 650, Op. 1, D. 2

30. Rodzianko, pages 56-57

31. Hall, *Little Mother*, page 273

32. Bing, page 302

33. Witte, page 50

34. Vorres, page 83

35. Mossolov, page 95

36. Abrikissow, pages 232-33

37. Steveni, page 305

38. Majolier, pages 76-79

39. Crawford and Crawford, pages 8-9

40. Vassili, page 239

41. Bing, page 213

42. Ibid., pages 230-31

43. Crawford and Crawford, pages 10-11

44. Ibid., pages 13-14

45. Ibid., page 35

46. Ibid., page 10

47. Vassili, page 240; Radziwill, *Dethroned Royalty*, page 91; Abrikissow, pages 231, 236

48. Alexander Mikhailovich, *Always*, pages 9-10

49. Crawford and Crawford, pages 77-107

50. Ibid., pages 125-26

51. Vyrubova, page 95

52. Bing, page 282

53. Ibid., pages 283-84

54. Alexander Mikhailovich, *Always*, pages 296-97

55. Crawford and Crawford, pages 127-30, 136; Radziwill, *Dethroned Royalty*, page 94; Vassili, pages 240-41

56. Cited, Crawford and Crawford, page 153

57. Maylunas and Mironenko, page 363

58. Alexandra Feodorovna to Nicholas II, March 4, 1915, in GARF. F. 601, Op. 1, D. 1149

59. Crawford and Crawford, page 172

60. Nicholas II to Alexandra Feodorovna, March 3, 1915, in GARF, F. 640, Op. 1, D. 105

61. Crawford and Crawford, page 175

62. Ibid., pages 192-93

63. Brusilov, page 288

64. Abrikossow, page 236

65. Crawford and Crawford, page 234

Chapter 4

1. Yusupov, *Lost Splendor*, page 157
2. Brayley Hodgetts, page 2:149
3. Intimacies, page 160
4. Buchanan, *Mission*, page 176
5. Vassili, page 244
6. Queen Marie of Romania, page 1:98; Grand Duchess George, page 43
7. Kleinmichel, page 201
8. Kleinmichel, page 201; Mossolov, page 98
9. Mossolov, page 98
10. Paleologue, *Ambassador's*, page 2:138
11. Buchanan, *Victorian Gallery*, page 56
12. Queen Marie of Romania, page 1:476
13. Russian Court Memoirs, pages 171-72
14. Vassili, page 243
15. Buchanan, *Mission*, page 176
16. Radziwill, *Dethroned Royalty*, pages 41, 47-48
17. Buchanan, *Dissolution*, page 47
18. See also Purishkevich, pages 87-88
19. Original in GARF, F. 468, Op. 46, D. 63, courtesy of Brien Horan
20. Vassili, page 243
21. Lehr, page 223
22. Paleologue, page 1:56
23. Russian Court Memoirs, page 171; Cantacuzene, *Revolutionary Days*, page 58
24. Grand Duke Andrei Vladimirovich, diary entry of September 19, 1915, in GARF, F. 650, Op. 1, D. 2
25. Stopford, page 22
26. Paleologue, *Ambassador's*, page 1:208
27. Kirill Vladimirovich, page 39
28. Alexander Mikhailovich, *Once*, page 144
29. Kirill Vladimirovich, page 168
30. Ibid., page 169
31. Queen Marie of Romania, page 1:189
32. Lee, *Empress Frederick*, page 179
33. Wimbles, "An Enduring Mystery," page 36
34. See Buchanan, *Mission*, pages 1:28, 1:176; Sullivan, page 153
35. Elsberry, page 61; Sullivan, pages 136, 182
36. Wimbles, "An Enduring Mystery," page 40; McLean, page 42
37. Wimbles, "An Enduring Mystery," page 43
38. Buchanan, *Mission*, page 1:36
39. Lee, *Queen Victoria*, page 504
40. Bing, page 158
41. Sullivan, pages 93, 114
42. Ibid., page 157
43. Kirill Vladimirovich, page 112
44. Quoted in Wimbles, "An Enduring Mystery," page 2
45. Maylunas and Mironenko, page 228
46. Sullivan, page 230
47. Kirill Vladimirovich, page 161
48. Ibid., page 181
49. Daisy, Princess of Pless, page 109
50. Kirill Vladimirovich, page 100
51. Mossolov, page 100; *New York Times*, October 17, 1905; Sullivan, page 236; Kirill Vladimirovich, pages 183-84
52. Kirill Vladimirovich, page 184
53. Cited in McKee, page 202
54. Van der Kiste, *Princess Victoria Melita*, page 90
55. Sullivan, page 237
56. Kirill Vladimirovich, page 183
57. Bing, page 165
58. Sullivan, page 243
59. John Van der Kiste and Béeche, page 12
60. Queen Marie of Romania, page 1:576
61. Cantacuzene, *Revolutionary Days*, page 188
62. Queen Marie of Romania, page 1:577
63. Russian Court Memoirs, page 180
64. Vassili, page 244
65. Russian Court Memoirs, page 179
66. Quoted in Van der Kiste and Béeche, page 14
67. Alexandra Feodorovna to Nicholas II, March 8, 1915, in GARF, F. 601, Op. 1, D. 1149
68. Radziwill, *Dethroned Royalty*, page 54
69. Queen Marie of Romania, page 1:338
70. Radziwill, *Dethroned Royalty*, page 54
71. Cockfield, page 3
72. Perry and Pleshakov, page 126
73. Ferrand, page 408. Boris Lacroix died in 1984.
74. Perry and Pleshakov, page 71
75. Ibid., page 70
76. Ular, page 90
77. Ibid.
78. Daisy, Princess of Pless, page 258
79. King, "Diaries of Grand Duke Andrei Vladimirovich," Diary entry of March 8, 1917, page 49
80. Perry and Pleshakov, page 84; Korneva and Cheboksarova, page 67
81. Korneva and Cheboksarova, page 63
82. Abrikossow, page 235
83. Knox, pages 2:430-31
84. Paleologue, *Ambassador's*, page 2:186
85. Chavchavadze, *Grand Dukes*, page 237
86. Alexandra Feodorovna to Nicholas II, February 13, 1916, in GARF, F. 601, Op. 1, D. 1150
87. Nijinska, pages 46-47
88. Teliakovsky, page 242
89. Hall, *Imperial Dancer*, page 70
90. Romanovsky-Krassinsky, page 103; Perry and Pleshakov, page 70; Hall, *Imperial Dancer*, page 85
91. Chavchavadze, *Grand Dukes*, page 216
92. In Romanov News No. 67
93. King, "Diaries of Grand Duke Andrei Vladimirovich," Diary entry of December 20, 1916, page 43
94. Buchanan, *Mission*, page 2:36
95. Cantacuzene, *Revolutionary Days*, page 95

96. Rodzianko, page 146
97. Nostitz, page 184
98 Perry and Pleshakov, page 140

Chapter 5

1. Queen Marie of Romania, page 1:7
2. King, *Court*, page 81
3. Alexander Mikhailovich, *Once*, page 140
4. Hough, page 55
5. Alexander Mikhailovich, *Once*, page 139
6. In Romanov News, No. 67
7. Queen Marie of Romania, page 1:87; Alexander Mikhailovich, *Once*, page 140
8. Marie Pavlovna, *Education*, page 32
9. Alexander Mikhailovich, *Once*, page 139
10. Vassili, *La Société*, page 29
11. Kudrina, page 88; Brayley Hodgetts, page 2:232; Ganz, page 60; Ular, pages 78-79
12. Mossolov, page 101
13. Millar, pages 91-92
14. Vassili, page 326; Radziwill, *Dethroned Royalty*, page 81
15. Van der Kiste, Romanovs, pages 162-63
16. Rohl, page 123
17. Warwick, page 164; Ular, pages 77-78
18. Cited, King, *Court*, page 81
19. Marie Pavlovna, *Education*, page 79
20. Ibid., page 17
21. King, *Court*, page 81
22. Dorr, pages 145-46
23. Mager, page 243
24. Quoted in Ashton, *"A Country,"* page 12
25. Vyrubova, pages 113-13
26. Alexandra Feodorovna to Nicholas II, June 16, 1915, in GARF, F. 601, Op. 1, D. 1149
27. Olsoufieff, page 32
28. Paleologue, *Ambassador's*, page 3:54
29. Yusupov, *Rasputin*, page 126
30. Volkov, page 2
31. Alexander Mikhailovich, *Once*, page 141
32. See Radziwill, *Dethroned Royalty*, page 68
33. Volkov, page 2
34. Grand Duchess George, page 29
35. Mager, page 142
36. Queen Marie of Romania, pages 1:214-15
37. Volkov, page 3
38. Marie Pavlovna, *Education*, page 11
39. Volkov, page 5
40. Russian Court Memoirs, page 178
41. Mossolov, page 81; Intimacies, page 149; Radziwill, *Dethroned Royalty*, pages 68-69
42. Intimacies, page 149
43. Bing, pages 169-70
44. Mossolov, page 81

45. Bing, pages 169-70
46. Cited, Perry and Pleshakov, page 71
47. Volkov, page 6; Mossolov, pages 81-82; Paleologue, *Three*, page 178
48. Mossolov, page 82
49. Vassiliev, page 437; Vassili, pages 237-38
50. Alexander Mikhailovich, *Once*, page 141
51. Cited in Lee and Davidson, page 160
52. Paleologue, *Three*, page 178
53. Maylunas and Mironenko, page 302
54. Lee and Davidson, page 160
55. Mossolov, page 82
56. Cited, King, *Court*, page 84
57. Alexandra Feodorovna to Nicholas II, June 14, 1915, in GARF, F. 601, Op. 1, D. 1149
58. Alexandra Feodorovna to Nicholas II, September 17, 1915, in GARF, F. 601, Op. 1, D. 1149
59. Alexandra Feodorovna to Nicholas II, April 6, 1915, in GARF, D. 601, Op. 1, D. 1149
60. Nicholas II to Alexandra Feodorovna, April 7, 1915, in GARF. F. 640, Op.1, D. 1149
61. Alexandra Feodorovna to Nicholas II, September 14, 1916, in GARF, F. 601, Op. 1, D. 1151
62. Marie Pavlovna, *Education*, page 311
63. Paley, pages 169-70
64. Alexandra Feodorovna to Nicholas II, September 3, 1915, in GARF, F. 601, Op. 1, D. 1149
65. Nicholas II to Alexandra Feodorovna, October 9, 1915, in GARF, F. 640, Op. 1, D. 1149
66. Knox, page 2:468
67. Alexandra Feodorovna to Nicholas II, November 7, 1915, in GARF, F, 601, Op. 1, D. 1150
68. Alexandra Feodorovna to Nicholas II, November 10, 1915, in GARF, F. 601, Op. 1, D. 1150
69. Alexandra Feodorovna to Nicholas II, November 15, 1915, in GARF, F. 601, Op. 1, D. 1150
70. Cited, Lee and Davidson, page 161
71. Alexandra Feodorovna to Nicholas II, May 28, 1916, in GARF, F. 601, Op. 1, D. 1151
72. Paley, pages 26-27
73. Marie Pavlovna, *Education*, page 3
74. Ibid., page 50
75. Ibid., page 19
76. Ibid., page 51
77. Cited in Montefiore, page 568
78. Lee, Dmitry Pavlovich
79. Ibid.
80. Buchanan, *Victorian Gallery*, pages 149-52
81. Yusupov, *Lost Splendor*, pages 154-55
82. Cited, Perry and Pleshakov, page 128
83. Alexandra Feodorovna to Nicholas II, April 17, 1915, in GARF, F. 601, Op. 1, D. 1149
84. Alexandra Feodorovna to Nicholas II, September 14, 1915, in GARF, F. 601, Op. 1, D. 1150
85. Alexandra Feodorovna to Nicholas II, January 8, 1916,

in GARF, F. 601, Op. 1, D. 1150; Alexandra Feodorovna to Nicholas II, March 10, 1916, in GARF, F. 601, Op. 1, D. 1150; Alexandra Feodorovna to Nicholas II, March 15, 1916, in GARF, F. 601, Op. 1, D. 1150

86. Alexandra Feodorovna to Nicholas II, February 13, 1916, in GARF, F. 601, Op. 1, D. 1150

87. Belyakova, *"Letters from Grand Duke Alexander Mikhailovich to Grand Duchess Xenia,"* letter of January 4, 1917, page 138

88. Shchegolev, page 4:232

89. King, *"Diaries of Grand Duke Andrei Vladimirovich,"* Diary entry of December 31, 1916, page 43

Chapter 6

1. Chavchavadze, *Grand Dukes*, page 69; Belyakova, *Romanov Legacy*, page 154

2. Cantacuzene, *Revolutionary Days*, page 385

3. Paleologue, *Ambassador's*, page 1:60

4. Witte, page 518

5. Grand Duchess George, page 84

6. Ignatiev, page 81

7. Cantacuzene, *Revolutionary Days*, pages 390-91

8. Ibid., page 387

9. Dehn, page 22

10. Vassili, page 247; Ferrand, pages 159-62; Witte, page 780

11. Witte, page 78

12. Alexander Mikhailovich, *Once*, page 145

13. Witte, page 200

14. Naryshkina-Kurakina, page 163

15. Witte, page 201

16. Naryshkina-Kurakina, page 163

17. Yusupov, *Lost Splendor*, page 62; Nostitz, page 144

18. Smitten, page 12:99; Radzinsky, page 90

19. Mossolov, page 88; Witte, page 186

20. Witte, page 196

21. Vassili, page 247; Naryshkina-Kurakina, page 163

22. Bing, pages 226-27

23. Maylunas and Mironenko, page 301

24. Cantacuzene, *Revolutionary Days*, page 390

25. Ibid., pages 31-32

26. Nicholas II to *Alexandra Feodorovna*, January 26, 1915, in GARF, F. 640, Op. D. 110

27. Cantacuzene, *Revolutionary Days*, page 66

28. Knox, page 1:334

29. Alexandra Feodorovna to Nicholas II, June 12, 1916, in GARF, F. 601, Op. 1, D. 1150

30. Grand Duke Andrei Vladimirovich, diary entry of September 6, 1915, in GARF, F. 650, Op. 1, D. 2

31. Grand Duke Andrei Vladimirovich, diary entry of August 25, 1915, in GARF, F. 650, Op. 1, D. 2

32. Alexander Mikhailovich, *Once*, page 269

33. Paleologue, *Ambassador's*, page 2:63

34. Pipes, page 269

Chapter 7

1. King and Wilson, *Gilded Prism*, page 45

2. GIAR, F. 435, Op. 1, D. 141, report of August 12, 1874; GIAR, F. 475, Op. 66, D. 675; Witte, pages 224-25

3. Ferrand, page 359

4. Ibid., page 358

5. Private information from Konstantinovichi descendants to Penny Wilson

6. Central State Archive of Uzbekistan; Alisher Navoi State Library, Tashkent, Uzbekistan, and information from Directing Librarian Rustam A. Alemov

7. Ferrand, page 361

8. Brayley Hodgetts, page 1:143

9. Barkovets, Federov and Krylov, pages 122-23

10. Information from Princess Vera Konstantinovna to Penny Wilson

11. http://en.tchaikovsky-research.net/pages/Grand_Duke_Konstantin_Konstantinovich

12. Radziwill, *Memories*, page 232

13. Vassili, page 246

14. Novikoff, pages 247-48

15. Grand Duke Andrei Vladimirovich, Diary entry of December 29, 1916, in GARF F. 650, Op. 1, D. 4

16. Grand Duke Konstantin Konstantinovich, Diary entry of September 12, 1904, in GARF F. 660, Op. 1, D. 53

17. Princess Vera Konstantinovna, Kadetskaya Pereklichka, page 24

18. Buxhoeveden, *Before the Storm*, page 225

19. Information from Princess Irina Bagration-Mukhransky to Penny Wilson

20. Bing page 263

21. Bokhanov et al, page 127

22. Information from Princess Vera Konstantinovna to Penny Wilson

23. Princess Vera Konstantinovna, Kadetskaya Pcrcklichka, page 26; information from Princess Irina Bagration-Mukhransky to Penny Wilson

24. Princess Vera Konstantinovna, Kadetskaya Pereklichka, page 26; information from Princess Irina Bagration-Mukhransky to Penny Wilson

25. Russian Court Memoirs, page 165

26. Cited in Horan

27. Gabriel Konstantinovich, page 286

28. Ibid., pages 286-287

29. Obolensky, pages 83-84

30. Ibid., page 84

31. Information from Princess Vera Konstantinovna to Penny Wilson

32. Cited in King and Wilson, *Gilded Prism*, page 156

33. King and Wilson, *Gilded Prism*, page 130; Gabriel Konstantinovich, page 26

34. King and Wilson, *Gilded Prism*, page 131; Gabriel Konstantinovich, page 101

35. Novikoff, page 259

36. *Moscow Times*, March 10, 2004
37. Grand Duke Andrei Vladimirovich, Diary entry of September 29, 1915, in GARF, F. 650, Op.1, D. 2
38. Ibid.
39. Gabriel Konstantinovich, page 267
40. Gabriel Konstantinovich, page 276; Svet, No. 259, October 1, 1914
41. Information from Princess Vera Konstantinovna to Penny Wilson
42. Novoe Vremya, No, 13851, October 3, 1914; Gabriel Konstantinovich, page 275
43. See Chizhkov for more information
44. Novikoff, pages 254-55
45. Kyasht, page 127
46. King and Wilson, *Gilded Prism*, page 156; information from Princess Vera Konstantinovna to Penny Wilson
47. King and Wilson, *Gilded Prism*, page 132
48. Ibid.
49. Princess Vera Konstantinovna, Kadetskaya Pereklichka, page 23
50. Information from Princess Vera Konstantinovna to Penny Wilson
51. Alexander Mikhailovich, *Once*, page 143
52. Mossolov, pages 84-85
53. Alexander Mikhailovich, *Once*, page 143

Chapter 8

1. Alexander Mikhailovich, *Once*, page 146; Mateos, page 12; Witte, page 304
2. Alexander Mikhailovich, *Once*, page 21
3. Cockfield, page 63
4. Alexander Mikhailovich to Grand Duchess Xenia Alexandrovna, January 4, 1917, in Belyakova, "Letters," page 138; King, *"Diaries of Grand Duke Andrei Vladimirovich,"* entry of December 29, 1916, page 42
5. Mossolov, page 93
6. Paleologue, *Ambassador's*, pages 1:342-3
7. Buchanan, *Mission*, page 1:177
8. Alexander Mikhailovich, *Once*, page 172
9. Troyat, page 621
10. Chavchavadze, *Grand Dukes*, page 171
11. Cockfield, page 61
12. Kleinmichel, page 161
13. Paleologue, *Ambassador's*, page 1:343
14. Alexander Mikhailovich, *Once*, page 148
15. Cockfield, pages 14-42
16. Grand Duke Nicholas Mikhailovich to Nicholas II, May 11, 1916, in *Nikolaya II v Velikii Knyazya*, page 146
17. Alexandra Feodorovna to Nicholas II, November 4, 1916, in GARF, F. 601, Op. 1, D. 1151
18. King, *"Diaries of Grand Duke Andrei Vladimirovich,"* Diary entry of March 8, 1917, page 49
19. Ibid diary entry of January 7, 1917, page 44
20. Alexander Mikhailovich, *Once*, page 149
21. Cockfield, page 17
22. Queen Victoria to Princess Victoria of Battenberg, letter of February 20, 1886, in Hough, page 80
23. Cockfield, page 32
24. Naryshkina-Kurakina, pages 112-13
25. Alexander Mikhailovich, *Once*, page 149
26. Cockfield, page 64
27. Becket and Alderman
28. de Stoeckl, *Not All Vanity*, page 68
29. Wynn, page 323
30. Daisy, Princess of Pless, page 165
31. For details see *Never Say Die*
32. Maylunas and Mironenko, page 312
33. Nicholas II to Alexandra Feodorovna, April 7, 1916, in GARF, F. 640, Op. 1, D. 111
34. Wynn, page 324
35. Yusupov, *Lost Splendor*, page 216
36. Crawford and Crawford, page 148
37. Ibid.
38. Russian Court Memoirs, page 176
39. Lehr, page 222
40. Yusupov, *Lost Splendor*, page 170
41. Alexander Mikhailovich, *Once*, page 128
42. Vorres, page 59
43. Empress Marie Feodorovna to Queen Louise of Denmark, letter of July 19, 1894, in Ulstrup, page 89
44. Maylunas and Mironenko, page 73
45. Kudrina, page 88
46. Nunes, pages 79-80
47. Alexander Mikhailovich, *Once*, pages 237-38
48. Ibid., page 232
49. Ibid., page 236
50. Hall and Van der Kiste, page 83
51. Vassili, page 245
52. Maylunas and Mironenko, page 385
53. Alexander Mikhailovich, *Once*, pages 283-84
54. Cantacuzene, *Revolutionary Days*, page 100
55. Alexander Mikhailovich, *Once*, page 18
56. Ibid., pages 149-50
57. Chavchavadze, *Crowns and Trenchcoats*, page 55
58. de Stoeckl, *Not all Vanity*, pages 140-41
59. Cockfield, page 196; Grand Duchess George, page 51; Chavchavadze, Grand Dukes, page 184
60. Grand Duchess George, page 175
61. Queen Marie of Romania, page 1:199
62. Grand Duchess George, page 79
63. Ibid., page 133
64. de Stoeckl, *Not all Vanity*, page 142
65. Daisy, Princess of Pless, page 170
66. de Stoeckl, *Not all Vanity*, page 145
67. Romanovsky-Krassinsky, page 63
68. *Nikolaya II v Velikii Knyazya*, page 170
69. Chavchavadze, *The Grand Dukes*, page 203
70. Romanovsky-Krassinsky, page 53

71. Ibid., page 89
72. Hall, *Imperial Dancer*, page 128
73. Knox, pages 1:271-74
74. Grand Duke Andrei Vladimirovich, Diary entry of May 12, 1915, in GARF F. 650, Op. 1, D. 36; Rodzianko, page 161
75. Alexandra Feodorovna to Nicholas II, June 25, 1915, in GARF, F. 601, Op.1, D. 1149; Alexandra Feodorovna to Nicholas II, January 9, 1916, in GARF, F. 601, Op. 1, D. 1150
76. Wilton, *Russia's Agony*, page 237

Chapter 9

1. Kleinmichel, page 64
2. Van der Kiste, *Kings of the Hellenes*, pages, 24-25; King and Wilson, Gilded Prism, page 37
3. Prince Christopher of Greece, page 32
4. Prince Nicholas of Greece, page 35
5. Marie Pavlovna, *Education*, page 79
6. King, *Princess Marina*, page 12
7. Grand Duchess George, page 1
8. Ponsonby, page 392
9. Christmas, page 404
10. Aronson, page 200
11. Vassili, pages 118-19
12. Queen Marie of Romania, page 1:28
13. Radziwill, *Royal Marriage Market*, page 343; Cornwallis-West, page 247
14. Cornwallis-West, page 237
15. Stanley, page 218
16. de Fontenoy, page 98
17. Abrash, page 393
18. Ibid.
19. Fulford, page 58
20. Longford, page 393
21. Corti, page 214
22. Mandache, page 6
23. Jerrold, page 199
24. Queen Marie of Romania, page 1:3
25. Erbach-Schonberg, page 173
26. Prince Nicholas of Greece, page 29
27. Buchanan, *Queen Victoria's Relations*, page 115
28. Radziwill, *Royal Marriage Market*, page 343
29. de Fontenoy, page 99
30. Pakula, page 33
31. Queen Marie of Romania, page 1:15
32. Prince Nicholas of Greece, page 39
33. Marie Pavlovna, *Education*, page 56
34. Queen Marie of Romania, page 1:4
35. Ibid., page 1:188
36. Lee, *Empress Frederick*, page 149
37. Jerrold, page 404
38. Lee, *Empress Frederick*, page 296
39. Eilers, page 62; Jerrold, page 404
40. Wimbles, *"Death and The Duchess,"* page 302
41. Lee, *Empress Frederick*, page 341
42. Quoted in Wimbles, *"Grand Duchess Marie Alexandrovna,"* page 53
43. Buchanan, *Victorian Gallery*, page 50
44. Zeepvat, *Camera*, page 90
45. Vickers, page 69
46. Yusupov, *Lost Splendor*, page 157
47. Daisy, Princess of Pless, page 82; Buxhoeveden, *Before the Storm*, page 217
48. Buchanan, *Victorian Gallery*, page 52
49. Maylunas and Mironenko, page 198
50. Prince Nicholas of Greece, page 194
51. Maylunas and Mironenko, page 215
52. Prince Nicholas of Greece, page 196
53. Béeche, page 125
54. Buchanan, *Victorian Gallery*, pages 55-56
55. Marie Pavlovna, *Education*, page 48
56. Perry and Pleshakov, page 74
57. Marie Pavlovna, *Education*, pages 19-20
58. Ibid., page 21
59. Ibid., page 78
60. Grand Duchess George, page 133
61. Russian Court Memoirs, page 85
62. Marie Pavlovna, *Education*, page 90
63. Ibid., pages 93-95
64. Ibid., page 97
65. Ibid., page 98
66. Ibid., page 107
67. Maylunas and Mironenko, page 302
68. Romanovsky-Krassinsky, page 108
69. Radziwill, *Royal Marriage Market*, pages 211-212
70. Perry and Pleshakov, page 104; *Radziwill, Royal Marriage Market*, page 212
71. Perry and Pleshakov, page 104
72. Menzies, page 143
73. Maylunas and Mironenko, page 383
74. Radziwill, *Royal Marriage Market*, page 214
75. Russian Court Memoirs, page 85
76. Marie Pavlovna, *Education*, page 180
77. Alexander Mikhailovich, *Once*, page 21
78. Zeepvat, *"Other Anastasia,"* page 3
79. Radziwill, *Disillusions*, pages 13-14
80. Alexander Mikhailovich, *Once*, page 22; Radziwill, *Disillusions*, page 14
81. Radziwill, *Disillusions*, page 16
82. Mateos, page 13
83. Cockfield, page 105
84. Mateos, page 14; Cockfield, page 16; Radziwill, *Disillusions*, page 19
85. Radziwill, *Disillusions*, page 31
86. Cockfield, page 105; Radziwill, *Disillusions*, page 34; *New York Times*, April 13, 1897, and April 15, 1897
87. Radziwill, *Disillusions*, page 37
88. See Ferrand for details
89. Daisy, Princes of Pless, page 112

90. Cockfield, page 17
91. Painter, page 210
92. Yusupov, *Lost Splendor*, page 252

Chapter 10

1. Alexander Mikhailovich, *Once*, page 151
2. Brayley Hodgetts, pages 2:229-30
3. Nicholas II to Alexandra Feodorovna, September 15, 1916, in GARF, F. 640, Op. D. 111
4. Witte, page 525
5. *New York Times*, October 26, 1909
6. Vassili, page 127
7. Vorres, page 90
8. Alexander Mikhailovich, *Once*, page 152
9. Queen Marie of Romania, page 2:119
10. Witte, pages 80-81
11. Vorres, page 50
12. Ibid., page 74
13. Vassili, page 246
14. Fisher, page 231
15. Russian Court Memoirs, pages 81-82
16. Vorres, page 86
17. Bing, page 148
18. Vorres, page 87
19. Belyakova, *"A Strange Prince,"* page 22; Phenix, page 52
20. Vassili, page 246
21. Belyakova, *Romanov Legacy*, page 89
22. Phenix, pages 46, 53; Vorres, page 84
23. Vorres, page 104
24. Ibid., page 105
25. Vassili, page 247
26. Washington Post, February 13, 1907
27. Alexandra Feodorovna to Nicholas II, January 29, 1915, in GARF, F. 601, Op. 1, D. 1149
28. Phenix, pages 91-92; Vorres, page 141; Russian Court Memoirs, page 16
29. Alexandra Feodorovna to Nicholas II, September 24, 1914, in GARF, F. 601, Op. 1, D. 1149
30. Alexandra Feodorovna to Nicholas II, March 17, 1916, in GARF, F. 601, Op. 1, D. 1150
31. Alexandra Feodorovna to Nicholas II, March 26, 1916, in GARF, F. 601, Op. 1, D. 1150
32. Nicholas II to Alexandra Feodorovna, April 27, 1916, in GARF, F. 640, Op. 1, D. 111
33. Vorres, page 151
34. Belyakova, *Letters from Grand Duke Alexander Mikhailovich to Grand Duchess Xenia,"* letter of November 5 1916, pages 136-37
35. Korneva and Cheboksarova, *Russia and Europe*, 55
36. Ibid., 54
37. Russian Court Memoirs, page 256

Epilogue

1. Shchegolev, page 5:38
2. Nicholas II, Diary entry of March 2, 1917, in GARF, F. 601, Op. 1, D. 265
3. Gilliard, page 216
4. Vyrubova, page 214
5. Nicholas II, Diary entry of March 15, 1918, in GARF, f. 601, op. 1, d. 266
6. Gilliard, page 257
7. King and Wilson, *Fate*, page 85
8. Ibid., pages 205-06
9. Nicholas II, Diary entry of May 19, 1918, in GARF, f. 601, op. 1, d. 26
10. Maylunas and Mironenko, page 639
11. Cockfield, pages 229-30
12. Grand Duchess George, page 215
13. Ibid., page 217
14. Information provided by Antonio Perez Caballero
15. Grand Duchess George, page 217
16. Ibid., page 227
17. King and Wilson, *Gilded Prism*, page 165
18. Ibid., pages 183, 188
19. Cockfield, pages 244-46
20. Information from two Konstantinovichi descendants and one Konstantinovichi relative-by-marriage to Penny Wilson
21. Hastings, page 51
22. Wynn, pages 326-27
23. Cockfield, pages 34, 138-9; Grand Duchess George, page 321
24. www.tashkent-info.narod.ru
25. King and Wilson, *Gilded Prism*, pages 181, 187
26. Ibid., page 170
27. King and Wilson, *Fate*, page 261
28. Information from Princess Vera Konstantinovna to Penny Wilson
29. King and Wilson, *Gilded Prism*, page 186
30. Details drawn from the Princess Elena of Serbia and Russia, Memoirs, Bakhmetiev Archive, MS Collection, Box 42, Columbia University
31. Alexander Mikhailovich, *Once*, page 296
32. Vorres, page 156
33. Ibid., page 159
34. Kirill Vladimirovich, page 206; Dehn, page 162
35. Dymin, pages 94-97; Paleologue, *Ambassador's*, page 3:259; Buchanan, *Mission*, page 2:101
36. Alexander Mikhailovich, *Once*, page 370; Sullivan, page 321
37. Hall, *Dancer*, page 201; Perry and Pleshakov, page 174
38. Hall, *Dancer*, pages 211-14
39 Perry and Pleshakov, pages 231-3

Bibliography

Materials utilized in this book draw on both published and unpublished sources.

Archives

Alisher Navoi State Library, Tashkent
Bakhmetiev Archive, Columbia University, New York
Central State Archive of Uzbekistan, Tashkent
Eurohistory Royal Photographic Collection, East Roichmond Heights, California
State Archives of the Russian Federation (Gosudarstvennyi Arkhiv Rossisskii Federatsii) (cited in chapter notes as GARF)
Gosudarstvennyi Istoricheskii Arkhiv Rossisskii (State Historical Archives of the Russian Federation), St. Petersburg (cited in chapter notes as GIAR)

Books

Abrikossow, Dmitri Ivanovich. *Revelations of a Russian Diplomat*. Seattle: University of Washington Press, 1964.
Alexander Mikhailovich, Grand Duke of Russia. *Once a Grand Duke*. New York: Farrar & Rinehart, 1932.
___ *Always a Grand Duke*. New York: Farrar & Rinehart, 1933.
Aronson, Theo. *Grandmama of Europe: The Crowned Descendants of Queen Victoria*. London: John Murray, 1973.
Barkovets, Olga, Feodor Federov and Alexander Krylov. *Peterhof is ein Traum: Deutsche Prinzessinnen in Russland*. Berlin: Quitessenz Verlag 2001.
Battiscombe, Georgina. *Queen Alexandra*. Boston: Houghton Mifflin, 1969.
Beéche, Arturo. *Dear Ellen: Royal Europpe Through the Photo Albums of HIH Grand Duchess Helen Vladimiurovna of Russia*. East Richmond Heights, CA: Eurohistory, 2011.
___ "Grand Duchess Elena Vladimirovna." In *The Grand Duchesses*. East Richmond Heights, CA: Eurohistory, 2004.
___ The Coburgs of Europe. East Richmond Heights, CA: Eurohistory, 2013.
Belyakova, Zoia. *The Romanov Legacy: The Palaces of St. Petersburg*. London: Hazar Publishing, 1994.
___ *Honour and Fidelity: The Russian Dukes of Leuchtenberg*. St. Petersburg: Logos Publishers, 2010.
Benckendorff, Count Paul von. *Last Days at Tsarskoe Selo*. London: Hutchinson, 1927.
Bing, Edward J., Editor. *The Secret Letters of the Last Tsar: Being the Confidential Correspondence between Nicholas II and His Mother, Dowager Empress Maria Feodorovna*. New York: Longmans, Green, 1938.
Boland, Terry. *Death of a Romanov Prince: The Promising Life and Early Death of Prince Oleg Konstantinovich of Russia*. East Richmond Heights, CA: Eurohistory, 2018.
Bokhanov, Alexander, Manfred Knodt, Vladimir Oustimenko, Zinaida Peregudova, and Lyubov Tyutyunnik. *Romanovs: Love, Power and Tragedy*. London: Leppi, 1993.
Botkin, Gleb. *The Real Romanovs*. New York: Fleming H. Revell Co., 1931.
Brayley Hodgetts, E. A. *The Court of Russia in the Nineteenth Century*. Two volumes. London: Methuen, 1908.
Brusilov, Alexei. *A Soldier's Notebook*. London: Macmillan, 1926.
Buchanan, Sir George. *My Mission to Russia and Other Diplomatic Memories*. Two volumes. London: Cassell, 1923.
Buchanan, Meriel. *Dissolution of an Empire*. London: Cassell, 1932.
___ *Queen Victoria's Relations*. London: Cassell, 1953.
___ *Victorian Gallery*. London: Cassell, 1956.
Buxhoeveden, Sophie. *Life and Tragedy of Alexandra Feodorovna, Empress of Russia*. London: Longmans, Green, 1928.
___ Before the Storm. London: Macmillan, 1938.
Cantacuzene, Princess J. *Revolutionary Days: Recollections Of Romanoffs And Bolsheviki, 1914-1917*. Boston: Small, Maynard & Co., 1919
___ *My Life Here and There*. New York: Charles Scribner's Sons, 1921.
Chavchavadze, Prince David. *The Grand Dukes*. New York: Atlantic International Publications, 1989.
___ *Crowns and Trenchcoats*. New York: Atlantic International Publications, 1990.
Chizhkov, A.B. *Podmoskovnie Usadbi Segodnya*. Moscow: Progress, 1996.
Christmas, Walter. *King George of Greece*. New York: McBride, Nast and Company, 1914.
Cockfield, Jamie. *White Crow: The Life and Times of the Grand Duke Nicholas Mikhailovich Romanov, 1859-1919*. Westport, CT: Praeger, 2002.
Cornwallis-West, Mrs. George. *The Reminiscences of Lady Randolph Churchill, Mrs. George Cornwallis-West*. New York: Century, 1908.

Corti, Egon Caesar, Count. *The Downfall of Three Dynasties*. London: Methuen, 1934.

Crawford, Rosemary and Donald Crawford. *Michael and Natasha: The Life and Love of the Last Tsar of Russia*. London: Weidenfeld & Nicolson, 1997.

Dehn, Lili. *The Real Tsaritsa*. Boston: Little, Brown, 1922.

Dorr, Rheta Childe. *Inside the Russian Revolution*. New York: MacMillan, 1918.

Dymin, Stanislav. *Romanovi Imperatorskii Dom*. Moscow: Progress, 1998.

Eagar, M. *Six Years at the Russian Court*. New York: Charles Bowman, 1906.

Eilers, Marlene. *Queen Victoria's Descendants*. Falköping, Sweden: Rosvall Royal Books, 1997.

Elchaninov, Major-General Andrei. *The Tsar and His People*. London: Hutchinson, 1914.

Elsberry, Terence. *Marie of Romania: The Intimate Life of a Twentieth Century Queen*. London: Cassell, 1973.

Enache, Nicolas. *La descendance de Pierre le Grand, Tsar de Russie*. SEDOPOLS: PAris, 1983.

Erbach-Schonberg, Princess Marie zu. *Reminiscences*. London: George Allen & Unwin, 1926.

Ferrand, Jacques. *Descendances naturelles des souverains et grands-ducs de Russie, de 1762 à 1910*. Paris: Répertoire Généalogique/Jaques Ferrand, 1995.

Fisher, Sir Jackie. *Memories*. London: Hodder and Stoughton, 1919.

de Fontenoy, Marquise. *Within Royal Palaces*. Philadelphia: Hubbards, 1892.

Fulford, Roger, Editor. *Darling Child: The Private Correspondence of Queen Victoria and the Crown Princess of Prussia, 1871-1878*. London: Evans Brothers, 1976.

Gabriel Konstantinovich, Grand Duke of Russia. *V Mramornom Dvortse: iz Kroniki Nashei Semyi*. New York: Izdatelstvo imeni Chekova, 1955.

Ganz, Hugo. *The Downfall of Russia*. London: Hodder and Stoughton, 1904.

Gelardi, Julia P. *From Splendor to Revolution: The Romanov Women 1847–1928*. New York: St. Martin's Press, 2011.

George, Grand Duchess of Russia. *A Romanov Diary*. New York: Atlantic International Publications, 1988.

Gibbes, Charles Sidney. *Memoirs*. Unpublished manuscript. Undated. In Authors' Collection.

Gilliard, Pierre. *Thirteen Years at the Russian Court*. New York: George H. Doran, 1921.

Grabbe, Paul and Beatrice Grabbe. *The Private World of the Last Tsar: In the Photographs of General Count Alexander Grabbe*. Boston: Little, Brown, 1984.

Gray, Pauline. *The Grand Duke's Woman*. London: Macdonald and Jane's, 1976.

Greece, Prince Christopher of. *Memoirs*. London: The Right Book Club, 1934.

Greece, Prince Nicholas of. *My Fifty Years*. Annotated and expanded by Arturo Beéche. East Richmond Heights, CA: Eurohistory, 2006.

Gurko, Vladimir. *Features and Figures of the Past; Government and Opinion in the Reign of Nicholas II*. Stanford: Stanford University Press, 1939.

Hall, Coryne. *Little Mother of Russia: A Biography of Empress Marie Feodorovna*. London: Shepheard-Walwyn, 2001.

___ *Imperial Dancer*. Stroud, Gloucestershire: Sutton, 2005.

Hall, Coryne and Arturo Beéche. *APAPA: King Christian IX of Denmark and His Descendants*. East Richmond Heights, CA: Eurohistory, 2014.

___ *The Romanovs (Royal Collections, Volume II)*. East Richmond Heights, CA: Eurohistory, 2017.

Hall, Coryne and John Van der Kiste. *Once A Grand Duchess: Xenia, Sister of Nicholas II*. Stroud, Gloucestershire: Sutton, 2002.

Hastings, Selena. *The Red Earl: The Extraordinary Life of the 16th Earl of Huntingdon*. London: Bloomsbury, 2014.

Hintze, Count Paul von. *The Health of Empress Alexandra of Russia*. Unpublished report to Kaiser Wilhelm II, 1910. In Authors' Collection.

Hough, Richard, Editor. *Advice to My Granddaughter: Letters from Queen Victoria to Princess Victoria of Hesse*. New York: Simon & Schuster, 1976.

Ignatiev, Alexei. *A Subaltern in Old Russia*. London: Hutchinson, 1944.

Intimacies of Court and Society. New York: Dodd, Mead, 1918.

Izwolsky, Alexander. *Recollections of a Foreign Minister*. New York: Doubleday, 1921.

Jerrold, Clare. *The Widowhood of Queen Victoria*. London: Eveleigh Nash, 1916.

King, Greg. *The Man Who Killed Rasputin*. Secaucus, N.J.: Citadel, 1995.

___ *The Court of the Last Tsar*. Hoboken, N. J.: John Wiley & Sons, 2006.

King, Greg and Janet Ashton. *A Life for the Tsar: Triumph and Tragedy at the Coronation of Emperor Nicholas II*. East Richmond Heights, CA: Eurohistory, 2016.

King, Greg and Penny Wilson. *The Fate of the Romanovs*. Hoboken, N. J.: John Wiley & Sons, 2003.

___ *Gilded Prism: The Konstantinovichi Grand Dukes and the Last Years of the Romanov Dynasty*. East Richmond Heights, CA: Eurohistory, 2006.

King, Stella. *Princess Marina*. London: Cassell, 1969.

Kirill Vladimirovich, Grand Duke of Russia. *My Life in Russia's Service, Then and Now*. London: Selwyn & Blount, 1939.

Kleinmichel, Countess Marie. *Memories of a Shipwrecked World*. London: Brentano's, 1923.

Knox, Major-General Sir Alfred. With the Russian Army, 1914-1917. Two volumes. London: Hutchinson, 1921.

Kokovtsov, Count Vladimir. *Out of My Past*. Stanford: Stanford University Press, 1935.

Korneva, Galina and Tatiana Cheboksarova. *Russia and Europe: Dynastic Ties*. East Richmond Heights, CA: Eurohistory, 2013.

___ *Grand Duchess Marie Pavlovna*. East Richmond Heights, CA: Eurohistory, 2014.

Krog, Ole Villumsen, and Dominic Lieven, Yulia Kudrina, Vladimir Dmitriev, Aliya Barkovetz, Preben Ulstrup, Bent Jensen, Alexander Golubev, Andrey Larianov, Andrey Yanovsky, Pastor Gennady Belovolov, Sergei Gontar, Mogens Bencard, Tatiana Muntian, William Clarke and Alexander Sokolov. *Marie Feodorovna, Empress of Russia: An Exhibition about the Danish Princess who Became Empress of Russia*. Exhibit catalogue. Copenhagen: Christiansborg Palace-der Kongelige Udstillingsfond, 1997.

Kudrina, Iulia. *Imperatritsa Maria Feodorovna*. Moscow: Olma Press, 2001.

Kyasht, Lydia. *Romantic Recollections*. New York: Brentano's, 1929.

Lee, Arthur Gould. *The Empress Frederick Writes to Sophie, Her Daughter Crown Princess and Later Queen of the Hellenes: Letters 1889-1902*. London: Faber & Faber, 1955.

Lee, Sir Sidney. *Queen Victoria: A Biography*. London: Smith, Elder, 1903.

Lee, Will and Lisa Davidson. "Grand Duke Paul Alexandrovich." In *The Grand Dukes*. East Richmond Heights, CA: Eurohistory, 2010.

Lehr, Elizabeth. *King Lehr and the Gilded Age*. London: Constable, 1935.

Lerche, Anna and Marcus Mandal. *A Royal Family: The Story of Christian IX and his European Descendants*. Copenhagen: Aschehoug, 2003.

Lieven, Dominic. *Nicholas II: Twilight of the Empire*. New York: St. Martin's Press, 1993.

Longford, Elizabeth. *Victoria R*. New York: Harper & Row, 1964.

Lowe, Charles. *Alexander III of Russia*. New York: Macmillan, 1895.

Mager, Hugo. *Elizabeth, Grand Duchess of Russia*. New York: Carroll & Graf, 1998.

Majolier, Nathalie. *Stepdaughter of Imperial Russia*. London: Stanley Paul, 1926.

Mandache, Diana. *Dearest Missy*. Falköping, Sweden: Rosvall Royal Books, 2011.

Marie Pavlovna, Grand Duchess of Russia. *Education of a Princess*. New York: Viking Press, 1931.

___ *A Princess in Exile*. New York: Viking Press, 1933.

Maylunas, Andrei, and Sergei Mironenko. *A Lifelong Passion: Nicholas & Alexandra, Their Own Story*. London: Weidenfeld & Nicolson, 1996.

McCormick, R. R. *With the Russian Army*. London: Hutchinson, 1915.

Menzies, Grant. "Grand Duchess Marie Pavlovna, Junior." In *The Grand Duchesses*. East Richmond Heights, CA: Eurohistory 2004.

Michael Mikhailovich, Grand Duke of Russia. *Never Say Die*. London: Collier, 1908.

Millar, Lubov. *Grand Duchess Elizabeth of Russia, New Martyr of the Communist Yoke*. Richfield Springs, NY: Nikodemos Orthodox Publication Society, 1991.

Miller, Ilana D. *The Four Graces: Queen Victoria's Hessian Granddaughters*. East Richmond Heights, CA: Eurohistory, 2011.

Montefiore, Simon Sebag. *The Romanovs, 1613-1918*. New York: Knopf, 2016.

Mossolov, A. A. *At the Court of the Last Tsar*. London: Methuen, 1935.

Moynihan, Brian. *Rasputin: The Saint Who Sinned*. New York: Random House, 1997.

Naryshkina-Kurakina, Princess Elizabeth. *Under Three Tsars*. New York: Dutton, 1931.

Nikolaya II v Velikii Knyazya. Moscow: State Publishing, 1925.

Nijinska, Bronislava. *Early Memoirs*. New York: Holt, Rinehart and Winston, 1981.

Nostitz, Countess Lili. *Romance and Revolutions*. London: Hutchinson, 1937.

Novikoff, Olga. *Russian Memories*. New York: Dutton, 1919.

Obolensky, Igor. *Le Destin de Beaute: Histoire de femmes Georgiennes*. Tblisi: Cezanne, 2010.

Olsoufieff, Countess Alexandra. *HIH Grand Duchess Elisabeth Feodorovna*. London: John Murray, 1923

Painter, George D. *Proust: The Later Years*. New York: Atlantic-Little, Brown, 1965.

Pakula, Hannah. *The Last Romantic: A Biography of Queen Marie of Romania*. New York: Simon and Schuster, 1985.

Paley, Princess. *Memories of Russia*. London: Herbert Jenkins, 1923.

Paleologue, Maurice. *An Ambassador's Memoirs*. Three volumes. New York: Doran, 1925.

___ *Three Critical Years*. New York: Robert Speller, 1957.

Papi, Stefano. *Jewels of the Romanovs: Family & Court*. London: Thames & Hudson, 2013.

Pares, Sir Bernard. *Fall of the Russian Monarchy*. New York: Knopf, 1939.

Perry, John Curtis, and Constantine Pleshakov. *The Flight of the Romanovs*. Old Saybrook, CT: Konecky and Konecky, 1999.

Phenix, Patricia. *Olga Romanov: Russia's Last Grand Duchess*. Toronto: Viking, 1999.

Pipes, Richard. *The Russian Revolution*. New York: Knopf, 1990.

Pless, Daisy, Princess of. *By Herself*. New York: Dutton, 1928.

Ponsonby, Sir Frederick, Editor. *Letters of the Empress Frederick*. London: Macmillan, 1928.

Purishkevich, Vladimir. *The Murder of Rasputin*. Ann Arbor, Michigan: Ardis, 1985.

Radzinsky, Edvard. *The Rasputin File*. New York: Doubleday, 2000.

Radziwill, Princess Catherine. *My Recollections*. New York: James Pott, 1904.

___ *Memories of Forty Years*. New York: Funk & Wagnalls, 1915

___ *The Royal Marriage Market of Europe*. New Yorl: Funk and Wagnalls, 1915.

___ *The Disillusions of a Crown Princess*. New York: John Lane, 1919.

___ *Secrets of Dethroned Royalty*. New York: John Lane, 1920.

___ *Nicholas II: The Last of the Tsars*. London: Cassell and Company, 1931.

Rappaport, Helen. *The Romanov Sisters*. New York: St. Martin's Press, 2014.

Rodzianko, Michael. *The Reign of Rasputin*. London: Philpot, 1927.

Rohl, John. *Wilhelm II: The Kaiser's Personal Monarchy*. Cambridge: Cambridge University Press, 2004.

Romanovsky-Krassinsky, Princess (Mathilde Kschessinska). *Dancing in Petersburg: The Memoirs of Kschessinska*. Garden City, NY: Doubleday, 1961.

Romania, Marie, Queen of. *The Story of My Life. Two volumes*. New York: Charles Scribner's Sons, 1934.

Russian Court Memoirs, 1914-1916. London: Herbert Jenkins, 1917.

Saenz, Jorge. *A Poet Among the Romanovs: Prince Vladimir Paley*. East Richmond Heights, CA: Eurohistory, 2004.

Salisbury, Harrison. *Black Night, White Snow: Russia's Revolutions, 1905-1917*. Garden City, NY: Doubleday, 1978.

Sazonov, Sergei. *The Fateful Years*. New York: Frederick A. Stokes, 1928.

Schelking, Eugene de. *Suicide of Monarchy: Recollections of a Diplomat*. Toronto: Macmillan, 1918.

Shchegolev, P. E. Editor. *Padenie Tsarskogo Rezhima, Stenografisheskie Otchety Doprosov i Pokazanii, Dannikh v 1917 g. v Chrezvychainoi Sledsvennoi Komissii Vremennogo Pravitel'stva*. Seven volumes. Moscow and Leningrad: State Publishing, 1924-1927.

Schleswig-Holstein, Princess Marie Louise of. *My Memories of Six Reigns*. London: Evans Brothers, 1956.

Shelayev, Yuri, Elizabeth Shelayeva, and Nicholas Semenov. *Nicholas Romanov: Life and Death*. St. Petersburg: Liki Rossii, 1998.

Spain, Infanta Eulalia of. *Court Life from Within*. New York: Dodd, Mead, 1916.

Spiridovich, Alexander. *Les Dernièèrs Années de la Cour de Tzarskoie-Selo. Two volumes*. Paris: Payot, 1928.

Stanley, Lady Augusta. *Later Letters of Lady Augusta Stanley, 1864-1876*. London: Jonathan Cape, 1929.

Steveni, William Barnes. *Petrograd, Past and Present*. Philadelphia J. B. Lippincott, 1916.

de Stoeckl, Baroness Agnes. *Not All Vanity*. London: John Murray, 1950.

___ *My Dear Marquis*. London: John Murray, 1952.

Stopford, Albert. *The Russian Diary of An Englishman*. London: Heinemann, 1919.

Sullivan, Michael John. *A Fatal Passion: The Story of the Uncrowned Last Empress of Russia*. New York: Random House, 1997.

Surguchev, I. *Detstvo Imperatora Nikolaia II*. Paris: Payot, 1953.

Taylor, Edmund. *The Fall of the Dynasties and the Collapse of the Old Order, 1905-1922*. Garden City, New York: Doubleday, 1963.

Teliakovsky, Vladimir. *Vospominaiia, 1898-1917*. Petrograd: Vremia, 1924.

Troyat, Henri. *Tolstoy*. New York: Doubleday, 1967.

Ular, Alexander. *Russia From Within*. New York: Henry Holt, 1905.

Ulstrup, Preben. *Treasures of Russia: Imperial Gifts*. Copenhagen: Amalienborg Palace, 2002.

Van der Kiste, John. *Princess Victoria Melita*. Stroud, Gloucestershire: Sutton, 1991.

___ *Kings of the Hellenes: The Greek Kings 1863–1974*. Stroud, Gloucestershire: Sutton, 1999.

___ *The Romanovs: 1818–1959*. Stroud, Gloucestershire: Sutton, 2004.

Van der Kiste, John, and Arturo Beéche. "Grand Duke Kirill Vladimirovich." In *The Other Grand Dukes*. East Richmond Heights, CA: Eurohistory, 2012.

Vacaresco, Hélène. *Kings and Queens I Have Known*. New York: Harper, 1904.

Vassili, Count Paul (Princess Catherine Radziwill). *La Société de Saint-Pétersbourg*. Paris: Chamerot, 1886.

___ *Behind the Veil at the Russian Court*. New York: John Lane Company, 1914.

Vassiliev, Alexandre. *Beauty in Exile: The Artists, Models, and Nobility who Fled the Russian Revolution and Influenced the World of Fashion*. New York: Harry N. Abrams, 2001.

Verner, Andrew. *The Crisis of Russian Autocracy: Nicholas II and the 1905 Revolution*. Princeton, NJ: Princeton University Press, 1990.

Vickers, Hugo. *Alice, Princess Andrew of Greece*. London: Hamish Hamilton, 2000.

Volkov, Alexei. *Souvenirs d'Alexis Volkov*. Paris: Payot, 1928.

Vorres, Ian. *The Last Grand Duchess*. London: Hutchinson, 1964.

Voyekov, Vladimir. *S Tsaryom i bez Tsarya*. Helsingfors, 1936.

Vyrubova, Anna. *Memories of the Russian Court*. New York: Macmillan, 1923.

Warth, Robert D. *Nicholas II*. Westport, CT: Praeger, 1997.

Warwick, Christopher. *Ella: Princess, Saint, and Martyr*. Chichester, UK: John Wiley & Sons, 2006.

Welch, Rachel. *The Russian Court at Sea: The voyage of HMS Marlborough, April 1919*. London: Short Books, 2011.

West, J. *Soldiers of the Tsar and other Sketches and Studies of the Russia of Today*. London: Hutchinson, 1915.

Wilton, Robert. *Russia's Agony*. New York: Dutton, 1918.

___ *The Last Days of the Romanovs*. New York: George H. Doran, 1920.

Wimbles, John. "Grand Duchess Marie Alexandrovna." In *The Grand Duchesses*. East Richmond Heights, CA: Eurohistory, 2004.

Witte, Sergei. *The Memoirs of Count Witte*. Armonk, NY: ME Sharpe, 1990.

Wortman, Richard. *Scenarios of Power: Myth and Ceremony in Russian Monarchy, Volume 2: From Alexander II to the Abdication of Nicholas II*. Princeton: Princeton University Press, 2000.

Yusupov, Felix. *Lost Splendor*. London: Jonathan Cape, 1953.

___ *Rasputin*. New York: Dial, 1927.

Zeepvat, Charlotte. *Romanov Autumn*. Stroud, Gloucestershire: Sutton, 2000.

___ *The Camera and the Tsars*. Stroud, Gloucestershire: Sutton, 2004.

Articles

Abrash, Merritt. *"A Curious Romance: The Queen's Son and the Tsar's Daughter."* In Slavonic and Eastern European Review, July 1969, Volume 47, No. 109.

Ashton, Janet. *"'A Country Where A Man of God Helps the Sovereign Will Never Be Lost:' A Look at Some of the Religious Ideas and Influences of Empress Alexandra Feodorovna."* In Atlantis Magazine, Volume 3, No. 4.

Belyakova, Zoia. *"Letters from Grand Duke Alexander Mikhailovich to Grand Duchess Xenia, 1916-1917."* In Royalty Digest, November 2004, Volume XIV, No. 5, Issue 161.

___ *"A Strange Prince: Prince Peter of Oldenburg and Grand Duchess Olga Alexandrovna."* In Royalty Digest, No. 2, 2007.

Horan, Brien. *"The Russian Succession in 2013."* Privately Printed. In the authors' collection.

King, Greg, editor. *"The Diaries of Grand Duke Andrei Vladimirovich, 1916-1917."* In Atlantis Magazine, Volume 5, No. 1.

Mateos Sainz de Madrano, Ricardo. *"A Child of The Caucasus."* In Royalty Digest, July 1993, Volume 3, No. 1.

McLean, Roderick R. *"Kaiser Wilhelm II and his Hessian Cousins: Intra-State Relations in the German Empire and International Dynastic Politics, 1890-1918."* In German History, Volume 19, No 1, 2001.

Nunes, Pepsi. *"The Evolution of the Imperial Russian Navy and the Grand Dukes, 1850-1917."* In Atlantis Magazine, Volume 2, No. 4.

Smitten, B. N. *"Poslednyi Vremenshchik Poslednago Tsaria."* In Voprosi Istorii, 1965, No. 12.

Vera Konstantinovna, Princess of Russia. *"Kadetskaya Pereklichka."* 1972, No. 3.

Wimbles, John. *"Death and The Duchess."* In Royalty Digest, April 2001, Volume X, No. 118, Issue 10.

___ *"An Enduring Mystery: The Divorce of Ernie and Ducky."* In Royalty Digest, 2007, No. 2.

Wynn, Marion. *"A Russian Grand Duke Resident in England: Grand Duke Michael Mikhailovich, Keele Hall, and Kenwood."* In Royalty Digest, May 2002, Volume XI, No. 11, Issue 131.

Other Media

Becket, Anne and David Alderman. *Grand Duke Michael at Keele*. Power-Point presentation, 2014.

Lee, Will. *"Dmitry Pavlovich, 1908-1914: Portrait of a Young Grand Duke."* At www.directarticle.org

McKee, Claire. *British Perceptions of Tsar Nicholas II and Empress Alexandra Feodorovna, 1894-1918.* Unpublished PhD Thesis. University College of London, 2016.

Romanov News, monthly PDF published by Paul and Ludmila Kulikovsky.

Sorenson, Thomas C. *The Thought and Policies of Konstantin Pobedonostsev.* Unpublished PhD Thesis. Seattle: University of Washington, 1977.

Tchaikovsky Research, at http://en.tchaikovsky-research.net/pages/Grand_Duke_Konstantin_Konstantinovich
www.tashkent-info.narod.ru

Newspapers and Periodicals

Dates are referenced within the individual citations

Krasnii Arkhiv, Moscow
Moscow Times
New York Times
Novoe Vremya
Svet, Moscow
The Times, London

Index

The Authors

Greg King is the author of many internationally published works of royal and social history, specializing in late Imperial Russia and Edwardian-era royalty. His books include: *The Last Empress, The Duchess of Windsor, The Fate of the Romanovs, Gilded Prism – The Konstantinovich Grand Dukes, The Court of the Last Tsar, A Life for the Tsar: The Coronation of Nicholas II,* and *The Assassination of the Archduke.* His work has appeared in Majesty Magazine, Royalty Magazine, the European Royal History Journal (Eurohistory), Royalty Digest, the Daily Mail, and the Washington Post, and he has served as a commentator for documentaries by National Geographic, the History Channel, the CBC, Channel 4, and Fox News. His previous book, *The Assassination of the Archduke,* which has been translated to several languages, reexamines what happened at Mayerling.

– // –

Penny Wilson is the author of numerous books on Russian Imperial, Royal, and social history. She has contributed to renowned publications like Majesty, Atlantis, History of Royals, and the European Royal History Journtal (Eurohistory). Her works include: *The Fate of the Romanovs, Gilded Prism – The Konstantinovich Grand Dukes, Resurrection of the Romanovs, Lusitania, and Twilight of Empire.* She is also a fitness expert, much-respected in the field.

THE EUROHISTORY COLLECTION

Here is the full list of Eurohistory books! Prices do not include shipping.

$48.95

$48.95

$48.95

SOLD OUT
$43.95

THE GRAND DUKES
$43.95

THE OTHER GRAND DUKES
$43.95

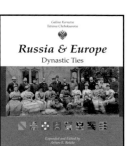
$48.95

$48.95

$48.95

The Four Graces
$43.95

The Gotha
SOLD OUT
$43.95

MY FIFTY YEARS
SOLD OUT
$43.95

SOLD OUT
$28.95

SOLD OUT
$43.95

$43.95

THE NASSAUS OF LUXEMBOURG
$48.95

Royal Exiles in Cannes
$48.95

THE ROYAL HELLENIC DYNASTY
$43.95

Maria Pia
$43.95

Gilded Prism
$43.95

Ella
$43.95

The Coburgs of Europe
SOLD OUT
$48.95

The Romanovs
SOLD OUT
$48.95

Albany
One Dynasty, Two Destinies
SOLD OUT
$48.95

NEW!
Death of a Romanov Prince
$48.95

Coming Soon:

The Royal House of Bavaria

Royal Gatherings
$43.95

Royal Gatherings
$48.95

Dear Ellen
$43.95

Michael I of Romania
$29.95